T0305016

STATES

OF

PLAY

STATES
OF
PLAY

How Sportswashing Took
Over Football

MIGUEL DELANEY

SEVEN DIALS

First published in Great Britain in 2024 by Seven Dials
an imprint of The Orion Publishing Group Ltd
Carmelite House, 50 Victoria Embankment
London EC4Y 0DZ

An Hachette UK Company

The authorised representative in the EEA is Hachette Ireland,
8 Castlecourt Centre, Dublin 15, D15 XTP3, Ireland (email: info@hbgi.ie)

3 5 7 9 10 8 6 4

A CIP catalogue record for this book is
available from the British Library.

ISBN (Hardback) 978 1 3996 1940 0
ISBN (Trade Paperback) 978 1 3996 1941 7
ISBN (eBook) 978 1 3996 1943 1
ISBN (Audio) 978 1 3996 1944 8

Typeset by Input Data Services Ltd, Somerset

Printed and bound in Great Britain by Clays Ltd, Elcograf S.p.A.

www.orionbooks.co.uk

To Paul. For Éabha.

CONTENTS

CAST OF CHARACTERS

Roman Abramovich: Russian businessman and former owner of Chelsea from 2003–2022.

AFC: The Asian Football Confederation, consisting of the continent's national associations. One of six continental confederations under FIFA responsible for governance and running of club competitions.

Andrea Agnelli: Former chairman of Juventus and part of the Agnelli family that founded FIAT, as well as a key figure in the European Super League.

Sheikh Tamim bin Hamad Al Thani: Emir of Qatar, who was influential in delivering 2022 World Cup as crown prince.

Sheikh Hamad bin Khalifa Al Thani: Former Emir of Qatar, in power at the time Qatar won the 2022 World Cup bid.

Nasser Al-Khelaifi: President of Paris Saint-Germain, chairman of beIN Media Group and Qatar Sports Investments, chairman of the European Club Association.

Khaldoon Al Mubarak: Chairman of Manchester City, chief executive officer and managing director of Abu Dhabi sovereign wealth fund Mubadala Investment Company, as well as chairman of the Executive Affairs Authority.

Yasir Al-Rumayyan: Governor of Saudi Arabia's Public Investment Fund, chairman of Saudi Aramco and chairman of Newcastle United.

Hassan Al Thawadi: Secretary General at Supreme Committee for Delivery and Legacy for the 2022 FIFA World Cup Qatar Local Organizing Committee.

David Beckham: Former Manchester United and England player who was also one of Real Madrid's *Galácticos*, while fostering a new level of fame for footballers.

Silvio Berlusconi: Media mogul who was owner of AC Milan from 1986–2017 and former prime minister of Italy.

Mohammed Bin Hammam: Former chairman of Qatar Football Association and president of Asian Football Confederation.

Sepp Blatter: President of FIFA from 1998–2015.

Jean-Marc Bosman: Former RFC Liège midfielder whose move to Dunkerque was blocked, ensuring he successfully took a case against RFC Liège, the Belgian Football Association and UEFA to the European Court of Justice for restraint of trade.

CAF: The Confederation of African Football, consisting of the continent's national associations.

Aleksander Čeferin: President of UEFA since 2016.

Clearlake Capital: American headquartered private equity firm who have been majority owners of Chelsea since 2022.

CONCACAF: The Confederation of North, Central America and Caribbean Association Football, consisting of the area's national associations.

CONMEBOL: The South American Football Confederation, standing for Confederación Sudamericana de Fútbol.

Court of Arbitration for Sport: International body founded to settle sporting disputes, established in 1984 and based in Lausanne.

Martin Edwards: Former chairman of Manchester United.

Recep Tayyip Erdoğan: Turkish president since 2014.

Sir Alex Ferguson: Former manager of Manchester United, considered by many to be the greatest football manager of all time.

FIFA: The International Federation of Association Football – Fédération Internationale de Football Association in French – the ultimate global body responsible for the governance and running of the game.

The Football Association: Governing body of English football and the oldest football association in the world, formed in 1863.

The Glazer family: Majority owners of Manchester United, having purchased the club with a leveraged buy-out in 2005, initially under late father Malcolm. Of six siblings, Joel and Avram are most involved in football.

Pep Guardiola: Manager of Manchester City, also considered by many to be the greatest football manager of all time. Previously the manager of Barcelona and Bayern Munich.

John Henry: Owner of Liverpool, through Fenway Sports Group.

Gianni Infantino: President of FIFA since 2016 and former UEFA General Secretary.

Boris Johnson: Prime Minister of the United Kingdom from 2019–2022.

Xi Jinping: President of China since 2013.

Jamal Khashoggi: Journalist and Saudi dissident, killed in 2018.

Stan Kroenke: Owner of Arsenal, through Kroenke Sports & Entertainment.

Daniel Levy: Chairman of Tottenham Hotspur since 2001.

Emmanuel Macron: President of France since 2017.

Roberto Mancini: Former Italian international and Manchester City manager, who is currently the manager of the Saudi Arabia national team.

Kylian Mbappé: French forward who moved from Paris Saint-Germain to Real Madrid in 2024.

Lionel Messi: Argentine footballer, considered to be the greatest footballer of all time, who played for Barcelona, Paris Saint-Germain and, currently, Inter Miami.

Massimo Moratti: Industrialist and former owner of Internazionale.

Rupert Murdoch: Media mogul who owned BskyB and was directly involved in initial talks over broadcasting the Premier League.

Sheikh Mansour bin Zayed Al Nahyan: Vice president and deputy prime minister of the United Arab Emirates, as well as brother of president Sheikh Mohamed bin Zayed Al Nahyan. Owner of Manchester City through Abu Dhabi United Group.

Sheikh Mohamed bin Zayed Al Nahyan: President of the United Arab Emirates and ruler of Abu Dhabi.

Neymar: Brazilian footballer who moved from Barcelona to Paris Saint-Germain in a world-record €222 million transfer.

OFC: Oceania Football Confederation, consisting of the area's national associations.

Florentino Pérez: President of Real Madrid 2000–2006 and 2009 to present.

Rui Pinto: Portuguese activist and whistleblower who created the Football Leaks website.

Public Investment Fund: Saudi Arabia's sovereign wealth fund.

Simon Pearce: Board member of City Football Group, who also serves as special advisor to the Chairman of the Executive Affairs Authority in Abu Dhabi, and the emirate's main communication advisor.

Michel Platini: Legendary French footballer who was president of UEFA from 2007–2015.

Vladimir Putin: President of Russia since 1999.

Qatar Sports Investments: Subsidiary of the Qatar Investment Authority sovereign wealth fund, founded to invest in sport.

Cristiano Ronaldo: Portuguese footballer who has played for Manchester United, Real Madrid and Juventus, eventually going to Al Nassr in the Saudi Pro League.

Karl-Heinz Rummenigge: Former German international who was Chairman of the Executive Board of Bayern Munich from 2002–2021. Served as chairman of the European Club Association from 2008–2017.

Mohammed bin Salman: Crown prince of the Kingdom of Saudi Arabia, popularly known as MBS.

Nicolas Sarkozy: President of France from 2007–2012.

Irving Scholar: Former chairman of Tottenham Hotspur who figured out a way to evade Rule 34 in English football and ensure the club became the first to float on the stock market in 1983.

Richard Scudamore: Chief executive of the Premier League from 1999–2018.

Thaksin Shinawatra: Former owner of Manchester City, 2007–2008, and former prime minister of Thailand from 2001–2006.

Ferran Soriano: Manchester City chief executive who formerly worked at Barcelona.

Amanda Staveley: British financier who was a minority owner of Newcastle United from 2021–2024.

Javier Tebas: President of La Liga since 2013.

UEFA: The Union of European Football Associations, consisting of the continent's national associations.

TIMELINE OF EVENTS

1863:	**December**	The Rules of Association Football are published.
1899:	**September**	English clubs must operate under a new regulation for new season, later codified as Rule 34, restricting dividends and preventing club directors from being paid.
1901:	**September**	Maximum wage introduced for the start of the new English season.
1904:	**May**	FIFA founded.
1932:	**September**	Kingdom of Saudi Arabia established.
1954:	**June**	UEFA founded.
1955:	**April**	The European Cup is organised in Paris, starting the following September.
1961:	**January**	The Professional Footballers' Association successfully challenges the maximum wage.
1971:	**September**	The State of Qatar is founded.
	December	The United Arab Emirates is founded.
1974:	**June**	João Havelange elected FIFA president.
1978:	**June**	Argentina hosts the World Cup, leading to criticism from Amnesty International for how Jorge Rafael Videla's military junta politically used the event.
1983:	**October**	Tottenham Hotspur become the first club

to float on the stock exchange, after Irving Scholar takes steps to evade Rule 34.

1985: May The Bradford City stadium fire sees 55 fans lose their lives, just two weeks before 39 supporters die at Heysel Stadium before the European Cup final.

1986: February Silvio Berlusconi buys AC Milan.

1987: September Diego Maradona's Napoli meet Real Madrid in a first-round European Cup tie that Berlusconi describes as 'economic nonsense'.

1989: April The Hillsborough disaster at the FA Cup semi-final, where 'negligent failures' from authorities saw 97 Liverpool supporters eventually lose their lives.

1990: January The Taylor Report is published, recommending huge changes to English football.

August Iraq invades Kuwait.

October The Spanish state introduced Law 10/1990 so football clubs become a special type of public limited company to ward off financial disaster, with only four allowed to remain member owned.

1991: April The European Commission agrees to the so-called 'foreigner rule' with UEFA, where teams competing in European competition can field just three foreign players, plus two 'assimilated', who had been in the country for five years.

June Manchester United are floated on the stock exchange.

1992:	May	The Premier League is formed, starting the following August.
	August	The European Cup becomes the Champions League.
1993:	September	La Liga clubs are permitted to sell broadcast rights individually, following a Spanish competition court ruling, allowing Real Madrid and Barcelona to dominate the market.
1994:	June	The World Cup is held in the United States.
1995:	December	The 'Bosman ruling' is published, bringing free movement for players within the European Union and ensuring the removal of foreign player restrictions.
1997:	August	The Champions League expands to feature runners-up from major leagues.
1998:	June	Sepp Blatter is elected FIFA president.
	October	The German football association rules on the so-called '50+1 rule'.
1999:	August	The Champions League expands to feature up to four clubs from the best-performing leagues.
2000:	July	Florentino Pérez becomes Real Madrid president, buying Barcelona's Luís Figo on a release clause as part of his election promise.
	September	The 'G14' is founded by the biggest clubs, a group that would later become the European Club Association (ECA).
2003:	July	Roman Abramovich buys Chelsea.
2005:	May	The Glazer family agree a deal for a leveraged buy-out of Manchester United.

2006:	**May**	'Calciopoli' influence-peddling scandal uncovered in Italy.
2007:	**July**	Thaksin Shinawatra buys Manchester City.
	August	Abu Dhabi 'Vision 2030' launched.
2008:	**July**	Pep Guardiola appointed as manager at Barcelona.
	September	Sheikh Mansour's Abu Dhabi United Group buy Manchester City; Lehman Brothers bank collapses, spiking the global financial crisis.
2010:	**May**	UEFA Executive Committee unanimously approves Financial Fair Play regulations, to come into action from the 2013–14 season.
	December	Russia wins the vote to host the 2018 World Cup; Qatar for the 2022 World Cup. Tunisian Mohamed Bouazizi self-immolates in protest at Zine El Abidine Ben Ali's dictatorship, sparking the Arab Spring.
2011:	**June**	Qatar Sports Investments buys Paris Saint-Germain.
2013:	**January**	City Football Group is founded, with Manchester City as the central club.
	February	Premier League negotiates overseas rights deals worth £5.5 billion for the next three-year cycle.
2014:	**May**	The first FFP investigations see UEFA announce 'settlements' with both Paris Saint-Germain and Manchester City that ultimately result in €20 million fines.
2015:	**March**	Saudi Arabia leads a coalition involving UAE in the Yemeni civil war, mere weeks after

		Mohammed bin Salman is put in charge of the military.
2015:	May	Swiss police arrest seven FIFA officials staying in the Baur au Lac hotel at the behest of American authorities, following a corruption investigation; Blatter is still re-elected president before standing down days later, amid more reports of bribery within FIFA.
	September	Swiss prosecutors find a 2 million franc payment from FIFA to UEFA president Michel Platini in 2011, first agreed in 1998, eventually forcing his resignation; Football Leaks website is created.
2016:	February	Gianni Infantino is elected FIFA president.
	April	Saudi Arabia 'Vision 2030' launched.
	May	Leicester City win the Premier League.
	August	The ECA use a vacuum at UEFA to agree Champions League 'royalties', where more money would be distributed to clubs based on appearances over 10 years.
	September	Aleksander Čeferin is elected UEFA president.
2017:	June	Gulf blockade starts; Mohammed bin Salman is appointed Crown Prince of Saudi Arabia.
	August	Paris Saint-Germain sign Neymar for a world-record €222 million, paying his release clause at Barcelona.
2018:	April	Infantino begins plans for an expanded Club World Cup.
	June	The World Cup starts in Russia, Infantino

is sat with Mohammed bin Salman and Vladimir Putin at the opening game; PSG escape serious sanction from a second FFP investigation on a technicality; USA wins bid to host the 2026 World Cup.

2018:	**July**	Elliott Management buy AC Milan.
	October	Journalist and Saudi dissident Jamal Khashoggi is killed.
	November	Football Leaks releases a series of emails from Manchester City that result in investigations into the club by UEFA and the Premier League over potential breaches of financial regulations.
2019:	**August**	Bury are expelled from the English Football League after 125 years due to financial collapse.
2020:	**February**	UEFA announce a two-year Champions League ban and €30 million fine for Manchester City for 'serious breaches' of FFP regulations.
	March	Covid-19 pandemic brings global shutdown in football for over two months.
	April	Mike Ashley initially agrees a deal to sell Newcastle United to a consortium led by Saudi Arabia's Public Investment Fund (PIF).
	July	The Court of Arbitration for Sport overturn Manchester City's two-year Champions League ban and reduce fine to €10 million, noting the club did 'fail to cooperate'.
2021:	**January**	Gulf blockade ends.

	April	European Super League launches and fails in the space of three days; PSG chairman Nasser Al-Khelaifi president elected chairman of ECA.
	August	Private equity firm CVC acquires a minority stake in La Liga; financial regulations and Barcelona's debt force Lionel Messi out of the club, as he agrees to join PSG.
	October	PIF complete purchase of 80 per cent of Newcastle United as part of an ownership consortium.
2022:	February	Russia invades Ukraine, seeing Roman Abramovich sanctioned by the UK government and therefore forced to sell Chelsea. Russian teams are also banned from UEFA competition, with the national team also banned from the World Cup.
	May	Clearlake Capital become majority owner of Chelsea.
	November	Qatar World Cup starts.
	December	Cristiano Ronaldo signs for Al-Nassr in Riyadh, which is followed in June 2023 by the Saudi Pro League announcing PIF have taken over the club and three others as part of a national project to make it one of the best leagues in the world.
2023:	February	Manchester City charged by the Premier League with over 100 breaches of Financial Fair Play rules, after a four-year investigation.
	October	FIFA announce that the centenary 2030 World Cup will open with three games

		in South America, before moving to Morocco-Portugal-Spain, leaving the way clear for Saudi Arabia to host the 2034 World Cup.
	December	Sir Jim Ratcliffe completes purchase of a minority stake in Manchester United, having seen off Qatari Sheikh Jassim's attempt at a full takeover; European Court of Justice ruling on Super League case calls for review of UEFA and FIFA procedures and governance.
2024:	June	Kylian Mbappé joins Real Madrid.
	September	Champions League expands again, with 36 teams in the new 'Swiss system'.

INTRODUCTION

It was a moment that Lionel Messi had imagined all his life, but he probably didn't picture it quite like this. As the Argentinian great waited to finally lift the World Cup, it had already been proclaimed as one of the most uplifting sporting storylines, alongside Muhammad Ali reclaiming the heavyweight title in 1974. The scene from the podium in Qatar's Lusail Stadium, however, suddenly raised eyebrows. With every previous World Cup trophy lift, the winning captain was in only their national colours, creating an image that becomes immortal for both their country and the game. This time, both the Argentina crest and the famous blue and white stripes were obscured. Messi had been adorned with a bisht, an honourable Arabic garment that would usually be a beautiful gesture. It was here impossible to separate from the fact it had been draped on Messi's shoulders by the Emir of Qatar. The state's autocratic ruler ensured the hosts intruded upon this moment of football history. The bisht may be entirely innocent but the bestowing of it was not. Lusail was now part of football lore, the Emir's gift front and centre, warmly associated with Messi's ascendance in the way Mexico's Azteca Stadium was with Pelé and Diego Maradona. This was despite the immense human cost of building the stadium and everything around it. That is influence that no amount of diplomacy or political force can secure. That the moment followed 40 minutes of the most spectacular sporting theatre, maybe even a perfect period of football, only deepened the power of it all. This would be talked about for ever.

Messi, understandably, didn't care. He was only looking at this dazzling gold trophy, the pinnacle of the sport. There couldn't have been a better metaphor for modern football. It is exactly why everyone else should care. An otherwise stirring moment had been captured and compromised by greater forces, like the game as a whole. It is now hard to watch a lot of elite football without being conscious that it is drastically changing in front of our eyes, while the very people the so-called 'people's game' is for are unable to do much about it. Football itself struggles to properly apply its own regulations, on the occasions it actually tries to. Instead, the game is increasingly used for questionable purposes, and primarily dominated by questionable forces. The general description for this is 'sportswashing', a phrase that has lamentably become part of football's language. Messi's World Cup lift was as basic an illustration as you can have.

As with the phrase itself, though, there is so much more going on than just image. Saudi Arabia and United Arab Emirates (UAE), who had led a blockade of Qatar between 2017 and 2021, were looking on enviously while sharpening their own plans. Meanwhile, Russia had been excluded from this World Cup for the invasion of Ukraine, having used their own hosting of 2018 as part of a national project similar to the 1936 Summer Olympics in Berlin. That conflict only emboldened Qatar, given how newly dependent the planet had become on the state's natural gas, sustaining a capitalist system that was in turn looking so hungrily at all the emotion that football creates. More than image, then, this was really about projection, security, hard power and the history of fossil fuels. It is all of the most serious issues on the planet, with football just another cultural good to be carelessly misused along the way.

That has so far left a game where: Abu Dhabi's Manchester City have won more trophies and games across seven years than any other English team in history; Qatar's Paris Saint-Germain have rendered the French league a joke and the global party of the World Cup has been held in countries where minorities fear to go and migrant workers have been abused in its staging. The sport's economy has meanwhile been upended, with state influence in every corner, and capitalist enterprises picking off everything in between.

None of this is what football is actually for. It doesn't actually exist to make a profit. It is still at its heart a mere game that is played to represent communities, not autocratic rulers. That is why an analysis of where the sport is, and an articulation of what sportswashing is, has never been more necessary. It is all the more surprising that there has never been a public discussion over states owning clubs, even in government discussions over the welfare of the sport. We are talking about the future of our game, but also how it is cynically used to change our world. What immediately becomes apparent when trying to untangle this, however, is that you can't talk about sportswashing without talking about where the game actually was and multiple other influences. The story of modern football is how it has been transformed and distorted by three main forces. One is geopolitics, with much of that emanating from a specific regional rivalry in the Gulf. Another is a distinctly Western hyper-capitalism, both from within football and outside. The third is a willing facilitation of all this by football's authorities, due to power structures that are not equipped to deal with any of it.

The story isn't, at its core, sportswashing. It is the extreme economic politicisation of football, where the sport has become a terrain for geopolitical positioning, that it should really have been protected from. The opposite happened. It has become a pawn for greater interests. Capitalist forces are trying to make as much money as possible out of football. Geopolitical powers are looking to put as much money as possible into it, in order to take over football's infrastructure. Many within that are only invested in their own interests, rather than the idea of protecting the game as a whole. This dynamic explains everything about modern football.

Since so much of this is about how wider political frameworks are imposed on sport, it is little surprise the cycle started when neoliberalism took hold of the planet in the 1980s.[1] Football has simply taken this to extremes that not even Ronald Reagan or Margaret Thatcher could have imagined, a reality which represents considerable irony given the latter's derisive attitude to the sport. The game's embrace of this creed saw it quickly grow to 'the single most popular activity that's ever been known by humanity', in the words of historian Tom Holland.[2] This was propelled through crucial moments like the Bosman ruling, as well as former Italian prime minister Silvio Berlusconi's idea of the 'television spectacular', ultimately given form by the founding of the Champions League and Premier League. The evolution of the internet then helped this race around the planet, to create a distinctive strand of super clubs whose immense global popularity brought a social capital attractive to autocracies. The game became so huge that its top end narrowed, to the point it was easily taken over, and entangled by geopolitical developments.

Gulf states looking to their own post-fossil fuel futures saw the sport as an asset, as well as an arena for their own regional rivalries, while registering how Roman Abramovich's 2003 purchase of Chelsea opened a new world. Ownership of clubs formed an important step in what was almost a playbook for sportswashing strategies, to go with the more classic approach of hosting tournaments. The controversial winning bids for the 2018 and 2022 World Cups are still described as forming the most influential moments in modern football, indeed reshaping the game and arguably the world. Qatar's victorious campaign was a direct factor in the Gulf blockade, where football became further collateral in a cold war. That directly led to Neymar's world-record transfer from Barcelona to PSG, which overturned the game's economy.

American commercial interest in football from the 1994 World Cup had meanwhile attuned the FBI to the clientelistic culture that led to the 2018 and 2022 campaigns, resulting in an overhaul of FIFA and UEFA that allowed the major clubs an even greater land grab. A direct consequence was the Super League, led by US-owned Manchester United and Liverpool, and driven by established powers like Real Madrid and Barcelona, desperately looking to secure the distorted world they had created. Camp Nou is the starting point for a line that runs through all of this. In 2008, Pep Guardiola created a team that offered such a perfect vision of football that every autocracy wanted to appropriate it. This wasn't just influence. It was global adulation. By 2024, Guardiola and most of Barcelona's key figures had worked under state ownerships, while the crisis-racked Catalan club were being investigated for accusations of payments to a former referee. That was one of a number of similar cases that threatened the very legitimacy of football, the most prominent of which was the investigation into Manchester City for 100-plus alleged breaches of Premier League financial rules. It all furthered the argument that the game couldn't govern itself. These fault lines were all growing until the Covid-19 pandemic widened them to cataclysmic levels. Much of the game began to plummet into the gaps, leaving the wealthiest to stand even stronger, visible in the paired peaks of the 2022 World Cup and the Premier League. Both represented logical conclusions of where football was going, in its two different levels of international and club.

Qatar 2022, held for the planet's wealthiest people but only made possible by the poorest, was an immoral tournament that merely took the game's carbon-fuelled capitalism to an extreme. The very staging of football caused human suffering, showing how it was being used at any cost. Saudi Arabia saw that and wanted their own. The Premier League had meanwhile become a super league, cannibalising the rest of the sport, before eventually distilling many of modern football's problems. This was the corrosive model of concentration that football had insisted upon, driven by a demented wage race.

Absolutely every metric shows the sport across Europe is more predictable than 30, 20 or even 10 years ago. Somehow, a world where the vast majority of teams can't compete has been normalised, along with state ownership. Many clubs are simply surviving. It again just mirrors the wider world, where globalisation has created billionaires at a faster pace than ever before. Football's apparent solution has been to invite even more billionaires in. This has all changed the DNA of the sport, and its culture. Many fans are priced out. Others just congregate around super clubs. Teams owned by autocratic states dominate, and a primary response has been applause. This has furthered the devolution of old fan rivalries into online slanging matches about finance and Gulf politics, in a way the game shouldn't even be touched by. It said much when human rights activist Iyad el-Baghdadi was talking about Gulf politics only to stop himself. 'It's crazy in twenty-first-century soccer that we're discussing tribal dynamics in the Middle East.' This is what runs a lot of football, as well as large sections of the global fossil fuel economy. Events of huge scale can come down to personal pettiness. So much of football is now being played in the name of autocracies. What are some of these regulatory cases, after all, but a product of the inevitable tension between the attempt to ensure a system of rules, and state actors whose entire thinking is they set the rules? Throw immense money and capitalist interests into this and you have far more than a mere sport can handle.

While football has never been completely clean, the last decade has witnessed more game-rocking controversies of a greater scale than the sport has arguably ever seen. The game's embrace of a world larger than its own has at the same time left it profoundly susceptible to global events, most visible in Abramovich's sanctioning after the invasion of Ukraine in February 2022. Given how football was used to facilitate Russia's geopolitical aims through the 2018 World Cup, the game should not be spared criticism for the real-world effects of all this. They are most visible in the empty spaces left by migrant workers in Qatar and other autocracies, the number of dead left disgracefully uncounted. That should be reflected in every trophy lifted.

All that makes it more important to remember why football actually matters, since that is what is being exploited. It is *a* beautiful game, right down to its very spirit. Other than just running or jumping, it is the one sport any child can play, only requiring something resembling a ball. 'That is why football is so popular,' Arsène Wenger says. That simplicity sets a universality that brings people together, be it one-on-one or thirty-five-a-side, right up to gatherings to watch games. The feeling of expression in kicking the ball fosters a connection when watching teams compete, especially when they represent your community. As well as a game anyone can play, it features matches anyone can win. The preciousness of a goal has ensured football is just low-scoring enough to strike the perfect balance between satisfying reward for performance and the right amount of surprises. That has translated into wider results for the majority of the game's history, so there have been spells where Bayern Munich's league titles have been punctuated by Kaiserslautern; where Cameroon can beat Argentina. Such vitality and variety has only added to the joy of the sport. It is not just about emotional investment but a sense of wonder at the colour of it all. Geography could be learnt through football. That will be familiar to anyone who has flicked through Subbuteo's different kits or the exotic names supplied by the board game's scoreboard. There's a Proustian element of nostalgia to all this, but that's what football should be about, nurturing a childlike enthusiasm that fills life with excitement. That sense of discovery is the spirit that invigorated the FA Cup, European football and the World Cup itself. It's what actually made football popular in the first place.

This is also what the embrace of neoliberalism, and capture by geopolitics, is directly eroding. It is for all the same reasons that the game is so good that it can be used for such bad. 'The biggest problem is that football is attractive to some of the worst people in the world, whether it is authoritarian regimes, private equity or toxic investors,' says Ronan Evain of Football Supporters Europe. 'Football is high on money. It's the illusion that there will be this perpetual growth, that there are no limits. It's an unsustainable model.'

And it is beginning to come to its limits. The game is at a point where those fault lines are now causing real tremors, and a huge discussion about what happens next is needed. It is not without some irony that conversation, despite a book like this extolling the variety of global football, must primarily focus on the elite end of the men's game. That is because it is there where all these forces come together and spread out from. They include hard geopolitics;

a very acute family rivalry; the rise and fall of great clubs and leagues; classic sporting corruption; the failure of sporting authorities; human rights abuses; fan mobilisation and political populism; the future of oil and late-stage capitalism. All of this characterised by the most sensationalist and salacious details that make football seem like a soap opera, but serve to obscure how serious much of this can be. Few could have pictured the game becoming like this, but it has never been more important to understand why.

1.

HOW FOOTBALL WAS
RIPE FOR TAKEOVER

Even by Florentino Pérez's standards, this was remarkable self-interest. It was the 2020–21 UEFA Champions League quarter-final, and the Real Madrid president had a sense of urgency as he prepared to meet his counterparts at Liverpool. The two clubs were opponents for this tie but also partners in the European Super League project, which was at that point only days from launch. The grand plan was for the wealthiest clubs to break away from the Champions League, and Pérez was eager to tell the world. He wanted to bring the announcement forward to the Thursday after the Real Madrid–Liverpool second leg. The problem was that date happened to be 15 April, so Liverpool were completely unwilling to launch. Pérez couldn't understand why not. It was diplomatically explained to him that this was the anniversary of the Hillsborough disaster, a solemn day when Liverpool remembered the 97 supporters who lost their lives in a crush at a 1989 FA Cup match.

Pérez accepted that, but was still a bit bemused that there was such concern over 'something that happened 30 years ago'. Those who remember the exchanges don't see it as Pérez being intentionally disrespectful. It was more that he can never see past what matters to Real Madrid, and never accepts anything that isn't guaranteed to keep the Spanish club at the top of the football pyramid. Rival executives even got used to a familiar Pérez refrain from meetings.

'Y así es,' the Real Madrid president would say, totally sure of his stance on anything as if it was a self-evident truth. *That's how it is.* That's how it has been for most of modern football history, at least. The great white sharks like Real Madrid and Barcelona got their way, with everything flowing down from there. Except, as Norwegian Football Federation president Lise Klaveness puts it, the game is in 'a time of unique change'. That resistance to regulation has created a world that is now moving beyond the control of Pérez and the European industrialists that defined half a century of European football. It was why Silvio Berlusconi got out, selling AC Milan in 2017.

Football's greed has caused the game to grow to a size where, as long forewarned, it is finally 'eating itself'. An increasing predictability is undeniable.[1] This comes from the apparent paradox that the game is at a point of unprecedented global popularity, but that popularity – and, consequently, money – is concentrated among a decreasing number of so-called 'super clubs'. A mere 12 clubs are responsible for a quarter of the total European football economy, at around €7 billion of €29 billion.[2]

Similar contradictions have been the engines driving the game to this point, where its universal human purity is now being exploited by the most questionable interests. The deepest of these contradictions is at the core of the sport. It is competition that is dependent on collaboration. Only one team can win but the value of winning comes from having many teams to play against. All of this fits into another unreconciled tension, which is how football is a community-based game that has also become big business.

Former Football Association chief executive Mark Palios argues that impetus between clubs adds further edge. 'If you're in business, the aim is to kill off the competition. In sport, it is to keep reinventing competition every season.' One of the most corrosive problems in football is that too many of the most influential voices lean towards the former. For all that other clubs complain about Pérez, most echo his attitude. As far back as 2016, one of the Premier League executives involved in the Super League came out with the following at a private dinner. 'We don't want too many Leicester Cities,' the official said, referencing the club's 2015–16 Premier League title victory, considered one of sport's most romantic stories. 'Football history suggests fans like big teams winning. A certain amount of unpredictability is good, but a more democratic league would be bad for business.'

That executive need not have worried. The Premier League's wealthiest clubs – known for years as 'the big six' – had already ensured that the famous 4,000-1 odds against Leicester's sensational victory have only lengthened since. Virtually every major governance decision over 40 years has further eroded that essential, but delicate, quality that is competitive balance. It's a key phrase, that basically means how likely it is any club can beat any other club, or win a trophy. Football is sold on this unpredictability, but instead got itself into a paradoxical situation where income matters more. It's now gone way beyond that, too. Modern football represents extreme economic neoliberalism distilled into sporting form. It sucks up money from everywhere but then redistributes it as narrowly as possible. No club with a revenue of less than €460 million has won the Champions League since 2013, and there aren't many with a greater revenue.

If the will is to bring everything back to business, one of football's foremost economists offers a succinct but concerning summation of where the game is. The University of Liverpool's David Forrest uses the common football obsession of American sport, with its draft picks and closed leagues, as a contrasting example. 'All discussion ultimately comes down to the prisoner's dilemma,' he says, pointing to a thought experiment from game theory where a non-cooperative attitude pays off. 'In America, they've overcome the prisoner's dilemma, because there has been collusion between all of the owners to set up arrangements which prevent them from taking individually beneficial decisions. Whereas in Europe, it's not quite mutually assured destruction, but . . .' it's as close to it as you can get. That language, so grimly linked to the Cold War, is apt, given how people within football talk about all of this. When one federation employee privately spoke about rule-bending, and how negotiations between clubs always descend into private whataboutery that are followed by public omertà, it was likened to a 'stand-off . . . but with nuclear weapons'. The most common description of all is an 'arms race'. It is an increasingly reckless one, with the weapons being ruinous squad wages. The flood of TV broadcasting money has caused clubs to offer more and more money to players, eventually blowing even the biggest names out of the water. There are cautionary tales about how distinguished institutions like Rangers, Everton and AC Milan were at the forefront of the grandest changes in football, only to fall victim to the Frankenstein's monsters they helped build. Many current super clubs may yet face the same fate, let alone hundreds of community institutions around the world.

This wage race has been another engine just ploughing through football. It's all the worse since UEFA's internal stance is that wages are not 'investment' but consumption, distorting the system and forcing everyone to overpay. Those same authorities should be protecting football from this, but another driving factor has been increasing deregulation. 'A lack of understanding is endemic in this industry,' one major club executive complains.

Part of the problem is that the major governing bodies have become 'competitors', as they organise highly lucrative events while notionally regulating the game. UEFA found itself in charge of club competitions almost by accident in the 1950s, when French newspaper *L'Équipe* came up with the concept of the European Cup – the Champions League's predecessor – and FIFA simply suggested the continental body organise it. This very idea came from another driving factor: pride. There was irritation that English newspapers were declaring Wolves the best team in Europe after beating Honvèd, a brilliant Hungarian club then on tour. That happenstance of history has further riled figures like Pérez, who feel the clubs should run all this themselves. He was once heard dismissing UEFA president Aleksander Čeferin as 'just some lawyer on €2 million a year'. Clubs now need a wage bill of £300 million to even compete. A constant sophism in football is that it has always been like this, and the big clubs have always won, but there are mountains of evidence to suggest otherwise. The reality is that the game has been a working illustration of the 'boiling frog' apologue. Incremental changes have gradually caused profound transformation without people realising. This is how it becomes normal for so many teams not to win, but it is something new. Between 1958 and 1977, the English title was never defended and 11 different clubs won it. By contrast, Manchester City were recently in the most intense period of dominance ever seen, following long dynasties by Manchester United and Liverpool. They are three of only seven clubs to have won the Premier League in 31 years. Until 2012, no German club had ever won more than three titles in a row, amid a huge variety of champions. Bayern Munich have since won 11 leagues in a row. In Spain, the millennium began with Deportivo La Coruña and Valencia sharing the title. Since 2004, there have only been two seasons when Real Madrid and Barcelona haven't won the league, and they were claimed by Atlético Madrid. One of the Super League clubs, Atlético are who counts as an 'underdog' these days.

It is like this across Europe, where half of the continent's domestic leagues have seen periods of historically unprecedented dominance in the last decade alone. Many of them have become uncompetitive one-team leagues. A huge cause of this is prize money from the Champions League, which stands atop the pyramid as the greatest illustration of the issue. It is no coincidence that 11 of Europe's 13 longest domestic winning streaks have overlapped with the competition's existence since 1992.

14 – Skonto Riga, Latvia, 1991–2004
14 – Lincoln Red Imps, Gibraltar, 2003–16
13 – Rosenborg, Norway, 1992–2004
13 – BATE Borisov, Belarus, 2006–18
13 – Ludogorets Razgrad, Bulgaria, 2012–present
11 – Dinamo Zagreb, Croatia, 2006–16
11 – Bayern Munich, Germany, 2013–23
10 – Red Bull Salzburg, Austria, 2014–present
10 – Sheriff Tiraspol, Moldova, 2001–10
10 – Pyunik, Armenia, 2001–10
10 – Dinamo Tbilisi, Georgia, 1990–99
10 – BFC Dynamo, East Germany, 1979–88
10 – MTK Budapest, Hungary, 1914–25

The 37 years of the old European Cup had 19 winners from nine different countries, with four new champions in its final six years: Yugoslavia's Red Star Belgrade, Romania's Steaua Bucharest, Portugal's FC Porto and the Netherlands' PSV Eindhoven. Scotland's Celtic had won it in 1967. That was a far truer reflection of what a continental competition was supposed to be about. Since 2004, no club from outside the five major leagues has reached the final. France, who didn't even win the original European Cup, have only had one representative and that was a club owned by Qatar. England and Spain have otherwise occupied 27 of the 40 final places, with their clubs winning 16 of the last 20 finals.

The greatest of trophies has itself become a great symbol of neo-liberalism. Leicester's Premier League title has meanwhile been held up as an illustration of football's joyous unpredictability, but it is that rarity that is so concerning. It is only very recently that it's been this astounding for a club outside the elite to win a title. Worse, La Liga president Javier Tebas argues that 2016 'was when the industry was not as financially polarised as it is now'. None of this is to romanticise the past as perfect. Football has always been 'dirty', in the words of many involved. Rather than paying players almost all the money it had, the game used to exploit them. Corruption has been rife. But, as one long-serving figure now regularly says, 'the main moral concern used to be a few bungs'.

That was accompanied by regulation that at least recognised the community role of the game and encouraged competitive balance. All of Spain's clubs used to be member-owned. For almost a century, English football was shaped by Rule 34 in the FA handbook, which was introduced in the 1890s to preserve clubs as non-profit community institutions that could not be asset-stripped or exploited. Directors were prohibited from being paid and dividends were restricted. The regulation was almost a resolution of that tension between sport and business from the very start.[3] It was meanwhile understood that watchable matches were needed to actually grow the new Football League, which meant games had to be unpredictable. So, to mitigate the potential power of big-city clubs, the competition ruled that a portion of gate receipts be shared with away teams.

It's a stance that's almost remarkable to consider now. At the very foundation of the game was a measure that would be seen as preposterously revolutionary in 2023, but the decree of a 20 per cent share actually lasted into the 1980s. This prevented clubs like Arsenal and Manchester United winning the number of titles that European counterparts such as Juventus and Real Madrid did. English football had something that went even further than the vaunted American system, but without ever realising it. It was how Burnley and Huddersfield Town won the league.

Far harsher to modern eyes, the draconian maximum wage served as a crude salary cap from 1904, which worked alongside the old retain-and-transfer system to keep the power with clubs rather than players. It was morally wrong to deny workers their agency but had an equalising sporting effect. 'Buying success' was close to impossible.

The real world had further influence. Foreign player restrictions across Europe meant clubs couldn't accumulate talent in the same way, ensuring an invigorating spread around the game and a higher concentration of domestic players within leagues. The Iron Curtain kept the best Eastern European players in their own countries long into their careers, while communist regimes saw investment in football as part of state projects. This was how Dynamo Kyiv could field one of the continent's best sides long before Andriy Shevchenko's emergence. Even when football began to be televised, more basic technology meant everyone could only watch their local league. Right into the 1990s, it was impossible to see much more than weekly highlights of clubs like Barcelona, quite a contrast to having them at your fingertips.

That plays into another simple factor. There just wasn't as much money in football. Gate receipts were still 90 per cent of a club's income into the 1980s. So, even if there were financial gaps, they couldn't grow. It allowed much more mobility. Brighton & Hove Albion had two of the highest earners in England during the 1980s in Michael Robinson and Steve Foster. The highest wage bill in the country was meanwhile just three times the size of the top tier's lowest, a gap that has since grown to seven times the size. There's a telling story from when England's wealthiest clubs first started looking to break away from this system and travelled to America's National Football League (NFL) for research. When the soccer contingent explained why they were seeking to 'generate more revenue', there was a cautionary response.

'If you think you've got problems now, wait until you have money,' an NFL executive said. It should be acknowledged that one of the main reasons all of this changed was because of a root impetus of sport. It's the same reason players dive, but also what inspires them to the highest level of performance: competitiveness. Sunderland chairman Sir Bob Murray explains it simply. 'There's a lot of self-interest because we have to win games.' For Palios, 'ambition is the lifeblood of the game'.

That's also precisely why the sport requires stringent regulation, to protect it from that innate will to push everything to the limit. Ambition has instead been unchecked for 40 years. It is no coincidence regulation within football started to corrode amid the Reaganomics of the early 1980s. Much of this may seem like dry off-field stories but the truth is that it is all easily tracked, with simple translations on the pitch. Every major development since then has been in service of the game's highly specific form of hyper-capitalism. 'Decisions are made without taking into account what the mid- and long-term effects are,' Tebas argues. Some of those decisions were even necessary in isolation, and it's worth stating that football's explosion did not just happen by accident. Coming together, they transformed the game's economic infrastructure.

A case in point was England's first major change. No one could dispute the Professional Footballers' Association's successful 1961 challenge of the maximum wage was an entirely justifiable labour right. It was just that the decisions that followed allowed uncontrolled wages to unravel the sport. In the early 1980s, steps were taken to remove the sharing of gate receipts. It was at the same time that England's old 'big five' – Manchester United, Liverpool, Arsenal, Tottenham Hotspur and Everton – started to meet informally. The group felt deepening frustration at football's resistance to any modernisation, and there was an undeniable argument that the game was no longer served by what were Victorian-era governing structures. An antiquated governance was possibly why there was no resistance to the next big step.

Spurs' Irving Scholar, having already innovated on advertising, was intent on floating the club on the stock market to improve commercial revenue. Rule 34 prohibited this . . . so Scholar simply set up a holding company to get around it. The FA never even responded to his letter suggesting such ideas. All of this occurred as the NFL's $2 billion television deal in 1982 fired imaginations. The big five felt they were due more than the £25,000 that the broadcasting deal at the time afforded their clubs, especially since it was the same figure that those in the Fourth Division received. It wasn't even as though there was much live football on TV, in what was an underdeveloped industry. State broadcasters like RAI and BBC had minimal competition to show games, meaning there was no incentive to increase the value of broadcasting deals. That was all to be swept away with the whirr of helicopter blades descending into the San Siro stadium. This was how Berlusconi chose to mark his 1986 purchase of AC Milan, as 'Ride of the Valkyries' played to add to the spectacle he wanted. 'I knew people would laugh,' Berlusconi said, 'but we needed to show Milan had a new way of thinking'.[4]

That thinking would show football a new world. It is no exaggeration to describe Berlusconi as one of the most influential figures in football history. A media tycoon who harboured political ambitions and would later become Italian prime minister, he was an archetype for men like Pérez. These were the patriarchal industrialists who shaped the game in the late twentieth century, before states and capitalist funds in the early twenty-first century. Berlusconi was a genuine football fan, who managers like Carlo Ancelotti credited with proper tactical insight. Berlusconi also intuited how the game could complement his ideas on private broadcasting. As a club owner, his most profound effect was integrating all of these ideas into the very infrastructure of the sport.

Technological evolution had fostered encrypted multi-channel satellite television, but the maintenance of this was hugely expensive. New broadcasters required content that people would first pay for and then, crucially, subscribe to. Movies and pornography were beneficial for the first part. It was the emotional connection to football, however, that proved essential to the second.

Berlusconi believed broadcasting rights could propel both his business and the game, creating what would be the industry's first 'virtuous cycle'. That phrase would be used again and again, by virtually all of the major clubs. It here meant fans would pay for games, broadcasters would invest more in football, and all of it would become more attractive. These virtuous cycles would have many negative consequences for the wider game, including even for AC Milan, but at that point they offered blockbusting colour TV in a world of grainy images. There was now competition – and ambition – in the industry, as similar models followed. Leo

Kirch's media group in Germany, Canal+ in France and Rupert Murdoch's Sky in Britain all used football to drive business in the same way. It was precisely this conflict of interest that would cause the UK government to prevent a Murdoch takeover of Manchester United in 1998.

If all of this allowed Berlusconi to become one of football's most influential figures, a first-round European Cup tie in September 1987 was inadvertently one of the most influential fixtures. It aptly involved Real Madrid, the continent's most successful club, who were drawn against Napoli, led by the world's greatest player in Diego Maradona. The two legs were to be among just six appearances for the Argentinian in the European Cup, as Madrid won 3-1 on aggregate. Berlusconi watched on and couldn't believe a game like this was just being wasted, especially as it meant one of either Northern Ireland's Linfield or Norway's Lillestrøm going further in the competition than the Italian champions. 'The European Cup has become a historical anachronism,' the Italian mogul said in a landmark interview with *World Soccer* in 1991. 'It is economic nonsense that a club such as Milan might be eliminated in the first round. It is not modern thinking.'[5] It was, however, the essence of sport: random chance, sudden death, unpredictability. Berlusconi was already seeking to erode much of that. He felt it absurd that the biggest clubs were not regularly meeting in more glamorous matches, believing football should be a 'television spectacular' freed from archaic parochial restrictions. London-based consultancy Saatchi & Saatchi were commissioned to come up with a model for a 'European Television League' that would replace the European Cup. Satellite television, like Berlusconi's own Canale 5, could naturally offer the perfect home for this. This whole idea represented the game's core ambition given full form, and it would shape football's future. The threat of it exerted a gravitational force on the sport. Everything that has happened since, from every reform to every distribution change, was all based on the 30-year threat of a Super League.

Crucially, Berlusconi was not alone. Rangers were just as aggravated as Berlusconi at big-spending clubs going out early. The 1980s alone saw them eliminated in the first round of all three continental competitions at the time. Rangers found they couldn't properly budget under such unpredictability, especially as they bought expensive English signings such as Terry Butcher and Trevor Francis. So, club general secretary Campbell Ogilvie drew up plans to present to UEFA that would bring more guaranteed matches in the form of group stages. It quickly gained support from other clubs, adding to the pressure from Berlusconi. England's 'Big Five' were meanwhile arriving at a similar conclusion as the AC Milan owner. They were pushing for a breakaway from the Football League.

All of these forces started to combine, and in some cases with events of far greater importance. As Victorian governing bodies oversaw Edwardian architecture, all amid the economic disparity of the 1980s, a series of tragedies occurred that seemed to symbolise how the infrastructure of the sport was crumbling. In 1985, 55 fans died in the Bradford City stadium fire. Just over two weeks later, in the European Cup final itself, 39 people – mostly Juventus supporters – died when a wall collapsed at the decrepit Heysel Stadium after a breach by Liverpool fans. Grave discussions in the aftermath only increased the impetus for change.

Modernisation would soon be imposed upon the game, although only after the most serious failure of all. On 15 April 1989, 'grossly negligent failures by police and ambulance services' led to a crush at Hillsborough that saw 97 innocent Liverpool supporters lose their lives.[6] The report on the tragedy by Lord Justice

Taylor called for widespread reform of British football, especially as regards the quality and safety of stadiums. UEFA meanwhile overhauled their requirements for staging games. The order for all-seater stadiums required significant investment, which made arguments for changes to the football economy even more persuasive. England's 'Big Five' could now claim their 'Premier League' idea was a necessity.[7] It was typical of the era. A social pursuit had been neglected to the point it needed profound reform, but that reform was co-opted by the most capitalistic interests.

It is why 1992 is one of those watersheds in history, a definitive point where the sporting element of football ceded majority space to the business side. That would be taken to extremes, escalating with every successive broadcasting deal for the new competitions created that year: the Champions League and Premier League. The first television contract was what really marked out the English breakaway. The initial £214 million deal with Sky was almost a five-fold increase on the previous £44 million Football League agreement, with a further £90 million coming from overseas deals and sponsorship. Even more enticingly for the 22 clubs, most of the earnings would be going to them, compared to just 75 per cent before.

What remains remarkable is the lack of resistance. Any breakaway actually needed permission from the FA to operate within the English football pyramid, so the governing body had considerable leverage to ask for all kinds of conditions. If the FA had said 'No', the Premier League could not have happened. Instead, as with the evasion of Rule 34, it was just waved through. Self-interest of a different kind dictated their response. The FA was at war with the Football League, in one of those bitter grudges that now looks like a relic. The Premier League was sanctioned as 'a way of putting the knife' into the Football League.[8] These were the words of later FA chairman Greg Dyke, who was scathing about his predecessors.

'As I'm just finding out, the biggest fuck-up in the world was the FA didn't ask for anything,' Dyke complained on taking the job. 'But the trouble was that Bert Millichip and Graham Kelly were not the brightest blokes . . .' The concession was that the new competition would be called the 'FA Premier League', but the first part was left off the Founder Members Agreement until Kelly, then chief executive of the governing body, put it in by hand.[9] Kelly would later admit they were 'guilty of a tremendous lack of vision'.[10] It could be an epitaph for football regulation.

UEFA's more technocratic leadership of Lennart Johansson and Gerhard Aigner at least sought to initially incorporate a more responsible Nordic economic policy into the new Champions League. Ogilvie's plan, in the words of Saatchi & Saatchi's Alex Fynn, 'offered a more practical solution' to Berlusconi's 'political threats'. For the 1991–92 season, UEFA adopted one of the Rangers secretary's secondary proposals, which was knock-outs leading up to two groups of four. It wasn't until 1992–93 that the European Cup actually became the Champions League, as UEFA took some of Berlusconi's idea for a television spectacular. TEAM Marketing AG were mandated to come up with glossy branding, devising the Starball logo and stirring anthem, based on George Frideric Handel's 'Zadok the Priest'. The classical theme suitably captured the gravitas of the old European Cup. Berlusconi's Fininvest then duly won the broadcasting rights for Italy, beating the state broadcaster RAI.

It was still unmistakably symbolic how the Champions League's first ever winners, an immensely talented Olympique Marseille, were almost instantly punished for match-fixing in Ligue 1. Owner Bernard Tapie, yet another business magnate with political ambitions, was described by a former parliamentary aide as 'a person who knows no limits – he would do anything to get to the top'.[11] Desperate to beat Berlusconi's AC Milan in the Champions League final, Marseille had arranged for payments to Valenciennes players to go easier in a crucial league match the weekend before. The club were eventually relegated from Ligue 1 but, in a typical UEFA fudge, were banned from the 1993–94 Champions League without being stripped of the title. Paris Saint-Germain were offered the place but declined because their owners, Canal+, didn't want to aggravate the many Marseille fans among their subscribers. None of it did any damage to the Champions League brand. When AC Milan were back for a third consecutive final in 1995, the overall viewer numbers for the competition had risen to 3.64 billion, up 61 per cent from the previous season.[12] Berlusconi was beaming, at least before a young Ajax beat them in that final. The glossy new products were proving increasingly attractive.

By 1996, Sky's deal with the Premier League went up to £670 million. By 2000, it was £1.1 billion. The increased exposure was in turn proving more attractive to commercial interests. Manchester United, having followed Spurs into the stock exchange, were the first to really capitalise on this by bringing all merchandising in-house. Their commercial revenue went up 180 per cent between 1993 and 1994, and total turnover by 1998 was more than Arsenal and Liverpool combined.[13] By then, United were worth even more than the New York Yankees, and consistently topping the newly commissioned Deloitte Football Money League.[14]

Almost as ubiquitous as the club's badge were UEFA's sponsors like Mastercard and Continental. The European body had adopted the FIFA model of centralised TV deals and exclusive contracts with blue-chip companies. The income ensured the Champions League structure changed again in 1994, so the first round proper was four groups of four, before another expansion in 1997. The latter was a landmark moment, as second-placed clubs from highest-ranking leagues were allowed in for the first time. It went against the competition's very name but, again, the brand wasn't affected. The Champions League only became more lucrative, beginning the process of hardwiring inequality into the European football structure. The 50 per cent of prize money that went to the wider game began to be reduced with every cycle of broadcast negotiations, as the threat of the Super League always provided the leverage. More money went towards mere participation, reinforcing the position of clubs who regularly qualified.

The decision for the biggest show in sport to be held in the home of all of these commercial issues couldn't have been more timely. The first FIFA World Cup in the United States, in 1994, is now seen as an under-appreciated influence in overwhelmingly changing the game. It was just the effects weren't felt for around a decade. For all the everyday power of the club game, it is still the World Cup that primarily shapes football's economic cycles because of the immense focus on the hosts and mega broadcasting contracts. USA 94, along with Qatar 2022, shaped so much more. FIFA's stated goal when the tournament was awarded was for football to 'grow in a very big way'.[15] That can now be witnessed. The biggest market on the planet directly saw how the rest of the world was obsessed with stars at big European clubs, like Juventus's Roberto Baggio or Barcelona's Romário. AC Milan duly supplied many of the Italy team beaten in the final by Brazil.

Berlusconi's home country, invigorated by its own World Cup in 1990, was appropriately enjoying the benefits of all this the most. Serie A was far and away the planet's dominant domestic league. It was enriched by both the country's national and football cultures, as well as the moguls and industrial families that defined the era. Berlusconi led a group that included steel magnate Massimo

Moratti at city rivals Inter Milan, as well as Fiat's Agnelli family at Juventus. Even previously modest clubs were fielding the most glamorous teams. At Parma, the wages of stars such as Gianluigi Buffon and Hernán Crespo were driven by the income from the Tanzi family's Parmalat food company. Such financial superiority ensured an Italian club featured in 9 out of 10 European Cup or Champions League finals from 1988–89 to 1997–98. The spending reached such a level that, when AC Milan broke the world transfer record for Torino's Gianluigi Lentini, Pope John Paul II called the £12 million fee an 'offence against the dignity of work'.[16] It's hard to decide what was more quaint, the price or the fact this was an era when Italian clubs could only field three foreign players. The famous AC Milan side fired by the Netherlands' Ruud Gullit, Marco van Basten and Frank Rijkaard is far less cosmopolitan than today's AFC Bournemouth team.

Although many countries had their own restrictions on foreign players, UEFA had sufficient concerns about such transfers diluting the game that they struck their own agreement with the European Commission in 1991.[17] This was the famous three-plus-two rule, where clubs in continental competition could only field three foreign players, but also two 'assimilated' that had been in a country for five years. Their implementation was brief, due to a development that had been a long time coming. The last columns of the old transfer system were demolished by European law. In 1990, Jean-Marc Bosman's contract with RFC Liège expired, but the Belgian club were still legally entitled to demand a transfer fee. The midfielder's preferred club of Dunkerque refused to meet the asking price, so RFC simply refused to release him, as his wages were cut by 70 per cent since he was no longer considered for the first team. Bosman suffered three years of frustration before his case was finally brought before the European Court of Justice in

October 1993, where he sued for restraint of trade against his club, the Belgian Football Association and UEFA.

Judging the case from the perspective of labour rights, the court had no choice but to rule in the player's favour. Judging from the perspective of sporting regulation, though, it was a classic case of unintended consequences. Football's failure to adapt had a ruinous effect on competitive balance. The so-called 'Bosman ruling' allowed players to move for free within the European Union at the end of their contracts, but also ensured UEFA had no choice but to remove foreign player restrictions.[18] The lament within both European law and sport is that 'nobody foresaw just how enormous a change would occur'. Rick Parry, the Premier League's first chief executive, describes it as 'an absolutely pivotal moment' in football history. What the Bosman ruling really did was create an almost completely open labour market – more than even international banking – for an industry where all financial safeguards were being eroded, at the exact same time as new floods of money were coming in. The game was only going one way, and was to be swept there at drastic speed. Even by 2024, one high-level UEFA meeting saw UEFA's most senior figures lament that Bosman 'made the European space impossible'.

The frustration is that, even by the late 1990s, the financial gaps still weren't as vast. At the time of the ruling in 1995, after all, Ajax were the European champions. Blackburn Rovers were English champions and Nantes the French champions. Bayern Munich finished sixth in the Bundesliga. Bosman would wedge everything apart. There is an argument that if regulation like UEFA's highly debated Financial Fair Play (FFP) rules had been brought in around then, it would have been much more beneficial. A competitive balance could have been preserved, as opposed to the financial superiority of a small group of clubs.

As it was, the first high-profile 'Bosman' signing was indicative. Edgar Davids moved from Ajax to AC Milan, the very club the Dutch team had beaten in the 1994–95 Champions League final. The midfielder became one of six players from that match who left Ajax within a year. By 1999, no one was left. The asset-stripping would only accelerate for the next club outside the five major leagues to win the Champions League, who would also turn out to be the last. FC Porto lost five players, as well as charismatic manager José Mourinho, in the weeks immediately after their 2003–04 victory over Monaco. A further 6 of the 14 who appeared in the final would leave the following year. The rate of departure had doubled from Ajax, from an average of two years to one.

Bosman had fully released the wage race, with clubs free to spend as much as they could and hoard as many players as they could. The system was now fully geared towards concentration, which further conditioned the rest of the game. 'It's that global element at the top that pulls everyone up,' Palios explains. 'Without any sort of bridle, that upward drag caused gaps underneath, and those gaps become tank traps.' Former Spurs chairman Alan Sugar typically had a more colourful description. He offered up his famous 'prune juice' analogy to describe how the vast majority of the game's money went straight out, and into players' pockets. That consistently amounted to around 60–70 per cent of all revenue across the Champions League era.

It was this dynamic, driven by the base ambition of the game, that necessitated FFP in the first place. Too many clubs were going bankrupt trying to keep up, with too many players outside the elite going unpaid. The 2000–01 Champions League semi-finalists Leeds United and Valencia infamously overextended themselves. Warnings had already come in a 1980s financial crisis that changed the fabric of Spanish football and forced the government to intervene.[19] Struggling to pay debts, most clubs were converted from 'sports associations' to companies, with only four allowed to remain fan-owned. They were the institutions with deeper regional representation: Osasuna, Athletic Bilbao, Barcelona and Real Madrid. It was to prove another social element that would contribute to commercial branding, especially for the latter two.

The Bosman ruling meanwhile made escalating media rights all the more influential, since money was inevitably attracted to the best players. The domestic markets of clubs like Ajax, Porto and Rangers were no longer big enough. Illustrating a recurring theme in modern football's history, this was only the world Rangers themselves had wanted. UEFA finally adopted Ogilvie's first model for the Champions League for the 1999–2000 season, which was a 32-team 8-group structure. The crucial difference was that it now included the top four clubs from the best performing leagues, who would inevitably be the wealthiest clubs. All of this was done under pressure from a new group they had formed in 1998, called the G14, who set out the most concrete plans to break away with a Super League. It was the most explicit threat up to that point, going so far as Media Partners group investigating the possibility of a closed competition.

'It's remained on the table since then, even when unsaid,' relays one official who has been in the room for such negotiations. There were often moments when UEFA employees would privately talk among themselves about how new reforms weren't good for football, but they knew that if they lost the big clubs it would split the game, while removing money from the rest. That was always the justification for every single decision. It was just another cycle, though. The big clubs argued they brought in the money, but the issue was the economic structures only reinforced their earning power. There was some resistance. When former Manchester

United chief executive Peter Kenyon mentioned a Super League idea at one meeting, he was met with an acerbic response from Chelsea's Ken Bates. 'Oh Peter, why don't you piss off out of the Premier League.'[20]

It was actually outside of the Premier League, despite its eventual unassailable power, that all of these forces were synthesised. Florentino Pérez was to prove Berlusconi's successor as the game's most forceful visionary, even if that vision wasn't beneficial to the game itself. His victory in the 2000 Real Madrid presidential race is another of those historic turning points. That campaign was built on the audacious gambit of promising the voting fans he would sign Luís Figo from Barcelona, or else pay for their annual memberships. As astounding as that pitch was, it was suitably central to a much grander strategy naturally built on spectacle. Pérez even had a branding that almost matched the name of 'Real Madrid' itself: *los Galácticos*. The idea was to move the notion of a team into the stratosphere, illuminated by real stars, which was perfect for a more globalised world.

Pérez first benefited from more local factors. Real Madrid's training ground was controversially sold to clear the club's substantial debt,[21] followed by constant accusations that similar deals represented illegal state aid.[22] 'The House of Pérez', in the words of one European official, had been created. The Madrid president was already looking beyond all that. Since Manchester United were at that point a listed company, Pérez pored over their accounts like a manager looking for players.[23] What immediately impressed him was how United divided their income into three areas – TV, stadium and commercial – but Pérez felt it wasn't far enough.[24] Sir Alex Ferguson used Manchester United's success to sign better players in order to win more trophies. Pérez felt the players themselves needed to drive everything, as the stars everyone wanted to watch. This was beyond Berlusconi's television spectacular. It was the big screen, as Real Madrid began to see themselves in the same mould as movie studios. They were the rivals now.

'Disney is a content producer, and we're another content producer,' Real Madrid marketing executive José Ángel Sánchez said around the time.[25] This was why world-record transfer fees were actually part of the branding. Like box-office figures from movie stars, they created the sense this was must-watch. The summer presentations for Galácticos like Zinedine Zidane, Ronaldo and David Beckham became events in themselves. It represented a new virtuous cycle – to a point. Between Figo's first season in 2000–01 and Beckham's first in 2003–04, Real Madrid's income went from €138.2 million to €236 million. By the next year, they were the first club to usurp Manchester United at the top of Deloitte's Football Money League. That was celebrated almost like a Champions League title. Beckham's fame was key to this, even if he didn't have an obvious tactical place in the actual football team.

Much of that was again aided by external forces. A Spanish competition court ruled in 1993 that La Liga would not be permitted to sell their broadcasting rights in the way the new Premier League had, which was as a single entity. That allowed clubs to sell individually, which had the unintended effect of destroying competition rather than serving it. For 14 years, until a European court ruling in 2007, Real Madrid and Barcelona were able to dominate almost all television income in Spain. This at one point amounted to 90 per cent of the total value of rights, which resulted in a duopoly where they regularly claimed over 90 points each.

Pérez might say that's how it should be. Others describe it as La Liga's 'wasted decade'. The internet was meanwhile speeding up and spreading, which led to Pérez talking of how 'technology works in our favour'.[26] By the end of 2005, a Nike advertisement featuring Barcelona's Ronaldinho became the first YouTube video to reach one million views. The instant reaction was that this would 'change everything'. It changed the parameters of football. A club's size used to be restricted by how many fans could get into their stadium, and then the size of the TV market. Now, like with the global transfer market, there were potentially no limits at all.

This was realised by American businessmen who had studiously noted the effect of USA 94. Billionaires like Malcolm Glazer similarly viewed sports clubs as media companies, akin to 'high-scale marketing', and they saw immense financial potential in Manchester United. This was especially felt after a period where the revenues of major clubs had already increased by 10 to 25 per cent, 'far higher than that seen in most industries', according to Manchester City chief executive Ferran Soriano.[27] The Glazers subsequently applied the most reductively capitalist approach possible to purchasing United in 2005. One of European football's greatest institutions was bought through a purchase as financially cynical as a leveraged buyout. This was an approach that typically spread through the deregulation of the 1980s and involved using a company's success against it. The Glazers borrowed £525 million of the £790 million needed to buy United, most of it against the club's future earnings.

It was one other area where a lack of regulation reshaped the game. The Premier League under chief executive Richard Scudamore described itself as 'ownership-model neutral'. Any investment was seen as good for the brand so long as it came from someone without a criminal conviction, which was basically the only requirement of the notorious 'fit and proper person's test' to buy clubs. There wasn't enough consideration about what any of this might mean for the future. The Glazers knew exactly what they had, though.

Malcolm Glazer's sons, Avram and Joel, repeatedly described United as 'the strongest brand name in the sports world'. Another arms race ensued, where all the major clubs chased commercial opportunity around the planet. Real Madrid were at that point benefiting from deals with European brands like Siemens, reflecting how the continent's biggest financial engine was in Germany. That area's major power, Bayern Munich, would meanwhile vote to make their football side a limited company in order to form strategic partnerships with a select group of major companies such as Adidas and Audi. The horizons would soon expand.

The Bundesliga's central broadcasting rights prevented Bayern from negotiating their own TV deals like the Spanish and Italian giants, although it later emerged they received secret bonus payments from Kirch's company for staying in the system. That system was, in any case, serving them. The Bundesliga has long been lauded for its community focus in the form of the '50+1' rule, where members hold 50 per cent of voting rights plus one more to ensure majority control. In terms of competition, though, this more parochial approach simply couldn't cope with Bayern's global dimension. The Champions League was by then being shown in over 200 countries, with UEFA beginning to pay out billions of euros in prize money to competing clubs. From 2003 to 2012, 45 per cent of that money went to just 12 clubs.[28]

The growth of that group started to cannibalise the rest of the game. The idealised global football pyramid under FIFA instead became a steep spike that dropped dramatically. The League of Ireland offered an early case study for the world. Up until the 1960s, the country's domestic fixtures had relatively healthy crowd attendances. English highlights show *Match of the Day* then became available through the BBC, and many Irish fans never looked back. They became known for travelling to clubs like Manchester United and Liverpool, setting a trend that would spread around the globe. This became the new culture of football. Going from Asia through Africa into Europe and even South America, many fans would look to the most glamorous clubs over their local teams. Even in Spain, a 2001 national poll found that Real Madrid were the most popular club in all but three cities.[29] They were of course Barcelona and the two Basque cities of Bilbao and San Sebastián.

The Champions League worsened this verticality, and not just through its ubiquity. The prize money created one-team domestic leagues that are 'disastrous' for television rights. It got to the point where competitions like the Latvian league had to pay broadcasters to show matches. This was all the more ruinous to the vitality of football since various studies have shown a 90 per cent correlation between wage bill and league position.[30] Success, in very direct terms, could now be bought. That became a further accelerator of the wage race. The biggest clubs wanted to spend more money, in turn becoming less inclined to give it away to the rest of the pyramid. UEFA 'solidarity money', which was that given out to the thousands of clubs not in European competition, began to be reduced. The attitude was already dismissive. It was as long ago as 1985 that Martin Edwards said 'smaller clubs . . . should be put to sleep'.[31] Soriano has since relayed the story of how an American sports manager once argued to him that clubs like Barcelona should be seeking to share more money with clubs like Villarreal for the commercial sake of their own matches. 'While I was listening to him I found it difficult to think about maximising any income of any kind, because all I wanted and cared for was for FC Barcelona to win all the matches, win and always win, independently of the "tournament overall income" or suchlike concepts.'[32]

The sadness is that the historic growth of the sport was never solely based on the 'great' clubs. Vitality used to be one of football's great virtues. In contrast to super clubs now attracting so many fans, it was the game's variety that used to dazzle. Many clubs that are no longer considered commercial giants had their time capturing the imagination. You can go even further than Eusebio's Benfica or Jock Stein's Celtic. There were periods when everyone wanted a glimpse of AS Saint-Étienne and FC Dinamo Tbilisi, both having been involved in electric continental ties with Liverpool.

Pelé's Santos, Zico's Flamengo and Juan Román Riquelme's Boca Juniors all eviscerated European champions in the old Intercontinental Cup, reflecting South America's historic status as the stage for football of a quality beyond Europe. These days, their best talent would have long left the continent, most of them before their twenties. South America became an export economy, as it had shrunk to one 10 times smaller than Europe. While the continent's adoration of the game has preserved a distinctive football culture, it isn't thriving, since even Argentina's league is made up of those not good enough to be sold abroad, or veterans returning. One academic study likened the transfer market to the coffee industry, in how wealthy countries earned so much from 'processing' the raw materials – in this case, the talent – rather than actually producing it.[33]

Tebas describes it as 'an ethical problem' since 'little by little, competitiveness is lost'. So much of the Champions League felt predetermined, as the wealthiest clubs built bigger and better squads. It would also bring them to new peaks. Concentration of talent inevitably meant concentration of success. Barcelona's transcendent 2008–09 treble – which represented the first time a Spanish club won La Liga, the Copa del Rey and Champions League in the same season – also marked the first of a series of similar records at the top of the game. Feats previously considered impossible were now achieved almost every season, sometimes with relative ease.

From 2008 to 2024, the five major leagues saw 11 types of trebles, where previously there had been just one. Manchester United's 1998–99 heroics had been unique. The biggest names were indeed more than just football clubs or 'entertainment providers', to use the language their commercial staff did when seeking sponsors through their 'global reach'. They were 'super clubs'.

It was that very scale, however, that would quickly usher in another era. It was one these same clubs couldn't quite control, paradoxically because of the hold they had over the planet. They had a unique social power. Eventual Arsenal owner Stan Kroenke noticed it on a business trip to Hong Kong. 'I walk up to a news-stand on the waterfront, pick up a magazine, and it's all about the English Premier League,' he told *Sports Illustrated*. 'Maybe we have something here.'[34]

An even wealthier but more taciturn individual sensed that something in 2003. The official story has always been that Abramovich had been struck by Real Madrid's wondrous 3-1 victory over Manchester United in the 2002–03 Champions League quarter-final first leg when watching on television, so wanted to attend the second leg in person. Agent Pini Zahavi was requested to sort it, but soon found himself asked to make inroads into something bigger. Abramovich was so taken by the game, which featured Ronaldo scoring an audacious hat-trick in a 4-3 Manchester United win, that he wanted to buy a football club. That was at least the official story, which also served as the perfect summation of the era in how a glamour occasion between the two biggest super clubs led to greater powers getting involved.

Manchester United were, at that point, not for sale. Real Madrid and Barcelona were ring-fenced by fan ownership. Chelsea, however, were available. They were another club who had financially overextended themselves and needed saving. It has become a matter of debate within football over whether Abramovich's takeover constituted 'sportswashing'. What is beyond doubt was that it transformed football, both in terms of ownership and the sport's relationship with money. Nothing like this had been seen before. The burgeoning Premier League hadn't previously involved an owner who wasn't either British or based in Britain, let alone one so remote and mysterious. This was someone of a global scale, with resources of unprecedented depth. It was football's first great disruption, in how the hundreds of millions of pounds that Abramovich immediately spent came directly from outside the game. Wages and fees were instantly inflated. The financial threshold to compete just got much higher. 'For the first time,' Parry argues, 'there was huge expenditure with little regard for profit or loss.' Families like Arsenal's Hill-Woods and Liverpool's Moores may have been wealthy, in the words of one executive, 'but they weren't oligarchs'.

This was what the game had left itself open to, ripe for takeover. Oligarch comes from the Ancient Greek word *oligarkhēs*, meaning 'rule by the few', and is primarily used to describe a class of mega-rich figures who exert immense power through quickly accumulated resources and political connections.[35] It is most commonly associated with Russia, since so many rose out of the shrapnel of the Iron Curtain. The supposed new freedoms from the death of communism actually afforded many cynical opportunists the freedom to plunder preposterous wealth from unregulated resources and the sale of former state assets.

That period, symbolised by the fall of the Berlin Wall, was celebrated as the final victory of free-market capitalism and liberal democracy – the same forces that had transformed football in the 1980s. It has by now become a cliche to refer to political scientist Francis Fukuyama at this point, as he declared 'the end of history' in how this economic structure would forever shape the future.

Except, in an evolution that would be clearly mirrored by the global game, the inequalities hardwired into that system would quickly bring economic divisions that forced greater fissures. Football had of course embraced this to an even greater degree, adopting this distinctive model of hyper-capitalism. There's an early line from Thomas Piketty's *Capital in the Twenty-First Century* that could aptly describe the game:

> When the rate of return on capital exceeds the rate of growth of output and income, as it did in the nineteenth century and seems quite likely to do again in the twenty-first, capitalism automatically generates arbitrary and unsustainable inequalities that radically undermine the meritocratic values on which democratic societies are based.[36]

In the wider world, this resulted in the 2008 economic crash. Banks began to collapse and had to be nationalised. The top end of football still stayed relatively robust. The Premier League's revenues grew by 20 per cent in 2008 and 9 per cent in 2009.[37] Even within that, though, individual clubs started to feel the pressure. Takeovers increased, especially from American owners. Various forces were again coalescing.

Western economies turned to the apparently limitless funds of Gulf sovereign wealth funds, who were ready and willing to invest as part of economic diversification programmes. Abu Dhabi, Qatar and Dubai became new centres of the global economy almost overnight.

'The British government was essentially going cap in hand to the Gulf looking for sovereign wealth injections to prop up our banking sector,' academic Chris Davidson explains.

Around that time, UK prime minister Gordon Brown and business secretary Peter Mandelson had a private dinner with the then Emir of Qatar, Hamad bin Khalifa Al Thani, and the then prime minister Hamad bin Jassim. As those at the table eased into conversation, there was a conspicuous early question.

'Are you thinking of buying a football club?'

2.

WHAT IS SPORTSWASHING?

If the feeling pervades that football is being taken over, and that the game has moved beyond the reach of the regular fan into something much more serious, it makes it all the more important to try and articulate what is actually happening. There is a lot going on, as is maybe summed up by one defining scene.

It was June 2023 on the pitch of Istanbul's Atatürk Stadium, and Pep Guardiola was intensely embracing his victorious Manchester City players. Nearby, chief executive Ferran Soriano was taking photos of chairman Khaldoon Al Mubarak, who was holding the European Cup itself. Far above them was City's named owner, Sheikh Mansour bin Zayed Al Nahyan, attending just his second ever match. He was happily sharing this family moment with his elder brother, Sheikh Mohamed bin Zayed Al Nahyan, the ruler of Abu Dhabi, who had arrived shortly before kick-off with a huge security detail and gone straight to his seat. There were many more humble family moments in the stands around them. There, City fans who had been going since the 1950s hugged children and grandchildren and just couldn't keep it in. Some openly admitted they couldn't have imagined this ever happening.

City, historically Manchester's second club, were champions of Europe as a result of unprecedented investment from Abu Dhabi. Many fans were talking about 'the greatest owners in the world'. Even those with more ambivalent feelings couldn't deny some sense of gratitude. They would be far from alone in that. Thousands of Newcastle United supporters celebrated the club's takeover by Saudi Arabia's Public Investment Fund in October 2021 with an open-air party around St James' Park. Chelsea fans sang Roman Abramovich's name even after he had been sanctioned by the British government for a 'close relationship' with Russian president Vladimir Putin. Argentina players still light up at the mere mention of Doha, because that was where their dreams came true of lifting the World Cup. It has a sense of magic for them. There is certainly some sleight of hand here, an act of distraction. It is understandably difficult to have too many rational thoughts about human rights amid the profound emotion of sporting victory. They are, well, washed away.

If the inclination is to describe this as the very essence of 'sportswashing', there's an argument that that phrase barely begins to convey what is actually happening. The concept the term seeks to articulate is now about so much more than supporter reaction, public relations or even the implied idea of image cleansing. Many of the states accused of sportswashing don't really care about obscuring anything.

Even the word seems too light for something that involves hard power and soft. Part of that comes from overuse, as awareness has spread through the game. Human rights activist Iyad el-Baghdadi believes 'a new word is needed'. Michael Page of Human Rights Watch says 'it's useful shorthand but doesn't deal with the scale of the problem'. Exploration of that scale is all the more important since the concept at the core of sportswashing has reshaped both the psychological and the sporting architecture of the game. That's quite the effect for a phrase that first appeared in media in 2015, about Azerbaijan. The term wasn't commonly used until 2018, when *Der Spiegel* reported on a sensational collection of leaked emails from Manchester City. Amnesty International even used quotation marks when referencing the concept in a statement for that game-changing story.[1]

'The UAE's enormous investment in Manchester City is one of football's most brazen attempts to "sportswash" a country's deeply tarnished image through the glamour of the game,' said Amnesty International's Devin Kenny at the time.

FairSquare's Nick McGeehan, one of the first activists to draw attention to the subject, believes the phrase was coined from trying to make sense of a dynamic that had gone under the radar but was having overt consequences. 'Amnesty used this term because they were troubled by what they were seeing, which was autocratic states getting involved in sport. They needed something to hang protests on, since it's not a human rights violation to buy a football club.'

A pertinent question is what does buying a football club actually mean for human rights? That's still only part of the dynamic, though. The impulse at the core of sportswashing goes back much further, to the 'bread and circuses' of Ancient Rome. The *Ludi*, or public games, were about superficial distraction and control. In other words, a primitive politicisation of spectacle. That idea can take many forms, but the fundamental motivation connects many different historic events. It's no coincidence Benito Mussolini's 1934 World Cup and Nazi Germany's 1936 Olympics both evoked Roman pageantry. Neither was about distraction or 'washing', although Adolf Hitler did issue a directive that anti-Semitic signs be removed from German main streets.[2] It was otherwise pure projection and propaganda. Autocratic states still want to stage World Cups for that purpose, but the idea has evolved way beyond these mega-events. That evolution has primarily come from the Gulf states. Through that, as well as the assessments of human rights activists and political experts, it feels possible to distil the concept this disputed phrase seeks to convey.

Sportswashing in this form is the centrally planned political use of sport to normalise autocratic states, for the purpose of perpetuating their authoritarian structures without the need for reform. That's also where the more benignly framed description of 'economic diversification' fits in. Immense wealth is essential to the concept. The obvious question is what they are trying to diversify for? The answer, put bluntly, is to keep dictatorships going. The answer that many in football give to such questions is instructive, meanwhile, since it's often to dismiss the idea. Several figures interviewed for this book, some of them having done business with the states most accused of sportswashing, say they 'don't believe' in it. Others are frustrated with how a greater responsibility appears to be put on football than any other industry, an argument that some supporters also make about their clubs. This was articulated by La Liga president Javier Tebas, who has otherwise been one of the biggest critics of state-owned clubs. 'We cannot always point the finger simply at football . . . and then on the other hand be selling weapons or conduct business with these countries'. That isn't quite true, though. There is a difference between the necessities of realpolitik for a government, who can still face criticisms, and the requirements for sporting regulation. The question of what sportswashing means as a phrase similarly cuts across the more philosophical question of what football is supposed to be for.

It isn't that the game faces greater social responsibility. It's that football has a responsibility to itself to examine the consequences of all this for the sport. There's also the very reason that states seek out football in the first place. It has 'a unique emotional and cultural appeal', in the words of Amnesty International's Steve Cockburn. 'It's far bigger than cricket or the Olympics.'

It is still the modern Olympics that illustrate how common that element of sportswashing can be. A significant motivation in the bidding for London 2012, according to some directly involved in the planning, was to improve the UK's image after aiding the US-led invasion of Iraq in 2003. The 2016 Rio Olympics then built on the perception of Brazil as fun that football had been crucial to creating, despite so many societal problems. James Lynch, who has worked for the UK government in the Gulf, believes the region's states would have 'absolutely looked at that branding'. 'It's classic sportswashing.'

The phrase itself is believed to have derived from 'greenwashing', where companies use environmental causes to detract from criticisms. That is partly why businesses seek to associate with sport as much as states. In 2012, Liverpool sponsors Standard Chartered had to pay €300 million for lapses in anti-money laundering procedures and were criticised for leaving 'the US financial system vulnerable to terrorists, weapons dealers, drug kingpins and corrupt regimes'.[3] This is where football's relationship with business entangles it in all manner of other politics. Some of the fortune Stan Kroenke used to pay for Arsenal came from Wal-Mart's business approach, where pay is so low that many staff have to be subsidised by the US state with food stamps and housing. Kroenke, who previously disclosed that he owned 2 per cent of the company's stock, donated almost $300,000 to the Republican Party between 2000 and 2013. George Bush, US President for the first eight years of that period, had previously been advised by strategist Karl Rove to buy Major League Baseball's Texas Rangers as it would give him 'exposure' and a prominence 'easily recalled by people'.[4]

Such is the subversion of football that if you were to draw one of those maps displaying geopolitical influence on the game, it would maybe only leave North Korea untouched. There was even a period in the 2010s when China looked like it would reshape the game, in what had been the most centralised national sporting programme since the Soviet Union. President Xi Jinping felt the growth of the country as a football power could complement its rise as an economic superpower. The problem, ironically, was that its programme wasn't centralised enough. There was almost no proper planning. The Chinese state soon realised football wasn't having any positive economic effect because money was just sluicing out of the country on huge wages to foreign stars like Carlos Tevez. A disengagement ensured China still hasn't been awarded a World Cup, despite widespread expectation within the game that it would host 2030. China never replicated Russia's influence in that way.

The long build-up to the 2018 World Cup, and what followed, now almost serves as a showcase for how modern sportswashing works in practice. Putin's regime perhaps wrote the modern play-book. There were even echoes of a cruder era. Argentina's hosting of the 1978 World Cup, used so bluntly by Jorge Videla's military junta, had its legacy softened by the fluttering white ticker tape that became so famous. Russia went gaudier for 2018. The tape that went up in the air as France lifted the trophy was gold. Some of those leaves are still on show at the FIFA museum in Zürich. Putin, however, didn't need to look as far as Argentina 1978 for influence. The former KGB agent had served in East Germany and directly witnessed how sport was politically used, realising its immense value in ensuring internal stability and international projection. A newly elected Putin had already told Russian athletes for the 2000 Olympics that 'victories in sport do more to cement the nation than one hundred political slogans'.[5] The 2018 World Cup was the culmination of a series of more classic event-hosting, and it has since been noted by political analysts how the initial invasion of

Ukraine came as Sochi staged the 2014 Winter Olympics. There was simultaneously huge investment in the domestic sporting infrastructure, with much of that spreading out to the wider football world. Gazprom, the state-owned energy corporation, took a controlling stake in Zenit St Petersburg in 2005. The club then won the old UEFA Cup in 2008 and became a regular presence in the Champions League. Zenit weren't quite as ubiquitous as their part-owners, since Gazprom sponsored UEFA's marquee tournament while also agreeing deals with Germany's Schalke 04 and Serbia's Red Star Belgrade.

There's almost an irony that Russian teams never took off due to the constraint of rules requiring a certain number of home nationals to be fielded, but club success wasn't a state motivation.[6] Among the biggest aims was one of the most under-appreciated aspects of sportswashing: direct political integration, to the point of profound influence. Several Russian state officials sat on the boards of international sports federations. Access to such influence was viewed as a key motivation in Gazprom's football deals, since a status as the world's largest supplier of natural gas didn't exactly require advertisement.[7] Alex Dyukov, the chief executive of Gazprom Neft, was voted to UEFA's executive committee through the presidency of the Russian Football Federation. The peak of this was Putin successfully presenting himself as an international statesman at the 2018 World Cup opening game, seated in a row with FIFA president Gianni Infantino and Saudi crown prince Mohammed bin Salman. It was all a façade. Bin Salman evidently liked what he saw, though. So did other premiers such as Hungary's Viktor Orban, who have mimicked some of this strategy.

The fact none of this was recognised as sportswashing at the time was just another illustration of the point. It's all the more effective if people don't realise it's happening. There were admittedly other reasons this wasn't applied to Putin. One well-placed football executive says, 'Russian money was not as offensive to powerful people in the game', especially since Putin's state was once an ally of governments like the UK's. Another factor was the semblance of democracy, which suggested a degree of separation with the state. Although liberal democracies are naturally concerned with image, their very nature means they can't pursue sportswashing strategies in the same way. Use of resources is accountable to the electorate. Norwegian voters would not be impressed if the country's oil wealth was used to sign Neymar.

If all of this only really suggests political influence on sport, there are a number of distinctive reasons why the sportswashing strategy became super charged in the Gulf. It was duly about scale. One factor was the immense wealth from fossil fuel economies. A second was the amount of direct power the rulers had. McGeehan puts that into suitable context, stating that 'few people in history have ever had the ability to deploy tremendous amounts of liquid assets at any one time without any checks'. It is a scale often overlooked, because it's so hard to comprehend. Aramco has consistently been making profits of $10 billion a month. Once these states had realised the power of football, it was inevitable this was going to be further driven by regional rivalries and politics. It is not a coincidence this era has run parallel to the Gulf blockade, where a clash over foreign policy saw Saudi Arabia and UAE lead an isolation of Qatar. All of this is why the Gulf has become the global centre for sportswashing.

Figures who have worked close to power in those countries insist that the effect of 11 September 2001 is underappreciated. Gulf academic Chris Davidson argues that the regional fragility created by subsequent military campaigns ensured the US was 'not seen as a reliable actor' any more. Young states quickly realised the need to stand up for themselves. This was especially true of Qatar and UAE, both founded in 1971 after the vacuum left by British withdrawal from the Gulf, and eventually Saudi Arabia. All three began to develop global aspirations, in the way less wealthy neighbours such as Bahrain, Oman and Kuwait couldn't. This, as should really go without saying, is really about oil. Just like 11 September 2001 and so many other major historic events, the story of modern football is actually that of hydrocarbon. Or, just as relevantly, that there's a relatively near future where hydrocarbon won't be as available or desirable. Vast income from fossil fuels allowed states like Saudi Arabia, UAE and Qatar to build up huge sovereign wealth funds, most founded in the early 2000s. They now needed to use the global capitalist system to maximise those funds for the future.

'My concern now,' Hamad bin Khalifa Al Thani, the former Emir of Qatar, said in 2007, 'is how to invest both internally and externally towards the benefit of our future generations.'[8] All of this was consolidated in huge projects outlined in documents that were each called 'Vision 2030'. Abu Dhabi's says it's 'essential' to 'create a more sustainable pattern of growth'.[9] The documents also paid particular attention to image.

It's remarkable to think in an era when the UK government was pushing for the Saudi takeover of Newcastle United, but the first few years of the millennium witnessed a reluctance from the West to embrace Gulf investment.[10] Human rights concerns were part of that but more relevant was the memory of gaudy expenditure in the 1970s and 1980s. They were seen as opportunistic moves to capitalise from high prices in the 1973 oil crisis,[11] to the point there were even attempts at state regulation.[12] By the 2000s, major Gulf states were seeking meetings with Western governments only for the response to amount to 'What do they want?' That abruptly changed with the 2008 economic crash. The response to such requests was to immediately clear space. The West needed the money to sustain its financial system.

The Gulf needed that financial system, too, as well as the West's evolving technologies. UAE's foreign minister, Abdullah bin Zayed Al-Nahyan, spoke about how membership in the global network 'entails obligations'.[13] The way was clear for Gulf states to invest far and wide, as deep as telecom lines and as high as the Shard in London. The Qatari-funded tower could almost serve as a signpost for the UK's willingness to open its doors wider than anyone else, with the Premier League an ideal space for negotiation. Investment in sport was part of the bigger plan laid out in the 'Vision' documents, but very quickly came to be a huge undertaking in itself. It helped that the Gulf was utterly football obsessed. Iran, Kuwait, Iraq, UAE and Saudi Arabia had previously qualified for the World Cup. Rulers used to see investment in the game as 'gifts' to the populations. It fostered the understanding of how powerful football is, even before it went to another level.

What actively changed the sport, though, was how the interaction between these states saw the dynamic escalate from sponsorship to outright club ownership, political influence and far wider plans. It inevitably developed into a race itself, with every new step adding more pages to the playbook. What is most striking is how all of the major states followed it to the letter, constantly copying each other. Saudi Arabia's decision to buy Newcastle United was a direct response to the purchases of Manchester City and PSG.

Part of this was cultural proximity. As well as monarchical structures, the Gulf states share languages, religions, values and even identity. There are families that straddle borders. Petty emotion plays a huge role. It's often overlooked how these geopolitical developments are mostly due to 'egotistical megalomaniacal figures', to quote McGeehan. 'Rivalries between interrelated elites, with feuds going back centuries, can't be understated,' Davidson adds. El-Baghdadi puts all this more bluntly. 'A lot of it is about one-upmanship.' That has meant constantly trying to outdo each other in the same fields, but often from the same advice. The proximity has fostered a shadow industry of international consultants. PR figures that worked for Qatar 2022 quickly decamped to Saudi Arabia 2034. As the most prominent example, Amanda Staveley finally worked with an English club through Saudi Arabia's Newcastle, having previously been involved in the sale of Manchester City to Abu Dhabi, after failing in similar attempts with Dubai. She got there eventually.

The UAE's most famous emirate has been completely overtaken by its neighbours, having initially set this race off. With their oil reserves amounting to about 4 per cent of Abu Dhabi's, Dubai had to think about diversification much earlier. Tourism has been a successful part of this, with Dubai long marketed as a glamorous city despite the rigidity of its Islamic legal system. There's an instructive story from Qatar's preparations for the World Cup, when the state sought to research media strategies against criticism. A focus group was asked whether they had ever been to the Gulf. The majority kept their hands down. They were then asked whether they had been to Dubai. Half put their hands up. For those that do know where Dubai is, the projection had been so successful that there is a general assumption the city is the capital of UAE, not Abu Dhabi.[14] This doubtless pleased Sheikh Mohammed al Maktoum, who came to another realisation. The Dubai ruler's prized Godolphin racing stables created positive association with the city. Some Western executives in the state airline, Emirates, felt Dubai wasn't advertising abroad anywhere near enough. The company was soon sponsoring the Asian Football Confederation, Olympiacos, AC Milan, Benfica, Hamburg, and Real Madrid, as well as Arsenal and their stadium. 'Oil is a commodity,' El-Baghdadi notes, 'but Dubai is a brand.' The first flag was up.

Qatar followed Dubai into sponsorship, most visibly with Barcelona. It was all the more of a shift since the Catalan club had historically never sullied their famous stripes with branding. This was eventually broken for UNICEF, before the charity was quietly moved to the back of the shirt to make space for the Qatar Foundation in 2010. All of the Gulf states began to stage events, with golf, tennis and Formula One the most forthcoming partners. Mohammed bin Zayed spoke of how the Abu Dhabi grand prix gives the emirate a 'global resonance'.[15] Football was always going to follow the money. The Asian Cup and Club World Cup were held in the Gulf before the Qatar 2022 World Cup bid in 2010. While all of this imposed the Gulf states onto global football, they weren't truly part of it. Ownership of clubs is another level entirely. It is control as well as appropriation of identity, while allowing full integration into the system.

Although such state takeovers now look like a logical step from what was happening, they represent a crucial evolution in football history. It was to put the club game on a different scale. Figures who have worked in the Gulf say initial suggestions again came from European consultants. It is conspicuous that Staveley was involved in the first attempt. Dubai International Capital, a sovereign wealth fund, attempted to buy Liverpool in 2006–07. It never went anywhere. Liverpool executives doubted whether Dubai ever had real conviction. The attempt came just a year before Abu Dhabi bailed out Dubai in the financial crisis. The Al Nahyans had been watching all this closely. 'That's a really key point in this story,' former diplomat Arthur Snell says. 'It used to be you went to

Dubai for the popular culture and Abu Dhabi for the high culture. At a certain point, there was a realisation that having a branch of the Louvre makes no difference. If you're going to play this game of cultural diplomacy, you have to be in the popular space.' Abu Dhabi started to look for 'proxy brands' for the nation, which had been a pillar in the state's 'Vision' document.[16] That was written by Australian public relations expert Simon Pearce, who had become an influential official within the state.

McGeehan believes it was impossible that he 'can't have seen the potential of having a club like Manchester City'. Abu Dhabi was also beginning to look at sport in the same way that firms like Goldman Sachs do: that it was worth the investment. Some of this evolved naturally from opportunity presenting itself. The UAE's decision-makers had been in increasing dialogue with the British state and there was an existing link with City owner Thaksin Shinawatra, a disgraced Thai politician who desperately needed a buyer by 2008. So, through Sheikh Mansour's Abu Dhabi United Group – ADUG – a state-linked entity owned a foreign football club for the first time in the history of the game. It was to be one of three, all from the Gulf. There was barely any discussion of what this actually meant at the time, because few even conceived of the possibility of state interest in a club. The purchase was largely seen as another super-wealthy individual seeking entertainment.

Virtually everyone with knowledge of the Gulf, from human rights activists to political analysts, uses the same word in response to the idea there is any separation from the state in such purchases: 'preposterous'. One executive who has directly worked with state clubs simply bursts out laughing at the notion. 'That's the worst argument I've ever heard.' City actually did make exactly that argument in their Financial Fair Play case at the Court of Arbitration for Sport, as a legal representative of the Finance

Ministry in Abu Dhabi claimed ADUG is 'completely unconnected' to the government of UAE or the emirate.[17] *Der Spiegel* later undermined that claim with leaks that revealed Abu Dhabi's Executive Affairs Authority, a government agency that sets strategy and is headed by City chairman Al Mubarak, managed accounts belonging to ADUG. The club even sent an invoice for sponsorship from Etisalat to Omar Awad, the finance director of the agency. 'Omar works for the EAA and is very important and helpful in facilitating our financial administration of City,' Pearce wrote.

Such details display how blurred the lines are in such autocracies, where the rulers have absolute power. The law in a country like the UK might have Sheikh Mansour as the named owner. The legal structure of Abu Dhabi works differently, since rulers can and have just appropriated what would be seen as private property in liberal democracies. 'They are the state,' Douglas London, a Georgetown University academic specialising on the Gulf, says. 'It's their property. Everything belongs to them.' FairSquare warned UEFA that, in the case of an attempt to buy Manchester United, 'a basic study of Qatar's political and economic system amply demonstrates the impossibility of any Qatari consortium proving itself independent of state influence'.[18] The Takeover Panel in the United Kingdom generally considers state influence when it comes to companies from Gulf monarchies. UEFA investigators meanwhile found it difficult to disentangle ownership when it came to looking at related parties in Financial Fair Play cases, as they often involved extended royal family members.

Snell is another who can't help but laugh at the idea. 'What's ironic is that on one level they say it's independent, there's no co-ordination and it's just coincidence they all decided to pump money into this one firm, then on the other hand, if something of note happens, there'll be a call to the British ambassador.'

Davidson outlines what is called 'Gulf capitalism', where there are no separations between government, business and individuals. 'These small ruling elites also style themselves as the heads of giant private sector conglomerates.' One US ambassador once described Qatar as 'a family business with a seat at the United Nations'.[19]

More fundamentally than any of this, all of Mansour's wealth is state wealth. Al Mubarak, the City chairman, is head of sovereign wealth fund Mubadala in addition to the EAA. 'He can sit in these two positions without them seeing any conflict of interest because they are one and the same,' McGeehan says. The phrases often used in Gulf countries, according to those who have worked in government, are 'front of window' and 'the hand behind the curtain'. The establishment of Qatar Sports Investments was expressly about the subtlety of being able to purchase assets while keeping the Emir's name out of the media. It created a perception of distance.

When big decisions are required, though, the description is of 'going to the fire' – the ruler. McGeehan goes even further, describing such autocracies as 'kleptocracies'. 'They're not seen as kleptocracies because the misappropriation of state resources doesn't visibly impoverish the population but there's zero transparency or accountability. Anyone who criticised that would find themselves in hot water.' This is the reason for this entire sportswashing era. It is that power extended into football, without football ever really considering what it means. Within those states, that autocratic nature has translated into what Amnesty International describes as 'systematic human rights abuses'. There are limited women's rights. Homosexuality is illegal. Power is enforced through methods that include torture, forced disappearance and a complete absence of fair trial. Human rights groups are not free to do research in either UAE or Saudi Arabia, although Qatar is more permissive. El-Baghdadi, a Palestinian national who grew up in UAE, has personal experience of how the state has ruthlessly shut down dissent. He was given a choice of immediate deportation or indefinite imprisonment. 'The sound of a human hand smashing into a face was very familiar,' El-Baghdadi says of his temporary detainment. Dr Ahmed Al Zaabi, a former university professor and judge, detailed how he was physically and psychologically abused by security forces.[20] 'There is no accountability because the court of public opinion doesn't really exist in these states,' McGeehan continues. 'There's no free press. Free speech is off the table. And, to make people stick to that in the UAE, there's this unbelievable electronic surveillance network.'

Capital punishment meanwhile remains one of Saudi Arabia's most recognisable problems, to the point Newcastle United manager Eddie Howe bristled when asked about it in press conferences. That has persisted under Mohammed bin Salman, who had been presented by Mohammed bin Zayed to Western powers as 'the great reformer'.

Perhaps the most callous issue, however, is a migrant labour system that the Business and Human Rights Resource Centre (BHRRC) describes as 'modern slavery'. It is also the phrase many of the workers themselves use. The problem is so central because the Gulf autocracies are literally built on this system, with limitless money going into gleaming towers rather than fair pay, directly worsening dismal circumstances. Despite profound resistance to reform, it is not as though this is any kind of historic cultural norm. The system was set up by British colonial authorities, who took the Islamic tradition of Kafala and the religious responsibility to 'guard' the vulnerable, warping it as a cost-effective way to control labour. It was eagerly taken up by the local rulers, who gradually ensured the global capitalist system was taken to its logical extremes: inconceivable disparity creating the space for migrant workers from the world's poorest countries to be systematically exploited by the wealthiest. This has been the way much of the world works, but the difference was the institutionalisation in law.

Isobel Archer of BHRRC describes it as a 'cycle of abuse' that invariably starts with illegal recruitment fees in workers' home countries, which are generally in sub-Saharan Africa or southern Asia. Impoverished individuals first arrive in exorbitant debt, ensuring companies that sponsor their employment have total control of their lives. That extends to accommodation that is generally squalid and overcrowded. Permission is required to leave, and that is rarely granted. Working days are often 12 hours long, and conducted in searing heat for long stretches of the year. It is then almost impossible to change jobs, since passports are confiscated. Medical issues are widespread, with death common, and worrying numbers of suicides. Many workers have complained of a lack of days off, and there are huge deductions from meagre salaries for mistakes, with 'wage theft' one of the most common problems. That wage is reported by numerous worker groups to differ based on nationality, and a UN report on Qatar ahead of the 2022 World Cup wrote of 'serious concerns of structural racial discrimination'.[21] This is a common complaint across Gulf autocracies. Amnesty International accused UAE in one case of having 'brutalised hundreds of individuals on the basis of their skin colour'.[22] Such discrimination makes it all the more shameless that autocratic states have the gall to accuse critics of this system as 'racist'. What is so frustrating for human rights groups is that there is ample money to easily overhaul the entire system. The will isn't there, though, since it is commonly seen as another form of control. While Qatar has initiated more reforms than other states, the criticism is they haven't gone anywhere near far enough. There is, consequently, a lot to 'wash'.

The idea behind sportswashing has never been so simplistic, though. Even Abu Dhabi's thinking on City evolved as the state saw how the takeover produced more publicity than multi-billion-pound pipeline deals.[23] 'It certainly became strategic,' McGeehan adds. 'Khaldoon Al Mubarak was soon giving interviews saying this is about telling the world who Abu Dhabi is.' That remains the root of the concept: geopolitical positioning and image projection. Sheikh Mohammed Al Maktoum described Gulf spending on sport as a multi-billion-dollar 'charm offensive' back in 2007.[24]

There is so much that is attractive for such states in football that the question isn't why they got involved but why it took so long. Association with something so popular brings influence and legitimacy. A proper stadium atmosphere affords authenticity. Winning a trophy as prestigious as the Champions League brings gratitude and status. States work their way into the sport's folk-lore. This used to be called 'soft power', which amounts to getting what you want through attraction rather than coercion. Qatar World Cup chief Hassan Al Thawadi even admitted there was 'an element' of that to their hosting.[25] He was right in the sense it's just one element. 'It's a classic example of work on what are brands,' Lynch explains, 'but they need foreign investment to make all these visions happen.' Sport allows a deeper integration through people's emotional connection.

On a basic level, people now talk about going to the Emirates or the Etihad stadiums without thinking. They're no longer just state airlines. They're part of the language of the game. They're also part of a grander presentation, where these clubs are draped in the sponsorship of companies from those states. 'It's becoming less and less about soft power and more and more about cold, hard global branding opportunities,' Davidson explains. 'They'll have to use their sovereign wealth in this very tight window of opportunity to springboard other sectors of their economy.' Football offers a huge lift for relatively small investment. There are multiple accounts of business deals being struck at major stadiums because two high-net-worth individuals were sitting beside each other. It's why Chelsea have been intent on completely open executive boxes. Such 'indirect benefits' have always been present in football, leading to all manner of interests seeking association. David Murray used to struggle to get people to take calls when he was just the chairman of Murray International Metals. No one ever refused when he was owner of Rangers. It extends to Bayer with Bayer Leverkusen and the Moores family with Liverpool and Everton. States, as with everything, simply take it to a new level. During the protracted sale of Newcastle United to PIF, MPs were inundated with letters demanding support. 'That's £300m for a massive cultural asset that probably brings far more political weight than it cost,' Cockburn adds. 'It's almost creating dependencies that make them feel indispensable to the region.' The Mayor of Greater Manchester, Andy Burnham, has similarly praised City's owners as 'huge partners for the city'. Football offers a foothold. It all helps to create an image, as Human Rights Watch's Adam Coogle puts it, 'that these are good business partners'. It's why Lynch feels the focus on the PR aspect of sportswashing is misplaced. 'These states don't need the approval of the West. But they do need companies to want to do business.' Sport makes investment seem safer. Staging events directly improves risk ratings. That is then pointed to on government committees, right up to approving arms sales. That reflects one of the main reasons for all of this: security.

Sport also fostered a sense of assurance, especially in a region perceived as turbulent. Iraq's 1991 invasion of Kuwait conditioned diplomacy for a generation, with many smaller countries fearful of similar fates. 'Buying weapons and sporting brands from the West increases the reliability of the security guarantee,' Davidson says. 'Basically what happened in 1991, where the West liberated Kuwait.' This was a particular concern of Qatar, as it found itself diplomatically isolated in the region. A view commonly articulated in football politics is that it's very difficult to invade a country that has just hosted a World Cup. The ever-shifting dynamics of the region mean all of the states have to consider this, especially amid a cold war between Saudi Arabia and Iran, and new tension between Bin Salman and Bin Zayed.

What these states are almost more mindful of than anything, however, is one of the main factors that led to the Gulf blockade. Qatar was accused of supporting political Islam, particularly groups like the Muslim Brotherhood. They had been influential in the Arab Spring, a series of protests and uprisings that spread across the region and transformed it. It is a confluence of history that the spark for it, the self-immolation of Mohamed Bouazizi in Tunisia, occurred a mere two weeks after the awarding of the 2022 World Cup in December 2010. The Gulf autocracies have been obsessed with preventing similar uprisings. This is where football is more classically and directly politicised. Repression in these states is increased, at the same time that investment in sport bestows legitimacy. That also applies to the social contract, where ruling families consolidate power by exchanging consent to rule and political participation for social benefits. International image buttresses that, especially among the internet-savvy younger generation. 'The ruling elite is seen as offering young people something exciting,' Davidson says. 'It diverts the population away from potentially more dangerous forces such as tribalism or conservative Islam.'

This more reductive bread and circuses element is especially important in Saudi Arabia, which has over 20 million people under the age of 30.[26] 'It's an amendment of the social contract,' Lynch explains. 'They can't rely on oil revenue to keep providing public sector jobs. It's a serious issue coming down the line. That's partly what the Saudi Pro League and concerts are all about.' That modernisation plan is another reason Bin Salman needs the West. 'Association with football gives the image of a country that is reforming, at the same time as oppression has got worse,' Cockburn surmises. 'That duality is really important. It's giving with one hand and taking with the other.' It's also why these states are able to weather occasional critical headlines, since they're a smaller proportion of a much larger discussion. Internet searches on Saudi Arabia, for example, now return many more results about football amid those for beheadings or Khashoggi. 'You win your reputation on the cheap,' Page says. 'Sportswashing makes total sense.' The conversation changes. It's the perfect example of normalisation. This is also precisely why there has never been any truth to the argument that cultural proximity to the West might bring long-term reform. The tail doesn't wag the dog. 'That was often the argument made about China and Putin's Russia,' Cockburn says. It might have more merit if football used some of its significant leverage. Proper human rights requirements for staging tournaments could have been hugely effective. Football has instead done the opposite, and empowered these states. Just months after the Newcastle takeover, Saudi Arabia executed 81 people in one day. The human rights situation in Abu Dhabi is worse in 2024 than it was in 2008. 'Sport is used to establish the idea they should not have to change,' Snell says.

It is all why the concept behind sportswashing works so well. States can carve out power bases. Abu Dhabi used the Manchester City takeover to launch a construction empire in Manchester, deepening political roots. Qatar have developed one of the most glamorous brands in the world, through PSG's collaboration with Air Jordan. There were then those scenes of joy at the Newcastle takeover. That's a reaction that the most sophisticated political strategies or even black ops can't produce.[27] Such images travel around the world a lot quicker than weighty arguments about human rights. Qatar's World Cup will go down in football history as the stage for one of the sport's greatest ever stories. Russia's World Cup, however, will go down in actual history as a modern 1936 Olympics. The conversation on sportswashing here becomes more complex for football. It is not just that sport is used for branding. It is that football is made complicit in so many of these issues, its very identity warped. That's why state ownership represents an extreme, more problematic for the game than even the worst financial interests. As McGeehan puts it, 'the Glazers aren't bombing Yemen'.

Page lays it out starkly. 'It certainly makes football complicit in trying to cover up or downplay human rights abuses. It helps silence any type of criticism.' The gratitude from fans here carries an even greater importance, especially if it means attacking critics. 'That does matter to these states,' Cockburn says. 'They want to make sure the fans see them as saviours.'

It is how sportswashing further corrupts what football is actually supposed to be for. Social institutions that play matches to proudly represent their area are used to also represent a state, directly contradicting their community role. 'This is something referred to in the UK government white paper,' McGeehan says. 'When abusive governments take clubs over, that's a misappropriation of something incredibly important. They've bought your name, they've bought your asset. It's the Dr Faustus story.'

It also makes the entire narrative of football very different.

'The game doesn't exist to make autocratic states look good,' Snell points out. And yet that's exactly what is happening, as football has become just another element in a rivalry between autocracies. It is just another social price of sportswashing, not as serious as real-world consequences but still important. Football is warped. Very few clubs can actually compete with the resources of oil states over the long term. These autocracies won't have any financial concerns for generations. It's why it's worth considering a world without the contentious Financial Fair Play regulations. States and state-linked individuals would just be able to pump in as much money as they want, obliterating any idea of competitive balance. That has happened in a more gradual way even with FFP, since these owners have no need to behave like normal companies. They have no financial risk, which itself fosters a huge advantage. They are not answerable to shareholders or staff. Even in this world, the scale of City's dominance has been unprecedented in English football history. The financial threshold has still been raised. PSG's €222 million signing of Neymar from Barcelona in 2017 massively inflated transfer fees and wages. It wasn't just that clubs had to pay more to keep up. They had to pay more to keep existing squads. One executive at a major club privately complains about how contract negotiations with a major star collapsed when a state-owned club offered four times his wage. Even in football terms, after all, billionaires have limits. The wealth of states is comparatively limitless. Silvio Berlusconi said as long ago as 2015 that it's clear football's traditional powers 'cannot compete with a state'. Tebas says this has a greater effect on the game than who wins competitions.

'Hundreds of millions of euro has been injected into the industry, which is not generated from within ... it harms other teams.' It is hyper-inflation of a scale the game can't cope with.

The widespread view, from Milan to Wimbledon, is that it's close to impossible to have responsibly run clubs and also compete in a sport that features state ownership.[28] The dynamic threatens the basic sustainability of the game. The bottom line is that if someone was designing a sport from scratch, nobody would pick football's current model. 'This is not a sensible or reliable policy for running sport,' former UEFA executive Alex Phillips argues. 'It's not viable.'

State ownership ultimately makes the sport less competitive, not more. Tebas, typically, is even blunter. 'This is destroying sport.' There is now some regret within the game that authorities 'didn't see something like this as inevitable'. That has been sharpened by outright concern for the norms of sport. Manchester City and PSG have both already had to pay huge fines for accusations of FFP breaches, with legal threats forcing UEFA into 'settlements' that were never part of the regulations. Russia initiated a state-sponsored doping programme for the Olympics.[29] As one well-placed lawyer puts it, 'a system designed to ensure fair play among participants sharing essential values will struggle to cope with sophisticated state actors whose whole philosophy is that they don't have to play by any rules they don't like'. Abu Dhabi, for one, has been accused by the United Nations' own reports of defying an arms embargo in Libya.[30] One source within a confederation complains that it has posed challenges beyond anything they've ever faced. 'You're not arguing with club executives. You're arguing with armies of lawyers, combined with the potential for misinformation. It's very different to a row with David Dein.' States will always have more substantial legal power, especially when sport lacks institutional protection.

An increasingly common view is that it's ludicrous to think football can regulate such owners when you have situations like

Bin Salman messaging the UK prime minister about the purchase of a football club,[31] and you have football club chairmen like Al Mubarak, in their role as state actors, threatening to block arms deals because of the government's stance on Islamist groups.[32] There is always far greater political power to be wielded. If football systems were never built for these challenges, there's then the extra problem of states infiltrating sporting infrastructures. Qatar has immense influence in European football through the multiple roles of Nasser Al-Khelaifi, who is chairman of PSG and through that chairman of the European Club Association. There is simultaneously a fear that the Saudi Pro League could serve as a launchpad for something similar in football to LIV Golf, which has upended that sport. 'It's partly a projection of power,' Cockburn argues. 'Saudi Arabia is making clear that they are a serious force to be dealt with, no matter the cost.'

One federation official just resignedly stated 'it's ultimately better to work with these interests rather than have them working against you'. Otherwise, it's 'total destruction'. The wider politics from state involvement are potentially even more harmful, though. Through a growing dependency on state money, the entire sport is left at the mercy of geopolitical shifts. A significant warning came with the air raid sirens of Kyiv. It is probably underestimated just how close Chelsea came to going out of business after Abramovich was sanctioned. It is far from inconceivable football could be forced to face similar discussions in the future. The historic irony of all this shouldn't be overlooked, of course. Much of this landscape was created by Western powers, particularly the British Empire. The economic model adopted ultimately led to the financial crisis of 2008, which was in turn exploited by oil powers wishing to expand, before the effects of that were also exploited. European clubs similarly sought to dominate the entire world, only for the real powers of that world to try and dominate European clubs.

It does not feel like 'sportswashing', as a phrase, comes anywhere close to describing what is happening.

3.

ALL PATHS LEAD FROM ROMAN

When the Premier League was informed that a Russian business-man called Roman Abramovich wanted to buy Chelsea in June 2003, there was no alarm, no special talks. There wasn't actually any discussion at all. The summer meeting had already taken place so most club executives were on holiday. The overriding emotion was one of 'bemusement' since nobody knew who this man was or what the significance would be. It wasn't seen as that big a deal.

That lasted about as long as the first bid for a player went in, which was immediately followed by the second, third, fourth . . . Arsenal were one of the few clubs to express concern, since there was an awareness early on that this might threaten the success of their self-sustaining model. For the rest of the Premier League and the wider game, the main response was one of dazzlement. Chelsea's immediate outlay of over £100 million was a level of spending no one could even conceive of, which was why the most common refrain was 'it's like fantasy football'. It was certainly expanding horizons. Abramovich's purchase of Chelsea instantly shifted the geography of the sport, bringing an unprecedented in-ternational dimension to ownership of clubs. This entire era can't be explained or framed without him. Abramovich was the first owner of a club who wasn't British or based in Britain, but that quickly felt like the most irrelevant fact about him. Much more sensational was the wealth he had and the mystery surrounding him, right up to reported connections with Vladimir Putin. This was a figure unlike any the game had known.

There was gradually some regret that the game's authorities didn't show more foresight on such issues. It should have been a lesson for football that Abramovich wanted Real Madrid and Barcelona first, only to find the Spanish clubs protected by fan ownership. That lesson feels all the harsher with the benefit of hindsight, as Chelsea were left completely unprotected by the time Abramovich was sanctioned by the UK government 19 years later. The purchase was an inevitable consequence of the Premier League's entire philosophy since the intention was to open it all up, and invite money from almost anywhere. Employees from the time claim they would only really learn of takeovers after the fact but this was where football was long headed, out of domestic markets and into the wider world. The Premier League's single barrier to ownership at all appeared to be criminal conviction. This would have been laughable if it wasn't so serious. By the time Thaksin Shinawatra bought Manchester City in 2007, his government in Thailand had been accused of over 2,000 extrajudicial killings by police during the 2003 'war on drugs'. Allegations also came to light that an arrest warrant had been issued in Russia in 1992 over Abramovich's counterfeiting of documents to obtain 55 train wagons' worth of diesel in the same year.[1] He has always denied the claim.

This single condition about criminal records came from the much-criticised Fit and Proper Person's Test, later to become the Owners' and Directors' Test. It was actually introduced after Abramovich's takeover, in 2004, to insulate the game from those with a track record of bankruptcy or a conviction for fraud. Owners just had to prove they had the money so that the club could fulfil fixtures and pay tax. Mere criminal charges didn't concern the Premier League. Neither did human rights, owners' backgrounds, their political affiliations, their ambitions, the identity of clubs, sporting culture or the potential effects for the future.

All that mattered was the money coming in, which fitted perfectly with the economic outlook of the New Labour government. It is no coincidence this happened during a period when Russian money was flooding into the UK and buying up swathes of London.[2] Tony Blair's government was inviting all foreign capital, as part of the 'Third Way' that sought to tread a path between social responsibility and economic liberalism.[3] The Premier League certainly warmed to the latter. Chief executive Richard Scudamore was one of the few in that first summer to immediately realise the significance of the Abramovich takeover. Having worked outside football, and especially in the US, he saw this as the moment the young competition had been waiting for. It was the first substantial foreign investment, transforming the Premier League from a wealthy but still parochial model into a global one. The leap from Jack Walker's £300 million that secured the 1994–95 league title for Blackburn Rovers to Abramovich's billions in 2003 certainly felt like it was of a greater scale than a mere 8 years.

When more investment inevitably arrived, Scudamore saw the competition as 'ownership model-neutral'. This essentially meant that no judgement was made on the form of buyer, be it an individual, public limited company or a consortium. Such parameters alone perhaps displayed the limits of the thinking at the time. Nobody was considering state actors. This still echoed the UK's position on foreign investment, and the Premier League developed a much deeper working relationship with the Foreign Office. Scudamore was described as a perfect political bedfellow for Blair. The existing club owners were themselves all too eager to follow, since they wanted to be able to sell to the highest bidders. Another argument was that the new money kept the Premier League 'competitive and compelling', which was the mantra repeated by staff from the early 2000s. That complemented an increased globalisation of the division, especially in terms of players and a new broadcasting strategy. The conceit was that they just had to comply with the rules of English football. There is derision towards that view now, especially in the myopia of thinking that having 20 local owners was in any way similar to majority foreign ownership. That was before you even got to nation states. 'Scudamore's shadow is long,' in the words of one executive.

The exact character of the Abramovich takeover is now a matter of considerable debate, especially since he was specifically sanctioned for his links to Vladimir Putin following the invasion of Ukraine in February 2022. Theories are still relayed in football about how it might have been an 'insurance policy' for the dangerous world of Russian politics, given that it's a lot more difficult for anyone to be 'disappeared' if they are the high-profile owners of an internationally popular football club. The sense of mystery reflects how seductive the purchase of Chelsea was at the time. It all felt so exotic. As was to become grimly normal, however, the laxness of the game brought a situation where Chelsea simply had to be sold. They were just another club that had overextended themselves, as was typical of that era across European football. The threat of bankruptcy weighed over Chelsea's 2002–03 season, with an £80 million debt making it a challenge to pay wages. In January, club executives had even borrowed against August's instalment of broadcasting money. Consequently, the final game of the season against Liverpool was not just a play-off for the last Champions League place. It was a play-off for the club's financial future. Lose, and things could have got a lot worse. Manager Claudio Ranieri was so concerned that he hired a US military veteran to give a team talk about facing fire from the Viet Cong.[4] Chelsea beat Liverpool, which was crucial, since it was at this exact time that Abramovich was investigating the purchase of a club – who he expressly wanted to be in the Champions League. Word had got back to him about Chelsea through football agent Pini Zahavi. The Israeli had seen the potential of the newly opened Russia from the early 1990s and worked on contacts there. A connection was eventually made with Abramovich by a member of the Council of the Russian Federation. When the name of the interested party was put to Chelsea executives, they attempted to do an internet search, but almost nothing came up. They didn't even know Abramovich was a billionaire. His stature was immediately obvious, however, when he turned up with advisors from firms like Citibank and Skadden Arps – as well as a security detail.[5]

A £60 million deal was struck on a straight cash offer in the space of just 20 minutes at the Dorchester in London. 'We don't want a big song and dance, just a quick deal,' Abramovich told then club chairman Ken Bates. It was celebrated with glasses of Evian water, before a helicopter trip over London.[6] One call still had to be made before signing, though. A close Putin aide, Aleksandr Voloshin, was informed of the developments.[7] It was impossible for a long time to even discuss Abramovich's relationship with the Russian president because the former Chelsea owner threatened legal action against anyone that raised it. The broad available facts were always instructive, though. In July 2000, not long after coming to power, Putin hosted a meeting of Russia's wealthiest oligarchs in his dacha outside Moscow. The billionaires were explicitly told by the president that absolute loyalty was a condition of their wealth.[8] They could get in line or lose everything, which was exactly what happened to some who bridled. Abramovich didn't just get to keep his fortune. He increased it. Indeed, the state had already aided his rise to mega-wealth. In 1995, Abramovich purchased oil producer Sibneft for a fraction of its true value, thanks to Boris Yeltsin's 'loan-for-shares' scheme. The initiative was a desperate attempt to secure influential political support through a fire sale of state assets. Sibneft were then in 2005 sold to state company Gazprom for its true value of $13.1 billion, making a crucial difference to how less quiescent oligarchs just had companies taken away from them. Abramovich already enjoyed direct political influence, though. In 1999, he vetted all of the candidates for Putin's first cabinet, in individual meetings at the Kremlin.[9]

'I respect him a lot,'[10] Abramovich said of Putin in an interview with Gazprom's media arm that same year. 'In my opinion, everything that Putin does, he does without making any mistakes.' Such public comments from Abramovich were rare, which was why there was shock in Russia when he made a move as conspicuous as buying Chelsea. He even explained why to the *Financial Times*. 'I'm looking at it as something to have fun with rather than having to realise a return.'[11] Catherine Belton put forward a different theory in the original print of her book, *Putin's People*, which Abramovich successfully took action against before the invasion of Ukraine.[12] 'According to business magnate Sergei Pugachev,' the book reads, 'Putin's Kremlin had accurately calculated that the way to gain acceptance in British society was through the country's greatest love, its national sport. In Pugachev's view, from the start the acquisition had been aimed at building a beachhead for Russian influence in the UK.'[13] The book also cites a Russian tycoon and former associate as saying 'it looked like Putin may have asked Abramovich to buy the club'.[14] Belton caveats the statements by saying there is no other supporting evidence for them, while a spokesperson for Abramovich denied the claims and pointed out Pugachev has been regarded as an unreliable witness in previous UK court proceedings.[15]

Even if the theory is incorrect as regards Abramovich, it offers an astute analysis of how football can be used. It is nevertheless worth noting that, a month before the invasion of Ukraine and in response to the legal action against Belton's book, Conservative MP David Davis used parliamentary privilege to state that 'it was alleged by associates of [Abramovich] that the purchase was done at the behest of the Kremlin'.[16] 'As a result of the purchase,' Davis went on, 'he now has enormous influence in the UK. I ask the House to come to its own conclusion about whether this man is acting at the behest of the Kremlin or Putin's Government.'

Whatever the truth, the Chelsea takeover was part of a wave of Russian investment into the United Kingdom. The estimated £27 billion spent by a series of oligarchs from the 1990s on led to the terms 'Londongrad' and 'Moscow-on-Thames'.[17] The taciturn Abramovich presided over the noisiest of these assets.

Tony Banks, the former Labour sports minister who was also a Chelsea supporter, was one of the few to bravely express scepticism at the time. 'We need to look at the source of his money, what his track record has been in Russia, to establish whether he is a fit and proper person to take over a football club in this country,'[18] said Banks. 'At the moment I don't like it.' Banks even referred to Russia as 'a country that has a reputation that is not savoury in terms of its financial situation'. The truth was that everyone was too busy gawking at the purchases made with that money, such as Abramovich's private Boeing 767 and luxury yachts that included the biggest in the world. This was a world away from local businessmen buying their club. Then the actual football spending started.

The outlay of over £100 million in a single transfer window was absurd for the time. It wasn't just the amount but the manner. At that time, in 2003, clubs generally paid transfer fees in instalments and many did so knowing full well they had yet to figure out how they were going to pay for the final two of three. This was a direct factor in the creation of Financial Fair Play rules, since football at that point didn't really have financial regulation at all. Abramovich's Chelsea did business rather differently, akin to the meeting to buy the club. No song and dance. When Chelsea asked about buying England star Joe Cole, West Ham United named a price and Abramovich's hierarchy instantly agreed to it. The full money was in West Ham's bank account almost immediately after the contracts were signed.

Mark Schwarzer, a goalkeeper for Middlesbrough at the time who later played for Chelsea, remembers newspapers featuring the latest bids being passed around to shocked players. 'It was like nothing we'd ever seen.' Every day brought new names, numbers and a wonder about what would come next. Abramovich himself genuinely loved the buzz of player trading more than almost anything else in football. He especially enjoyed testing the limits of counterparts, like when a business dinner with steel magnate Massimo Moratti resulted in an unsuccessful bid for Internazionale's Christian Vieri. An offer was of course made for the Premier League's biggest star, Arsenal's Thierry Henry.

Little seemed off-limits, except Chelsea's own executive lounges. They immediately had airport security installed, which irritated executives at other clubs, who felt it was disrespectful. One even considered doing the same at their stadium out of petty revenge. A further indication of how football was now in a different world was when Abramovich's security guards tried to bring guns to Premier League matches. This didn't impress local police forces, either. It was at least appreciated that Abramovich deviated from his usual uniform of jeans when certain away stadiums had a dress code, and even wore a tie. This wasn't true of every executive.

Abramovich otherwise represented a new owner that fans couldn't get near to. It was barely known what they were thinking, something that clearly clashed with the community ethos of clubs. This opaqueness extended to when Abramovich sat in the dressing room beside players at matches, barely saying anything. Conscious of backlash in Russia, he did make sure to announce he would spend $65 million on a new stadium for CSKA Moscow.[19] His long-time lawyer, Bruce Buck, meanwhile became one of the most influential figures in the Premier League. That extended to having a significant say in how money was spent in every cycle, due to his membership of the Premier League audit and remuneration committee. Buck developed such a strong friendship with Scudamore that he even delivered the speech to Premier League staff on the chief executive's resignation. He had been in the office virtually every week. The new Chelsea hierarchy were always conscious of the politics, which is probably just as well given how many clubs they aggravated with transfer bids.

But not yet with trophies. Chelsea didn't actually win anything in that 2003–04 season, which spoke to the strength of the Manchester United–Arsenal duopoly. They had finished top two for five of six seasons, with the era elevated by United's treble and ended by Arsène Wenger's team being crowned the 'Invincibles' for winning the 2003–04 Premier League while going undefeated. It was why Arsenal were among the few to express reservations about Abramovich. It was also why the overriding feeling elsewhere was excitement at a new challenger. Chelsea even defeated Arsenal 3-2 on aggregate in the Champions League quarter-finals that season, only to be surprisingly eliminated by AS Monaco, who were themselves eviscerated 3-0 by FC Porto in the final. The

Portuguese side remain the only club from outside Europe's five major leagues to even reach UEFA's showpiece since 1996.

The man responsible for this alchemy was the captivating José Mourinho. The Portuguese manager had of course already spoken to Abramovich about taking the Chelsea job, as befitting the new order. Abramovich had first tried to undiplomatically prise Sven-Göran Eriksson from the England national team, which was just something not done at the time. Ranieri, an Italian widely seen as a 'gentleman', was sacked in a decision that many in football considered unnecessarily ruthless. It was all the worse that it had been widely expected for months, especially after a surprising interview Ranieri had given to Spanish newspaper *Marca*. In addition to saying 'Abramovich knows nothing about football,' the Italian was asked whether such owners were good for the game.[20] 'No,' Ranieri responded, 'but what can I do about it? Money talks in football.' By the weekend after the Champions League final, Mourinho was on Abramovich's yacht *Pelorus* in the French Riviera, forensically outlining how the club would win trophies. Another £90 million in transfer expenditure that season also helped.

Mourinho then charmed England, too. Posterity demands that it be recorded how the new manager declared himself 'a special one' in his first press conference. Headlines were sorted, with the entire episode setting the image of a Chelsea that went beyond glamour to glory. An Abramovich mantra was 'failure isn't an option'. That eventually evolved into the club's various managers receiving messages about selection decisions. Mourinho didn't initially need those, as Chelsea immediately ended a 55-year club wait to be English champions, to go with a League Cup victory. What was really striking was the thoroughness. The Premier League title had been secured with 95 points, which was 4 more than the previous record and 13 more than the average.

This was one of the most obvious ways that a new profile of owner was reshaping the game. The threshold to compete had been raised. Inflation in wages led to inflation in points at the top, as financial gaps between clubs were stretched. There was now much less margin for error in order to challenge. It used to be that the league could be won through a haul of 80 points, with a late winning run enough to lift the trophy. No more. Even Sir Alex Ferguson had to change how he prepared for seasons, ensuring his team were relentless from the off. That was only after another re-calculation on how to time a challenge against Chelsea. Although United were one of the clubs with the commercial income to at least compete, Ferguson realised it was pointless to try and go for instant success in the way Abramovich did. He instead focused on building a young core of players who would evolve over time, led by Wayne Rooney and Cristiano Ronaldo. The Glazers, for their part, trusted Ferguson with this on buying United in 2005.

Arsenal had meanwhile settled on a hinge decision. The English game's 'establishment club' doubled down on a financial plan that was entirely based on money generated from within the sport, taking on a massive debt to build a new stadium. By the time it was ready, in 2006, Abramovich had transformed the game with money from the outside. All of Wenger's plans were suited to a world that no longer existed. It wasn't long until he coined the phrase 'financial doping'. A telling moment then came when Chelsea signed highly rated left-back Ashley Cole from Arsenal by offering him far higher wages, although only after Abramovich's club were accused of 'tapping up' the player through an approach that was against the rules, and were subsequently found guilty.[21] It created huge enmity between the clubs.

That did clash with Abramovich's aim to make Chelsea revered around the world in the way that Real Madrid were. He had already removed Trevor Birch as chief executive for saying that might take four decades, replacing him with Manchester United's Peter Kenyon. The negotiation was a customary tactic. Kenyon's salary was doubled. Abramovich was nevertheless increasingly drawn to something money couldn't quite buy, at least not in the direct way he intended. Barcelona, who used to employ Mourinho as a translator, were cast as the grand aesthetic contrast to the Portuguese's more brutalist style of play. The Chelsea manager even sparked another rivalry, by accusing Barcelona counterpart Frank Rijkaard of attending referee Anders Frisk's dressing room at half-time of a 2004–05 clash. The Catalans got revenge by beating Chelsea on the way to the 2005–06 Champions League, with Ronaldinho and a young Leo Messi illuminating the tie. Abramovich found this far more exhilarating than the pragmatic football he was watching. When results turned for Mourinho in his fourth season, the Russian made a change.

A line was already being drawn in this new era of football, and not just on the pitch between the more attacking ideology developing in Spain and the counter-attacking approach of before. Abramovich foreshadowed a lot of what would happen at City, particularly as regards spending, success and the remoteness of the owners. It wasn't quite on the same level, though. There was still this constant sense of drama at Chelsea, seen as symptomatic of the owners idiosyncrasies, that was only partly overcome by spending more. Abramovich became even more involved in transfers, as one close advisor complained 'he is starting to think he understands football'. Mourinho's exit was followed by the surprising interim appointment of the unknown Avram Grant. A brilliant squad still got to the 2008 Champions League final, but Ferguson's long-term approach was vindicated as United won on penalties. Chelsea would finally win the competition under another interim manager, former player Roberto Di Matteo, in 2012. The squad remained strong enough.

Few could actually build teams to compete at that level, though. If Abramovich represented a new trend in ownership, the financial situation at Chelsea that led to his takeover represented a new trend in the game. The wage race was accelerated. Many figures who defined the previous ownership eras of local millionaires decided it was time to cash out. 'Abramovich turned it all into the "business of soccer",'[22] former Newcastle United owner Sir John Hall later said. 'I was not prepared to throw unlimited money at it to compete with him, because I couldn't.'

Of the 30 clubs that competed in the Premier League between Abramovich's takeover in 2003 and Mansour's in 2008, a total of 11 went through changes of majority owner. Ten saw English owners sell up. Coming in were nine different nationalities. The most common was American, with billionaires from the US buying Manchester United, Liverpool, Aston Villa, Leicester City and Sunderland through that period. They would all have different economic plans, but most were centred on the capitalisation of the clubs. New Liverpool owners, George Gillett and Tom Hicks, promised not to 'do a Glazers' only to try and do exactly that.[23] Their attempt to load debt onto the club was blocked by the Anfield hierarchy. Scudamore still described the prospect of more takeovers as 'irresistible'.[24] The Football Association still said nothing.

This was maybe Abramovich's main legacy, even more than the money. The takeover of Chelsea had shown that England was the easiest country to buy football clubs in, that had the most effect. A new strand of owner had taken notice. Proof of that was how the Russian was mentioned in Sheikh Mansour's negotiations to buy Manchester City. 'Nobody had ever heard of Roman Abramovich until he bought Chelsea,' City chief executive Garry Cook told the Abu Dhabi delegation.[25] City would eventually become everything Abramovich wanted, right down to replicating Barcelona on a grand scale. There was at least a bit more noise about the next step.

4.

CITY STATE

There could scarcely be a better illustration of the new world that football had moved into. Little more than a month after Sheikh Mansour bin Zayed Al Nahyan had bought Manchester City, his brother, Sheikh Abdullah bin Zayed Al Nahyan, was at the United Nations in New York meeting David Miliband. The foreign ministers of the United Arab Emirates and the United Kingdom were there to discuss issues such as terrorism in Iraq, but one of the first subjects that came up was football. Sheikh Abdullah lamented how a lot of money had already been spent on Manchester City but results were still disappointing. The discussion continued with the Emirati talking about how important the purchase was – all of this between the walls of a building constructed to settle the weightiest issues on the planet.

It shows the centrality of Manchester City to the Gulf state's vision from the start. It also shows how they were already thinking about how much was going to be required to make the club the biggest in the world, beyond even Real Madrid or Manchester United. That seemed a ludicrous prospect even after the takeover, since the club still had a complex about their famous neighbours. It informed the infamous description of 'Cityitis', a phrase coined by former player and manager Joe Royle that captured a farcical but endearing fatalism. It wasn't just that everything that could go wrong would go wrong, in the words of club legend Vincent

Kompany.[1] It was that it would go wrong in the most astoundingly slapstick manner. When Manchester City needed a win to avoid relegation from the Premier League on the last day of the 1995–96 season, word somehow got around Maine Road, their old stadium, that the 2-2 score with Liverpool would be enough due to results elsewhere. It led to the tragicomic sight of the substituted Niall Quinn tearing up the touchline to tell Steve Lomas to stop time-wasting. Manchester City were relegated, and eventually went down to the third tier of English football.

Such depths only added to the shock of the takeover. City went from being the butt of every Manchester United joke to winning every single trophy, and that in the most clinical manner the game has ever seen. Mansour's hierarchy quickly learnt to convert near limitless money from Abu Dhabi into records that transformed the parameters of the sport.

That takeover on 1 September 2008 was to prove an entirely new form of ownership, although it did have echoes of both Roman Abramovich and even Abu Dhabi's immediate predecessor. The Russian's fantasy football spending at Chelsea first ensured that Manchester City's didn't feel anywhere near as 'explosive', in the words of agent Jonathan Barnett. The brief spell under former Thai Prime Minister Thaksin Shinawatra then featured elements of how the Gulf state have politically used the club, while marking the first time human rights groups raised serious questions about an English club ownership.

If that was new, the circumstances that led to Shinawatra's takeover were dismally familiar. City badly needed to be sold. The last Manchester-based major shareholder, John Wardle, had been propping up the club for years with partner David Makin. They couldn't keep going, though. Jobs were at stake. A sense of desperation ensured there were virtually no questions about

Shinawatra's money. The politician had been seeking to buy a club for some time. A Liverpool delegation met him twice in 2006, but they told each other it 'didn't feel right'. Shinawatra later insisted he came into football out of pure 'love' for the game, and the Premier League is admittedly huge in Thailand.[2] That also meant the game had a convenient political benefit, particularly after Shinawatra had been ousted after five years as prime minister by a military coup in September 2006. He used the international exposure from the Premier League to keep his image out there. It also served as a way to move some of his considerable wealth out of the country.

That image had a lot of stains. Shinawatra's government had faced allegations of authoritarianism, torture,[3] treason, conflicts of interest and suppression of the press.[4] The murders perpetrated during his 'war on drugs' campaign already alarmed the United Nations, with Shinawatra declaring 'there is nothing under the sun which the Thai police cannot do'.[5] Among the dead were a 16-month-old baby in her mother's arms and a nine-year-old boy. The suppression of an insurgency in the south of the country was meanwhile reported to have led to the death of hundreds of ethnic Malay Muslims.[6] Shinawatra was still considered a fit and proper person by the Premier League, despite Human Rights Watch declaring him a 'human rights abuser of the worst kind',[7] and writing a letter to the competition.

'In light of the widespread, serious and systematic human rights abuses perpetrated in Thailand under Mr Thaksin's leadership, we are very concerned that you concluded that he is a "fit and proper person" to purchase Manchester City Football Club,'[8] wrote Brad Adams, the body's executive director for Asia. 'We hope you would agree that the integrity of the Premier League depends in large part on the integrity of its owners. The rules concerning who is "fit and proper" should ensure that serious human rights abusers are not among the league's owners.'

It was far from the last time a human rights body would comment on the Premier League, since the game willingly passed the buck. Scudamore wrote back saying such questions were so 'extremely important' that 'they fall to the UK Government, statutory authorities and the European Union to consider'.[9] City's directors, chaired by John Wardle, recommended all club shareholders sell to Shinawatra on the same day he was charged with corruption in Thailand.[10] The stance was that, as a public limited company, they only had to consider whether the offer represented fair value. 'All the boxes were ticked and the money was there,'[11] Wardle told David Conn for his book on the club, *Richer Than God*. 'It was clean as a whistle. I didn't have any concerns.'

There weren't too many misgivings in general, although one former editor of the club magazine swore to never attend a game again.[12] Shinawatra immediately started using the populist plays he had been criticised for when trying to win votes in rural Thailand.[13] Themed events were put on, with free noodles. Shinawatra was dubbed 'Frank', as in Sinatra, when he turned up to sing 'Blue Moon'. There were some sophisticated intentions, mind, that would similarly foreshadow Abu Dhabi ambition. Shinawatra wanted a global brand that would move Thailand away from the market for counterfeit goods. He also wanted a club for the whole of the country to support, that could be rolled into his political ambitions. Former defender Nedum Onuoha describes how Shinawatra 'had players from Thailand training with the first team' as the hierarchy 'were trying to implement lots of Thai ideas within the club'. Dignitaries and politicians were entertained at what was then the City of Manchester Stadium, while the scoreboard was used for messages celebrating the king of Thailand.

It helped that the results alongside those messages were initially good. City started the season well, with new manager Sven-Göran Eriksson and signings such as Elano and Martin Petrov bringing a sense of spectacle after drab recent seasons. City even did the double over Manchester United. If much of this was about image, though, it was a mirage. Performances got so bad that City were defeated 8-1 at Middlesbrough on the last day of the season, leading to Eriksson's sacking. Shinawatra hadn't actually invested much into the club. The money for transfers had been from loans, with interest of almost 12 per cent. All of this was laid bare after Shinawatra's wife, Potjaman, was sentenced to three years in prison for violating Thai land sale laws in July 2008. She and Shinawatra instantly violated bail by going to the Beijing Olympics, before heading to England. The owner of Manchester City was a fugitive from justice.[14] An increasingly engaged UK Foreign Office eventually told the Premier League this was 'a problem'. Shinawatra's assets were frozen, meaning City faced ruin. As with Chelsea before Abramovich, the club had to mortgage future TV contract payments. 'It was very unlucky for me,' Shinawatra later said.[15]

City were in an even more perilous situation than the year before. Garry Cook, who had just been headhunted from Nike, couldn't believe what he had taken on. He had already caused embarrassment when asked about the various allegations against Shinawatra in an interview with the *Guardian*.[16] 'Is he a nice guy? Yes. Is he a great guy to play golf with? Yes. Does he have plenty of money to run a football club? Yes. I really care only about those three things.' In that same interview, Cook also came out with the following when speaking about 'Thaksin's ambitions'. 'Can we be as big, or bigger, than Manchester United? Yes. Can we win the Premier League? Yes. Can we win the Champions League? It will take time, probably 10 years or more. But if I didn't think that, I wouldn't be here.'

Almost all of that would turn out to be true, right down to the timing, although not in a way anyone could imagine at that point. City still badly needed to be sold in summer 2008. It should have been another shame of English football. There were everyday concerns for people. Employees didn't know if they would be paid. Cook felt that one of football's great names was going to 'collapse', and Shinawatra gave him permission to speak to buyers at the end of June 2008.[17] There were few coming forward, because City didn't look especially attractive. They were known as Manchester's second club, for one, and had a huge wage bill but little land. The stadium, built for the 2002 Commonwealth Games, had been bestowed on City by Manchester City Council.

In one of football's ironic twists, all of those factors actually proved attractive to a very distinctive buyer. Sheikh Mansour was at that point exploring plans to buy a foreign club. There had already been tentative talks between Arsenal's David Dein and City's eventual chairman, Khaldoon Al Mubarak, about investment in the years before. Dein claimed 'the timing wasn't right',[18] but it wasn't long after that the UAE hosted the 2007 Gulf Cup and lifted the trophy. The rulers had watched many of its four million population celebrate on the streets, in what was a rare national moment for a young country. The social power of football was sinking in. The national league was relaunched in 2008, before the 2009 and 2010 Club World Cups were hosted with the intention of attracting more foreign fans.

At the same time, City had engaged Amanda Staveley in the sale process. The financier was seen as having contacts in the Gulf from the Dubai bid for Liverpool. She had also helped Sheikh Mansour acquire a £3.5 billion stake as part of the bail-out of Barclays that same year, and it is claimed she at one point just exclaimed: 'Why don't we get into football?' Staveley certainly had an appreciation for the exposure the game brought. The common view was that she blew the Liverpool sale as 'she couldn't help but be in the public eye'. That perception worsened when it became apparent Dubai weren't as committed to buying a club as had been thought. That wasn't to be the case with Abu Dhabi. The idea was passed to a close advisor of Mansour, Ali Jassim. He eventually sat with Staveley and Cook for a 45-minute meeting before City's first home game of the 2008–09 season, against West Ham United. What the club and city could do for the state was very much pushed. 'If you're developing your nation and you're looking to be on a global stage, we are your proxy brand for the nation,'[19] Cook said.

It was also important to the Abu Dhabi side that City had good crowds. Mansour was viewed as having little interest in football, although he had invested into Emirati club Al Jazira in the same period. The idea certainly fit into Vision 2030. Mansour went ahead with the purchase through Abu Dhabi United Group, a company founded that summer. Shinawatra made a personal profit of around £90 million, according to documents from a Dubai court case that revealed the club had been bought for £150 million.[20] The UAE's second emirate had given Shinawatra political asylum. So much for his luck, as he put it. So much for 'Cityitis', too. Just at the point that everything was going as wrong as it could, the entire history of the club was changed. So was its identity. City had the wealthiest owner in football, of a different order of magnitude to even Abramovich. Since that meant due diligence could be worried about afterwards, the deal was concluded within mere days at the Emirates Palace Hotel in Abu Dhabi. The Premier League, in the words of one insider, 'almost fell over themselves' given 'the Thaksin problem'. There were no difficult questions or even the sort of noise that Shinawatra's purchase produced. Few knew who Mansour was.

Details were soon offered in a generally well-measured letter to fans on 18 September 2008. After a few paragraphs talking about the plans, there was an acknowledgement of the whys. 'In cold business terms, Premiership football is one of the best entertainment products in the world and we see this as a sound business investment.'[21] There was then some important context. 'I should perhaps also explain that despite what you may have read, I have bought the club in a private capacity and as part of my personal business strategy to hold a wide portfolio of business investments.' Mansour's letter said he was 'a football fan' and 'now also a Manchester City fan' but 'also a long-term investor' as it was confirmed 'we are here for the long haul'. It was then explained Mansour couldn't be at the next fixture against Portsmouth, although he wouldn't actually appear at a match until a home game against Liverpool on 23 August 2010. A banner read 'Manchester thanks you Sheikh Mansour'. It was his last appearance until the 2023 Champions League final. Al Mubarak explained Mansour enjoyed that first trip, if not the 'fuss' as 'he isn't going to be left alone'. This despite state-level security. Mansour is one of the highest royals in the UAE as the fifth of 19 sons of revered state founder Sheikh Zayed. More importantly, he was one of the 'Bani Fatima', the six sons of Sheikh Zayed's favourite wife, who are described within political circles as 'ruling the country in every way possible'. One of Mansour's full brothers is Sheikh Abdullah, of the football chats with Miliband. Another is Sheikh Mohammed bin Zayed, now President of the UAE but who was then the crown prince and was already being described by a US diplomatic cable as the 'de facto ruler' of the country.[22] That afforded Mansour a huge fortune, which all came from a royal family fortune that went into the trillions. This was almost entirely generated through oil that makes up 7–9 per cent of the world's reserves.

It was one of those strange little quirks that a story of such global significance started with a famous man in speedos. Deep sea explorer Jacques Cousteau was the first person to detect oil in Abu Dhabi, having been commissioned by a British expedition to look for signs on the ocean floor.[23] Britain didn't stick around for the spoils, though, having decided they could no longer afford to militarily oversee the region in 1971. This left an opening for Sheikh Zayed to shape the seven emirates into a nation state that same year, having already taken power in Abu Dhabi in 1966. He had an impressive vision for the new UAE and its wealth, but also quite rigorous ideas about how to achieve it. Sheikh Zayed described democracy as 'transitory and incomplete'.[24] He also realised that such order could only be achieved through a patronage system that was to become typical of the region's monarchies, where that wealth was shared with the population in the form of infrastructure and even money on marriage. One of his sons, Sheikh Saif bin Zayed Al Nahyan, would go on to say that 'loyalty is a condition of citizenship'.[25]

This evolved into a climate that brought an international outcry over another son, Sheikh Issa bin Zayed Al Nahyan, being acquitted by an Abu Dhabi court despite the leak of a 'torture tape'.[26] A video released by American businessman Bassam Nabulsi showed the royal shooting at an Afghan man, setting him on fire, electrocuting him, pouring salt into the wounds and eventually having him driven over. While Sheikh Issa's lawyer said that the trial showed 'everyone in the country can be put in front of the law', Nabulsi said 'they act like Al Capone in the 1920s – no one can stop them'. The UAE have since built one of the largest surveillance states in the world, commonly described as 'Orwellian'.

Mansour had a lofty position in that state, with a US cable describing him as 'a powerful behind-the-scenes player in controlling access to Sheikh Zayed through an early role as head of his father's presidential office'.[27] For some time the City purchase was still reiterated as being in a 'private capacity'. It was conspicuous that Al Mubarak repeatedly stressed the point to Conn, while insisting 'it has nothing to do with any of the government investment companies'.[28] This is an argument rejected by virtually all experts, as backed by documents from Football Leaks, and those with knowledge of the purchase insist the initial decision to buy went wider than Mansour. The state influence was quickly undeniable, too, even beyond all the company branding. Al Mubarak's very presence was testament to that.

His brief predecessor as front man was Sulaiman al Fahim, a real-estate millionaire who fronted the Emirati equivalent of *The Apprentice*. He spent three days acting as if he were the owner, bragging about how City would now buy stars like Fernando Torres and Cristiano Ronaldo, and become 'bigger than both Manchester United and Real Madrid'. There was an obvious question at the next Premier League meeting. 'Who is this clown?' Such headlines made Abu Dhabi executives quickly realise that owning a football club brought a far greater level of exposure than anything else associated with their name. Al Fahim's comments went against the respectful and understated image the emirate was cultivating. Al Mubarak outright stated much of this in comments to Conn that seemed to blur the lines drawn in his statement about a private purchase. The Emirati said 'everything we do' is about 'telling the world' about 'the true essence of who Abu Dhabi is'. 'There is almost a personification of the values we hold as Abu Dhabi, with the values of the club ... this is something new, something we didn't really plan for, but it is becoming an important part of this.'

Proving all of that, Al Fahim was swiftly removed, never to be seen near City again. Al Mubarak replaced him, ensuring that one of the most influential figures in the UAE ran the club. Through his role as chairman of the centrally powerful Executive Affairs Authority, Al Mubarak is often described as the de facto prime minister of the state. He is one of Mohammed bin Zayed's most trusted advisors and always present when the ruler meets world leaders, such as Vladimir Putin. In a 2014 meeting, when the UAE wanted the UK to take a harder stance on the Muslim Brotherhood political group, it was Al Mubarak who warned that the government would 'need to consider the political implications' and that 'difficult conversations' could 'become far more difficult'.[29]

Such approaches are why, in the words of Foreign Office staff, the UAE are a 'strategic partner' but 'these are not cosy relationships'. It also emphasises the extra value of having a huge cultural asset in a major English city. Al Mubarak has regularly shown a deft ability for marrying such assertiveness with measure while at Manchester City. He is the son of the UAE's former ambassador to France, Khalifa Ahmad Mubarak, who was assassinated in 1984. Noted as a talent from a young age, Al Mubarak was part of a generation that Sheikh Zayed insisted go to the best foreign universities so the burgeoning Abu Dhabi could develop an intelligentsia beyond the ruling family. Al Mubarak went to Tufts University, where he studied economics and finance. It was quite a contrast to Mansour's two years at Santa Barbara College, whose most famous alumnus is Katy Perry.[30] Al Mubarak was eventually handpicked to lead Mubadala, one of UAE's biggest sovereign wealth funds.

Reporting to him at Manchester City was Simon Pearce, who was commonly seen as Mohammed bin Zayed's main communications advisor. The forthright Anglo-Australian had come from Burson-Marsteller, a PR firm infamous for representing clients like Romanian dictator Nicolae Ceaușescu and the Argentininan military junta.[31] It meant City had on its board the men with primary responsibility for Abu Dhabi's budget, its international strategy and its image. 'That shows the importance of Man City to Abu Dhabi,' McGeehan argues. 'Those are the top guys.' This reflects how the UAE foreign minister, who had no official connection to the club, was discussing it as a high-priority issue at the UN.

As with Abramovich, it would take significant external developments years later for any of this to be discussed. There wasn't any mention of soft power or state vehicles for some time. The perception of Mansour as another self-indulgently wealthy super-billionaire meant there was no debate about the migrant workers who had laboured in indentured servitude to turn Abu Dhabi from largely open desert into a gleaming metropolis in the space of 40 years. The immediate headlines on 1 September 2008 played their part in that, since they were so astonishing it was all hard to take in. Mark Hughes, who had replaced Sven-Göran Eriksson as manager, sprinted from a round of golf to check the television. Football executives were again left googling a new owner. Cook had already been instructed to sign a superstar. He had less than a day, since the transfer window was about to close. Other European clubs were left bemused as City sent faxes around with what seemed like absurd offers. There was even a bid for Leo Messi. Two options emerged as the most realistic. One was Dimitar Berbatov, who Tottenham Hotspur were negotiating to finally sell to Manchester United for £30.75 million after a summer of tension. When Berbatov was told of City's interest, he just said 'fuck off'. United was his dream. That decision would have repercussions.

City were already up against another major club for the second name. Abramovich's latest big move was to be Real Madrid's Robinho, a young Brazilian forward spoken about as Pelé's successor, but negotiations with Chelsea were fraught. City went in strong but couldn't get a commitment. There was then another twist. Robinho appeared on the Chelsea website before anything was agreed. Real Madrid were livid. City had an opening. Fans had already turned up at the stadium to celebrate. By midnight, Robinho was pictured holding up City's shirt in their London offices. Those present felt it was possible he didn't actually know which club he'd signed for.

Then again, this was no longer the old Manchester City.

5.

DRINKING IT IN

When Garry Cook laid out Manchester City's plans for 2009 onwards, it genuinely shocked people. This was basically the world XI at the time, and there seemed little barrier to assembling it since they'd essentially told Real Madrid to name their price for Robinho. The Spanish club couldn't believe they'd got €42 million in that year's market. Although Manchester City knew they needed a statement like that, and Cook was all too willing to talk about stars, it gave completely the wrong impression of what the club would become. The image was immediately of the flashiest names and superficiality. The reality was to go much deeper. This wasn't to fit with the expectation people had of a Gulf royal throwing money around. Al Mubarak quickly instructed Simon Pearce and consultants Booz Allen and Co to go through every centimetre and examine what was required to 'become one of the top clubs in the world'.[1] The eventual recommendation was to change everything. The new hierarchy were shocked at what they found, which included a gym that had just one boxing glove. They couldn't believe this was the level of a club in the famous Premier League.

What followed was a showcase in how you build an elite club from scratch, with unlimited resources. Abu Dhabi were attempting something of a scale that had never been seen in football before, because nobody had the means to even imagine it. This was the difference with state-level thinking. City's new owners had the usual four-year plan but this was, entirely unusually for football, within the context of thirty- to fifty-year plans. Al Mubarak literally described the purchase as a 'value proposition in football that has not yet been accomplished'.[2] The Abu Dhabi hierarchy wanted to invest as much money as was necessary to turn the club into a brand the level of Real Madrid or Manchester United, with Al Mubarak referring outright to 'the financial resources we are able to make available'.[3] The old Manchester City were essentially a 'host', a blank slate for creating something that was going way beyond their local identity. It already had the identity of Abu Dhabi bolted on to it. City, for the first time in football, were a club that represented another state as well as their community.

Amid such a scale, there had to be basic steps. Mark Hughes flew out to Sheikh Mansour's palace to be interviewed for his own job. Al Mubarak was impressed with how straightforward the manager was, but complications soon came. Learning the nuances of football was to be a key part of year one, alongside overhauling the club infrastructure. The guiding standard for everything and everyone was 'best in class'.[4] Each member of staff was asked what they thought was needed in their specific role to be the finest in that field. Each prospective appointment was given the full vision. Brian Marwood, the former Arsenal player headhunted to co-ordinate all this, was 'blown away'.[5] He was soon going around a number of different sports to research world-class standards.

'They wanted to see how the best do it,' Nedum Onuoha says. 'That quest to be the best. "Do they have places for players to sleep? How many fields do they have?"' The ownership were leaving nothing to chance, as the staff drastically expanded with a number of new departments. The squad didn't have to concern themselves with anything except performing, since every aspect of their lives was catered for. The scale of change was illustrated by how some players went away for one international break and came back to a new state-of-the-art gym as part of a £3 million overhaul of the training complex. There were motivational messages on the wall, including one from Lance Armstrong. 'Pain is temporary. It may last a minute, an hour, a day or a year but eventually it will subside and something else will take its place. If I quit, it lasts for ever.' They expected most of the pain to be gone by year two. That was when the club planned to compete for a Champions League place, with year three to be when they started winning trophies. Year four was to be the Premier League title.

These targets were all met within the timescale. That's in large part because the team was backed by over £1 billion of expenditure on the squad over the same period.[6] It was much more forensic than the frantic first day, too. As well as the most advanced analytics, City's choices were partly driven by another aim. They wanted to strengthen their own squad while also weakening direct opponents.[7] With Aston Villa, Everton and Arsenal blocking the way to the Champions League, City blew holes in each of them. All of Gareth Barry, Joleon Lescott, Emmanuel Adebayor and Kolo Touré were signed. 'They ripped the heart out of Arsenal,' was a common sentiment, since five of City's first 23 signings came from Arsène Wenger's team. Showing how much had changed, Sir Alex Ferguson expressed concern for his old rival.

It had an effect on the wider market, too. The old 'big four' of Manchester United, Chelsea, Arsenal and Liverpool had finished in the Champions League places for four successive seasons, but were finally broken up. Tottenham were actually City's direct rivals for the final top-four place in the 2009–10 season and even beat them in the decisive game. It was seen as one of those hinge matches that could reshape the future. It only delayed the inevitable. Spurs couldn't match the financial power. City beat them to the signings of Barry, Craig Bellamy and Patrick Vieira. They were 'blowing everyone out of the water' with offers. When players were hesitant to join because of City's modest history, they were told they could instead shape the future. Cook even accused AC Milan of 'bottling it' for not selling Brazilian star Kaká.

Ferran Soriano, who at that point had just left Barcelona, described it as another 'inflation craze'.[8] It wasn't long until even United felt the tremors from the changed landscape – right down to a barb over Manchester's geography. Carlos Tevez had been key to United's Champions League victory in 2007–08, but was personally put out when Ferguson brought in Dimitar Berbatov. The Argentinian's two-year loan was up in 2009, and the United manager didn't want to renegotiate with the player's agent, Kia Joorabchian. Although City didn't have Tevez in their detailed plans, they realised the huge opportunity for a statement. Documents leaked to *Der Spiegel* indicate that City agreed to pay a total of €51.25 million for Tevez to Harlem Springs, a company reported to hold the player's economic rights, and owned by Joorabchian.[9] The player himself signed a contract worth just under £200,000 a week, with huge bonuses, as well as a condition he always be the best-paid player at the club. Even the United squad were amazed by the numbers. One senior figure at Old Trafford described it as 'the first moment of clarity' as regards City's power. This would all be signposted – literally.

Manchester United are actually based in the borough of Trafford, part of Greater Manchester, but distinct to the borough of Manchester itself. At the border between the two, City put up a huge and provocative billboard. The image was of Tevez with his arms outstretched, in sky blue, with three words: 'Welcome to Manchester.' City fans were thrilled. Players were astounded, and Onuoha admits it made him feel 'uncomfortable'. Some in the hierarchy felt the same, since Abu Dhabi's ethos at that point was to be respectful.[10] There was still relish – and laughter – when they realised they'd got to Ferguson. 'It's City isn't it? They are a small club with a small mentality,'[11] the manager spat. 'All they can talk about is Manchester United; they can't get away from it . . . They think taking Carlos Tevez away from Manchester United is a triumph. It is poor stuff.'

It was also, however, 'content'. This was how senior staff at City started to speak, as they echoed the super clubs in seeing themselves like a media company. They wanted to be in the news, and 'disruptive'. It was progress if a figure like Ferguson was talking about them, especially if it was with fury. He bellowed at City staff about the banner, and even told players not to fraternise with friends there. Ferguson himself went as far as referring to City as 'a noisy neighbour' after the first Manchester derby following Tevez's switch. That was of course a United victory, at 4-3, and a vintage late winner. Michael Owen's 96th-minute goal was one of four late strikes United would score against City over the next year and a half. This had just been the way of things. Abu Dhabi executives were shocked at how that fatalism affected the fans, especially when it came to United. They were determined to change it.

The results at that stage were the wrong type of content, though. Hughes only won another three Premier League games after the United defeat, and the new ownership made their first managerial change. It was admittedly later than anyone expected, but still brought rare complaints from supporters. The fact Hughes had been left to manage a last game against Sunderland after the news leaked was viewed as callous.

This was the other side of the best-laid plans. City's huge turnover of players meant an unsettled and unwieldy squad. Robinho became an issue. There just weren't enough moments like a brilliant chip against Arsenal, that brought out that thumb-sucking celebration. He instead became part of a Brazilian clique that would often threaten to throw their toys out. Robinho even suggested other players do more running for him. When teammates like Bellamy or an increasingly influential Kompany attempted to call this out, Elano would stand in front of Robinho and threaten to 'tell the Sheikh'.[12]

The team needed shape and discipline. They would get more than that with Roberto Mancini, an Italian playing legend, who was the ownership's first managerial appointment. They also got real pedigree and a record of three Serie A titles as a coach. If it still seemed early in the ownership that a figure of Mancini's standing was joining, the money helped. The new manager signed a contract worth a base salary of £1.45 million a year, with £4 million of bonuses and incentives possible.[13] On the same day, according to *Der Spiegel*'s leaked documents, Mancini also signed a £1.75 million contract for 'consulting' with Sheikh Mansour's Emirati club, Al Jazira.[14] The payment went to an offshore shell company in Mauritius called Sparkleglow Holdings.[15] Such revelations would later add another significant strand to the City story, to go with sportswashing and how you build an ideal club. Mancini also brought a more fundamental football theme. That is how a team can succeed despite hating the manager.

That's a fact that has surprised many, especially given how charming Mancini was in the media. Even Ferguson spoke of enjoying his company. The glamour of the name was amplified by the image of the 'fancy scarf' – as the players put it – and the bicycle he rode to the training ground. Such media-friendly flourishes aggravated the squad more. Mancini immediately disabused the ownership of one image. Although the hierarchy wanted flamboyant football to improve the 'brand', he told them they first needed defensive discipline. Mancini imposed this in distinctive ways. The first XI would be set up in formation on a training pitch, but with no one in front of them. They would then be ordered to play through the team, until the forward just kicked the ball into an empty net. While bemusing the players, the idea was for the team to internalise positions. Slight deviations enraged Mancini. So did jokes. Training was not 'fun'. The backline, led by Kompany and Pablo Zabaleta, at least started to relish a will for defending. They kept four clean sheets in Mancini's first six games. Robinho's refusal to run wasn't tolerated, with Mancini immediately despising him.

The Brazilian wasn't alone there. Every morning would usually start with Mancini getting onto the exercise bike as the medical team gave standard updates on squad fitness. This almost always led to an explosion and all manner of accusations from the manager. 'He thought people were conspiring against him,' Onuoha says. Popular staff members were forced out. If things went wrong, it was because of you not him, with 'you' potentially being anyone. Mancini didn't care in the slightest about building any sort of bond, or anyone liking him. Players were berated in the most brutal ways. He would question aspects of their body shape and their basic talent. Accomplished players were frequently told it looked like they'd never played football before. This was not delivered as a joke. 'Never speak to me again,' was a common Mancini conclusion to discussion about errors. Samir Nasri and Mario Balotelli were among those who came to physical confrontation with the manager.

Mancini, for his part, would still pick them. The ultimate example of this was the club's poster boy. Although Mancini had guided City to their first ever Champions League qualification in 2010–11, tension had grown with Tevez. The Argentinian gave everything on the pitch but was a poor trainer, with staff members believing Mancini's ego resented the amount of attention the star signing got. Tevez certainly created headlines that summer, when he said he would not return to Manchester as the city only had two restaurants, 'everything's small' and 'it rains all the time'.[16] Tevez still went back but was left on the bench for a huge away game against Bayern Munich in September 2011. City were 2-0 down at half-time so Mancini told Tevez to warm up. The player said he already had but then argued he didn't feel right, in part because he was irritated at not being introduced earlier. The response went as expected. Mancini had to be held back from Tevez in the dressing room and later unleashed to the media. The Argentinian was the latest that would apparently never play for City again – although the fact that the claim was this time stated in public made it legally contentious. Tevez was fined four weeks' wages, eventually reduced to two after representations by the Professional Footballers' Association. He again decamped to Argentina, complaining how Mancini treated him 'like a dog'.[17] It looked insoluble, especially since City's relationship with Joorabchian had become strained. Further complicating the controversy was how players felt Tevez couldn't be captain any more, but were still irritated by how Mancini portrayed the incident to the media. Such disgruntlement was a major reason why Mancini was sacked just a year after winning the title. The players just stopped responding. Mancini's own attitude to his superiors didn't help. Some figures say he spoke to the hierarchy with a 'disdain' they'd never experienced before. 'He didn't manage up well.'

He was still capable of sudden decisions that could serve the team, as with Tevez. City refused to sell the Argentinian, and the owners' resources meant they didn't have to think like a normal club and cut their losses. The players also felt Tevez could win them the title. So, after protracted talks, Mancini was persuaded to compromise. On Tevez's return, the manager immediately had him weighed. Mancini might have seemed to resent the majority of players, but he appreciated what the most talented could do. On taking over as manager, the Italian insisted City had two world-class players in every position. City beat Real Madrid to Atlético Madrid's Sergio Agüero and Manchester United to Nasri, as Wenger expressed increasing concern about financial force. Nasri later regretted his decision, solely due to his relationship with Mancini. It was a classic case of tension producing success. That and tens of millions of pounds.

Tevez, for his part, was always willing to give his all on the pitch no matter what. He was also central to the ownership's first big moment. That was, naturally, a win over United. Tevez scored twice as City came from behind to win 2-1 in the 2009–10 League Cup semi-final first leg. He celebrated by making a shushing gesture at Gary Neville, who had said he wasn't worth the money, before the Argentinian later called his former teammate a 'moron'.[18] That meant United savoured it all the more when they won the second leg 3-1 with yet another stoppage-time winner. This time it was Wayne Rooney, whom City tried to sign later that year. United were now their direct competitors, as well as the standard. Marwood even used to take detours past Old Trafford to remind himself of the level City needed to reach.[19]

City's initial rise can similarly be measured in results against their rivals, before they passed them by. It only added to the motivation that senior United figures used to make barbs about never catching up. They would be remembered. It wasn't even that long until City achieved a properly memorable victory. Mancini's side beat United 1-0 in the 2010–11 FA Cup semi-final, with expensive new signing Yaya Touré scoring the goal. City still needed to beat Stoke City in the final to ensure it really mattered, but there was never any doubt about that once United had been exorcised. Kompany believed that was when 'the change in mentality' happened.[20] Touré scored the only goal in the final, too, and City won their first trophy in 35 years.

That number had been gleefully showcased on a notorious banner at Old Trafford known as 'the ticker', that now had to be taken down for the next time City visited. They then took United apart, humiliating their rivals 6-1. With three of the goals coming after the 89th minute, it was like City were distilling years of pain into one exquisite victory that subjected United to even worse punishment. It wasn't even to be the last punishment that season. City actually found numerous ways to humble United, in turn inverting so much of the rivalry. There was first that Mancini's team came back from eight points behind in the title race, hauling back a faltering United in the way Ferguson had done to so many. Tevez was central to that, returning to the team after a 1-0 defeat at Arsenal that had seemed to settle it. Even Mancini was deflated. Al Mubarak calmly sat him down and asked what was needed. Tevez proved the solution. City won all of their last seven games, with the Argentinian scoring four in the next two matches, a 4-0 against West Brom and 6-1 away to Norwich City. The fifth of those victories was a decisive 1-0 at home against United, that meant City had the title in their own hands for the first time in months. Kompany's winning header almost felt as humbling as David Silva's divine passes in the 6-1, since Ferguson had played such a hugely defensive team.

On the final day, having defeated United in multiple different ways, City had just one more team to beat to make the title theirs. It wasn't really opposition team Queens Park Rangers, even as victory over the London club would confirm a first league title in 44 years. Those stakes ensured City really had to play themselves, their own history. This was what figures like Al Mubarak meant when pointing to the lack of belief among supporters. That would become apparent through the day itself. Only adding to the portentousness of it all was the presence of so many ghosts from City's past. Hughes was the QPR manager, with former players Onuoha, Shaun Wright-Phillips and Joey Barton part of his team. Legends from the days before Mansour were invited back. For all that had changed, the game started in the way these moments of truth always do. There was initial raucous excitement, and then extended anxiety. It didn't help that Rooney scored for United at Sunderland after 20 minutes, ensuring the title was going to Old Trafford as it stood. City needed to score, with Zabaleta doing just that on 39 minutes.

That should have been enough, only for Cityitis to spread like a virus. Results elsewhere suddenly meant QPR were going to be relegated so had to raise it. Within three minutes of the second half starting, Djibril Cissé equalised. City just needed to impose a sense of normality on the game, but the opposite happened. Within another seven minutes, Barton was sent off for a confrontation with Agüero. The extra man should have helped City, but the chaos only brought further distortion, especially as Barton confronted Kompany and Balotelli. Within another 11 minutes, Jamie Mackie made it 2-1 to QPR. This was everything City fans feared, as tears were visible in the stands with over 20 minutes left to play.

Mancini only made this worse. As the club was suffering a collective psychological collapse, he wasn't exactly displaying a 'winner's steel'. He was instead running out from the bench to aggressively berate anyone in his eye line. 'Fuck you. Fuck you. And fuck you.' It was extraordinary. It also seemed to further freeze the players. They stopped going through Mancini's methodically planned drills, with every desperate long shot like throwing coal into the furnace of his anger. Mancini's abuse of his team became more personalised. Players and staff still find that part of the day difficult to discuss. The hierarchy would remember. In the end, even against the fatalism in the stands, a squad with two world-class players in every position had too much quality. Abu Dhabi's utter assurance overrode even an identity as ingrained as City's. Mancini reached for the £27 million Edin Džeko and £24 million Balotelli. City's many crosses finally had an outlet, as Džeko scored in the 92nd minute. City were alive.

It was close to that exact moment that United's win over Sunderland was confirmed. Michael Carrick said that it was the first time he let himself believe they had a chance of winning the league.[21] Then, just as United had done to so many, just as City had suffered more than any, a stoppage-time winner came with what felt like cosmic force. As the clock ticked towards 93 minutes and 20 seconds of the signalled 95, Balotelli worked the ball to Agüero. The Argentinian instinctively evaded Taye Taiwo's challenge, before lashing the ball with all the force of 44 years. Sky Sports commentator Martin Tyler started saying Agüero's name the millisecond the forward took that first touch and finished with a roaring crescendo as the ball hit the net. 'I swear, you'll never see anything like this ever again! So watch it. Drink it in!'

There was so much to consume. On the most immediate level, this was vintage sport, as the will of elite athletes pushed them over the line amid grander narratives. Euphoric fans invaded the pitch. A wait was ended, a weight lifted, along with the trophy. Cityitis had been banished. There was now a before and after. Ferguson described it as his worst setback. Many United players still can't watch 'the Agüero moment'. Many City players, meanwhile, can't watch any of the minutes that led up to it. Most don't want to talk about Mancini. The Premier League couldn't stop replaying it. The competition finally had its signature moment in its twentieth season, an equivalent of the Michael Thomas goal that helped launch it. That was when Arsenal won the league at Liverpool with the last kick of the 1988–89 season, a Friday night 'television spectacular' that happened at the same time as both clubs were pushing for a breakaway. A month after Agüero's goal, the Premier League confirmed a new domestic TV deal worth £3 billion. It was a 70 per cent increase on the previous deal and a ten-fold increase on the 1992 deal.[22] Such numbers echoed the major significance of the Agüero moment, which was that over a billion pounds-worth of investment can quickly change an identity that has lasted for decades. City's very DNA had been mutated. The playbook had another chapter.

Abu Dhabi had their moment, too, even if nobody was talking about sportswashing at the time. This was the 'content' people like Cook spoke about, but so much more. The footage would go down in sporting history. You can immediately see the 'Etihad' branding when rewatching, to go with all the other state-linked sponsors like Etisalat, Aabar and just Abu Dhabi itself. Positive association had been taken to a euphoric degree. Everyday business had to be attended to, which meant Al Mubarak and Pearce left for Abu Dhabi before the parade.[23] There, Sheikh Mansour celebrated with a cake decorated with the City crest and a trophy. He shared it with his brother, Mohammed bin Zayed.

As significant as the title victory was to the very psychology of Manchester City, there were less sensational developments around the season that were just as important to the club's ambition. The ownership were already looking further afield, and mainly to Barcelona. September of the 2011–12 season saw the announcement of plans for a new football campus on a derelict 80-acre site across from the stadium. It was a remarkable investment given the Carrington site had been overhauled just three years beforehand. The campus would eventually feature 16 pitches, as well as a 7,000-seater stadium for academy teams. 'Money was no object.' The entire club would be based there, with office staff able to look out at training. This was another idea taken from the world search of world-class sporting institutions, but a primary influence was La Masia at Barcelona. The cost was estimated at around £200 million.[24] It was also in 2011 that Abu Dhabi entered into a £1 billion-plus deal with Manchester City Council and the regeneration body, New East Manchester.[25] Crucial context was the cuts that came from the Conservative government's austerity policy. Tom Russell, of New East Manchester, is reported by Conn to have said they wouldn't necessarily have built elite sporting facilities if allowed to choose how to use such money.[26] This was all while the enhanced arena overlooking everything was renamed 'Etihad Stadium' as a key condition of a renegotiation on the lease from the council on a 'fully repairing basis'.

Those attending saw an enhanced squad, too, with City spending over £75 million net to win the Premier League again in 2013–14. That title race is best remembered for Steven Gerrard's slip as Liverpool lost 2-0 to Chelsea in a decisive defeat. New Chilean manager Manuel Pellegrini was more taciturn than Mancini but his football more expressive. This was more like it, with 102 goals scored. The ownership had by then fallen under the same spell as Abramovich, as they had watched Pep Guardiola's Barcelona and saw attacking football as they felt it should be played. City had the means to do more than try and sign the manager and some players, though. They wanted to appropriate the whole idea. It was something that was obvious to those able to think on that scale, but impossible for anyone else. On leaving Barcelona in 2012, however, Guardiola initially decided to go to Bayern Munich. Pellegrini presented a temporary alternative, as City went about putting in place an infrastructure that was idealised for Guardiola.

The ownership had actually tried to appoint Barcelona's former business genius, Ferran Soriano, in the months after the takeover. Known as 'the computer' for his forensically analytical mind, the six-foot-three Catalan had been crucial to increasing the club's income from €123 million to €309 million through capitalisation of the club's identity. Soriano had been sceptical of the City ownership model, and in his book even derided the club's 'irrational investment'.[27] Contact was maintained, though, and Soriano gradually realised this was a unique opportunity for a huge idea he had. He wanted to create football's first multi-national. It was something Soriano divined early on at Barcelona, when he was one of the first to realise the implications of the sport's rapid globalisation. That was 'a startling gap between the clubs that had become entertainment providers with global brands' and those 'limited to their local markets'. Soriano felt that Barcelona's widely admired values – especially the philosophy and identity – could be franchised to branches around the world. His presentations of course referred to 'global entertainment companies like Walt Disney',[28] and how big clubs could 'capture the growth and become global franchises'. Soriano's book basically offers the blueprint.

'So, why don't they create different franchises and have teams that play in other leagues, like the Japanese or North American leagues?'[29] The problem at Barcelona was they were still wedded to their role as a conduit for Catalan identity, and felt this plan went against that ideal. City were all too willing to let Soriano bring his book to life. By the time he met the club again in April 2012, they all felt they could marry Sheikh Mansour's unlimited wealth and generational commitment with Soriano's global vision to make City the number one club in the world. 'And I mean one,' Soriano told Giles Tremlett. 'Not number two or three'.[30]

On 10 January 2013, a few months after Soriano started work, City Football Group (CFG) was founded.[31] The ethos behind the project is described as 'glocalisation' – adapting a global product to local markets.[32] The first expansion was of course in the biggest market of all. New York City was founded in May 2013 after a deal with the New York Yankees. Melbourne Heart were then acquired in January 2014 and made into Melbourne City, as executives realised how ideal the suffix of 'City' was for the plan. That didn't come without some resistance, as there was bristling in Australian football over the rebrand.[33] India's Mumbai City and Uruguay's Montevideo City Torque soon followed, along with majority ownership of Troyes in France, Lommel in Belgium, Palermo in Italy, and Bahia in Brazil, as well as minority stakes in Spain's Girona, China's Sichuan Jiuniu and Japan's Yokohama F. Marinos.

This afforded many advantages beyond footprints in crucial markets. Yokohama allowed a partnership with Nissan. Torque, according to an internal presentation reported by *Der Spiegel*, gave access to an 'attractive location due to the concentration of quality footballers and limited budgets of local teams'.[34] Even within the well of South America, the club's analysis illustrated Uruguay was the biggest per-capita exporter of players. 'Business number two,' Soriano said of the project, 'is player development.'[35]

On the other side, the branding of the Premier League aided the pace of it all. In October 2015, two months after Chinese president and UAE ally Xi Jinping visited Manchester City with UK Prime Minister David Cameron, state-backed China Media Capital bought 13 per cent of CFG for £265 million. This touched on another benefit, which made Soriano's pitch all the more timely. The CFG idea inflated the financial size of the institution around the club while spreading costs and bringing income through player sales, all during a period when UEFA were preparing to hugely restrict external investment.

In 2013, just months after the group was founded, the new Financial Fair Play rules came into force. The regulations attempted to link spending to income, only allowing clubs a loss of €45 million for the 2011–12 and 2012–13 seasons that could be covered by the owner. Potential sanctions went up to bans from the Champions League. It was going to be a huge readjustment for a club that had previously spent without restraint.

On 7 January 2014, City were informed in writing they had been selected for compliance assessment by UEFA. It would have huge repercussions.

6.

HOW THE WORLD CUP
WAS BOUGHT

Sepp Blatter was getting aggravated, which was ironic given he was trying to show that football could heal the planet. The FIFA president wanted the 2018 and 2022 World Cups to be held in Russia and USA, respectively, but with one important extra element. The two Local Organising Committees would be one, so they could work together. Having grown up during the Cold War, Blatter had visions of being the first person to bring the two superpowers together in a global common project. There could even be a symbolic handshake to the handover. This would surely secure the Nobel Peace Prize that Blatter so desired. In reality, the process contributed to another cold war and almost split the game apart, through a moment that had a greater chain reaction than almost any in football history.

Blatter still puts much of this down to a decision made by his one-time protégé, Michel Platini, then the UEFA president. Just days before the voting for the hosts of those two World Cups, on 2 December 2010, Platini called Blatter.[1] This was the source of his aggravation. Platini told the Swiss official they had 'a problem' and that he couldn't 'support' him. Platini's vote for 2022 would go to Qatar. Blatter, and many others, attribute that decision to a high-level lunch at the Élysée Palace in Paris on 23 November.[2] Platini had arrived on the request of French President Nicolas

Sarkozy, only to see two of the most senior figures in Qatar. They were Sheikh Tamim bin Hamad Al Thani, the then crown prince who would succeed his father as emir in 2013, and Sheikh Hamad bin Jassim Al Thani, the highly influential prime minister. Also present was Sébastien Bazin of Colony Capital, the American fund that owned 98 per cent of Paris Saint-Germain (PSG), the struggling Ligue 1 club that Sarkozy supported. The French president arrived late, completing a table that involved influential figures from football history, football politics, Western politics, Western capital and Gulf autocracy. They were also meeting in the middle of deepening ties between France and Qatar following the 2008 financial crash. Once Sarkozy got into the discussion, according to the most common version of events, he told Platini 'it would be a good thing' if he switched his vote for the 2022 World Cup from the USA to this tiny Gulf state.[3] Platini has always denied any external influence on his eventual choice, and insisted he came to the decision himself. He had already met Sheikh Tamim for dinner in Geneva the month before.[4]

Whatever the truth, huge consequences followed. Ten days after that meeting, Qatar won the vote to host the 2022 World Cup. Seven months later, Qatar Sports Investments (QSI) purchased a majority stake in PSG. A year after that, beIN SPORTS was launched in France by Qatar's Al Jazeera Media Network. The new channel had purchased a package to broadcast Ligue 1, posing serious competition to long-time rights holders Canal+, who Sarkozy reportedly hated.[5] France was meanwhile negotiating even more Qatari investment. Everyone at the meeting denies any connection between these events, which a *France Football* investigation naturally termed 'Qatargate'.[6] What is indisputable, however, is that a lot of modern football can be linked back to 2 December 2010. Qatar's improbable victory provoked a storm of controversy, and huge questions about corruption. The fall-out caused regime change at both FIFA and UEFA, while damaging Platini's reputation as one of football's great players. It had far wider geopolitical consequences, as Saudi Arabia and UAE looked on Qatar with envy. The World Cup is cited as a significant factor in the Gulf blockade.

Against all of that, it's incongruous there has been so much focus on 'brown envelopes', as one executive put it. The US justice department did release an indictment stating there had been 'bribe payments in exchange' for votes.[7] The reality is that events of such scale can't happen without far, far higher-level developments. The hosting of the World Cup wasn't just won with relatively petty bribes but with trade agreements, arms deals and high politics. From that vantage point, and a lot of hindsight, the decision on 2 December 2010 looks anything but improbable. It looks inevitable.

The first time that many people in modern football say they had even heard of Qatar was when the country's national team appeared in the first edition of the *FIFA International Soccer* computer game in 1993. It might now appear an unusual choice for one of the five Asian Football Confederation teams included, but Qatar were ranked 52nd in the world after victory in the 1992 Arabian Gulf Cup. Iraq had been banned from that competition due to the 1990 invasion of Kuwait, and a fear of suffering similar aggression was the main worry for most states in the region. It was an acute concern for Qatar, since the country was so small and forgettable. The FIFA game came out when, as a joke in foreign relations used to go, Qatar was best known for not being known at all.[8]

It could easily have been just another emirate in the UAE when the latter was founded in 1971, after Britain announced its retreat from all military bases 'east of Suez'.[9] Qatar was one of many countries that now needed protection. The emir at that time, Sheikh Ahmad bin Ali Al Thani, had broached entry into the UAE due to his family's long links with Abu Dhabi's Al Nahyans.[10] Qatar then had just 100,000 inhabitants, living in a poorly developed area the size of Yorkshire. Historically reliant on pearl diving, the state had oil but not as much as its neighbours. Military protection had been offered by Saudi Arabia, which was where the Al Thanis originated, but the relationship was complicated. So were the internal politics. When the emir went on a hunting trip to Iran in 1972, his cousin took the chance to depose him. The new emir, Sheikh Khalifa bin Hamad Al Thani, centralised a stagnant state around himself but made one crucial choice. His son, Sheikh Hamad bin Khalifa Al Thani, had been given responsibility for fossil fuel development. The younger royal had a more modern world view from attending the Royal Military Academy at Sandhurst, and realised the country was not achieving its potential.[11] That potential instantly became immense in 1971, when one of the world's largest gas fields was discovered at the bottom of the Persian Gulf, shared between Qatar and Iran. The only issue was that gas required a lot of long-term development, but Sheikh Hamad was already working on that. The future was being transformed, although partly because history repeated itself. When the emir made one of his own regular trips to Switzerland in 1995, Sheikh Hamad seized power.

The transformation of the country was like flicking a switch. Between 1998 and 2008, Qatar accumulated enough gas to heat Western Europe for centuries, becoming the largest exporter of liquefied natural gas (LNG) in the world by the month of the World Cup vote.[12] Tankers the size of aircraft carriers were bringing in over £100 billion a year. The GDP per citizen grew to the highest in the world at around €700,000, which was a hundred times greater than some of the home countries of the migrant workers now building Doha's new metropolis.[13] These workers were denied citizenship, although even citizens lacked freedom of political expression. Like other Gulf autocracies, a patronage system demanded loyalty. The riches of Qatar's system, where a third of the wealth went to citizens, actually made it the most stable state in the region. The emir could theoretically do what he wanted, but sought consensus from clearly defined hierarchies established beneath him. This period was Qatar's true foundation. The state, in the words of a cable from the US embassy in Doha, had 'more money than it knows what to do with'.[14] The new emir actually knew exactly what he wanted to do. He wanted Qatar to make its mark on history, to stand out between bigger neighbours like Saudi Arabia and Iran.

Qatar sought to broadcast all of this, literally. Al Jazeera was founded in 1996, with the establishment of an actual news channel an unusually progressive step for the Gulf autocracies. The emir predicted it would 'help put tiny Qatar on the map'.[15] Al Jazeera's forthright reporting – on everything except Qatar's own rulers – made it the most important news source in the region, attracting more than 30 million viewers within two years. The station also gained traction in the West, albeit with the nickname of 'terror TV' due to the broadcast of kidnap videos. The nature of the reporting horrified the UAE and Saudi Arabia perhaps even more, since this was one of the Gulf's own countries willingly publicising the region's issues. The two states had already backed a failed coup in Qatar in 1996. 'Al Jazeera completely changed the way the region interacted with current affairs,' says Arthur Snell, a former diplomat. 'It also meant Qatar, which was seen as a bit of a joke, assumed this amazing influence. Every other Gulf country hates that.'

The emir didn't care about aggravating neighbours but he did develop a new foreign policy around becoming an international mediator and what was termed 'the Switzerland of the Gulf'. Militarily, Qatar insulated themselves by signing a defence agreement with the USA after the first Gulf War in 1991. That evolved into the construction of the Al Udeid Air Base in 1996, which the US military used as its headquarters in Asia. The site was the launching ground for bombing missions in Afghanistan and Syria. Summing up Qatar's Janus-like strategy, Palestinian military group Hamas had an office in Doha by 2012. The US approved due to the possibility for back-channel negotiations.

Qatar's money remained front and centre. The purchase of assets and institutions in the West was complemented by museums and galleries within Doha, while the new Education City district attracted branches of distinguished universities from USA, Great Britain and France. That meant Qatar hosted academic thinking on geopolitics from three of the five permanent members of the United Nations Security Council.[16]

Those who worked with the royal family say they didn't need any research on football's power. The then emir and his sons were fans. One difference with Abu Dhabi was displayed by Qatar's significant investment in the domestic league from 2003. This became an arena for rivalry between the brothers, who each had a club, all broadcast on the newly established Al Jazeera Sport. Sheikh Jassim was crown prince at the time and known in Qatar's higher circles as 'Mr Football'. He abdicated in 2003 to pursue other interests, with Sheikh Tamim replacing him. The fraternal rivalry still persisted in transfers, and a competition to attract the biggest names. Each club was allocated $10 million, which was enough to attract a generation of stars at the end of their careers, like Pep Guardiola and Gabriel Batistuta.[17] In 2003, the Q-League was rebranded the Qatar Stars League, although some games had more players than supporters. The brothers still had higher aspirations. David Beckham was an obsession.

That pointed to where their interest really lay, since the brothers had also been educated at Sandhurst. The Premier League was already so prominent that Sheikh Tamim asked about purchasing a club. Pitches were made to him about Newcastle United, Everton and Manchester City, but the response was 'wrong club, wrong city, wrong colour'. The main attraction was Manchester United, a prestige name that would be seen as the equivalent of Qatar's purchase of Harrods. Initial interest went nowhere in 2009–10. There were also some informal discussions about buying shares in AC Milan. The view at the top of the state was still that buying clubs just burnt money. This was what was articulated to Gordon Brown by the Qatari delegation at that dinner in 2008: 'No, we don't think they're very good investments.'

The thinking was shaped by influential former prime minister Sheikh Hamad bin Jassim, who had no interest in football. He had once been bemused when introduced to Beckham by his awestruck son, Sheikh Jassim, who later fronted a bid to buy United himself. Any project had to be 'in the national interest', which was how they were presented to the emir. The state still felt money could be made out of sport more generally, which could then be reinvested in Qatar. This was where they started to replicate UAE. Qatar Sports Investments (QSI) was founded in 2005, specifically so the monarchy's faces wouldn't be on anything. The body ensured prices wouldn't be instantly increased and royals would be insulated from criticism. It was in meetings around 2003, as Qatar discussed long-term strategy for sport, that hosting the World Cup was first mentioned while just sitting on sofas. The initial suggestion was floated as an 'end game' years in the future. Something struck, though. Within a week, after consultation among the brothers, Sheikh Tamim announced 'we want it – it will be a great thing'. Work started the next day. Since it had been announced in 2003 that the 2014 World Cup would be held in South America, with Brazil eventually winning, Qatar aimed for the next bidding process. The attitude fitted with the pace of change in Doha, where new skyscrapers were shooting up. One early argument internally used in favour of a complicated project was that hosting a World Cup would bring the focus of a deadline for the construction of grander infrastructure. The country would have a mission.

A number of smaller sporting competitions, such as the 2006 Asian Games, were used as road tests. QSI began to get involved in planning, number-crunching on what facilities would be required. They also realised they would need a competitive football team. Qatar were at that point floating between 60th and 100th in the FIFA world rankings. The team's best period actually came around the time that the first FIFA video game was released. Qatar just missed out on qualification for the 1990 World Cup, and got to the quarter-finals of the 1992 Olympics tournament. The country was too small to sustain that, though.

Qatar had already naturalised Kenyan athletes as part of a parallel project for the Olympics, that also involved a failed bid for the 2016 Games. The football association attempted similar moves ahead of 2006 World Cup qualification. Huge money was offered to three German-based Brazilians with no previous links to Qatar, including Werder Bremen striker Aílton. An emergency FIFA committee ruled that players must have a 'clear connection' to a country to be capped.[18]

A typically audacious idea was instead developed called the Aspire Academy, an expansive £1 billion sporting institute in Doha. Suitably, Pelé and Diego Maradona were paid to appear at the official opening in 2005, along with Cirque du Soleil acrobats.[19]

Trials were held to assess every young boy in the country. That produced a tiny group that had national-team potential, which was an inevitability given a population of under 850,000. Running alongside this was an international search for talent, grandly titled the Aspire Football Dreams programme. The best players from abroad were to be given scholarships and the suggestion at the start was that they would become naturalised so as to perhaps play for Qatar.[20] There was a grim symbolism to this given the state's dependence on migrant workers who were denied basic rights. Eighteen countries were scouted, all of them representing huge contrasts to Qatar in terms of wealth and population.[21] The first trip was to Africa, with trials broadcast as a reality TV show on Al Jazeera.[22] Sheikh Jassim talked of this as a humanitarian programme, but there were also constant descriptions of the biggest scouting project in history, larger than any club.[23]

It was precisely because Football Dreams wasn't a professional club that it was not subject to FIFA's rules on under-18s moving country. There were accusations of trafficking, with even Blatter expressing concerns in a private letter.[24] The FIFA president changed his stance to one that was 'supportive' after a trip to Doha in February 2008, at the invitation of Mohamed Bin Hammam.[25] The Qatari official was then a Blatter ally on FIFA's 24-man Executive Committee, the highly powerful body known as the ExCo that voted on the hosts of the World Cup.

Qatar still had to change their own stance, after FIFA pushed through a rule change where any player seeking to switch to a new country had to live there for five years after the age of 18. Aspire has long since insisted there was never any plan for foreign players to be capped by Qatar.[26] Only one of the country's eventual 2022 World Cup squad came through Aspire, which was Almoez Ali, originally from Sudan.

The academy could still aid Qatari football in other ways. Foreign talent was intended to raise the standard of locals. Sheikh Jassim celebrated on the pitch with players after an Aspire team beat a Barcelona youth side. The Catalan club were forging deeper links with Qatar, and eventual Camp Nou president Sandro Rosell was an influential figure in the programme. During one visit of a Brazilian youth team, a waif-like player dazzled. The name was Neymar.[27] In a piece of foreshadowing, his team didn't win.

There was maybe other forward thinking with Aspire, however. It later became noted how Football Dreams opened 15 programmes around the world, and five of them were in countries represented by officials on the ExCo.[28] If it was that cynical, it would be in keeping with state strategy. One diplomat recalls a conversation with a senior official in the emir's administrative office. 'The reason we put LNG ports in our key strategic partners is because we need you to help us in the event of a disaster,' he said of the UK. By the time of Blatter's visit to Aspire in 2008, Qatar's great ambition was an open secret. The FIFA president even played along at a private dinner with the emir and Bin Hammam. 'We are going to bring the World Cup to Qatar,'[29] Blatter declared. Qatar knew better than to just trust a man described by rote as a 'wily old fox'. Bin Hammam was unsettled by the pace of developments. He tried to talk the emir out of the idea. So, crucially, did the heads of state from Qatar's Gulf neighbours. The main argument was that defeat in the ballot risked humiliation.

Qatar remained serious about it. The idea of regional unity was even raised after the formal bids for hosting the World Cup were registered at FIFA on 16 March 2009. 'We believe it is time to bring the World Cup to the Middle East for the very first time,'[30] said the emir's fifth son, Sheikh Mohammed, who had been made public head of the bid team. The emir himself was even open to inviting neighbouring countries into the bid, an idea they put in writing to Blatter.[31] The other states remained reticent. The idea of spreading the World Cup around the Gulf was later raised in a very different context. It is possible that the initial suggestion came from the realisation of how difficult this plan was going to be. Qatar had 21 months to convince the ExCo that a tiny country with little football legacy could host the World Cup, and that in a punishing desert summer. The country's football federation first had to establish a women's team just to be eligible.

From the very start, though, the process was unusual. This was to be the first time in the modern voting system that the hosts of two different World Cups were to be decided on the same day. Blatter's rationale was that 'it could be profitable for the bidders and all of football',[32] on the basis that it guaranteed long-term broadcast revenues amid a financial crisis. Others pointed out the commissions FIFA officials would receive. Blatter did also mention how 'the host nations could even help each other with how to organise it'.[33]

Russia and Qatar were instead to share one of football's greatest controversies. What the double bidding process certainly did was facilitate collusion and voting deals. That was against FIFA's rules, but then this was to be a secret ballot, typical of the governing body's lack of transparency. That was further layered by the World Cup rotation policy, meaning a country couldn't host the tournament if its continent had hosted either of the previous two World Cups.[34] Brazil 2014 ruled South America out of the whole process. Europe was widely expected to stage 2018, making that a tough race between England, Spain-Portugal, Russia and Belgium-Netherlands. USA was the stand-out for 2022 due to the immense commercial appeal, with Bill Clinton adding political clout. If Japan, Korea and Australia were seen as having little chance, Qatar was not considered credible at all.

The Gulf bid, however, was already thinking of every angle. A substantial team was first assembled under chief executive Hassan Al Thawadi, one of Qatar's rising stars and already the legal director of the Qatar Investment Authority. Just 30 years old, he was the son of a former ambassador to Spain, whose upbringing had seen him complete secondary-level education in Scunthorpe before studying law at Sheffield University.[35] Al Thawadi claimed to check the scores of both Scunthorpe United and Sheffield United even when legal director of Qatar's most successful club, Al Sadd. The real political force was Sheikh Jassim. Bin Hammam, who was by then aiming to become FIFA president, was regularly consulted.

Football legends were hired as ambassadors. Zinedine Zidane protested at one point that the contract 'wasn't even a third' of the '10, 11, 12, 13 million euros' reported.[36] The sentiment wasn't as confused as that from Guardiola, who said people in Qatar have 'all the freedoms of the world, within the frame that the government gives them'.[37] The real substance to Qatar's bid, however, was way above all of this. It was at state level and strategic geopolitical deals. 'They went big picture,' in the words of one executive. The emir had a number of huge levers to pull, from gas to air routes, and he used all of them. That, according to almost everyone that directly saw it play out, is where the World Cup bids were really won. If so, it cuts to the core of the sportswashing concept: influence through infrastructure.

FIFA's own executive presidential structure afforded Blatter immense power, with just two notional checks. One was FIFA Congress, which was the annual gathering of all member associations. The other was the ExCo, which met a few times a year. The luxuries they became accustomed to were amped up by Blatter when he was elected FIFA president in 1998. Under him, the ExCo consisted of eight vice-presidents and 15 members appointed by the confederations. All of the wider debate could actually be ignored. Bidders only had to convince 13 of these men and the World Cup would be theirs. Qatar started strong. On 7 January 2010, the Confederation of African Football (CAF) announced it had struck an exclusive $1.8 million sponsorship deal with the Qatar 2022 bid for its congress in Angola at the end of that month.[38] No other bid was allowed to make presentations.[39] Meanwhile, Football Dreams programmes had been developed in Cameroon, Guatemala, Nigeria, Paraguay and Thailand, who all had ExCo members.[40] In the Garcia Report that later investigated the process, Qatar denied any link between Aspire and the bidding for 2022, saying the allegations were 'disproven by a neutral version of history'.[41]

In the same month as the CAF conference, the emir joined Aspire officials to meet Argentinian ExCo senior vice-president, Julio Grondona, as well as Paraguay's Nicolás Leoz, Brazil's Ricardo Teixeira and former FIFA president João Havelange at Itanhangá Golf Club in Rio.[42] In March 2010, state airline Qatar Airways announced daily flights from Doha to Sao Paulo and Buenos Aires from that June.[43] There was little business logic, as one insider puts it, and the routes were heavily subsidised. The flights may at least have been useful for a prestige friendly between Argentina and Brazil on 17 November just two weeks before the vote. It was arranged to be the centrepiece of a conference driving support for Qatar 2022,[44] and privately sponsored by a conglomerate owned by Ghanim bin Saad Al Saad. He was the managing director of the emir's global property firm, Qatari Diar. Both the Argentinian and Brazilian federations received significant payments.[45] There were even denials from all parties about a *Wall Street Journal* story that Qatar had paid £44 million to ease the Argentinian federation's financial difficulties.[46]

By spring 2010, Thai state energy company PTT realised

that a February 2008 bulk deal to buy LNG from Qatar for a fixed price over 10 years was going to cost them billions due to the market plummeting.[47] They needed the security of a long-term deal, however, to get the new Map Ta Phut port up and running.[48] Thailand consequently needed Qatar to sell gas to PTT at a cheaper spot price but also be willing to enter a new long-term contract at a lower fixed price.[49] A meeting involving Qatar energy minister Abdullah bin Hamad Al Attiyah and Thai businessman Joe Sim in August 2010 nevertheless went well. Sim was a football networker who knew Sir Alex Ferguson and advised the Thai football association. An email he sent to Al Attiyah afterwards, as reported by *The Ugly Game*, even mentioned 'bilateral co-operations in soccer developments' between the two countries.[50] Qatar and Thailand eventually signed a 20-year deal in December 2012, PTT buying at the lowest market prices.[51]

Perhaps the most significant trade deal, however, was struck with Russia. Putin's regime, as one FIFA source cryptically put it about the 2018 bidding process, 'did it another way'. Although there was persistent suspicion about a voting pact between Spain-Portugal 2018 and Qatar 2022, the campaign that the English bid were most concerned about was Russia. It did have an emotional appeal to go with a football legacy, as 2018 could be the first World Cup behind the old Iron Curtain. The votes didn't really work on romance, though. There were instead throwbacks to Cold War fiction. The England 2018 bid hired an agency with British secret service links to conduct surveillance on competitors, but believed Russia were doing similar.[52] Offices were even swept for bugs.

It wasn't until just before the 2010 World Cup, however, that Russia got serious. Putin became personally involved. He wasn't a football enthusiast but was even less of an enthusiast for national humiliation. Russian ExCo member Vitaly Mutko hadn't been making progress, so Putin summoned the oligarchs. Roman Abramovich was an obvious call given his football links. The Chelsea owner was immediately dispatched to Johannesburg for the FIFA Congress, where there was an exhibition of the bidders for 2018 and 2022. Rumours quickly spread he was offering the use of his private jet. Abramovich was also conspicuously suited and ebullient, whereas he was normally aloof and in jeans.[53] When one England 2018 member saw the oligarch corral Blatter into a private meeting, the thought was 'we're fucked'.[54]

'They were much cleverer,' said one testimony on the Russian bid to a 2013 Select Parliamentary Enquiry into the process. 'It was conducted at such a high government level ... don't expect me or anyone else to produce a document with Putin's signature saying please X bribe Y with this amount in this way ... Putin is an ex-intelligence officer. Everything he does has to be deniable.' Much later, the Garcia Report only ever secured limited co-operation from Russia, who used a diplomatic spat with the US to prevent lawyer Michael Garcia from entering the country.[55] His Swiss deputy, Cornel Borbély, was notoriously told all computers had been destroyed.

It was subsequently revealed Russia had drawn up dossiers featuring psychological profiles of the ExCo members, and who might be susceptible to bribery.[56] The leaked documents came from a hacking group called BlackMirror, and were published in *Der Spiegel* and *Off the Pitch*.[57] The infamous Jack Warner was described as 'the most odious and scandalous member'. Claims were made that Platini and Belgium's Michel D'Hooghe received priceless paintings from the Russian state collection.[58] The UEFA president strenuously denied this but D'Hooghe admitted he had accepted a 'small painting'.[59]

The US Department of Justice eventually stated in 2020 that

representatives working for Russia had bribed FIFA ExCo members.[60] Indictments revealed Warner had received $5 million, with some of the money coming 'from companies based in the United States that performed work on behalf of the 2018 Russia World Cup bid'.[61] Russia denied the claims. Farcically, the process featured the bizarre scene of USA's Chuck Blazer high-fiving Putin after the Russian president told him he looked like Karl Marx.[62]

Most importantly, there was another warm greeting on 2 November 2010, just a month before the vote. That was a handshake between the emir and Putin at a meeting discussing general co-operation between Russia and Qatar.[63] This was the dream Blatter had for Russia-USA made into his nightmare. Almost 12 years later, just a month before the 2022 World Cup itself, the next emir praised Putin for his 'great support', especially 'with the organising committee'.[64]

This all came after a huge gas deal that English intelligence said was 'significantly related to the World Cup'.[65] In April 2010, Deputy Prime Minister Igor Sechin went to Qatar to discuss a gas extraction project in the Yamal Peninsula.[66] Russia's World Cup team also travelled to Doha at almost exactly the same time.[67] *The Ugly Game* details how Mutko even wrote to Bin Hammam saying he was 'happy that leaders of our countries enjoy very good relations', with the Qatari official forwarding the email to Al Thawadi.[68] That same period saw a deal announced by Al Attiyah and Sechin, allowing Qatar access to immense fields of gas.

The England bid's analysis was that, although Qatar had agreed to trade votes with Spain-Portugal for 2018, the Iberian bid would not last to the third round.[69] After that, Qatar and Russia's agreement would come into play. An ex-MI6 source, widely believed to be Christopher Steele, told the British parliament that 'if there was collusion, it was done through the energy sector'.[70] Against that, it now actually seems incredible that other bids even felt they had a chance, and that was despite their own controversies. Handbags, which the English bid handed out, weren't going to cut it.[71] They maybe should have realised the scale of what they were up against when Nicolàs Leoz demanded a knighthood and asked that the FA Cup be named after him.[72] An official from another bid now laughs at how they couldn't have threatened to cut off exports if a country's ExCo member didn't vote for them. 'You can't do that in a democracy.' The UK was the European democracy Qatar had invested most in, with France next.[73] In 2008, Sarkozy made the first trip to Doha by a French president in more than 10 years.[74] This was what Platini was really walking into for that lunch. Qatar had bought properties and stakes in companies all over France, including Suez Energy Group.[75] Over €15bn was spent on French fighter jets and Airbus airliners.[76] On the other side, Sarkozy was seen as having influence over Francophone Africa. Platini potentially influenced four UEFA votes as president of the confederation, although he had previously been extremely resistant to Qatar's bid. He didn't so much dismiss it as deride it, privately insisting it would be a disaster for FIFA.[77] Platini said he wasn't asked outright to vote for Qatar, although Sarkozy made his desire clear. Blatter is insistent Platini was swayed by extreme pressure and claimed his protégé told him so.[78] The former UEFA president did admit he had voted for Qatar but only on the romantic realisation that a winter World Cup in the Gulf would be 'beautiful'.[79] Platini responded strongly to suggestions it had anything to do with the Élysée Palace lunch, describing them as 'lies' and that he did 'not rule out legal action against anyone who casts doubt on the honesty of my vote'.[80]

The noise nevertheless changed the perception of a genuine football great, and it all rose again when he was detained but not charged in 2019 by French investigators looking into the meeting.[81] The eventual call to Blatter caused a rift between the two men who had a mentor–protégé relationship going back to the Swiss official's first presidential bid in 1998. Blatter at the time intuited that the support of such a legend would be invaluable. He persuaded Platini with a simple question. 'Can you imagine being FIFA president?'[82] Blatter promised Platini he would give him a job as an international advisor if he became president. That agreement finally tore FIFA apart 17 years later.[83]

Back in 1998, Platini was also made deputy chairman of the new GOAL programme, which was probably Blatter's most inspired political move. This was the initiative that saw FIFA use its immense wealth to spread annual grants to every football federation. Since the figures were transformative for smaller member associations, it also served as a classic piece of clientelism to accumulate support. The need to fund this is partly why competitions have kept expanding. Bin Hammam had similarly been made chairman of GOAL, from where his own political base grew. He began to imagine becoming FIFA president himself. That was another development that would later cause a destructive tension.

Separate to that, but just like with Russia, the US Department of Justice eventually said representatives for Qatar had made bribes as part of the World Cup campaigns. Grondona, Teixeira and Leoz were all accused of being paid to vote for Qatar.[84] A leaked email meanwhile revealed FIFA Secretary General Jerome Valcke wrote that Qatar 'bought' the World Cup, although he would later claim he just meant using their immense wealth within the rules.[85] The state has long denied all accusations, but particularly those of the bid's former media officer, Phaedra Almajid. She was eventually identified as a source for one of many claims in the *Sunday Times*' groundbreaking series of reports on the 2022 World Cup, alleging Qatar paid bribes worth $1.5 million to the federations of African

ExCo members at meetings around the CAF congress that the bid sponsored.[86]

The campaign reacted furiously and Almajid later signed an affidavit retracting the claims. She explained why she did so in the *FIFA Uncovered* documentary, where the allegations were repeated, claiming she started to get 'threats, anonymous calls, emails, social media'.[87] 'I was basically told either you sign an affidavit stating that you lied or else we are legally going to come after you.' The ExCo members referenced were Cameroon's Issa Hayatou, Ivory Coast's Jacques Anouma and Nigeria's Amos Adamu. 'It was just so simple,' Almajid said. '"We will give you this money for your football federation, you give us your vote and thank you so much."'[88] Adamu wouldn't even get to vote. The Nigerian official and Tahiti's Reynald Temarii, the president of the Oceania Football Confederation, were surreptitiously recorded by a *Sunday Times* sting offering to sell their votes. Both, for their part, were seeking to develop football in their territories.[89] The very context was another sign of football's growing economic divide. Adamu and Temarii were suspended, reducing the ExCo to 22 members. It ensured the entire process was publicly undercut by scandal before it even got under way. Of that 22, as many as 17 eventually found themselves accused, banned or indicted over allegations of bad practice or corruption.

There was one more blow to come for Qatar. The absurdity of a summer bid from the Gulf was summed up in FIFA's own technical evaluations of the nine bids going for 2018 and 2022, led by Harold Mayne-Nicholls, the former head of the Chilean federation. Russia had actually been deemed the second worst due to poor infrastructure. Qatar wasn't just the worst but the only one deemed high risk. All the talk of state-of-the-art cooling technology and a 'global village' didn't really cut it.[90] The primary concerns were that it was too small, had too little infrastructure and was just too hot. Fans would have found it 'impossible to do anything on the street'.[91]

There was still one more document that could have been decisive. Another *Sunday Times* report revealed Qatar was assessed by FIFA as also being at high risk from a terrorist attack due to proximity to countries with an Al-Qaeda presence.[92] The small scale of the tournament made it more of a problem since a single incident could paralyse the whole event.[93] The report, ordered by Valcke, was presented to the ExCo on the eve of the vote. There was also a presentation by Mayne-Nicholls. He noted that only one of the voters actually asked for his full report.[94]

There was laughter among some of the other bids at the naivety of the England 2018 team. That was perhaps illustrated by the extreme confidence of victory, as well as the response to a final development that really should have ended hope.

Three days before the vote, BBC aired a documentary by investigative journalist Andrew Jennings, who had been digging into FIFA for years. The programme accused Teixeira, Leoz and Hayatou of accepting millions of dollars in bribes from International Sport and Leisure.[95] The marketing firm was established by Adidas scion Horst Dassler and is viewed as the originator of modern sports business lobbying. The documentary also claimed Warner attempted to sell $84,240 worth of tickets for the 2010 World Cup to touts.[96] The English bid's response was to send an obsequious letter to the ExCo members expressing 'solidarity' and pleading 'not to be judged negatively due to the activities of individual media organisations'.[97] The documentary was meanwhile dismissed as 'unpatriotic' and 'an embarrassment'.[98] Colleagues of the late Jennings remain angry about the response to him.

Putin declared himself 'saddened' and said he would 'refrain from attending' the vote out of 'respect' so as to give the ExCo 'an opportunity to make an unbiased decision calmly and without any outside pressure'.[99] It's remarkable now that this was taken as a sign Putin feared humiliation. There were certainly nerves in other governments. Although the USA had been confident for 2022 since their bid was Blatter's preference, President Barack Obama rang his FIFA counterpart the night before the vote. 'Mr President, it will be difficult,'[100] Blatter responded. FIFA insiders say 'key people knew' what would happen. There were already panicked discussions about what it might mean for the governing body if Russia and Qatar won. Some figures in the English bid had wavered over the long campaign, but there were suddenly concrete reasons for confidence. Seven ExCo members expressly promised their vote, all with handshakes for one of the so-called 'three lions' of Prince William, David Beckham and UK Prime Minister David Cameron. Clinton brought Morgan Freeman, Australia had Elle McPherson. FIFA officials lined up for photos with the megastars beside a huge Christmas tree at the luxurious Baur au Lac hotel on Lake Zürich, where the frantic final hours of lobbying took place.

On the morning of 2 December 2010, the campaigns moved to the new FIFA Headquarters. The governing body's base is commonly described as like a villainous lair, because of how deep five of its eight floors descend underground from its sharply angled main building. That is all centred on a windowless meeting room for the ExCo, that does indeed look like the War Room in *Dr Strangelove*.

'Places where people make decisions should only contain indirect light because the light should come from the people themselves who are assembled there,'[101] Blatter grandly said on the building's 2007 opening. Attendees were grateful for the seclusion given how snowy it was in Zürich on that Thursday. They'd arrived for final pitches before the 2 p.m. ballot, after which the results would be announced in an auditorium five floors down. The mood had shifted. Putin's statement had already changed perception on Russia and there was now a spreading thought on Qatar: 'not even the ExCo could give it to a tiny desert country in the middle of summer'.

A buzzer went shortly before 4 p.m. It was followed by another moment of alarm. As bid officials went in, they saw Abramovich coming out smiling. By the time that Blatter started a rambling speech about how football is a 'school of life', the English bid was already 'ashen-faced'. ExCo Vice President Geoff Thompson had come out of the meeting room in a fury and told his team they'd been knocked out in the first round with just two votes. The promises meant nothing. Some ExCo members just shrugged when confronted. Only Hayatou had stayed with England, to add to Thompson's vote.[102]

Dmitry Chernyshenko, the chief executive of the Winter Olympic Games in Sochi, then tweeted in celebration. 'Yesss! We are the champions! Hooray!!!!' Moments later, Blatter confirmed as much by pulling Russia's name out of the gold-engraved envelope. Putin was already preparing an immediate trip to Zürich. On stage, his deputy Prime Minister Igor Shuvalov promised it was a decision 'you will never regret'. Qatar's name was announced six minutes later, but Al Jazeera had already been reporting victory for 30 minutes. The royal family, including the emir, jumped up in celebration. They did it right beside Clinton, who was understood to be furious. 'Quatar' and 'Katar' began to trend on Twitter.

'Take it in your hands,' a stilted-sounding Blatter said to the emir, gesturing to the World Cup itself. Back in Qatar, there were scenes of euphoria akin to a sporting victory, with car horns blared and the maroon flag waved. Qatar had got 11 of the 12 necessary votes in the first round, and won all four rounds emphatically.

Some of the defeated bids began to see solace in that. The feeling was that the narrative would no longer be about defeat but how exactly these two campaigns won. There were immediately questions about corruption. Beckham was especially furious in private but calmed down in public. By Qatar 2022 itself, he had signed a deal worth a reported £150 million to become an ambassador.[103] Freeman was another star who witnessed the anger of his US colleagues, only to end up speaking at the 2022 World Cup's opening ceremony.

The most theatrically aggrieved was Boris Johnson, who was then London mayor and part of the delegation. At a drinks function afterwards, said to be like a wake, Johnson got up on a table. 'I feel very proud to be English,' he began. 'And you know what? As far as I'm concerned, they're all a bunch of crooks and we should take our bloody ball and never work with FIFA again.' Cameron remained diplomatic. While others in the England bid wanted to start asking questions, the feeling that went around government departments was that it was better to move on. Russia and Qatar were allies. 'That,' as one involved figure sums up, 'is real power.'

Putin meanwhile showed how power in Russia worked. He conducted an hour-long press conference where a smiling Abramovich was gestured to when asked who would pay for new stadiums. 'It's no big deal,'[104] Putin said. 'He won't feel the pinch.' There's no big mystery to 2 December 2010, either. A flawed democratic process was won by the only two countries that weren't true democracies. This isn't to say it would have been clean anyway. The entire system had long been nurtured by Western democracies. A bribery investigation against German officials for the 2006 World Cup – which included the late Franz Beckenbauer, a 2010 ExCo member – was only closed due to new rules on the statute of limitations.[105] Some still mutter suspiciously about the other bids. 'It was the culmination of the whole Blatter system,' says Michael Page of Human Rights Watch. It went full circle in how it actually went against Blatter's desired outcome. There was an instructive coda to the day. Valcke, sitting in a shuttle with his face in his hands, simply declared: 'this is the end of FIFA.'[106]

There was then a coda to the wider story, too, that would itself start a new era in Gulf politics. On 17 December, in the provincial Tunisian town of Sidi Bouzid, a 26-year-old named Mohamed Bouazizi self-immolated in protest at Zine El Abidine Ben Ali's dictatorship.[107] It sparked the Arab Spring, and severely widened a split between the Gulf powers. Qatar's rivals were already envious of the World Cup. Their previously negligible neighbour now seemed to be backing the Islamic movements that threatened to overthrow the regional status quo.

All of this was escalating as Qatar immediately had a primer for the World Cup. Just a month after the vote, on 7 January 2011, the Asian Cup started in Doha. The city was naturally decorated in wordless posters of the emir lifting the World Cup. On that same day, Blatter became the first official figure to raise the prospect of moving the tournament to winter.[108]

Bin Hammam, just re-elected as AFC president, shot back. 'Our business is to organise a comfortable World Cup in June and July,' the Qatari asserted.[109] There had already been concern among football's political class at Blatter's unexpected announcement that he wanted to set up an anti-corruption committee.[110] The FIFA president then dropped a bomb by saying 'there was a bundle of votes between Spain and Qatar'.[111] The back-and-forth was all build-up to a momentous presidential battle between the two men. In the meantime, Qatar couldn't actually fill the stadiums for an Asian

Cup eventually won by Japan. It added to the questions about a hosting that still needed to build an entirely new infrastructure, including nine new stadiums.

The task would fall upon hundreds of thousands of migrant workers. It is maybe indicative of football's culture that the prospective human cost didn't even really come up when the bids were assessed. It fed into how Qatar, in the words of many political figures, didn't realise there was an issue at all. That was about to change. Qatar now had something to sportswash. It was just as well another project was already in place.

7.

PARIS SYNDROME

The way those at Paris Saint-Germain tell it, Sheikh Tamim can spot a player. It was the Qatari royal who supposedly noticed Marco Verratti playing with Pescara in Italy's Serie B, before his signing was sanctioned in 2012. That's all the more impressive given Sheikh Tamim's role as crown prince at the time was the day-to-day running of Qatar. He still needed to get sign-off for anything from the emir, his father, which was relevant to why Sheikh Tamim was scouting in the first place. The crown prince can spot a deal, too.

Sheikh Tamim sensed an opportunity when the idea of buying PSG was raised. Qatar's line is that the prospect was actually raised a year before the infamous lunch at the Élysée Palace. Either way, as with Michel Platini's World Cup vote, it was obvious what French president Nicolas Sarkozy wanted. That's why Sébastien Bazin of Colony Capital was there. The club had been losing €20 million a year, so were seeking investment for some time. The claim in *France Football* was that Sheikh Tamim offered to buy PSG if Platini voted for Qatar 2022.[1] Again, all involved have long denied any connection. It's obvious that Sheikh Tamim saw longer-term benefits. His previous interest in buying a club had seen PSG broached in 2004. There was now an obvious argument about the national interest he could present to his father, whom he would replace as emir in June 2013. Football was booming. Qatar's neighbours in Abu Dhabi were already enjoying an increased profile with Manchester City. It was felt a club could offer that same 'image tool', with all sorts of other potential. The family were also Francophiles, while PSG looked hugely undervalued. They were the single Parisian club in what was a global alpha-plus city of profound cultural importance. PSG were actually just a year older than the state of Qatar, having been founded in 1970, and had won a mere two French titles. This was all waiting to be built up.

'Paris is the city of fashion, of food, of the arts and of great museums,' eventual club president Nasser Al-Khelaifi told a Harvard study.[2] 'We saw the opportunity, and wanted to create a top club in France.' It all fitted with the national vision. As part of a general Qatari expansion, there were two other club purchases. The first had actually been six months before the World Cup vote, although by a distant member of the royal family. Sheikh Abdullah Bin Nasser Al Thani took over Málaga CF in June 2010, and immediately enlivened Spanish football by spending around €60 million on nine players including Santi Cazorla and Ruud van Nistelrooy. It was part of a wave that seemed to be constantly upending football at the time. Sheikh Abdullah's distance from the royal family, however, was illustrated by an inability to keep spending. Fans of Belgium's K.A.S. Eupen had similar visions about signing stars when the Aspire Zone Foundation bought the obscure second-tier club in June 2012, but this was intended as a launchpad for the Qatari youth academy's graduates.

PSG was much more central to the state. 'Ici c'est Paris' was the club's slogan: this is Paris. It was now also Qatar, who came up with a new motto: 'Dream bigger.' The club wanted to win the Champions League by 2018 and to have a brand worth €1 billion.[3] The latter was aided by reach and investment of another kind. In 2012, beIN SPORTS was founded, with an immediate footprint in France. Rights for the Champions League and European Championships were also bought up, as the group expanded into 43 countries across five continents, including the US.[4] By 2014, the French league rights were renewed and inflated to €726 million a season.[5] Canal+ went to the regulator with complaints that echoed those made about PSG, as beIN ran at a loss and undercut rivals.[6] Qatar consequently owned the most powerful club and an increasingly influential broadcaster.

The circumstances quickly fostered a number of theories about why beIN had been set up. One was that it was an indirect way of compensating the European club game for the disruption from the World Cup. Another was that it was a way of economically inflating PSG and French football, with Financial Fair Play rules coming. A third theory was that it was a favour to Sarkozy to stabilise French football. Within Qatar, naturally, the explanation is benign. BeIN was a personal project of Sheikh Tamim, who wanted to gift football to the Arabic-speaking world. The channel is now broadcast in more than 20 countries across the region.[7] It was through Sheikh Tamim that Al-Khelaifi became one of the most influential people in global sport. A former Davis Cup tennis player, Al-Khelaifi had been the crown prince's tennis coach. That established a trust, which saw Al-Khelaifi rise to chairman of QSI, chairman of PSG and chairman of beIN. It also made him the conduit for decisions that went to the highest levels, although PSG were quickly surrounded by a wider circle of royals and other senior figures. That created a constant 'noise' that ensured it was never quiet within the club.

The noise at Parc des Princes was diminished, though. Civil war had developed between the two ends of PSG's stadium, as the Boulogne end leaned towards the far right and the opposite Auteuil became multi-ethnic. With two fans having died in the five years before the takeover, the new owners were intent on stamping out violence as part of a plan to make the club an extension of the Paris cultural scene. Tickets were increased by 70 per cent and almost 4,000 more VIP seats installed, while 13,000 fans were banned.[8] It meshed with Sarkozy's law-and-order agenda, which was struggling with football. The effect was so drastic, however, that players complained about a lack of atmosphere. Although 2,000 were returned, it all reflected an edge that clashed with the club's pretences.

Sheikh Tamim has only attended for select fixtures, but has regularly watched training. That has informed the state's main influence on the football side, which is in managerial appointments. Former player Antoine Koumbouaré's December 2011 dismissal felt all the more unfair given PSG were top of the league. The first choice, for years, was Arsène Wenger. He was never ready to leave Arsenal. The money available did bring a coup in Carlo Ancelotti. Negotiations didn't even involve questions on playing philosophy, PSG just wanted the name. This was crucial to the early Qatari strategy. They were another club to follow the Real Madrid model of buying stars to increase commercial appeal, bringing an obvious name: *Les Galactiques*. Javier Pastore had been PSG's Robinho as a €39 million purchase from Palermo, in an initial €70 million spree. It still wasn't enough to finish ahead of little Montpellier, who won their first title without spending anything on transfers.

PSG responded by bringing in Zlatan Ibrahimović from AC Milan as part of a higher level of signing. The Swede was intended to improve the mentality of the squad, and it was something a self-confessed egotist threw himself into. Fights at training were followed by overhead kicks that brought unanimous applause. Such theatrics led to a new verb in French football, 'to zlataner'. He would then tell teammates and opposition alike they should be happy to be on the same pitch as him. It was partly why Thiago Silva was given the captaincy, although his very signing illustrated PSG's own new bluntness. The Brazilian centre-half was the first of their stars to reject Europe's establishment. Thiago Silva 'always wished' to play for Barcelona, but PSG's offer of €12 million a year was too much to turn down.[9]

If that changed the profile of the team, the owners had someone specific to amplify the profile of the club. 'David Beckham goes beyond the sport,'[10] Al-Khelaifi told *L'Équipe*. 'He is an ambassador, he is a brand ...' Within a month of Beckham's signing, in February 2013, the crest was altered so 'Paris' was made bigger. If more fans were now going to look at the club, this was the time to make the association clear. In a vintage Beckham move, he also decided his salary would go to a local children's charity.[11] This was even without any questions about human rights in Qatar.

The exalted level of player did bring a new expectation. Although Ancelotti had been absolved for the Montpellier failure, he was given a bizarre ultimatum the following December. The Italian was told he had to win a meaningless Champions League group game against FC Porto.[12] Ancelotti claimed Al-Khelaifi and sporting director Leonardo were not happy with how 'the project' was going. PSG won the game 2-1 and won Qatar's first league title by 12 points, but they lost the manager's trust. Ancelotti went to Real Madrid and, the very next season in 2013–14, lifted their long-awaited 10th Champions League title.

PSG's failure to win that competition characterised much of the Qatar era. A humiliating trend was even set in that 2013–14 season, under the more pragmatic Laurent Blanc. PSG beat Chelsea 3-1 in the quarter-final first leg, only to collapse 2-0 in the return and go out. Chelsea had more European experience, having gone through a similar quest in the Champions League to finally win it in 2011–12. They also had the returned José Mourinho, whom PSG had approached along with Fabio Capello, Guus Hiddink, Manuel Pellegrini and – of course – Wenger.

'We didn't manage to play our game tonight,' said seasoned midfielder Thiago Motta, 'and I don't know why.' That became a common question. One reason was obvious. Disproportionate Qatari wealth ensured most games in France were too easy. PSG won four successive titles, never by less than eight points. For Blanc's last league title, in 2015–16, the gap to runners-up Lyon was 31 points. There was a brief challenge when Russian oligarch Dmitry Rybolovlev bought a 66 per cent stake in AS Monaco and followed with €140 million-worth of signings, bringing stars like Radamel Falcao. Some at PSG were even happy with the competition, as well as the scrutiny on someone else's spending. PSG still beat them to the 2013–14 title by nine points. A perceived sense of entitlement was perpetuated by Ibrahimović telling a referee 'they don't even deserve PSG in this country'.[13] The problem was the team didn't perform that well outside it. Highlight reels of Ibrahimović scoring volleyed back-heels against Bastia or beating Troyes 9-0 didn't seem so impressive when PSG went out of the Champions League in the quarter-finals for four successive seasons. This was despite a wage bill that was already one of the biggest in world sport, just as clubs had to conform to new Financial Fair Play rules. As with City, there was increasing suspicion within the game. Mourinho typically stoked the fire before the 2013–14 Champions League meeting, saying Chelsea 'cannot spend what PSG have because we're playing by the rules'.[14] When Bayern Munich chairman Karl-Heinz Rummenigge said it was 'hard to imagine' PSG were complying, Al-Khelaifi told him 'not to tell any other club's business'.[15] They were more than words, though. A simulation exercise for FFP in February 2013 had PSG and City as 2 of 20 clubs whose losses far exceeded the acceptable total of €45 million for three seasons up to 2011.

'They know the rules are that they have to generate revenues to cover their costs without cheating,'[16] then UEFA General Secretary Gianni Infantino said of PSG. The French club had income of €398 million for 2012–13 but an estimated €200 million of that came from the Qatar Tourism Authority. There was a constant question over whether such deals would be so high if they were not state-linked companies. As with City, UEFA eventually wrote to PSG looking for more rigorous answers.

Given the theatre that happens on the pitch, it says something that an element as dry as financial regulation has provoked more emotion in football than some of the most dramatic late winners. Such rules do dictate what actually happens in games, though.

In 2013, the same summer that PSG signed Edinson Cavani for €64 million and City sacked Roberto Mancini, UEFA's new Financial Fair Play regulations came into force. This was a long-discussed idea, given form by Platini, to link spending to income so as to fight the ruinous effects of the wage race. He wanted a legacy as a football leader, in the same way a Euro 84 medal with France was his legacy as a player. Platini felt his influence on the game should be greater than any bureaucrat, who many felt he was oddly envious of. One idea was revolutionary. Platini wanted to revert the Champions League to an open knock-out with 256 teams. The big clubs instantly resisted. There was already an argument he listened to them too much, and he certainly listened on FFP. There were far more voices in his ear than that, though.

The consequences of FFP have ensured vested interests try to spin all manner of narratives about its creation, especially as regards protecting the status quo. The factors were actually more prosaic, if admittedly pressured by greater forces. The lack of regulation after Bosman had escalated the wage race to the point that the game's economy was almost out of control. More clubs were on the brink of going bust. More wages and transfer instalments were going unpaid. This was the genesis of the 'fair play' in the name, rather than anything to do with the idea of 'competitive balance'. Clubs would often agree transfers knowing full well they could only pay the first instalment, while hoping the new players would increase revenue. This was accompanied by the growing concern about what it would mean for football's reputation if a club went bust in the middle of a season.

UEFA had actually explored the introduction of a hard salary cap in 1999 but needed to create a legal framework first. The information accumulated in that process evolved into the licensing rules, where clubs had to fulfil criteria like stadium conditions and financial discipline to play in European competition. The idea was the prudent running of clubs, which was the foundation of FFP.

It was while this was being undertaken that the industry was overturned by the Abramovich takeover. Rummenigge was livid that a club like Bayern Munich, who he barked had once won three successive European Cups, could lose a star like Michael Ballack to some outfit with little history like Chelsea. 'Some clubs are just doing whatever they want,' was the roar from one executive at a UEFA meeting. This was where there was some merit to arguments that FFP preserved the elite, but it wasn't as simple as that. Although the debate is always dominated by the top end of the game, it is those at the bottom of the pyramid who feel the most lasting effects.

Staff who drafted the rules remembered horror stories from lower divisions or leagues like Ireland, where wage inflation from the next level up meant clubs had to stretch themselves to just stay at the same level. That often meant missed payments and players being unable to afford Christmas presents. Hyper-inflation caused by oligarchs and states, without cost control, would have been ruinous. Too few saw that it was all connected. It wasn't all consistent, though. Another element that aggravated Rummenigge, and eventually Platini, was that the German and French leagues had much tougher regulation than other countries. That was to the benefit of their clubs in terms of financial health, but it represented a huge disadvantage in the market. Foreign opposition had much greater leeway.

On becoming UEFA president, Platini told staff to create an equivalent of France's Direction Nationale du Contrôle de Gestion (DNCG). UEFA still wanted a direct salary cap, but found European law wouldn't allow it. The FFP formula was more workable, with crucial support coming from the European Union's Competition Commissioner Joaquin Almunia.[17] Tellingly, he was a supporter of Athletic Bilbao, the Basque club in La Liga who only fielded players with a link to the region. They were the definition of self-sustainable. Platini also went directly to club owners, since there had been tension with the executives. Just like City and PSG later on, Chelsea were among those clubs that felt the rules were specifically about them. There was anger that debt of the nature that the Glazers had loaded onto United wasn't targeted. Chelsea's Peter Kenyon had even pointed to how Abramovich's financing was different. 'Look, the money is good, the money is not debt,'[18] he told Platini. 'If Roman left, the club is in a great position.' The sanctions of 2022 would illustrate otherwise.

Even Abramovich and Inter's Massimo Moratti eventually agreed a perpetual wage race didn't make sense. Former UEFA executive Alex Phillips believes this is something that has always been missed. 'What UEFA was seeking was true to the principles of the game, the traditions and concepts.' The stated objectives of FFP do sound reasonable: (a) to improve the economic and financial capability of the clubs, increasing their transparency and credibility; (b) to place the necessary importance on the protection of creditors and to ensure that clubs settle their liabilities with players, social/tax authorities and other clubs punctually; (c) to introduce more discipline and rationality in club football finances; (d) to encourage clubs to operate on the basis of their own revenues; (e) to encourage responsible spending for the long-term benefit of football; (f) to protect the long-term viability and sustainability of European club football.[19]

They ultimately amounted to an indirect salary cap, restricting expenditure according to what clubs earned. The summer that FFP was announced showed this was never more necessary. In 2009, City had the chance to go on their first huge spending spree. Platini was even asked at the presentation whether the expenditure actually made the game more competitive. The UEFA president rejected this and gestured to Infantino. 'We think that the opposite will happen because, if you have a rich sugar daddy coming in and throwing money around, this is unhealthy in the medium and long term,'[20] the UEFA General Secretary said. Otherwise, Infantino went on, it is just 'an artificial bubble which inflates the system'.

City still suspected it was all about them. They felt they were shunned at initial UEFA meetings. There were also grumbles about how Manchester United's David Gill has become more involved at UEFA. 'Financial doping', a phrase coined by Wenger, began to become fashionable. Others did recognise potential flaws in FFP. One was that it wasn't immediately complemented by competitive balance measures like better distribution of prize money or even players. Platini and Infantino claimed it was never about that but would then drop it in when convenient.

At one initial presentation, a senior football official sparked a half-hour argument with UEFA's Andrea Traverso, saying 'you're going to fuck up the whole system, all you're going to do is have Man United, Barcelona, Real Madrid and Bayern there every year'. Two other senior figures privately claim that some at UEFA weren't even concerned about this, and didn't properly consider it, partly because the brands were hugely lucrative. Even Infantino referenced the supposed persistence of the established order while defending FFP. 'Big clubs have always existed, this will not change.'

These were arguments that would keep coming back, although in different forms. In the meantime, City and PSG argued their losses were covered by owners, which was a contrast to how Manchester United and Real Madrid were allowed to carry huge debt. UEFA said they would look at the issue, but were already pointing to successes of FFP. In the first cycle, aggregate losses of European clubs fell from €1.7 billion to €800 million.[21] That illustrated the logic in restricting spending, especially in a world where there was such a correlation between wage expenditure and success. Few clubs would be able to keep up with City's outlay. In 2011, the Abu Dhabi-owned club made the largest single-season loss in English football at £197 million.

For the following two years, clubs would only be allowed a loss of €45 million, to be covered by the owner. Then, from 2013–16, permissible losses would be restricted to €30 million. The first cycle covering 2011–13 was to be assessed during the 2013–14 season, with sanctions ranging from fines to exclusion from continental competition. The threat of a ban was to ensure wealthy clubs didn't just take a meaningless fine. There was a difficult balance to it.

Wenger criticised the complexity of the regulations, admitting that even someone with his experience couldn't explain it, let alone people 'in the street'.[22] He also recognised the new constraints that football was working in, with an insight that was to prove prescient. 'UEFA has lost power because of Europe, because you can have alternatives to go to court outside of UEFA, and not everybody accepts the decisions from UEFA,' Wenger said. 'So UEFA has to be a bit cautious as well because of television's financial power.'[23] That was perhaps one reason why UEFA constantly struck a conciliatory tone when its executive committee unanimously approved the new regulations in May 2010. Platini insisted the intention was 'not to punish' clubs, 'but to protect them'.[24]

This was the repeated message in investigations, too. Clubs were provided with all background materials and told what information was required. That work was carried out by the Club Financial Control Body (CFCB), the UEFA panel which monitored adherence to FFP through two separate units. The Investigatory Chamber conducts proceedings and can propose penalties. The Adjudicatory Chamber gives the final verdict. Platini had grasped that independence was required, and it was temporarily felt that these tasks should go to another body. UEFA just didn't fully commit. Both chambers are notionally independent, with no influence on their work supposed to come from the ExCo or president's office, but they were in practice completely dependent on UEFA's power. Investigations were as often started by staff emailing each other relevant media reports.

At the end of the first cycle, in 2014, the clubs that warranted added assessments were City, PSG, Galatasaray, Trabzonspor, Bursaspor, Zenit St Petersburg, Anzhi Makhachkala, Rubin Kazan and Levski Sofia,[25] while there were also audits of Barcelona and AC Milan. It was the two Gulf-owned clubs, however, that looked like they would pose the most work. Independent audits were required, with PwC doing City and Deloitte doing PSG. The approach was still conciliatory. 'It wasn't like Eliot Ness,' one involved figure says. UEFA even decided they would only focus on massive outliers rather than every detail. Financial information was submitted to a custom-made UEFA portal, with expenditure on sustainable elements like infrastructure stripped out. Beckham's PSG salary was excluded since it went to charity. Clubs were meanwhile required to verify that sponsorship contracts with companies that were 'controlled, jointly controlled or significantly influenced' by their owners – termed 'related parties' – were not overvalued. The suspicion already raised within football was that such deals could allow evasion of the rules, and that it was only possible with state-linked ownership. PSG's mega-deal with the Qatar Tourism Authority appeared to be the most extreme example.

Some who worked on FFP felt the entire idea of related parties and 'fair market value' was inherently problematic when it came to autocracies, since it was based on a false premise. 'It all ultimately comes from the same pot of money,' was the assessment of one. Investigators found it too difficult to determine separation and flow of money, especially with companies owned by large royal families. The frustration was that it wouldn't be accepted if an owner just gave a club £30 million and put their name on the shirt. Except, as one investigator complained, 'if you just stick a brand in the middle of it, it's apparently fine'. Some lobbied that any related party should be considered equity and not sponsorship.

The central question of 'fair market value' nevertheless made the PSG case more straightforward than City's. In 2012, over a year after the takeover, a five-year deal was signed with the Qatar Tourism Authority for 'the promotion of the image of Qatar'.[26] PSG were to receive an average of €215 million a season. For that, they didn't even have to put advertising in the Parc des Princes, let alone on the shirts. The five-page agreement spelled out how PSG were simply to help Qatar become 'a major player in the sporting world'. It was described by the club executives as 'nation branding', which is of 'another scale compared to traditional sponsoring contracts'.[27]

One suspicion from the investigators was that Qatar believed if they simply invented a new category of deal, it couldn't be assessed. Branding was admittedly more important given the increasing scrutiny on Qatar over migrant labour rights. By comparison, when the state's own Qatar Airways extended their shirt deal with Barcelona in 2016, the annual value went up to €35 million.[28] The Qatar Tourist Authority deal was consequently viewed as absurd. According to those with knowledge of the investigations, the body's advertising budget was €38 million. Their annual report didn't even mention PSG. The club were said to be abrasive in discussions with UEFA. 'Our contract with Qatar Tourism Authority is not some accounting trick,'[29] Al-Khelaifi said. 'It's the same contract we have with Emirates. There's no reason for UEFA to disagree.'

Sports marketing agency Octagon did disagree, assessing the 'fair market value' at a mere €2.78 million, while saying 'no rational sponsor would pay such money for that kind of exposure'.[30] It was damning. PSG's losses from 2011 to 2013 were instead calculated to be over €200 million. This was a number that was supposed to bring a ban.

Far from the CFCB operating with independence, though, the Football Leaks documents reported by *Der Spiegel* indicate a series of meetings between the club and UEFA executives from February through to April 2014. Al-Khelaifi is even reported as asking Platini if he really wanted to launch an attack on Qatar through PSG.[31] The Élysée Palace meeting carried an even greater resonance. PSG executives eventually demanded that a resolution could only be agreed at 'the top level', in what would have been a clear circumvention of the regulations.[32] PSG's executives weren't even willing to agree to an admission they violated FFP. It pointed to how image was so important. Infantino, according to *Der Spiegel*, wanted PSG to reduce the value of the Qatar Tourism contract to €100 million a year.[33]

On 16 May, UEFA's CFCB announced a 'settlement', even though this was never a provision in the original regulations.[34] PSG were to be fined €60 million with €40 million withheld, and their Champions League squad reduced from 25 players to 21. PSG still insisted on arguing the punishment represented a 'tremendous handicap' in competing at Champions League level, while saying they deplored the fact that UEFA had not recognised the full value of their Qatar Tourism Authority deal.[35]

Most of the other clubs investigated used it as 'a learning experience', but City's attitude was described as a 'level of aggression' way beyond PSG. Simple comparisons had raised similar complaints to PSG's Qatar Tourism Authority deal. City's originally reported £400 million 10-year sponsorship with Etihad Airways in 2011 was more than double the previous sporting record, which was the £187 million decade-long agreement between JPMorgan Chase and Madison Square Garden.[36] UEFA also had concerns about deals that raised £47 million in 2012–13 from image rights and intellectual property. City executives had realised by 2012 they would struggle to meet FFP requirements.[37] A report of an internal presentation revealed a warning that said 'compliance WILL NOT be achieved' unless 'significant additional revenues' were secured.[38] Details such as this came from the Football Leaks published by *Der Spiegel*, to which City consistently offered the same response. 'We will not be providing any comment on out-of-context materials purported to have been hacked or stolen . . . the attempt to damage the club's reputation is organised and clear.'

UEFA and their independent auditors did not have access to any of this information in 2014, four years before the leaks, but there were still a lot of red flags. One prominent deal was a £15 million-a-year sponsorship with Aabar, an investment vehicle owned by the International Petroleum Investment Company, of which Sheikh Mansour is chairman. A note in the PwC report for UEFA states the sponsorship contract provided – which went across years covered by the FFP investigation – had 'not been signed' by any representative on behalf of the company. Another deal with Etisalat already raised eyebrows given that an Emirati mobile operator can't have had any customers outside the UAE. The PwC report said they could 'not verify any payments prior to February 2013 to bank records'. The contract provided hadn't been signed by any representative on behalf of Etisalat, either.

The PwC report noted the contract for the Etihad deal similarly hadn't been signed by a representative of the airline and 'was also missing a signature from the Chief Commercial and Operating Officer of the Licensee'. It was added that Etihad Airways board member Mohamed Al Mazrouei was also a City board member. This was privately described as 'highly unusual' but not unprecedented. All of this was met with what investigators felt was 'the worst animosity' they'd encountered. Among the claims thrown around were: 'You have been looking to make an example of us from day one' and 'We'll hire the best lawyers, you'll never have anything hit you from a legal perspective like this'. The immediate perception was that City just wanted to fight back and go legal.

Such battle lines marked quite a change from how 'blasé' City had been perceived at the start of the process. PwC auditors found that the club had come up with their own amortisation formula for signings, despite UEFA outlining the maths used and requiring those submitting the information to complete a course beforehand. The alternative approaches made a significant difference. 'Manchester City has included costs relating to the amortisation of capitalised player transfer fees incurred in the final year to May 2012,' the report said. 'This is not permitted under "ANNEX XI". As a consequence, Manchester City cannot include amortisation of €36,903k (£31,404k) in this calculation.'

City later said there was 'a fundamental disagreement' about how those regulations should be interpreted.[39] With bank statements, some of the figures would be shown in the account, but officials were then unable to show where they came from. This was despite the expertise City had working for them, including specialists such as Alex Byars and Martyn Hawkins. They had joined the club from Deloitte Sports Business Group, which helped UEFA set up FFP regulations.[40]

Another point was made about the creation of two new companies under City Football Group when the overall group was established in 2013. These were a scouting and research business, City Football Services Limited (CFS), and a marketing and media business, City Sports Marketing Limited (CSM), later renamed City Football Marketing Limited. The club argued that they were independent companies and could be commissioned by anyone. The auditors responded that they were off-the-shelf companies, all registered to City's London office. The PwC report considered that CFS and CSM were 'inaccurately excluded from the reporting perimeter', which would have increased the break-even deficit. For CFG's part, the group did consultancy work for developing football areas years later. Singapore's national league was one competition that sought advice.

UEFA primarily focused on amortisation and commercial

deals. The PwC report 'identified a number of apparent variances between reported revenues and individual sponsors and the contract amounts payable'. Fair market valuations were assessed by RepuCom, since bought by Nielsen, with UEFA then double-checking through Octagon. City had benchmarked deals to Arsenal's with Emirates, but this was when the Abu Dhabi-owned club had nowhere near the commercial profile of the London club. What's more, 84 per cent of 'other commercial income' came from Abu Dhabi sponsors. Octagon found that the deals with the four Abu Dhabi companies were up to 80 per cent higher than their actual market value.

Investigators felt a ban was inevitable. It never got that far, with everything significantly slowed. UEFA were repeatedly threatened with legal action. *Der Spiegel*'s leaks show City were considering fighting UEFA 'on all legal fronts' if there wasn't a 'sensible settlement'.[41] The end of April then saw another leaked line that has become infamous. Al Mubarak, according to an email by City legal chief Simon Cliff, had told Infantino 'he would rather spend 30 million on the 50 best lawyers in the world to sue them for the next 10 years' than accept a financial penalty.[42] UEFA, the email went on, had the choice 'to avoid the destruction of their rules and organization'.[43] Cliff at one point wanted to take Platini and Infantino to court for conflicts of interest and abuse of office.[44]

PwC's report does say 'we acknowledge that Manchester City was fully cooperative during the compliance visit'. The club later told UEFA that the report was 'seriously flawed in that it contains numerous erroneous interpretations of the Regulations, false assumptions of fact, errors of law and erroneous conclusions'.[45] There was a genuine fear that the case was going to go to the European Court of Justice, with UEFA staff forensically poring over documents in preparation for that eventuality.

It instead played out in a similar way to PSG. A series of meetings saw UEFA move towards a settlement, although City were adamant on not admitting any misconduct.[46] It was another tightrope for UEFA, although the club seemed to be setting how high it was. City were only willing to accept a settlement that was 'more than a warning' and could be 'seen as effective/dissuasive' but did 'not affect dramatically MCFC business'.[47] This was described at the time as a 'plea-bargaining period', and it's remarkable to think now that City could have faced an even stiffer punishment if they rejected a settlement and the decision went to the CFCB's adjudicatory panel.

Infantino had instead sent an obsequious email to Mubarak at 11.50 p.m. on 2 May 2014. 'You will see that I've sometimes chosen a wording which "looks" more "strong",' the then UEFA General Secretary said. 'Please read the document in this spirit.'

'Finally, I would also like to thank you for your trust. You know you can trust me. Let's be positive!'

Platini followed Infantino by passing on a message through club representative Patrick Vieira at the 2013–14 Europa League final in Turin. 'Please tell your owners in Abu Dhabi they have to trust me. We understand and like what they are doing with the club.'[48] Platini was under immense external pressure, particularly given the ongoing controversy over the Qatar World Cup. Sarkozy's aide had even been copied into one email from Infantino to Al Mubarak.[49]

A settlement followed the day after that 2014 Europa League final, the same as with PSG: a €60 million fine with €40 million withheld, and a reduction of the Champions League squad to 21 players from 25.[50] The English champions were internally satisfied but couldn't resist some pointed remarks in their statement. 'In normal circumstances the club would wish to pursue its case and present its position through every avenue of recourse.'[51]

At the same time as all of this, according to the CAS judgment six years later, City knew that Etisalat, specifically, hadn't yet paid anything. That, according to one involved figure, could be construed as 'wilfully misleading'. The entire situation can meanwhile be interpreted as two clubs owned by autocracies pressuring a governing body into a secret deal. The decisions caused shock in football, both among rival clubs pushing for punishment and even within UEFA. Brian Quinn, who is described as knowing regulation inside out from his experience with the Bank of England, resigned as chair of the CFCB. Other staff followed. The view of many people within football is that the settlements were just another hinge moment. FFP was completely neutered on its very first application, since the punishments amounted to little more than a tariff. 'A blind eye was turned,' in the words of one staff member. It was felt that the hierarchies of PSG and City were 'emboldened' by the outcome, rather than the settlements proving in any way 'dissuasive'.

On the other side, it was argued that the outcome was UEFA rectifying rules that weren't fair in the first place. City and PSG certainly reinforced arguments that wealthy owners shouldn't be punished for investment, a point raised in an October meeting. There was already a lot of spin, a lot of lobbying. There was also a realisation: football's institutions were weak.

8.

CIRQUE DU QATAR

During Neymar's six years at Paris Saint-Germain, he was re-nowned among teammates as a lazy trainer who hosted incredible parties, but there is one surprise from that predictable image. The Brazilian felt the club was 'not professional'. It says a lot about what PSG had become. Neymar certainly came to define an era, but just not in the way anyone intended. Qatar had far greater plans for what remains the most expensive transfer in history at €222 million. Most went unfulfilled, although the effect on the game was profound. So much of that, as with so many such stories, was driven by wounded pride.

On 8 March 2017, PSG suffered the biggest comeback in Champions League history, which also made it the most punitive humiliation. Unai Emery's lavish team had eviscerated Barcelona 4-0 in the last-16 first leg just three weeks beforehand, for what seemed an arrival moment. Instead, the issues illustrated in pre-vious failures were about to get worse. Barcelona won the second leg 6-1, a victory simply known as 'la remontada': the comeback. No team in 62 years of the European Cup or Champions League had ever lost a four-goal first-leg lead. PSG really lost the tie twice. They quickly went down 3-0 only for Edinson Cavani to silence a raucous Camp Nou. Since the rules at the time ensured away goals counted double in an aggregate draw, Barcelona still needed three goals going into the 88th minute. They claimed them all, Sergi

Roberto scoring with the last meaningful kick of the game.

The entire match was a psychodrama that illustrated how mentality conditions elite sport, while telling greater narratives about the two clubs. In a cavernous stadium that had witnessed so much football history, Barcelona appeared to draw on that deeper identity. The squad had talked of persevering with the 'Barcelona way' all through the build-up. In one of many prophetic comments, manager Luis Enrique insisted 'if a team can score four times against us, we can score six times'. Against that zeal, there seemed a sense of fatalism about PSG. Midfielder Blaise Matuidi later wondered whether they played with 'too much fear'.[1]

It apparently proved the moral hollowness of a gaudy project, one that just didn't have the meaning of a great club like Barcelona. That inspired Neymar, who took command amid pandemonium. He'd scored Barcelona's goals in the 88th and 91st minutes, before delivering the perfect curved pass for Sergi Roberto's winner. Leo Messi even gave Neymar the penalty to make it 5-1, in a moment that would later carry greater significance, just like the night's most publicised photo. Neymar had given a career performance, and yet the enduring image was Messi standing above an adoring crowd.

It was a fall-out that accelerated Neymar's doubt about his own status. The playmaker complained to Brazil national teammates about how he'd done everything in the match but all the front pages were about 'Messi, Messi, Messi'. He felt he could never be 'number one' at Barcelona. PSG were more than willing to respond in the only way they knew: if you couldn't beat them, buy them.

The Qatari project had actually gone for Neymar in 2016, when they were looking for a star to replace Zlatan Ibrahimović. Barcelona wouldn't countenance a deal, but PSG were made aware of a €222 million release clause. That meant if a club deposited the necessary amount with La Liga, and the player wanted to go, there was no stopping a transfer. The usual deterrent was that such moves were considered a declaration of war amid the delicate diplomacy between the major clubs. By the summer of 2017, however, there was considerable tension between Barcelona and PSG, sharpened by the perception of the aristocracy against the nouveau riche. Barcelona had already tried to go for major PSG players like Thiago Silva and Marco Verratti, and the French champions couldn't bear the dismissive comparisons after *la remontada*. They were, according to one 'insider', traumatised. The emir sanctioned the most extreme retail therapy.

PSG were just going to pay Neymar's clause, with that willingness all the more remarkable since it would more than double the previous world transfer record of Paul Pogba's €105 million move from Juventus to Manchester United. The scale of the decision started to weigh on the player, though. A media storm whipped up, putting more pressure on the then 25-year-old. Messi and Uruguayan star Luis Suárez got Neymar into a room and spent two hours trying to convince him to stay. 'If you want the Ballon D'Or, I can help you,' Messi said. Neymar was at one point in tears.

PSG appealed to a deeper emotion, though. They were going to make him the face of the project, and literally put his name on the Eiffel Tower. His name was soon on a contract, as PSG made out a cheque worth €222 million to Barcelona on 2 August 2017. Football Leaks later revealed that €10.5 million also went to the player's father, Neymar Sr, as Neymar himself earned over €1 million a week. He insisted it wasn't about the money, at an unveiling organised like a film premiere. PSG chairman Nasser Al-Khelaifi claimed it had an audience of 85 million in Brazil, while describing Neymar as 'an international brand'.[2] French president Emmanuel Macron said the signing was 'good news'.[3]

It wasn't necessarily so for football. As with Chelsea in the summer of 2003, this was money the established powers had never come close to spending. It was the wage race going nuclear, while triggering hyper-inflation. Barcelona spent all of the Neymar money by January, culminating in a €120 million deal for Liverpool's Philippe Coutinho, who was paid a guaranteed €440,000 a week.[4] The English club then used £75 million of that on Southampton's Virgil van Dijk. There was such concern, even from German Chancellor Angela Merkel, that UEFA president Aleksander Čeferin went to the European Commission wondering about greater regulation.[5] Major clubs complained all negotiations were 'insane'. Barcelona even made bizarre decisions when not buying, like passing on a 17-year-old everyone else wanted. Kylian Mbappé had been AS Monaco's revelation in subjecting PSG to a rare second place in Ligue 1, but Barcelona felt he didn't yet warrant the €100 million fee.[6]

PSG saw the worth, all the more so as the teenager was a local fan. Al-Khelaifi's staff were shocked when he said they were going to add Mbappé to Neymar, especially since UEFA had explicitly warned the club of potential FFP sanctions in the last week of the transfer window.[7] There was a possible solution, though. Despite the fact that AS Monaco were defending French champions, they were offered a season-long loan, that involved an obligation to buy Mbappé for an eventual €180 million in the 2018 summer window. Monaco preferred to sell abroad, but the player only wanted Paris at that point, and could leave for much less the following year. The French champions settled on the compromise. Al-Khelaifi said money was never mentioned in talks with Mbappé's parents, but the teenager signed a deal that guaranteed almost €50 million over five seasons.[8]

This excess was exactly what many in football feared from the

2014 FFP settlements, as if the club had been emboldened. So much for chief executive Jean-Claude Blanc's later claim that the regulations had 'really slowed us down'.[9] UEFA were actually forced to speed up their customary FFP assessments and announce a formal investigation into PSG the day after the window closed, because there had been so many complaints within the game.[10] The step was intended to encourage faith in the regulations, when most people in football considered them a joke. Much of the agitation came from Spain, as articulated by La Liga president Javier Tebas.

'PSG are laughing at FFP, aren't they,'[11] he said. 'What we have done is caught them pissing in the bed, or the swimming pool. Neymar's gone on the diving board and now he's taken a piss.' As much as such comments caused huge tension for PSG, headlines like this arguably served their owners. The immense interest in Neymar and later Mbappé certainly did. This was Qatar waving a huge flag, at a time when the country was surrounded on all sides.

Buying Neymar wasn't the emir's idea, since it was Al-Khelaifi who brought it to him, but the timing might have been perfect. That was because of what happened two months beforehand. On 5 June 2017, Saudi Arabia, UAE, Yemen, Egypt, Bahrain and the Maldives announced they were cutting diplomatic ties with Qatar, including the closing of borders. That made it quite a moment for Qatar to get everyone talking about their destabilising influence on the planet's most popular sport. The detonation of the transfer market became collateral in a cold war. It was all the more important as Qatar was being made invisible in their own region. Qatar Airways, who were banned from flying over Saudi airspace, had their sponsorship of Barcelona shirts pasted over in the blockading countries. Bahrain, UAE and Saudi Arabia meanwhile passed laws imposing 15-year prison sentences on anyone expressing 'sympathy' for Qatar.[12]

Neymar and Mbappé, then, were a guarantee of rolling news.

It is oddly fitting all of this was bookended by football, since the blockade changed the sport. The crisis emanated from that moment just 15 days after the World Cup vote in 2010, when Mohamed Bouazizi set himself on fire in Tunisia to spark the Arab Spring. Put simply, Qatar was perceived as willing to accommodate the political Islam that drove the uprisings, and give it a platform on Al Jazeera. The blockading states, particularly UAE, wanted to destroy such movements over fears for their own futures. That divide had crystallised growing differences between the ruling families from years before. Qatar was for a long time seen as so negligible that it was treated as an extension of Saudi Arabia.[13] The kingdom was the mothership of the Gulf, exerting the largest influence on economics, international relations and even religion.

One of the reasons Sheikh Hamad deposed his father in 1995 was his will for Qatar to forge its own path. This was in turn why Saudi Arabia and UAE supported a counter-coup, to bring a pup of a state to heel. It was bad enough for the other rulers that the new emir was talking about evolving towards a British-style constitutional monarchy. They didn't want a showcase of such liberalism on their doorstep. Worse was Qatar positioning itself as a regional intermediary, extending contact to Saddam Hussein's Iraq and developing better relations with Iran, Saudi Arabia's main rival. Doha did point out it had to share a gas field with Iran, making diplomacy essential. Exportation of that gas meanwhile powered much of the region, with the logistics bringing Qatar into proximity with political Islamic groups. Doha felt it was better to engage in dialogue.[14]

This was a huge departure from the other states, who saw such movements as potential instigators of rebellion. The UAE just wanted them crushed. They would instead turn on Al Jazeera and see these dissidents given an audience of millions. It got to the point where the station was viewed as such a source of agitation that Mohamed bin Zayed, when crown prince of UAE, was recorded by a US cable to have asked the US in jest to bomb Al Jazeera's offices during the war in Afghanistan.[15]

The Arab Spring brought all of this to a head. The will for rebellion spread around the region, but most significantly to Egypt, where football ultras formed a prominent voice in the protests against Hosni Mubarak.[16] The country is probably the example that best explains the blockade. Fearful of a chain reaction where their own regimes were toppled, Saudi Arabia and UAE sought to buttress Mubarak. The primary agitators were the Muslim Brotherhood, an Egyptian group founded in the 1920s who cast themselves against the region's hereditary monarchies.[17] They had been banned in many Gulf states, but there they were on Al Jazeera, receiving what appeared to be positive coverage.[18] Qatar had already been supporting the protestors, as well as Egypt's first democratically elected president in Mohamed Morsi. There was a real chance that the politics that Saudi Arabia and UAE feared most were going to take hold in a hugely influential Arabic state, backed by Qatar. It was seen as unacceptable.

Saudi Arabia and UAE backed a counter-coup that resulted in hundreds of deaths at Raba Square, and put Abdel Fattah El-Sisi in power. It didn't reflect the strongest confidence in the patronage system. UAE started to respond more aggressively to mild calls for greater democratic representation. It was in this context that Khaldoon Al Mubarak, in his state role, warned the UK that billion-pound arms deals would be blocked if there was not more action against the Brotherhood.[19] The Manchester City Chairman described 'an existential threat not just to the UAE but to the region'.

Sheikh Hamad attempted to explain that Qatar had only ever backed the 'popular will', and that it had offered economic support to Egypt before the Brotherhood took office.[20] It had nevertheless been noted how Doha refused to back El-Sisi when he was later elected president. On the other side, liberals worried that Qatar's immense resources were distorting political discussion in favour of religiosity in what were formative democracies, as the Brotherhood's political influence had also seen a rise in violent internal division.[21] Saudi Arabia and UAE were by then outright criticising their neighbour for supporting 'terrorism'.[22]

With tension growing, Sheikh Hamad attempted to calm the situation by abdicating in 2013. The accession of Sheikh Tamim instead only heralded a new generation of rulers that brought fresh acrimony. Mohamed bin Zayed became the de facto ruler of Abu Dhabi when his brother suffered a stroke in 2014, and accentuated the contrast between the two sides of the state. Alongside a peaceful nuclear programme and vibrant cultural scene was an aggressive military expansion, underlined by the employment of figures such as Erik Prince, the founder of private security contractor Blackwater.[23]

'Mohamed bin Zayed is a zealot where political Islam is concerned,' FairSquare's Nick McGeehan says. 'It gains no foothold anywhere near him. He hated the Al Thanis anyway and, in the aftermath of the Arab Spring, it has just got worse.' This deepened when Mohammed bin Salman rose to become Crown Prince of Saudi Arabia in 2017. As minister of defence, he had already brought the UAE into a disastrous war in Yemen, widely seen as a proxy against Iran. Bin Zayed meanwhile considered Bin Salman a protégé, with both viewing Donald Trump's election as US president as an opportunity to influence American policy. UAE and Saudi Arabia had been infuriated by Barack Obama's nuclear deal with Iran. In May 2017, Trump was invited to Riyadh for his first foreign trip as president, and treated like a royal. It was amid this flattery that he was repeatedly told about Qatar's perceived support for terrorism, the context drastically simplified to appeal to Trump's emotion. 'During my recent trip to the Middle East I stated that there can no longer be funding of Radical Ideology,' the US president – of course – tweeted. 'Leaders pointed to Qatar – look!'[24]

Eyes were certainly drawn to a story that appeared on the Qatar News Agency on 24 May 2017. The report on the official state outlet purportedly quoted Sheikh Tamim as telling a military ceremony that Qatar had 'tensions' with the US, while appearing to laud Iran.[25] The emir was also reported to have said relations with Israel were 'good', while calling Hamas the 'legitimate representative of the Palestinian people'. It was all false. The story was taken down within minutes, but had already spread in seconds. Qatar quickly released a statement saying the agency had been hacked by an 'unknown entity', but they were already convinced Saudi Arabia and UAE were involved. A Russian cyber-mercenary group were later found to be responsible, but Western intelligence agencies believed it was probably ordered by the UAE.[26] This came as all three Gulf countries began to invest in sophisticated technology for what amounted to a cyber war. The UAE even signed a deal with the Israel-based NSO Group to use its powerful Pegasus software.[27]

Just two weeks after Trump's visit, with the Gulf states emboldened by the US president's attitude, the blockade of Qatar began. It was a crisis unlike any the region had seen, especially as Saudi Arabia had never been so abrasive. Civilians in Doha genuinely feared invasion, as an idea was even floated for Saudi Arabia to dig a 40-mile trench around the border with Qatar and fill it with nuclear waste.[28] Doha ran out of essential goods because basic imports stopped.

It was only three weeks into the blockade that the coalition finally issued 13 demands. Among them were that Al Jazeera was to be shut down, ties were to be broken with Iran and reparations paid for support of groups like the Muslim Brotherhood.[29] Qatar was basically being asked to abandon any idea of independent foreign policy. Gulf experts say the coalition felt considerable satisfaction in making Qatar squirm, particularly given a perceived arrogance.[30] Striking out on their own represented a strident move in the Gulf, stepping on toes when leaders were so insistent on saving face.

This was why the awarding of the 2022 World Cup was so influential. 'That bid, as far as I'm aware, absolutely infuriated the UAE,' Gulf academic Chris Davidson posits. 'Certainly, Qatar's hosting of the World Cup was a major factor in launching the blockade.' Hassan Al Thawadi, secretary general of the Qatar 2022 Supreme Committee, even admitted 'certain actions seem to indicate that's the case'.[31] The anger was perhaps worse since Qatar had invited neighbours into the bid, only to be told they would humiliate themselves. It was instead a nation-building moment. That was all the more important when Qatar had just 10,000 troops compared to Saudi Arabia's 200,000.[32] Davidson adds that 'there was even the projection the blockade would be enough to prevent Qatar staging the World Cup'.

That didn't work, and neither did the blockade itself. While Trump had openly supported the move, the State Department and Pentagon didn't. The US almost immediately signed off on $12 billion to supply Qatar with F-15 fighter jets, with the UK following in September by agreeing to an initial £8.6 billion order for 24

Typhoon aircraft.[33] Iran and Turkey meanwhile stepped in with imports, with 4,000 cows flown in from Europe for a self-sustaining dairy farm.[34] Far from subduing the tiny state, the entire episode became a case study in how financial diplomacy can greatly expand influence. One pithy description, referencing the currency, was 'riyal politik'.[35] If the crisis had the opposite outcome than intended, one side effect was escalating the rivalry in football. The game became another proxy in this battle for global influence. 'It's a competition between tremendously egotistical megalomaniacal figures for prestige, reputation and power,' McGeehan says. Some of the game's most significant modern developments came out of this.

One of the most prominent early responses was the campaign to expand the World Cup to 48 teams, a decision that would have made it impossible for Qatar to stage the tournament on its own. FIFA president Gianni Infantino publicly announced this in October 2018, stating it was being discussed with the hosts 'and other friends in the region'.

'You know me,'[36] Infantino said. 'It is possible. Why not?' The suggestion might well have served a few interests. FIFA had been perturbed by the 2022 vote since Blatter opened that envelope. The new hierarchy under Infantino were meanwhile highly conscious of so much controversy about alleged corruption and migrant labour abuses. The latter had become the most prominent criticism with Qatar, although the blockade suddenly offered an opportunity to turn this flashpoint issue on their neighbours by pointing to their own planned reforms. The long-held argument from the Infantino regime was that they 'inherited' Qatar, and one claim from within FIFA is that the governing body initially looked for ways to use corruption claims to move the tournament to a different host nation. The immense legal complications meant this was almost immediately set aside. The 48-team idea was instead put in familiar terms: a peace project.

'If it can help all the people in the Gulf and all the countries in the world develop football and bring a positive message to the world about football, then you should give it a try,'[37] Infantino declared. This was all as Infantino was developing a closer relationship with Mohammed bin Salman, having met the Saudi leadership four times in the months after the blockade was launched. Al Thawadi diplomatically admitted they were looking at the feasibility of the plan, but Qatar were ultimately totally reluctant to share their jewel while the blockade was happening.

It was even less likely amid a widespread influence campaign undermining the hosting. This was revealed by *The Intercept* news website's leak of emails from Yousef Al Otaiba, UAE's ambassador to the US.[38] One plan, conspicuously, was even to force the sharing of the tournament precisely by convincing FIFA it would 'display football as a tool to stabilise the region'.[39] Unknown activist groups began to pop up questioning Qatar's human rights record. One London-based consultancy called Cornerstone Global managed significant media cut-through with a purported insider report claiming it was uncertain the World Cup would even be staged in Qatar.[40]

In response, the hosts got football greats like Xavi and Iker Casillas to put up social media posts calling for an end to the blockade. Previous ambassador Pep Guardiola was this time not one of them, since he'd gone to Abu Dhabi's Manchester City. The football side of the crisis had of course moved to the most direct information battleground of all: television. Qatar's beIN SPORT broadcast the Gulf's most popular sport to virtually all of the region, which posed considerable political quandaries for the blockading countries. Here was one huge Qatari symbol on screens when the display of such emblems was punishable with jail. BeIN was even the broadcaster for Saudi Arabia's first World Cup qualification in 12 years, as the national team beat Japan 1-0 in 2017. One of their reporters was still questioned by authorities at the King Abdullah Sports City stadium while having some equipment confiscated.[41]

During the 2018 World Cup itself, Saudi Arabia's head of sport Turki Al Sheikh said the kingdom would take legal action for what it perceived as biased commentary on the national team's 5-0 defeat to Russia.[42] BeIN's Arabic-language commentators often derided the blockade on air. By that point, however, there was a remarkable workaround. Saudi Arabia had banned beIN from selling subscriptions before a new pirate station appeared, bootlegging games. The name, beoutQ, was as pugnacious as some of the logistics. It was all of beIN's content but without the graphics, and the transmission delayed by 10 seconds so contentious commentary could be edited out. Decoder boxes were sold in the region for £80.[43] An independent report confirmed 'without question' that beoutQ was using the satellite infrastructure owned by Arabsat, a Riyadh-based provider part owned by the Saudi government.[44] The Premier League, FIFA and UEFA spoke out against the piracy since broadcasting rights were central to their business model. It was still noted in other bodies how Al Sheikh described Infantino as 'a dear friend for whom the Kingdom and I hold a great respect'.[45] It reflected the awkward situation that associations were now being put in. They couldn't even take legal action since no firm in Saudi Arabia was willing to act on their behalf.[46]

BeIN meanwhile barely made it to the 2019 Asian Cup at all, despite holding the rights. That was because it was held in UAE, but that still wasn't half the story. Qatar had qualified and were drawn in a group against Saudi Arabia. The squad had to get in through Kuwait after special clearance, since exclusion would have seen UAE booted out of global football. The clearances weren't extended to beIN's Qatari staff though, and the station had to use reporters from other nations. Several stadiums meanwhile had banners with flags of the UAE and Saudi Arabia, featuring a set of shaking hands. Like much else about the blockade, the difficulties ended up affording Qatar the most satisfying of victories. This was classic sport as 'war without the guns'. Qatar won the tournament outright, while beating both Saudi Arabia and UAE along the way. The hosts were humiliated 4-0, with the crowd throwing shoes. One response from UAE was a complaint that two of the finalists' players, including Sudan-born top scorer Almoez Ali, were ineligible. Qatar were cleared and beat Japan 3-1 in the final. Emirati officials stayed away from the award ceremony, not wanting to be pictured at their rivals' success. Qatar's players knew to be restrained. There was some measure of revenge when the blockading states surprisingly decided to compete in the Gulf Cup in Doha later that year. Saudi Arabia beat Qatar in the semi-final before Bahrain won it all.

The expected election of Joe Biden as US president began to help smooth the situation, with the blockade formally ended in January 2021. Nevertheless, tensions persisted. There was still a stage that meant more than such international tournaments, too, at least in terms of global visibility. That was the real theatre that was the European club game. 'The big stress,' according to one figure at PSG, was 'who was going to win the Champions League first'. In the 2020–21 semi-finals, four months after the blockade ended but for the first time since it started, Manchester City met PSG. This was behind closed doors due to Covid-19 restrictions, although the few people at the game still say a 'tension' was felt. A difference between the projects was also witnessed. With Mbappé injured, PSG couldn't cope with City's superior collective. The Abu Dhabi-owned team won both games, making it 4-1 on aggregate. The contrast was even seen by experts as reflecting differences between the two autocracies. Abu Dhabi was viewed as a more sophisticated machine, 'more covert than overt'. Qatar was less structured, often looking to spend its way to solutions. City were a proper team, who became an illustration of the extremes that could be reached with unlimited wealth. PSG were an extreme in a very different way.

Thomas Tuchel couldn't believe what he was hearing. It was the Anfield dressing room for the first game of the 2018–19 Champions League season and the German coach was trying to get his €600 million Paris Saint-Germain team to just run more. One of the answers that came back was 'Why?'

'Because it's Liverpool and it's Anfield, one of the best teams in the world in one of the most demanding stadiums in the world,' an exasperated Tuchel responded. By the time PSG got out onto the pitch, Tuchel couldn't believe what he was seeing. He stood on the touchline just going 'Guys, what is this?!' Liverpool won 3-2, Roberto Firmino scoring a 91st-minute winner. The goal came from the Brazilian forward forcing a few extra yards of space. Liverpool were able to run for longer and, evidently, further. It's precisely why many who were at PSG have uttered the same refrain. 'It's not a football club.' Other common descriptions are 'a vanity project' and 'a circus'.

What PSG actually are is a state project, but that has curiously had the opposite effect as at Manchester City. Whereas Abu Dhabi's billions gradually ensured an extreme level of efficiency, Qatar's money has brought an obscene wastefulness and extreme chaos. There is an argument that PSG has been the most tumultu-ous club the game has ever seen. There have been flocks of prima donnas rather than just one or two. There have been fights. There have been the pettiest little disagreements. The chasm between the expenditure and what has actually been achieved has almost served as a modern football morality tale, although whether it's been worth it is a relative question. PSG have certainly offered a lot of value to neutral observers. Since so many clubs talk about how they are competing with film studios, this isn't so much a soap opera but one of those expensively cataclysmic film productions such as *Waterworld*.

The excess was all the more striking when players and manag-ers arrived at the old training ground. That had been the homely Camp des Loges, in quaint woodland just outside Paris. PSG have since constructed a £257 million complex with therapeutic pools and the usual trappings, but they probably needed it. Argentinian manager Mauricio Pochettino's first response on seeing Camp des Loges was 'this is shit'. Physios only had two seats, even though these were the employees who had the responsibility of keeping Mbappé in prime condition. Tuchel thought the place was filthy and, when Al-Khelaifi asked him what he needed, the German's first answer was 'a skip'. It was all the more remarkable given there was still equipment so the emir could watch training from Doha.

The communal areas weren't much better, with little more than a Smeg fridge. So much for linking the club to Parisian high cuisine. The canteen itself featured one long table, and then a small one. They weren't exactly arranged according to group psychology, as now frequently happens at elite clubs. It was nevertheless at those tables where one of the most compelling aspects of the modern PSG took form. That was the classroom squad dynamics. Or, as one former coach put it, 'where someone was often crying because someone has looked at him funny, where he isn't talking to him because one hasn't passed him the ball'.

That was when the players were actually there. Managers often had little control over when stars took holidays, and sometimes had to 'negotiate' returns for pre-season. In the summer of 2018, Tuchel had Cavani coming back one week and Neymar the next, at which point he turned to the newly signed veteran goalkeeper Gianluigi Buffon. 'Gigi, what is this?'

'I have never seen anything like this – it would not be allowed at Juventus.' That makes it less of a mystery why it has been so difficult for successive managers to co-ordinate pressing drills. Pochettino agreed to go to PSG in 2020 on the assurance that they were going to change approach and develop a younger squad. His first and only summer window featured the most star-laden and wage-heavy window any team had seen, as all of Gianluigi Donnarumma, Sergio Ramos, Gini Wijnaldum and Leo Messi arrived on free transfers. Pochettino immediately knew it would be a problem. He had been promised a streamlined squad but at one point had 42 first-team players.

Managers would usually have new stars just dropped on them, and it was always about reputation rather than strategic planning. The early days of Neymar and Mbappé brought a desperation for branding, which was why an 'MCN' with Cavani was pushed to match Real Madrid's 'BBC' (Gareth Bale, Karim Benzema, Cristiano Ronaldo). There was of course a photoshoot in Doha's West Bay, Thiago Silva taking a selfie with the trio behind him. The first notable moment the triumvirate produced on the pitch was a dispute over who got to take penalties, that further undermined former manager Unai Emery's authority.

That MC Escher-style power structure – at least underneath

Al-Khelaifi and the emir – had been the main reason for problems in the dressing room. The general pattern has gone like this: a manager would attempt to get a certain player to do something, only to get frustrated as there was no sense of obligation or consequence. The manager would then seek to punish the player, only for the player to go to a friendly executive or director. PSG have notoriously had this circle of officials underneath Al-Khelaifi, each of them close to different individuals or groups in the squad. The hierarchy had generally paid huge amounts to convince players to come, so the culture was one of indulgence. A series of sporting directors sided with players over managers. And on the cycle went, until eventually the manager was sacked.

Those players who believed their signing was sanctioned by the emir, meanwhile, felt they could get away with anything. There's an illustrative story that former squad members still tell. One highly paid international once responded to the news that he was on the bench by just putting his clothes back on and then silently zipping up his jacket. The manager was more than willing to leave him sitting in the dressing room, only to quickly get a call from one of the directors requesting an explanation. The player wasn't talking to his manager, but he'd already been on to his agent.

Fingers were constantly pointed. Numerous players were hammered as 'bad professionals', but that depended on the clique they were in. Leonardo was seen as the sporting director who managers had the most problems with, but Tuchel also had a combustible relationship with Antero Henrique. Almost every manager has meanwhile been dismissed as not having the charisma or the experience for the job. Emery was derided by one player's camp as 'a coach to play in the Europa League'.

PSG were for a long time a club where too many influential figures wanted too many different things, which is ruinous for a sports team. The most over-performing modern clubs have a unity of vision. Henrique was a classic example of the issue. He was appointed as sporting director because of his work unearthing talent from South America at FC Porto, but that wasn't how PSG built their squads. On leaving Paris, Emery made the comparison to Pep Guardiola. 'At Manchester City, Pep is in charge. At PSG, Neymar has to be.'[47]

For all the inevitable focus on the biggest stars, PSG's managers usually found the greatest difficulty was the well-paid 'middle class' underneath. The feeling was that they usually developed an unwarranted 'arrogance' due to pay that had often been quadrupled from previous clubs. Some complained their motivation had been affected because club publicity gave them a lower profile. One line used in the game was that if major players wanted to go to PSG, they probably weren't worth signing. 'No serious player wants to go there.' Or, at least, stay there.

A telling example came from one of their many Champions League collapses, this time the 3-2 aggregate defeat to Real Madrid in the 2021–22 season. As Karim Benzema was leading a stirring comeback at the Santiago Bernabéu, Pochettino and his staff turned to the bench to try and change something. The feeling was that most of the players, many of them on wages of between €100,000 and €250,000 a week, just 'didn't fancy it'. That isn't to say the stars didn't bring issues. Two regular starters openly despised each other. Although one was more important to the team's tactics, he was the player sold, because the other was friendlier with the megastars.

While Neymar was actually seen as a nice lad, who had a humility when alone, his huge entourage fostered egotism. Emery once faced a dispute over whether the Brazilian had to carry the official club washbag.[48] The fear within the club was that Neymar's lifestyle was more like that of a pop star than an elite athlete.[49] Players used to joke he would return overweight from one of his many trips to Brazil, occasionally appearing at mates' barbecues. Neymar's parties became legendary, even resulting in images of a hard-working trainer like Cavani dancing until 5 a.m. in black tie.[50] Managers would mull over whether it was appropriate to attend, or if an attempt at creating some distance would be seen as a snub. Neymar inevitably felt he had to defend himself from such discussion.

'When I can party, I will ... no one tells me what to do,'[51] he said in an interview with TF1. 'I'm a guy who knows when I can and when I can't ... you can't just be 100 per cent with your head focused on football the way I do, you'll end up exploding.' Some of PSG's own staff may dispute the logic. An internal analysis of Neymar's performances in 2018–19, as reported by the *Daily Telegraph*, showed he was generally only playing at 60 per cent capacity.[52]

A primary problem was that the very context didn't 'push anyone to sporting excellence'. Coaches found that their main task was facilitating egos, since it was impossible to impose any real tactics. The evolution of the modern game has demanded submission to systems. Guardiola's 2008 appointment at Barcelona represented a watershed in that regard, which was why so much of the sport's more recent history revolved around Camp Nou. His philosophy was so spectacularly successful that everyone else had to follow or fall behind.

PSG for years didn't heed this. There, even a more pragmatic manager like Emery struggled to get players to stay focused while watching analysis videos. It was perhaps indicative of the simplistic football thinking that PSG saw how Emery was a cup specialist with his three successive Europa League victories and felt this could just be bolted on to their squad to win the Champions League. The game doesn't work like that. Tuchel is meanwhile someone who thinks about how the game works as much as anyone, including Guardiola, constantly configuring tactical pictures in his mind. He couldn't make them that detailed for PSG. Pochettino then got the job on account of a high-pressing system where the ideal is that the entire team hounds the opposition into submission, as his Tottenham Hotspur exemplified. At PSG, he had to reduce this to eight players around three floating stars.

Managers instead relied on individual inspiration in single games, that did occasionally happen. PSG beat Liverpool 2-1 in that 2018–19 return game. Mbappé scored an audacious hat-trick in a 4-1 win over Barcelona in February 2021, that drew comparisons with the Brazilian Ronaldo. It was just that none of it was sustainable. It was even worse that the French title became so dispensable. Emery was lucky to survive finishing second to Mbappé's Monaco in 2016–17 after the 6-1 defeat to Barcelona, but PSG responded by winning the next two titles, by 13 and 16 points respectively. PSG scored six, seven, eight and nine goals in repeated thrashings of teams like Dijon, who never spent more than €2 million on a player. Many of these games involved the attackers just weaving through mismatched defences, in highlights that were less sport than empty 'content'. The immense wealth disparity ensured Ligue 1 came to be seen as a 'joke' by elite managers and players. Even Mbappé tried to ironically use the 'farmers' league' dismissal in one rare season of European success. The reality is illustrated by how executives at other French clubs talk about how they no longer aim to win the league. This isn't normal. Former Lyon manager Bruno Genesio once plaintively said that what the club misses most 'is that feeling of winning a title'.[53]

It is one of the most corrosive effects of this level of wealth, and has affected both the broadcast value of Ligue 1 and PSG's own Champions League performance. Tuchel once said success in the competition is necessary to 'give credibility to our project'.[54] The Champions League has instead only ravaged respectability. PSG's record somehow got worse than regular quarter-final eliminations. Over a third of the Champions League campaigns in the Qatar era ended with one of those infamous collapses. Four successive managers found themselves at least two goals ahead in the second leg of a tie only to still go out. It became difficult not to connect it to the fact these were among the few games in a PSG season that actually meant something, bringing histrionics to go with the lack of history. The gravitas of established clubs ensured their players expected to win. PSG feared defeat.

Another pattern emerged in how Neymar was often unfit for the last-16 stage, with jokes doing the rounds about keeping himself fresh for carnival in Brazil. He pretty much wanted to leave PSG as soon as he arrived, with Real Madrid's Florentino Pérez mulling a bid just months after Neymar had left Barcelona. There were repeated attempts to get him to Manchester United. The most tempting call was from Camp Nou, though. Neymar even messaged a WhatsApp group he still had with Messi and Suárez to say he wanted back in. The Argentinian told Neymar they needed him to reclaim the Champions League,[55] before instructing new Barcelona president Josep Bartomeu to make it happen. The truth was that the Catalan club didn't have the €200 million required and didn't want to raise it, either. Neymar at that point had a court case against Barcelona over, yes, an unpaid loyalty bonus.[56] He was by then so desperate to leave PSG he was willing to forgo €20 million. Barcelona instead went for Atlético Madrid's Antoine Griezmann, in a decision that would have repercussions for their relationship with Messi.

There were many ironies to this given some of Neymar's motivations for leaving Barcelona. He had wanted to be 'number one', only to realise PSG soon envisaged that role for Mbappé. An early friendship between the two, where Neymar was the 'big brother', became more complicated. Al-Khelaifi even appeared to implicitly criticise the Brazilian through this saga, saying he didn't want 'players who do the job only when it suits them – they are not here to have fun'.[57] Tuchel was nevertheless intent on convincing Neymar to stay. The manager himself felt he might have made a mistake in joining PSG on being picked by the emir, but decided to knuckle down. He appealed to this mentality with Neymar, affording him new responsibility as they spoke about winning the Champions League. Tuchel realised that a little freedom brought a lot of return, including with his own tactics. That 2019–20 season was perhaps the one time that iteration of PSG looked like it could work. As early as February, one of the club's black-tie birthday parties brought the endearing sight of Cavani, Neymar and Keylor Navas singing about winning the Champions League.[58] It was the season they finally got to the final, albeit after a truncated knockout stage in Lisbon due to the Covid-19 disruption. Tuchel told people Neymar carried them that far. PSG were narrowly beaten 1-0 by Bayern Munich in a tense final, Neymar brushing the trophy with his fingers as he went by.

It was illustrative of this PSG that, having got so close, they accelerated away in another direction. By December, Tuchel was gone, having fallen out with the returning Leonardo. By the following summer, after promising Pochettino 'a new project', they doubled down on stars. The Messi transfer, for PSG's part, was always going to happen. It had long been attempted. There was first of all the unique appeal of the Qatari-owned club having perhaps the greatest player in history for Qatar's World Cup. There was then just the fact he is perhaps the greatest in history. It was impossible to resist if you could afford Messi, but that was part of the reason he was available. Almost nobody could afford him, including his own club, Barcelona. They had to let him go due to the Argentinian's contract running out and an inability to re-register him amid La Liga's strict financial regulations. The rules were introduced in part to combat the inflation created by clubs such as PSG. Messi ended up being paid a €25 million signing-on fee and €25 million net per year. It was the *reductio ad absurdum* of football's economy, where a player everyone wanted had no choice on where to go due to his own market rate. The counterpoint is that Messi could have simply lowered his demands.

PSG insist they made huge money off the deal, because of how the Argentinian amplified the club's profile. There was also the one-upmanship over Abu Dhabi given that Manchester City had long been expected to reunite Guardiola and Messi, and were willing to make it happen in 2020. The Argentinian didn't seem to share the glee. It was a marriage of convenience that always looked like it put Messi out. Those at PSG say he never actually got over leaving his boyhood club. It was worse when they signed a symbol of Barcelona's great rivals in Real Madrid's Sergio Ramos, whom Messi never got on with. PSG felt it was one of the smartest transfer windows in history.[59] It immediately became apparent to Pochettino's staff why it didn't make sense.

Just putting three megastars together wasn't how you created fantasy football any more. Mbappé wanted the game played at speed with space to run into. Messi wanted it slowed down with a lot of passes. Neymar just wanted to be on the ball. Individual inspiration was again required in the absence of collective construction. After one match against Montpellier, Mbappé was lip-read complaining about Neymar. 'This tramp, he does not give me the pass.'[60] None of them were giving much in terms of pressing. It was little wonder it all ended in acrimony. Messi and Neymar were booted out of the club in 2023. One squad member said 'they didn't feel safe' amid attention from ultras. Neymar even said he and Messi 'lived through hell'.[61]

It is really one of the game's great mysteries how PSG haven't used Qatar's immense resources to produce something that works. They even have the profound advantage of Paris representing one of the three most fertile areas for footballers in the world, along with São Paulo and south London. PSG have repeatedly spoken of their will to nurture this, while broadcasting the fact they have academy operations in over 60 cities across 15 countries.[62] Young players were to be coached in the 'PSG way', which has often led to quips within the game.[63] There was a sense by 2024 that this had finally started to change. A young PSG team, hewn by Luis Enrique's high pressing, reached the Champions League semi-final. Maybe so many football lessons had started to sink in. Al-Khelaifi had repeatedly spoken about cultural resets that never happened, periodically declaring that 'superstar behaviour is over'[64] and they 'don't want flashy, bling-bling any more'.[65] He was widely seen as one of the main reasons this never happened. Under the emir, Al-Khelaifi sits as the most influential figure on a board with four other members, albeit with a wider circle around it constantly seeking to assert influence. He is generally viewed as a canny operator who is good on a personal level, but hasn't always presented in the best way because so many decisions have been dictated by this sense of wounded pride. While many pointed to the series of contracts given to Mbappé when he wanted to leave, more telling was a manager they no longer wanted.

There was huge interest in Pochettino from both Tottenham Hotspur and Manchester United in the summer of 2021, and it could have offered a deal that suited everyone given that both PSG and the coach sensed they didn't fit. Al-Khelaifi's hierarchy were still insistent on keeping the Argentinian for another year due to the potential perception from losing such a figure to a Premier League club. PSG, in the words of someone who was involved, 'wanted to show the world how big they are'.

There was then the more visceral wounded pride of defeat in a big game. After that 2021–22 defeat to Real Madrid, Al-Khelaifi, his bodyguard and Leonardo went straight to the dressing room of referee Danny Makkelie to complain about decisions in 'aggressive' fashion.[66] The official's own report revealed that they had 'blocked the door' after being asked to leave, and that an assistant's flag had been broken. While Leonardo was punished, there was nothing for Al-Khelaifi, whose behaviour Makkelie reported was worse.[67] The Qatari official had by that point risen to become one of the most powerful figures in European football, which included a seat on UEFA's Executive Committee. Given he also headed a significant broadcast partner, there were constant complaints about 'too many conflicts of interest', especially from Spanish league president Javier Tebas.[68] Some figures within UEFA did object to the Qatari's rise to the Executive Committee, specifically pointing to conflict-of-interest articles in the statutes. Čeferin still insisted Al-Khelaifi stay on the UEFA board even when the PSG president faced a corruption case in Switzerland, of which he was eventually cleared.

Al-Khelaifi's role maybe illustrates the greatest benefit to Qatar of club ownership, which is huge influence at the very top end of Western cultural infrastructure. The state has even benefited from the circus. Al-Khelaifi once declared in one of his customary resets that 'it's the end of the glitter'.[69] They'd already spread enough around. The noise brought attention and distraction. Irrespective of these descriptions of whether they were a football club or a vanity project, they'd certainly built a fashion brand.

If you walk out on the street, regardless of where you are in the world, there's a fair chance you will see a PSG shirt. There's a better chance you'll see PSG clothing with Nike's famous 'Jumpman' branding. Despite there being no connection between basketball legend Michael Jordan and football, let alone PSG, the link-up with Air Jordan has been spectacularly successful for both parties. LeBron James and Rita Ora have been among those pictured in PSG gear.

It is also the one area, beyond creating headlines, where Qatari PSG have enjoyed undeniable success from their principal objectives. If 'iconic players' are a 'fantastic accelerator', as brand director Fabien Allègre told the *Daily Telegraph*, Nike's Air Jordan has been rocket fuel.[70] Before the takeover, PSG sold around 40,000 shirts a year. By the first week of the exclusive football partnership with Jordan in 2018, 40,000 items were sold out in a week.[71] There were long queues outside their Paris stores but what most elated the club's commercial staff was how half the sales for the collection in 2018–19 came from outside France. 'We're truly global,' chief partnerships officer Marc Armstrong enthused in a Harvard study, where the title said enough: 'Paris Saint-Germain: Building One of the World's Top Sports Brands'. Insiders believe the one reason it was immediately such a massive success was because it was a rare area at PSG where elite appointments were left to their own devices. The more disruptive influences around the club were more interested in where players were going to party, not in flow-charts about reach. PSG are seen as a marketing machine like no other, who have occupied that football fashion 'space' the esteemed

Italian clubs used to specialise in, but expanded it to unimaginable size.

Since they didn't have the pedigree of Real Madrid or AC Milan, PSG were going to go in directions those clubs couldn't. Some had nothing to do with football at all. It was now about taking over the next generation's lifestyle, rather than just a pastime. As well as tie-ins with brands like Dior, PSG have sought 'collaborations' with youthful designers, artists and musicians. It's why many previous managers are right. They aren't a football club, or at least just a football club. They're an entity that has used the popularity of football to become everything from a fashion brand to an influencer space, producing merchandise such as headphones that someone like Sir Alex Ferguson would probably roll their eyes at.[72] When PSG did a promotion with Warner Bros for the release of *Justice League*, their stars were cast alongside some of the film's superheroes.[73] There was only one choice for Neymar, since he is such a fan of Batman that he has the Bat-Signal on the chairs of his helicopters.

One model of trainers, the AJ4 PSGs, were inevitably in Qatar's maroon colours. The executives – even if indirectly – had succeeded in making a hereditary monarchy with a hugely criticised human rights record 'cool', to use Allègre's own word. Most of that has been based on maximising the unique appeal of Paris, as the ownership realised how powerful the one-club city aspect could be. 'Paris means fashion, style, design and diversity,' Al-Khelaifi told the Harvard study.[74] He also wanted to make the club uniquely symbolic of the city. One reason behind expanding the 'Paris' in the club crest was to make PSG's name the European equivalent of a New York Yankees cap with 'NY'.

PSG inevitably appeared at Paris fashion week, but the real inspiration that came out of that was bringing fashion week to the Parc des Princes. Every week. The club wanted to make their matches like a New York Knicks basketball game, where every celebrity in town would want to appear.

The VIP experience was refashioned to become like going to the most exquisite private members club. 'Le Cercle' was its centrepiece, where seats cost €1,600 per game. That brought access to the presidential lounge and fine dining. Publicity agents relentlessly contact the club looking for tickets. As one staff member put it, 'if you manage to get a seat in Le Cercle, you're somebody'. Those who have include Leonardo DiCaprio, Beyoncé, Jay-Z, Rihanna, Mick Jagger, Naomi Campbell, Gigi Hadid and Kendall Jenner. Even UEFA asked PSG how they manage it. Given this desire for 'panache', it's difficult to see, say, how José Mourinho's football would have fitted. The image of Jenner and DiCaprio watching the Portuguese berate a referee after a bad-tempered 0-0 draw is nevertheless amusing. The match these celebrities attend is really a combination of different events. There's an incongruity in how the limited number of ultras create an impressive and authentic noise, only for a soundtrack more in keeping with a fashion show to crank up. All of this has made the club worth over €4 billion, although it would not have been possible without immense investment. 'We are disrupting the world of football, on and off the pitch, in a uniquely Parisian style,' chief digital officer Russel Stopford says in the Harvard study. 'That's the story we want to tell.'

Others tell a different one.

It is actually a story that has been replayed a few times. In the rest of European football, as well as within UEFA, there remains incredulity that PSG again escaped serious sanction from the second FFP investigation into the club. The former European Court of Justice judge who chaired UEFA's adjudicatory panel, José Narciso da Cunha Rodrigues, even criticised the process. 'The decision to close the case,' he was quoted as saying in a *New York Times* report, 'was manifestly erroneous.'[75]

The primary focus was again on state-linked sponsors, and particularly the arrangement with the Qatar Tourism Authority, to go with a group of deals that included telecom company Ooredoo and the Qatar National Bank. One of PSG's main arguments was that such contracts had facilitated the signings of Mbappé and Neymar within the rules, and – crucially – that these companies should not be considered as state-owned or state-controlled, and consequently not considered 'related parties'. This was why PSG hadn't put these deals through fair-value assessments. Auditors insisted that, by UEFA's definition, all of those agreements should have been disclosed as related-party income. It led to some 'bizarre' exchanges. 'That's UEFA's interpretation,' was one PSG employee's line

'But that's exactly what you're being assessed on,' came the incredulous response, as the UEFA definition was literally read out. The scope of Deloitte's work didn't include fair-value assessments, but it was flagged that the process should involve precisely that. There were even questions about the independence of the process at that point, which didn't make auditors comfortable. The remit of companies like Deloitte was to look at various elements and see whether they matched, in order to remove ambiguity or politics, but it was then found that UEFA always sent at least one person from club licensing and FFP to the club. UEFA officials even had meetings with PSG's finance director. This was described as discussing 'wider aspects'. There were questions as to why this was happening when external companies were onsite.

The feeling from many of these auditors was that the FFP regulations were quite strong in legal terms, but only as effective as their enforcement. Big clubs were widely seen as too powerful. Auditors in turn often felt powerless. When they would submit the first draft of a report to UEFA, there were requests to reword it. This caused frustration since they weren't UEFA-branded documents. A frequent grumble was that 'they almost just wanted a brand like Deloitte or PwC to rubber-stamp their reports'. PSG eventually accepted they were related parties, but one difference from 2014 was that they were allowed to hire independent parties to value their deals. They went with Nielsen, whose valuation was far closer to the club's accounted figure of €200 million. Octagon had it at less than €5 million. The chief investigator was former Belgian prime minister Yves Leterme but, rather than request a third assessment, he went closer to the Nielsen figures.[76] This rankled with members of his investigative committee and shocked Cunha Rodrigues. The latter complained that Leterme had given no reasons why the Octagon report should be disregarded but noted how the investigator had actually increased PSG's sponsorship income higher than Nielsen's calculations.

Leterme had sole discretion in cases put to his committee so, on 18 June 2018, it was announced PSG had fallen inside the allowed losses by €6 million.[77] Punishment was avoided. The Adjudicatory Chamber were so shocked that they called for the Investigatory Chamber to repeat the process, the first time that had ever happened. Before that could even get under way, though, PSG announced an appeal. They argued there was no justification to dismiss Leterme's decision, and that Cunha Rodrigues had missed a 10-day deadline to conduct a review. The former ECJ judge, according to the *New York Times*, described this as a 'logical absurdity' since the limit only applied to starting a review not concluding it. Turkish club Galatasaray had at the same time filed a similar appeal to the Court of Arbitration for Sport (CAS), after Cunha Rodrigues also wanted their settlement with Leterme scrapped. PSG and UEFA agreed to wait for the result of that, which ultimately saw the governing body side with Galatarasay's interpretation that the 10-day limit applied to the conclusion of the review. There wasn't any further argument. UEFA didn't defend their own Adjudicatory Chamber. PSG got off, on what was felt to be an 'extreme technicality'.

Several members of the Adjudicatory Chamber resigned, including legal expert Petros Mavroidis, who is also a professor at Columbia Law School. 'I understand that my thinking of football does not coincide totally with the thinking of the European football authorities,' he says. UEFA did subsequently clarify its rules so that the adjudicatory panel subsequently had 10 days to call in a case and 20 to review it.[78] The clear stance from many within the game, typically stressed most forcefully by Tebas, was that FFP was 'dead'.[79] Even UEFA insiders were surprised at the interpretations. The feeling was that 'teething problems' in 2014 might have been acceptable but that '2018 was the same if not worse'. 'What's the point of rules if you're not going to implement them?'

The entire episode articulated one of the major tensions in modern football, which was the establishment against new money. So much for the previous belief that such clubs would never catch up. The concern was now that this went beyond state-linked clubs buying up the best players. There was a fear that PSG were intentionally driving up transfer fees and wages because they knew, in the long term, only a handful of rivals would be able to compete. Gulf expert Chris Davidson believes that would completely tally with existing strategies in other industries. 'The Gulf state-owned airlines were able to offer far more luxurious aircraft at the same price. They pretended or claimed they were private companies, but they weren't. The US airlines complained this was unfair competition. It almost brought them to bankruptcy.'

There are parallels with football. The Neymar deal is now seen as a landmark that was deeply destructive for competitive balance. 'That reset the benchmark,' financial expert Rob Wilson says. Before Neymar, there were only two transfers that breached €100 million, and the first of those was as far back as 2013, with Gareth Bale's move from Tottenham Hotspur to Real Madrid. In the seven years since Neymar, before the summer of 2024, there have been 15. That's only taking into account transfer fees, too, not extra payments like agent commissions. This was the 'artificial inflation' many football economists speak of.

'The money was not generated by the football industry,' Tebas argues. 'So you are injecting hundreds of millions into the sector. Atlético Madrid wanted to keep their goalkeeper Jan Oblak, PSG wanted him, so Atlético had to raise his salary . . . it harms clubs who do not have this money coming in.' One major club complained of contract talks with a star collapsing when PSG offered a deal that quadrupled his wages. If true, it somewhat undermines Al-Khelaifi's words in 2022, that he is 'the first who would sign for a cap on salaries'.[80]

A confluence of events, not least the end of the Messi-Cristiano Ronaldo era, ensured it was the big Spanish two who endured the most visible impact. Both had new choices to make, and new relationships with PSG. For Real Madrid, there were tense stand-offs over Neymar and then Mbappé. Pérez never went all out for the French star, leaving it in Mbappé's hands before he eventually joined on a Bosman. The interpretation of this was that Pérez was mindful of what PSG did to Barcelona in 2017. That relationship was much more complex, partly because of what the Catalan club represent to so many. Guardiola's Barcelona made such a lasting impression on the game that everyone, and particularly state-linked clubs, wanted a piece of it. This great feat of creativity led to the destruction of the club, at least in its purest form. Barcelona were far from blameless in this. They made bad decision after bad decision, as if sent mad by the new world.

Barcelona played a huge part in legitimising Qatar in sport, for one, becoming one of the first and biggest platforms for the state's advertising. That initially took the form of the Qatar Foundation, which was the philanthropic organisation of Sheikha Moza bint Nasser Al Missned, one of the former emir's consorts. The two brothers, Sheikh Tamim and Sheikh Jassim, were delighted it pleased their mother. The intention was always for the space to go to a state company, though, which was eventually Qatar Airways. If the argument at that point was that Barcelona had lost their soul, the club was soon to be completely hollowed out. It wasn't just PSG buying their players. Such was the worldwide fascination with Barcelona's approach that the hierarchy tricked themselves into thinking they had developed a formula to solve football. Their youth philosophy would keep producing stars, and the admiration for that would attract the biggest names in the game. It was intended to be the most virtuous of cycles. The problem, as often happens in such situations, was believing that most of this was down to design rather than luck. While it's obviously true that Barcelona had the best academy set-up in the world, there was a generational level of fortune in how a historically good group came together at the same time. Xavi, Andrés Iniesta and Sergio Busquets spun the carousel that Messi stood on top of. This was always going to be impossible to recreate.

Barcelona had become high on their own supply, but that supply didn't reach a high enough level. The club also became obsessed with star power, to the point that the squad became ludicrously top heavy. They symbolised the game's capacity for eating itself.

Barcelona had spent so much on players that they couldn't keep the greatest in their history. By the summer of Messi's departure for PSG, in 2021, the re-elected club president Joan Laporta revealed their total debt stood at €1.35 billion. It almost exactly summed up a point by a rival executive. 'You could give Barcelona €1 million tomorrow and they'd spend €1.2 billion on players.' Barcelona had taken the modern game to an extreme. PSG had taken their best players. City had taken their idea.

Barcelona and Real Madrid were suffering from the world they created. One response was to come up with an idea to change that world again.

9.

FLAWED PERFECTION

Pep Guardiola was already the perfect appointment for Manchester City, but this somehow made it even better. Manchester United were speaking to the Catalan late into 2015, and felt they were close to agreeing a deal. It had got that far. Instead, there was 'genuine shock' within Old Trafford when it was learnt that Guardiola would be joining City for summer 2016. That was relished, since those at the Etihad remembered senior United figures dismissing the new project, openly talking about how they'd never catch up. It was to be one of many expensive mistakes.

United ultimately felt they couldn't match their neighbours' proposal, which was saying something for the highest-earning club in the world. City always knew they had their man. It was about more than making him the best-paid manager in football, or even working with close colleagues from Barcelona. City were able to offer Guardiola his idealised coaching environment. Those who know the Catalan say it is like a genius afforded perfect laboratory conditions. What Guardiola's City have really become is a vision of what happens when a state has unlimited funds to build the ideal club. There is an inevitability to success, since the team have come as close as you can get to taking unpredictability out of games. A series of records have been broken, while the standard necessary to compete has been drastically raised. City have won the treble, a first ever English domestic treble and a record six Premier League titles out of seven, with the first being an unprecedented 100-point season and the last ensuring they became the first English side to win four in a row. Guardiola has turned the Premier League into the Bundesliga, the German championship he similarly brutalised with Bayern Munich. This has all been aided by well over £1 billion-worth of expenditure on the team in fees and wages in his time alone, alongside a huge outlay on what represents the most lavishly funded football project ever seen. That isn't to diminish Guardiola, since the empowerment of such a historic great is the perfect illustration of how the club aims for 'best in class' in everything. And yet, as the Catalan has often complained, City don't get the appreciation he feels they deserve.[1] He should be able to work out why.

The expenditure is only one aspect. There are persistent criticisms over what this is all for, since it is essentially making a football club an extension of an autocracy. City have had to pay €30 million in fines from two investigations into breaches of financial rules, with a third investigation, in the Premier League, resulting in over 100 alleged breaches – another record. The club insist upon their innocence but suspicion reigns within the game. There's a respect for what City do on the pitch but none of the reverence Guardiola enjoyed at Barcelona. City's frequent eviscerations of opponents can feel like cold exhibitions to be admired on an intellectual level rather than an emotional level, unless you are a supporter. They're too smooth, too perfect. They're also a plundering, a facsimile, a genetic clone and an evolution of that Barcelona all at once.

And yet, for all that, this City don't feel as high a sum of the parts. It is a flawed perfection.

For the City hierarchy, it was always building up to Guardiola. That meant it was always going to be based on Ferran Soriano's vision. This was what other clubs never got in this race to recreate Barcelona 2008–11. Then again, other clubs couldn't afford it, bar Paris Saint-Germain. If Guardiola was the final piece, Soriano offered the blueprint. The story of this City is in part how they gave the executive a blank cheque to bring his book to reality.

Soriano was only one of many former Barcelona staff appointed, to go with Marc Boixasa, Joan Patsy, Txiki Begiristain and Omar Berrada. Camp Nou president Sandro Rosell complained in 2013 about 'offensive approaches from City, at all levels' of the club, to the point 'there were no fish left'.[2] The biggest was actually still to come. The romantic explanation for Guardiola's choice is that, on coming to England, he was only ever going to join the same club as Begiristain. A debt was owed. Begiristain had been Barcelona sporting director in 2008, when a cultural reset was required.[3] He saw the hand of Johan Cruyff in the precocious B team manager, who happened to be his teammate from the 1991–92 European Cup winners. 'You haven't got the balls,' Guardiola famously told the Barcelona hierarchy when approached for the main job. He was forever grateful that Begiristain pushed for his appointment when 'nobody else would take a risk'.[4]

There was a more hard-nosed side to joining City, too. A *Der Spiegel* leak revealed Guardiola signed a contract worth £13.5 million, rising to £16.75 million, as early as October 2015.[5] No wonder City felt United never had a chance. It was the project taking its final form, after less than a decade of ownership.

Even rivals who hated City regarded their structures as the best in the world. Begiristain had already started identifying players who would fit Guardiola's 'concepts', with staff working off an advanced database that allowed long-term succession planning. City usually knew who they wanted 18 months in advance, so no transfer was ever rushed. This was how Rodri so seamlessly succeeded

Fernandinho. Begiristain would hold regular recruitment meetings with Soriano and Al Mubarak, the latter often flying in for games on a private jet. The chairman would request signings be explained to him but trusted the judgement of the Catalans.

Throughout all of this, Soriano referred to boat races, and how those behind the leader must try a different course to get in front. City consequently went much bigger than PSG or Chelsea, with the ambition amplified by Soriano's constant stream of ideas. The 'golden rule' the chief executive set was that no decisions be made in the 24 hours after a game. 'Go put your head in the fridge' has been another guiding phrase. That hierarchy also trusted that Guardiola thinks about the game to a level beyond anyone in history, and they were going to give him the best environment for that. This pointed to the greater lesson of this era at City. It wasn't that victory was inevitable. It was that, as Soriano enthused, the impact of pure luck was hugely eroded.

At half-time of the 2022 FA Cup semi-final against Liverpool, a Manchester City side who had been second best came into the dressing room expecting fury from Guardiola. They found the opposite. There was Guardiola silently moving one of the counters on the tactics board by a matter of centimetres. Such intricacies were precisely why Karl-Heinz Rummenigge once said that watching the Catalan for even 15 minutes at Bayern Munich was to 'witness a search for football perfection'.[6] Guardiola set his players what seemed impossible targets so as to push the outer limits of the game.

That has given him a claim to being the most influential manager of all time, perhaps only surpassed by Cruyff. In reinterpreting his mentor's Total Football for the modern era, Guardiola has changed the way football is played. You can now go to almost any pitch in Europe and see teams of every age playing out from the back. This profound transformation in the tactical psychology of the game comes from a mindset where the Catalan supposedly can't go longer than 31 minutes without thinking about football.[7] Guardiola is revered as someone who has a perception of space unparalleled in his field. His players talk of how he sees movements no one else can.

There is an argument, given that Guardiola is praised as a renaissance man into chess and high cuisine (if also Coldplay), that he could do with thinking about some important subjects a bit more. The Catalan has been an ambassador for Qatar 2022 and never offered many thoughts on Abu Dhabi's human rights record. Instead, he's acted painfully offended on the very rare occasions he's been questioned by journalists. It's for all these reasons that no account of modern football can be complete without a portrait of Guardiola himself. He is the figure everyone sought, but Manchester City got, anchoring their entire football identity to him.

Guardiola has been the face of the club since he arrived in 2016. Even on the occasions when he's been involved in flashpoints, such as in one tunnel confrontation against Antonio Conte's Chelsea, City have been desperate to keep his name out of the headlines. This is notionally sportswashing in the most highly specific form. It's as if Guardiola's place in football history granted this City prestige, although there's a counter-argument that the union diminishes his own greatness.

Manchester City have instead created an environment where Guardiola is left to think only about football. 'I have everything a manager could dream of,'[8] he has said. There isn't the 'oven' of Barcelona, as the City hierarchy put it, where a Catalan like Guardiola felt all of the pressure of his notoriously volatile boyhood club. There isn't the haughtiness of Bayern Munich, so convinced their way is the right way. There was only a pristine canvas at City, where every brush was at Guardiola's disposal. From 2015 to 2017, the club spent almost half a billion net on transfers to build the manager his perfect team. There had never been such expenditure exactly tailored to one coach. Even the dressing room was oval on his recommendation.[9] City director Brian Marwood described 'a ready-made environment for Guardiola'.[10]

Except, the manager then made his squad completely relearn the game. Guardiola's preferred term for his ideology is '*juego de posición*' – positional play – with a method to learn it initially involving splitting the pitch into 20 boxes.[11] His players then internalise that map, as well as their position relative to other areas, teammates, opposition and the ball. This was the source of so many passing moves that looked organic. It still takes a lot of mental effort, and Guardiola has been quick to discard players he feels would never understand it. Goalkeeper Joe Hart was one, with the manager insisting the club legend had to go. The other side of that, where Guardiola saw a player worth persevering with, was witnessed in John Stones. The young centre-half had been signed the year before the manager arrived, for £47.5 million, and initially lacked belief he had the necessary composure. Guardiola insisted the then 22-year-old ignore all criticism and all instructions from his youth. He was never to send the ball long. The message was the same to everyone: 'Don't worry about mistakes so long as you're doing what I want.'[12]

And there were big mistakes, especially in 2016–17, the first season the Catalan won nothing in his career. After a calamitous 4-2 defeat at Leicester City, Guardiola notoriously asked 'what is tackles?' It was seen as an admission of how he would have to adapt to the intensity of the Premier League. One of Guardiola's most fervent disciples, Xavi Hernandez, still insisted 'Pep will change English football'.[13]

That started with Stones. Within a year, he was the corner-stone of a treble team. Within seven, Stones excelled in the pivot role that Guardiola himself perfected as a player with Barcelona. Such symmetry looks seamless but comes from immense effort. Guardiola, in the words of many players, can be 'hard work'. His broad tactical plan is clear but his instructions for individuals can be complex, and delivered intensively. One of the crucial elements of his management, however, is specifically designed drills that deepen the players' understanding. If Guardiola sees an opposition side can be exploited on one flank, his staff concentrate on precisely the moves required until they're automatic. Discipline is naturally crucial, going down to the tiny margins with which Guardiola moved the tactics board. Players are punished if even a minute late for training, with weight scrutinised to the kilogram. Such minutiae are essential to Guardiola's maximal demands, as his pressing requires players running up to 12 kilometres a game. That can't be done indefinitely so the manager empowers fitness coach Lorenzo Buenaventura to tailor programmes that allow City to come to physical peaks in the crucial periods of December and April. Guardiola himself is obsessed with nutrition and injury prevention, drinking hot water after meals because he believes it aids digestion.[14]

He isn't close to the squad. Players never know where they stand, but know not to make jokes at the manager's expense. João Cancelo was seen as showing insufficient respect, so was one of many abruptly jettisoned. That is where the ideal environment aids the search for perfection in a way that's almost impossible elsewhere. When Guardiola quickly decided Claudio Bravo wasn't suitable as goalkeeper, having just discarded Hart, he was allowed to buy Ederson for £34.9 million. The manager especially adored how Ederson is capable of playing a long-range pass that can travel 80 yards just a half-metre off the ground.

Such obsessiveness is maybe best illustrated in how Guardiola devotes the same attention to match preparation regardless of opposition. He will confine himself to an almost spartan office, perhaps some incense burning, watching previous games and visualising the next. The Catalan will occasionally come out to jog his mind, sometimes barefoot. What follows is like a scene out of *The Office*. Guardiola will make eye contact with someone or wander into a communal area just staring into the distance, but then walk off without saying anything because he's so consumed in thought. Sergio Agüero told Lu Martin and Pol Ballus how he would 'piss himself laughing' at such moments.[15] This is why golf is for Guardiola what horseracing is for Sir Alex Ferguson. It is the only time when he is immersed in something enough that he can switch off from football. Some at City actually think Guardiola should be less obsessive with most games, and there are occasional dressing-room questions like 'what is he doing now?' They all know it's his greatest strength, though.

Eventually, as he put it in 2011, 'the flash of inspiration arrives . . . the moment that makes sense of my profession'.[16] That may feel a bit much when it's a League Cup game against Oxford United. That also explains how Guardiola's teams reach the level of relentlessness they do. In seven seasons from August 2017 to May 2024, City accumulated a massive 79.9 per cent of all available points in the Premier League – 638 of 798. Guardiola's side also won almost half of all major trophies they competed in, 13 of 28. These are returns never before seen in English football over periods so long. The 2022–23 treble of Premier League, FA Cup and Champions League suitably crowned a supreme level of dominance that was a fitting extension of the football itself. The principles of Guardiola's philosophy are his team using possession to expand the pitch when they have the ball, and then to constrict it to the smallest space possible when they don't. It is almost perfect control, much like the entire project at Manchester City. Guardiola's team have had by far the highest average possession in the Premier League, at 66.3 per cent for his first seven seasons according to FBREF. It amounted to death by a thousand passes for opposition, so many moves ending in a simple cut-back. No Premier League team has scored as many goals inside the box.

Guardiola would of course encourage individual flourishes within this, be they David Silva's divine control, Raheem Sterling's runs or – above all – Kevin De Bruyne's deliveries. Guardiola then enhanced all of that with his own insights. Fabian Delph was re-trained as a left-back. De Bruyne was nurtured to be one of the best players in the world, which was precisely what the manager told him he should be in their first ever meeting.[17] Guardiola showed the midfielder where to move to 'drive' games, as well as a new way of looking at the pitch.

As could be seen with such football, but was also said by the hierarchy of the manager's moods, Guardiola has 'very high highs'. There is a profound satisfaction if a performance goes as idealised. That's why the first title win was so vindicating. 'This kind of play, we can do it in England,'[18] Guardiola exclaimed after beating Manchester United 2-1 in December 2017. 'That's why I'm so happy . . .'

The other side is 'very low lows'. Guardiola takes defeat very badly, and he has suffered most in the competition he prizes most, the Champions League. The sight of the City manager dropping to his knees in anguish became strikingly common on European nights. In the week after an elimination, players wondered whether it would be OK to smile. It went beyond the meaning to the club. As with PSG, the owners knew a trophy of such prestige afforded unique legitimacy. As a Barcelona obsessive, though, Guardiola grew up with the European Cup seen as Real Madrid's trophy. They'd won it more than anyone else. This permanent testament to Real Madrid's greatness was also a persistent stage for Barcelona's worst moments. One was when Guardiola was a ball boy at the club, as Barcelona lost the 1986 final in Seville to Steaua Bucharest on penalties. When they finally won it for the first time as late as 1992, Guardiola echoed former Catalan president Josep Tarradellas when presenting the trophy to fans. 'Citizens of Catalonia, here I am,' proclaimed Tarradellas on his return from exile after the death of General Franco. 'Citizens of Catalonia,' Guardiola beamed, 'here it is.'

The Champions League was all the more tantalisingly elusive because knock-out football has a far greater element of chance. A manager obsessed with control often saw games go out of control in single bad moments. At City alone, a series of eliminations involved sudden flurries of goals conceded. It seemed to point to a core flaw that compounded Guardiola's propensity for ruminating on games to the extent that he seemed to think himself out of clarity. For the defeat to Liverpool in 2017–18, he went too open. For the next season's elimination against Tottenham Hotspur, he went too cautious. Guardiola then tried a five-man defensive system with Rodri and Fernandinho in the 2019–20 quarter-final loss to Lyon, only to not play any holding midfielders at all in the 2021 final against Chelsea. Thomas Tuchel, the opposing manager, was shocked when he saw the line-up. It was one of the few occasions that City players acknowledged Guardiola might 'overthink' big games.

Although he occasionally responded with fury to such defeats, the usual response was to withdraw into himself. Worsening his mood was the argument, which Guardiola was all too aware of, that both of his previous Champions League titles at Barcelona were won because of Leo Messi. It made the manager reluctant to move for the Argentinian even though the hierarchy were willing to sanction it. City did eventually sign the club's first true superstar in Erling Haaland but, until then, the Champions League failures seemed the one element that couldn't be controlled with money.

This was most visible in the culmination of all these factors, a 2021–22 semi-final elimination at Real Madrid. At 2-0 up in the 90th minute, City somehow conceded three goals in five minutes. Real Madrid secured their 14th Champions League title, in what was seen as a defiant victory for football heritage. That semi-final comeback was their third in succession, all coming against the major clubs owned by states or oligarchs: PSG, Chelsea, Manchester City. 'That's what happens when you wear this shirt,' said Rodrygo, who scored two goals in stoppage time against City.

Such romantic notions were vaporised the following season. Three of the most successful clubs in European Cup history, in Bayern Munich, Internazionale and Real Madrid, were just swept away. It was all part of an unrelenting run to the treble, where City went 25 games unbeaten in all competitions. On that run, their last challengers in Liverpool were thrashed 4-1. Their new challengers in Arsenal were thrashed 4-1. Any sense of sporting tension was brutalised. In the 4-0 semi-final win over Real Madrid, it took 24 minutes for the Spanish side to even complete a pass in City's half, and that was a kick-off after Bernardo Silva's first goal.

Despite that, there was credence in Guardiola's comments that such matches were 'the flip of a coin'. This time against Real Madrid they scored early, but it could have gone the other way, as was the case in previous seasons and then in 2023–24 between the

two sides. The point was that putting perhaps the greatest manager ever in ideal conditions was always going to make it likely
they eventually got it right. They instead got it perfect. Haaland,
signed for a clause of £51 million but also huge agent fees of £31
million, aided that with more than his 52 goals.[19] The striker ensured Guardiola had to work his tactics back from that position,
offering instant clarity to the team. A clear-the-air in the dressing
room helped, after Guardiola questioned his team's hunger by
calling them 'happy flowers'. He won his players back around, as
his vision always did.

In the Champions League final against Internazionale, Rodri
scored the only goal. 'Now, nobody asks me if we will win the
Champions League,' Guardiola said. The talk was instead how
he'd become the first manager to win the treble with two different
clubs. He'd finally emulated Barcelona. 'It's like watching the same
team,'[20] Begiristain enthused to a friend after a 6-0 over Chelsea
in 2019. 'He's done it again!' It wasn't seen the same way, though.
There didn't feel the same emotional legacy as with that 2008–11
Barcelona. That was partly because of another more complicated
legacy, as well as a landmark beyond trebles. This was the first time
a state-linked club had won the Champions League. It was part of
other reservations related to off-field issues. Privately, Guardiola
was understood to be affected by this, given he is very much concerned with his own historical legacy and the idea of records. Late
in the season, the manager closed one team talk with a clear point.
'I want my warriors,' the Catalan roared. 'Because everything we
have won, guys, has been on the pitch, always!'[21]

In some ways, one mistake the Manchester City project made
was becoming almost flawless. Sporting achievement is enriched
by jeopardy, but there have been many achievements where

Guardiola's side have barely felt in trouble at all. A perception of financial advantage fostered growing unease within the game, which festered into outright fury with Football Leaks and a series of Financial Fair Play cases. The 2023 Champions League final and 2023–24 Premier League were won amid the uncertainty of a Premier League investigation over alleged rule breaches, although there was a feeling the February announcement motivated the squad.

No other Premier League club offered official congratulations on their social media after either the treble victory or four-in-a-row. Some at City argue this is just envy. It does go beyond self-interest, though. Football figures who greatly respect Guardiola lament what a 'shame' it is that feats so momentous were quickly forgotten. Chris Davidson believes it almost reflects a crucial cultural difference. 'The Gulf view would be "we created the best club ever, everyone should love it", but that might be a miscalculation. It's maybe a lack of a cultural understanding of the underdog.'

That touches on another debate about City's legacy, and why a sense of sporting jeopardy is so important. It fosters drama, which creates narrative. All of the most revered sporting feats express something greater than just some talented athletes overachieving. Manchester United's 1998–99 treble was about a group of locally produced players evoking the club's emotional history in the Champions League. Guardiola's with Barcelona was about the triumph of a philosophy with a new generation. What was City's legacy? It was essentially a senior royal looking around at what worked in football, paying for it, and investing as much money as possible until that paid off. That's not a story, it's an equation. If it did have greater meaning, it was only the victory of politics in football, especially with how it happened in the same season as the Qatar World Cup. It otherwise felt processed, or industrialised.

It's another reason why Guardiola has become so singularly important to City's legacy. His philosophy is a key step in football's most admired ideological lineage, going back to Ajax, which lends the project a part in something greater. But it's only lending it. Guardiola's part really belongs to Barcelona. That has been appropriated, to produce a much more expensive re-creation. That isn't unique to football, either. In the midst of City's treble celebrations, Jack Grealish posted a photo of himself with arms outstretched in the rain. His caption, to much amusement, was 'hang it in the Loooouvre'.[22] Which one? Abu Dhabi has its own branch of the Louvre. The squad is as expensive as the world's most expensive art. The net spend from the summer of 2015 to January 2018 was £441.65 million, which had represented the most ever paid out in putting a team together, even going beyond PSG's in the time around Neymar's signing. Only Chelsea across 2022 and 2023 spent more, but they didn't go close in terms of wages. By 2019–20, City's accounts revealed they were by far the highest payers in English football, at £351 million a year.[23] Other clubs felt City started to make decisions on opposition requirements as much as their own. Although Guardiola did want a striker in 2021, Tottenham Hotspur executives felt interest in Harry Kane was dropped when no one else bid for him. Old Trafford counterparts believed City only bought Grealish because Manchester United were close to signing him. The playmaker started just 22 of 38 Premier League games that season. Grealish said that was due to learning Guardiola's system. One rival coach complained 'only City can sign a £100 million player and he's on the bench'.

It was similarly noted how City were the only Premier League club never to lose a star to Barcelona or Real Madrid. De Bruyne was repeatedly wanted but Al Mubarak declared that a 'red line'.

The Belgian's importance made it all the more remarkable that City won the treble in 2018–19 despite the midfielder appearing in only half their Premier League games. Guardiola enjoyed such depth he could rotate a series of players signed for £30–80 million. and retain the same performance level.

Such expenditure isn't a guarantee of success, of course. United were proof of that. Such expenditure guided by the game's best intelligence on a state scale, however, gives as good a chance as possible. This was the cost of the Guardiola era for the lifeblood of the sport: competitiveness. City might offer great football but it isn't necessarily good for football. The threshold to even challenge is significantly raised. City, as Guardiola himself put it, 'destroyed the Premier League'.[24] One chief executive complained how clubs can't really think of consistently competing, since you probably require at least 90 points every season. That can be done once or twice but is very difficult to make a trend in the way Guardiola has. He enjoys fewer variables. Rivals almost have to just put themselves in the best position for the rare occasions that Guardiola has an off-season. Jürgen Klopp just couldn't allow himself to think this way, though. His Liverpool were quickly cast as the anti-City, especially since the German was one of the few major figures to speak critically on state-owned clubs.[25] Klopp had already represented almost an anti-Guardiola in terms of tactics, as his *gegenpressing* literally meant counter-pressing. That created a raucousness that contrasted with City's smoothness, producing some of the greatest games of the era. The rivalry was further fired by a genuine enmity between the clubs.

There is admittedly an absurdity to an establishment club like Liverpool, owned by venture capitalists like Fenway Sports Group, being cast as upstarts. This is nevertheless modern football. Liverpool had a similar cutting-edge approach to City as well as an era-defining manager, but just didn't have the same scale. This was almost the tragic element of Klopp's era, that displays how high the threshold is. Even allowing for the club's status in football's 1 per cent, the German drastically overperformed. His Liverpool got over 90 points in three different seasons, claiming 85.9 per cent of all points over 2018–19 and 2019–20. In another era, this would have been a glorious dynasty to go with their Champions League victory. In this era, it was enough for only one league title. City twice beat Liverpool by a point. In 2018–19, it literally came down to millimetres. Stones cleared the ball off the line at a crucial moment during City's pulsating 2-1 home win over Liverpool. Klopp's side pushed themselves to their own outer limits and it wasn't enough. City always just had more, as they showed by coming back from 2-0 down to beat Aston Villa 3-2 on the final day in 2021–22. It was the same when City claimed 89 points to finish ahead of Arsenal in 2022–23 and then, when Arsenal rose to that number the next season, City just went to 91. Some at Anfield were glad another club were seeing what it was like.

Vincent Kompany said he was surprised Liverpool went to such levels, but that he always felt City had greater depth.[26] That maybe has greater meaning than intended. In the decade before the start of the 2020–21 season, an analysis by Nick Harris revealed City benefited from £1.7 billion in commercial income.[27] This outstripped all of Liverpool, Arsenal and Chelsea, who averaged £1.1 billion. A major difference was that, as a consequence of the ownership, City had numerous sponsors from the UAE. By 2019–20, despite a decade of success and a superstar manager, UAE-based companies still accounted for 56 per cent of commercial revenue. Happily, all of Etihad Airways, e& (formerly known as Etisalat telecoms), Experience Abu Dhabi, Emirates Palace Mandarin Oriental, Aldar of Abu Dhabi, Healthpoint of Abu Dhabi and Noon of Abu Dhabi share the club's vision for commercial development.[28] Other sponsors are not based in Abu Dhabi but still have links to the emirate. Korea's Nexen Tire have a memorandum of understanding with Mubadala Investment Fund, which is run by City chairman Al Mubarak.[29] A statement on Mubadala's website said the fund had made a 'direct investment into Nexen'.[30] Illustrating a web of business relationships, City Football Group (CFG) employees appear on the boards of businesses that sponsor the club. City director Marty Edelman is on the board of Aldar, Soriano a director at Wix. Such a network of deals, as well as the opaque nature of ownership in Gulf autocracies, has led to agitation among rivals.[31] The argument frequently made in Premier League meetings is that, since City are presented as a vehicle for Abu Dhabi's image, they might not have benefited from such income if dealing with arms-length companies.

As early as 2018–19, City were looking for a shirt deal worth £50–60 million, a rate usually charged by Real Madrid and Barcelona. City's justification was that they had developed the most powerful intellectual property in football. Soriano spoke of how he'd just show potential sponsors a web page with stats like most points and goals.[32] Companies didn't feel the same, and were put off by the price. Etihad Airways remained the shirt sponsor into 2023–24, stretching back to 2009. City similarly pale in terms of broadcasting audience compared to the legacy clubs, according to studies conducted by football economist David Forrest. Manchester United and Liverpool generally raised audiences by 75 per cent.

Despite that, City's commercial revenue outstripped every single English rival in Deloitte's Football Money League 2024.[33] The club are admittedly described as so forward-thinking that they make other commercial departments look dated. City are especially embracing new technological markets and opportunities, such as virtual reality.

It's possible that CFG as an idea might be the most disruptive innovation of all, though. Few of the multi-club groups that have followed can match the influence of their refashioned blue shirts – although it isn't all positive for the clubs purchased. With ownership transferred to the Abu Dhabi-registered and Mansour-owned Newton Investment and Development in 2021, four clubs on three different continents have been national champions in the time since alone. They include Melbourne City, Mumbai City, New York City and Yokohama, with Girona becoming the 'fairytale' of La Liga as they pushed for the 2023–24 title. The upstart Catalan club are 47 per cent owned by CFG, 35 per cent owned by Marcelo Claure and 16 per cent owned by Girona Football Group. The latter are led by Pep Guardiola's brother Pere, while Claure is president of Club Bolivar, a Bolivian team who became a partner of CFG. He has also been executive chairman of City sponsors WeWork, who have had a partnership with Abu Dhabi tech company Hub71, whose other partners include Mubadala.[34] Claure has meanwhile been chief operating officer of Softbank, who have benefited from a $15 billion investment from Mubadala. Girona were initially planned as a 'finishing school' for CFG young players, but such loan arrangements were inevitably criticised by Tebas. At one football summit, he publicly outlined how La Liga made Girona register players at a higher value than they had been, to comply with the competition's stringent financial rules. Spanish clubs have their budgets centrally set by percentage of income, with this recalculation ensuring Girona had 4 per cent less money to spend on wages.

'Girona put the five players that were being loaned from Manchester City on the books for a certain amount of money, which we didn't believe was a real amount of money that these players should be on the books for in terms of their salaries,'[35] Tebas said. This was categorically denied by CFG, who threatened legal action. Among the players was Douglas Luiz, who was for a long time one of the group's few elite successes with how he rose to play for Aston Villa. That was until 2024, when Sávio became the first player to progress through the group's various clubs to sign for Manchester City. He had actually been Troyes' record signing, but never played for them, as he went on loan to Girona. Such a low return wasn't quite living up to Soriano's 'make-or-buy' policy. 'It's like venture capital in that if you invest 10 million each in 10 players, you just need one to get to the top who is going to be worth 100 million,' he told the *Guardian*.

The description of young players as 'venture capital' has raised alarms within the game. It was the phrase used in other internal documents revealed by *Der Spiegel*.[36] Although the club has been praised for a fine coaching education, that education can appear to view players as commodities. Young recruits are given a category based on their potential, which they are not told about, such as 'emerging talent player'. Target sale prices are then set for certain points in their career. If they are not seen as good enough for the Premier League, a pathway will be mapped through CFG until there is eventually an external bidder and players become numbers on the books.

Separate to that, established players and staff are moved around the group freely, leading many rivals to see the entire project's primary value as spreading costs to get around FFP rules. Tebas, of course, says precisely this. 'They hide these costs elsewhere,' he claims. CFG have always strenuously denied this, and it should be stressed that only non-playing and coaching staff wages can be split across groups.[37] Nevertheless, while Manchester City contributed £713 million of CFG's record revenue of £877 million in 2022–23, the losses of £127 million before tax added up to total losses from the group of £1.4 billion.[38]

There are still other football benefits that cut back to Soriano's original idea of franchising an identity. Since City have never had United's international fanbase, the project allows them to develop it at source. Having a local City-affiliated club while Haaland appears on television in sky blue can sway a lot of young fans, as football's global popularity only accelerates. They are now thinking way beyond Manchester or even Europe, and want to just create this global entity. City executives claimed vindication when 10 per cent of CFG was sold to US private equity firm Silver Lake for £389 million in November 2019, increasing the overall value to £3.73 billion.[39] Less than a year later, Silver Lake received a $2 billion investment from Mubadala.

City have also tried to increase income in other ways. Soriano was for a long time viewed as one of the main drivers in attempts to change broadcast money distribution in favour of the Premier League's 'big six'. The Catalan was viewed as especially 'arrogant' by other clubs, as resentment grew.[40] José Mourinho grumbled to one executive when at Manchester United that he was up against 'a state', in a sentiment that was widely echoed. All of this would soon be given a release. Or, rather, a leak.

Elite football is filled with egos who think they are invincible but, between December 2016 and November 2018, many were fretting about what was coming next. This was due to a series of sensational news reports by media partners of the European Investigative Collaborations, all based on terabytes of information fed by whistleblower Rui Pinto. He was the activist who created the Football Leaks website, which had quite an opening declaration. 'This project aims to disclose the hidden part of football. Unfortunately, the sport we love so much is rotten and it's time to say enough is enough.' Over those 23 months, a number of big players and clubs were embarrassed as details were revealed on everything from transfers to tax affairs. It was probably City who felt the most lasting effects. In the long term, the leaks brought investigations from UEFA and the Premier League that have hung over the club. In the short term, it changed the perception of the project. Leaks made the links between Manchester City and the Abu Dhabi state transparent, to prompt the first ever time any human rights body – in this case Amnesty – used the phrase 'sportswashing' about the ownership.[41] Up to then, commentary had been rare. Guardiola, of all people, had inadvertently invited scrutiny a few months before the leaks. The manager had taken to wearing a yellow ribbon in support of Catalan independence leaders, most visibly at the 2017–18 League Cup final. Since Guardiola spoke about political freedoms and 'the humanity', reporter Rob Harris asked him how he reconciled that with his gratitude to Sheikh Mansour, a leader in a country 'criticised for not respecting freedoms'. The City manager gave a garbled answer about how 'every country decides the way they want to live for themselves'.

It was all the worse for the club that attention came through their most celebrated figure, since the ownership had previously been so conscious of not inviting criticism that they didn't pursue the construction of a stadium in New York. Leaked internal emails revealed a fear of a 'very public fight' on 'vulnerabilities' such as 'gay [rights], wealth, women, Israel'.[42] In this case, it brought some criticism for Guardiola's perceived hypocrisy, but the pervading sense was still that Mansour was a private billionaire.[43] That changed with Football Leaks, which portrayed the image of something much more sophisticated. It wasn't long until 'state-run' and 'sportswashing' were as much part of the game's language as 'Etihad Stadium'.

Scrutiny even came on other purported benefits of Abu Dhabi investment into Manchester, such as the construction empire developed from 2013. As late as June 2023, shortly after City's treble, Manchester mayor Andy Burnham praised the club owners as 'huge partners', imploring people to compare East Manchester to photos from 30 years ago.[44] When pressed on Abu Dhabi human rights issues in the *Pod Save the UK* show, Burnham said he had to judge on 'what they do to improve life' in Manchester. That benign view had already been challenged by a 2019 *Sunday Times* report titled 'Manchester, the city that sold out to Abu Dhabi'.[45] It opened by detailing how references to the council 'selling out' to UAE had been removed from a commemoration of the Peterloo massacre, where 18 people died protesting for parliamentary reform. That reflected sensitivity over a business relationship that saw ADUG develop a £330 million-plus property portfolio through the leasing of publicly owned land, mostly near the stadium. It was a familiar story, since Manchester's regeneration had stalled after the financial crash. While council leader Sir Richard Leese gushed about ADUG's 'support', the newspaper reported that the council received none of the £10 million annual rent yields, with money only coming back through 'long-term profit-sharing arrangements'. These were criticised as 'sweetheart deals', especially since the land was not offered on the market via a tendering process. What's more, the developments from Manchester Life – as the partnership was called – didn't meet the council's own policy objectives over affordable housing. None of the rents were lower than 80 per cent of the local market rate. John Leech, of the Liberal Democrats, told the newspaper he would question the deal's 'benefit to the people'. All of this came amid a homelessness crisis as, by 2022, the council admitted that 4,000 of the city's children sleep in temporary accommodation every night.[46]

So, while the photos might have shown an area more pleasant to walk through, it coincided with tents spreading around the city.[47] A prominent Abu Dhabi royal had meanwhile extended the purchase of a football club to a joint venture with the British state structure.[48] Football historian David Goldblatt bluntly describes it all as 'a subsidy to a foreign state'. Leese wrote a letter to the *Sunday Times* complaining that the report didn't reflect the benefits 'to the city and its people'.[49] And yet a first thorough study of the Manchester Life scheme, conducted by the University of Sheffield in 2022 and titled 'Manchester Offshored', painted an even worse picture that included a reference to 'city-washing'.[50] The study was 'unable to identify any income received by the council from its joint venture stakes' despite being exposed to the risks. It similarly outlines how, under the terms of the deal, the council allowed ADUG to hold all land leaseholds, property assets and income rights through subsidiaries registered in 'the secrecy jurisdiction of Jersey'. The report details how the venture's management company paid only £4,000 Corporation Tax in 2021 on rental income of £10.1 million. The assessment of the researchers was that Manchester City Council 'sold the family silver too cheap' in a deal that 'represents a transfer of public wealth to private hands that is difficult to justify as prudent', while raising 'key questions of transparency, accountability and local democracy'.

In 2017, CFG named their new Strategic Development Advisor as the late Sir Howard Bernstein, who was central to the council's regeneration plans.[51] The Abu Dhabi links were meanwhile beginning to come into full view. Three weeks after *Der Spiegel*'s leaks, British academic Matthew Hedges was shockingly given a life sentence by the UAE for spying, his trial lasting five minutes with no lawyer present.[52] Hedges was quickly pardoned after 'intense lobbying' by the British Foreign Office. Even broadcaster Piers Morgan argued that every City fan should boycott games until Sheikh Mansour intervened.[53] Human rights groups began to draw attention to political prisoners in the UAE through this prism, displaying the more complicated nature of the sportswashing concept. One was human rights lawyer Dr Mohammed Al-Roken, whose 2011 calls for democratic reforms saw him convicted in a mass trial of activists known as the UAE94 and given a 10-year prison sentence that hasn't yet ended.[54] Another was Ahmed Mansoor, whose campaigning saw him jailed and kept in solitary confinement from 2017 for charges that included 'insulting the status and prestige of the UAE and its symbols'.[55] On 25 November 2023, during one of those pulsating Manchester City–Liverpool matches, Amnesty International flew a plane over the Etihad with the message 'UAE – Free Ahmed Mansoor'. Even Haaland was asked about the UAE imprisoning their own citizens in one of his first international calls up for Norway after joining City.

'I think the words you are using are too strong,' Haaland responded.[56] Such incidents are often put forward as why sportswashing doesn't work, because it raises these awkward questions, but the opposite is really true. The questions are washed away amid a sea of games. It doesn't stop anyone wanting to watch a box-office star like Haaland for City. Players are often spared criticism of such transfers on the basis they have a short career, and Frank Conde Tangberg of Amnesty Norway stresses they shouldn't 'have a responsibility in terms of international human rights'. 'But nor does that mean they should put their head in the sand.' Most don't realise or care about such questions. Players generally only look at the wages and possibility for trophies. Kompany, in contrast to the studies on the construction empire, praised the 'phenomenal' impact of the project.[57]

If anyone in football discussed other sides of this, there was usually a common response. When Klopp said 'there are three clubs in world football who can do what they want financially', an anonymous briefing linked to City described the Liverpool manager's comments as 'borderline xenophobic'.[58] It wasn't the first time similar defences had been propagated. When Tebas referenced City and PSG as 'playthings of a state' in May 2019,[59] Al Mubarak described it as 'ugly' while stating 'there's something deeply wrong in bringing ethnicity into the conversation'.[60] Tebas hadn't actually brought ethnicity into it at all. Klopp meanwhile referenced 'three clubs' because there were only three major clubs owned by states, all with fossil fuel economies. McGeehan describes such responses as consistent with Abu Dhabi's general strategy of attacking criticism 'as the best form of defence', since both were initially set by Simon Pearce.[61]

Istanbul was where many roads converged. That wasn't quite literal, since the actual travel to the Ataturk Stadium for the 2022–23 Champions League final was a shambles.[62] UEFA received huge criticism for the organisation. The federation still allowed their showpiece to become a showcase for what football had evolved into. Turkish president Recep Erdoğan at last had his grand event, at the same time that his government was being criticised for 'deteriorating democracy'.[63] Watching on was Sheikh Mansour, attending just his second Manchester City match, but more significant was the man beside him. There was his elder brother, the ruler of the UAE, Mohamed bin Zayed Al-Nahyan. Those in the lounge say they barely interacted with anyone else, although partly because there were more 'security staff than VIPs'. There was greater interaction months later, as CFG announced a collaborative agreement with İstanbul Başakşehir, who are viewed as being aligned to Erdoğan. On the night, they watched Rodri score. Everyone else saw the power in full glare.

After the victory, the UAE Minister of Interior and Deputy Prime Minister Saif bin Zayed Al Nahyan put up a social media post that lauded 'His Highness Sheikh Mohammed bin Zayed' for how this achievement was secured 'under your patronage and presence'.[64] He then congratulated Mansour before saying 'congratulations to all Emiratis and all football fans'. The video he posted as part of it then focused on Mohammed bin Zayed. By that point, even the British Foreign Office were discussing developments related to Manchester City, but for reasons that were far less celebrated.[65]

As everyone in football pored over *Der Spiegel*'s jaw-dropping re-ports in the first week of November 2018, a widespread feeling was that City and PSG were 'finally' going to be punished after years of suspicion. That was only after shock at the language used.[66]

Simon Pearce: 'Of course, we can do what we want.'[67]

Ferran Soriano: 'We will need to fight this . . . and do it in a way that is not visible, or we will be pointed out as the global enemies of football.'[68]

Then, most callously, there was chief legal advisor Simon Cliff on the death of UEFA FFP investigator Jean-Luc Dehaene through illness in early 2014: '1 down, 6 to go.'[69]

That last leak especially hurt those who worked on the Investigatory Chamber, since they had got to know Dehaene and his family. If there was 'almost a personification of the club with the values we hold as Abu Dhabi',[70] as Al Mubarak once claimed, what was this? City have never commented on the content of the emails other than to repeat the same line about how 'the attempt to damage the club's reputation is organised and clear'. There was no dispute about the authenticity, but City say the emails were taken 'out of context'.[71] Rui Pinto denied the club's view that the leaks were 'criminally obtained'.[72]

More consequential was the detailed content that allegedly showed manipulation of finances through backdated and inflated sponsorship deals with companies related to the owners in Abu Dhabi, in order to avoid breaches of rules. Investigators for the FFP case in 2014 found the new information 'incredibly frustrating', as they felt it was clear they had been deliberately misled. They had already called for a Champions League ban without this. The suspicion within the game was that funds were directly coming from the owners.

Now, a number of other lines in the leaks stood out. Among them were Finance Director Andrew Widdowson writing in an email how money is 'routed through the partners and they then forward on to us'.[73] In April 2010, around eight months after Michel Platini had first presented plans for FFP, there was an email from Simon Pearce regarding a £15 million-a-year sponsorship deal with Aabar. 'As we discussed, the annual direct obligation for Aabar is GBP 3 million,'[74] Pearce wrote. 'The remaining 12 million GBP requirement will come from alternative sources provided by His Highness.' The last line led to the primary allegation, that equity from Mansour had been disguised as sponsorship.

During the 2012–13 season, Chief Financial Officer Jorge Chumillas wrote in an internal email that the club 'will have a shortfall of 9.9m pounds in order to comply with UEFA FFP'.[75] Chumillas wrote that 'the only solution left would be an additional amount of AD [Abu Dhabi] sponsorship revenues that covers this gap'. So, Pearce suggested, they 'could do a backdated deal for the next two years' – 'paid up front'.[76] Ten days after the just-finished season, Chumillas suggested that the sponsorship contracts for the same campaign should be adjusted so Etihad was now to pay £1.5 million more, Aabar £0.5 million more and the Abu Dhabi tourist authority a surplus of £5.5 million.[77] If this looked like a club setting the budget of sponsors, it was there the response 'of course, we can do what we want' came.[78] More detail seemed to be revealed about this in an email sent by Pearce to Chumillas on 29 August 2013, as reported by the YouTube documentary, *Britain's Biggest Football Scandal?* It was in response to a question about how additional sponsorship money could be accounted for. 'Jorge, we have to show that the money is required for the ADUG P&L but we can't show the payment routes,'[79] Pearce wrote. 'So it's funding income that we should call partner funding and we should show the total and timing requirements for receipt, but we should not include any more detail than that.'

A further email, as detailed in the YouTube documentary, has then Chief Financial Officer Graham Wallace writing to Pearce stating that what they 'therefore need is that the money we are attributing to Etisalat, [redacted] and Etihad, as shown, are physically remitted to us by those businesses, as opposed to a combined receipt of partner/equity funding all remitted in one lump'.[80] 'It is important for us to effect this for audit purposes,'[81] Wallace wrote.

Just weeks before the initial UEFA investigation even started, in December 2013, Pearce wrote an email saying 'Etihad's direct contribution remains constant at 8m'.[82] That was when the airline's annual sponsoring obligation was £35 million. A 2015 email from Chumillas to Pearce about the Etihad sponsorship then stated: 'Please note that out of those 67.5m pounds, 8m pounds should be funded directly by Etihad and 59.5 by ADUG.'[83] Also notable was that the email was sent in 2015, after City's initial FFP fine from a settlement with UEFA.

There was similarly evidence of a 'creative solution', merrily called 'Project Longbow', which Cliff explained in an email was 'the weapon the English used to beat the French at Crécy and Agincourt'.[84] 'The French' in this case represented UEFA president Michel Platini, whose legacy idea was FFP. One scheme took around £40 million off the wage bill by selling City players' image rights to an offshore company called Fordham Sports Management, which then paid the players from those rights.[85] The club was allegedly then able to announce income of €30 million for selling the marketing rights, with the closed loop completed by ADUG paying Fordham the money needed.[86] Two experts brought in were Jonathan Rowland and his father David, an investment specialist who had been a Conservative Party donor. *Der Spiegel* reported how the ownership of Fordham went through the British Virgin Islands and the Rowland family trust. 'We need to know that AD is fully behind it this is the most important thing,'[87] Jonathan Rowland wrote to Pearce in April 2013. The response was: 'Regarding the ongoing operating costs, every year we will send in advance the cash of approximately 11 million.'

The 2014 settlement between UEFA and City didn't name Fordham, but analysts from PwC later noted how it looked 'a very good deal' for the club when auditing for UEFA. By the time of the leaks, the initial investigators felt it was obvious why bank records hadn't been supplied in 2014. Tebas was typically the most outspoken critic. La Liga had already made a complaint to UEFA in 2017, arguing that City had 'uncommonly high commercial revenue', with several sponsors 'directly controlled' by the UAE.[88] Tebas was now strident, saying it was 'crystal clear' that both City and PSG were 'making dirty tricks'.[89] Executives at other clubs were meanwhile pointing to income City were alleged to have made from the deals investigated and comparing them to transfer fees paid for players, arguing this laid the platform even for seasons not covered by the leaks. UEFA later estimated it was £204 million for the four years between 2012 and 2016.[90]

On the day that City completed the domestic treble by eviscerating Watford 6-0 in the 2019 FA Cup final, Guardiola was even asked if he had received additional third-party payments, in the way the leaks had alleged about predecessor Roberto Mancini. The Catalan was visibly furious. 'Honestly, do you think I deserve to have this type of question, the day we won the treble, did I receive money?' The controversy prompted further debate about FFP, as well the counterpoint that anyone who disagreed should have just lobbied for change, which UEFA were actually considering. This was all a sideshow. The eventual UEFA and Premier League investigations into the club, both confirmed by 2019, were actually about something much more serious than FFP. They were about fraud, 'truthful reporting' of required information and whether club directors had wilfully misled football authorities.[91] City vociferously insist on their innocence, mirroring the immense strength of feeling about it in the rest of the game. A story had started that distilled so many of the issues defining and dividing twenty-first-century football.

In lighter moments, investigators couldn't help but laugh at the differences between words and actions. Manchester City had stated that the club 'welcomes a formal UEFA investigation' in order to prove the 'accusation of financial irregularities are entirely false'.[92] They just didn't act especially welcoming. The Club Financial Control Body (CFCB), who were investigating for UEFA under statutes that called for assistance, found the club repeatedly obstructive. City's justification was the legal principle that the information was 'hacked or stolen'[93] and that the time had expired on some of the allegations.[94] The *New York Times* reported that one of the investigating team discovered a tracking device had been attached to his car.[95] There was no evidence it had anything to do with the case, but it contributed to an atmosphere of tension and paranoia. Some investigators worried about scrutinising an autocratic state, and many major accounting firms were unwilling to work on the case as they didn't want to affect relationships in the Gulf. UEFA ended up using an individual in Noel Lindsay, with the Court of Arbitration for Sport later describing how the CFCB had 'limited investigative means'. Against that, City had three firms of solicitors and two Queen's Counsels. The club even tried to block the case at CAS after early media reports said the investigation could lead to a Champions League ban, on the basis that leaks undermined its integrity.[96] The attempts were dismissed.[97]

It wasn't all tension, mind. In November 2019, UEFA president Aleksander Čeferin attended Manchester City's Champions League home match with Shakhtar Donetsk as a guest of Al Mubarak.[98] Soriano later made a point of differentiating the investigators from UEFA as an institution, saying the body 'is much bigger than this FFP chamber'.[99] There were nevertheless periods when UEFA were getting multiple legal letters from different firms. It was described as completely different to PSG, who co-operated, and eventually accepted their sponsorship deals were related parties.

City never accepted anything, so their case never went as far as whether the sponsors were related parties. That took the club's legal team aback, to the point they sent letters of complaint. The feeling was this was what they were geared up to fight. Investigators thought the issue was a 'rabbit hole', since it didn't really matter whether sponsors were related if the question was over whether the sponsors hadn't actually paid the money to the club in three years.

Over six months, the CFCB assiduously went over the six leaked emails downloaded from *Der Spiegel*'s website, and cross-examined City's hierarchy. Requests for more documents were blocked. The investigation centred on two main deals.[100] One was with Etisalat, who had an arrangement with the club from 2012 onwards, and for which there was more information. On City's own admission, ADUG 'caused' for £30 million to be paid by a third party on behalf of the telecom company in 2012 and 2013. Etisalat didn't actually pay anything until 2015. It was later alleged that this was paid by a person named 'Jaber Mohamed', who a Manchester City lawyer stated was 'a person in the business of providing financial and brokering services to commercial entities in the UAE'. This was first reported in 2023 by the YouTube documentary, which also published details of the unreleased Adjudicatory Chamber report for the first time.[101] The latter adds that 'the obvious question, not answered at any point in the club's submission and evidence, [is] why either Etisalat or ADUG should have needed any financial assistance from a broker in paying the Etisalat sponsorship liabilities'. City hadn't even concluded a contract with Etisalat until 2015 but one had been agreed in principle. The payments were still recorded in City's financial statements – as provided to the English FA for UEFA's licensing process – as sponsorship.

The Adjudicatory Chamber concluded that this was 'disguised equity funding'.[102] City's defence was that Etisalat had reimbursed the £30 million in 2015 and that these payments were properly accounted for because they were credited against invoices to the telecoms company. Another obvious question is, given City's insistence these were not related parties, why a club would allow a sponsor to enter this kind of arrangement but continue to enjoy the rights? Additionally, UEFA had entered into the 2014 settlement agreement – which fixed the value of the Etisalat sponsorship and acknowledged it – on the assumption that it had been properly paid for. The second example centred on the allegation that ADUG also funded the sponsorship from Etihad, and the emails reported by *Der Spiegel* that were alleged to show the airline was paying only £8 million of sponsorships worth £35 million, £65 million and £67.5 million from 2012–13, 2013–14 and 2015–16, respectively. The rest was argued to come from ADUG.

The CFCB only had emails in this case, not accounting information, but found the evidence credible because Etihad had made two separate payments for the 2015–16 sponsorship worth £67.5 million that tallied with the amounts set out in the email. Since City refused to hand over further emails or allow relevant individuals to give evidence, representing a failure to co-operate, the chamber was entitled in Swiss law to infer the same patterns of behaviour as with Etisalat.

In relation to a deal with Aabar, the CFCB were struck by the line used by Pearce that £12 million from a £15 million sponsorship would come from 'alternative sources provided by his highness'.[103] Pearce denied any wrongdoing and said the 'alternative sources' were 'grants' made available by the Abu Dhabi Tourist Authority and that 'his highness' was not Mansour but another senior royal. It was never explained who this was. As regards Chumillas' line about the structuring of payments through Etihad, Pearce said that his chief financial officer was incorrect and that appeared to reflect his continuous misunderstanding on the source of the funds.[104] UEFA noted that this misunderstanding was never corrected.

The initial outcome, on Valentine's Day of 2020, was a two-year Champions League ban and €30 million fine for 'serious breaches' of FFP regulations.[105] It was also outlined that City had breached regulations by failing to co-operate. The Adjudicatory Chamber's report, according to the YouTube documentary, said the club did not truthfully declare its sponsorship income.[106] It also said they were comfortably satisfied the leaked emails were authentic. The description was 'a sophisticated, thoughtful and fundamental attempt to circumvent or violate the financial fair play rules'. It was for that reason the punishment had been the harshest ever handed out, in order to 'protect the integrity of UEFA club competition'.[107] UEFA informed City of their verdict around 2 p.m. in the afternoon and, amid the initial fury, the club rushed to tell Guardiola and the players before the news leaked. The squad was stunned, since the feeling had been the case would just amount to a fine. Executives insisted the ban would be overturned. City had already made it clear to UEFA they would respond as aggressively as required. No one requested to leave, although the club feared players could be worried about how their achievements might be delegitimised. Guardiola immediately made it known he would stay, even if City were 'in League Two', standing by his long-asserted 'trust' in the club.[108] The Catalan reaffirmed a message to his players that would become familiar, that they just had to keep showing it on the pitch. The Abu Dhabi hierarchy were understood to be furious. Headlines about cheating weren't good for soft power. Suspicion reigned. City had already noted how PSG had escaped sanctions in 2019, while assembling 'a dossier' on the financial dealings of rivals.[109] The club's official statement was just as biting when the news was announced, stating they were 'disappointed but not surprised' before criticising a 'flawed and consistently leaked process' and the apparent conflict of interest of 'a case initiated by UEFA, prosecuted by UEFA and judged by UEFA'.[110]

Tebas of course had his say, which was 'better later than never'.[111] The 'outcome' was still one of many moments when it felt the case was actually never-ending. City were already preparing to go to CAS. Soriano similarly stated that, in providing what they believed was 'irrefutable evidence', the club 'did co-operate with this process'. That assertion was one of the few that CAS went against.

In contrast to all the emotion around the CAS case, the hearing largely occurred in the most sterile surroundings possible. It took place on 8–10 June 2020, amid restrictions enforced because of the Covid-19 pandemic. City's team still needed more social distancing space. They had 11 lawyers and one expert witness, compared to UEFA's four representatives, with two British counsel attending by video call. The governing body's defence team was still more sparse than it might have been. Although the CFCB discipline the clubs independently, they are not the party that argues at CAS. That reverts to UEFA's in-house legal team.[112]

CAS has always occupied a curious place in the sporting legal infrastructure. It is seen as suitable for binary issues like doping, but not for complex cases where it simply can't commit the time that a high-court trial can. The European Court of Justice rarely pays attention to its judgments, and the general feeling is that it isn't accountable or transparent enough. In the City case, CAS said no one requested a public hearing. On its first day, City's ample defence team initially felt it was going against them. That changed 24 hours later, as the club began to add witnesses and evidence not available to the original hearing. The main theory, that equity was disguised as sponsorship, was described by the club's defence as 'nonsense' and amounting to a 'pointless self-defeating conspiracy.'[113] Pearce dialled in from Australia, insisting the six emails had been incorrectly interpreted.

In a first key development, UEFA's expert witness, forensic accountant Noel Linsday, was asked if he'd seen enough evidence from City to clarify payment routes. 'No,' he replied, 'I feel I've been shown in essence the tip of the iceberg.'[114] Lindsay said he'd not been given access to Etihad or Etisalat's accounts, something that UEFA's in-house team surprisingly declined to pursue despite the legal requirement that City assist fully with all financial disclosure. The belief among the CFCB was that this was 'the killer for the case' and no one knew who made that decision.

Another major development came down to the subjective interpretation of the three judges. City disagreed with the parameters set for UEFA's five-year time-scale, but CAS decided on their own date. This was to be five years back from when UEFA first brought charges, so May 2014 to May 2019. Where that got contentious, however, was whether the cut-off would apply to the date of payment or date of submission.

The accounts for the more illustrative Etisalat example had been submitted inside the May 2014 time limit, but the payments had been made earlier. The judges ruled that it was payments that mattered, by a majority of 2-1. This baffled investigators since deals were done on rolling three-year cycles. It was also crucial since it made all Etisalat evidence time-barred, with that also ensuring it couldn't be used to draw inference for the Etihad case. Since UEFA had stopped pursuing emails, too, CAS couldn't rule that City were refusing to submit information. That meant no inference could be drawn from that, either. Investigators felt it was wrong that statutes of limitations apply when the information was hidden. The club meanwhile always drew confidence from the dates, with others believing that should have set off alarm bells for UEFA. Since City had refused to offer further information on Etihad, it meant UEFA only had the emails, which were deemed insufficient.

The panel felt the testimonies to the court were more credible. CAS wrote in their summary that an alternative reading would 'require the conclusion' that the evidence of 'several high-ranking officials of large international commercial enterprises such as Mr

[James] Hogan [former president and CEO of Etihad], Mr Pearce were false'. City's explanation was seen as not incredible. CAS consequently found, with UEFA agreeing, that there was 'insufficient conclusive evidence' to uphold the Champions League ban. A statement said 'most of the alleged breaches' were 'either not established or time-barred'. The ban was thrown out. City were still fined €10 million for a lack of co-operation, with CAS saying they should be 'severely reproached'.[115]

Some figures, such as Miguel Maduro, felt this was virtually a reward.[116] Björn Hessert, a University of Zürich research assistant for one of the judges but writing in a personal capacity, went even further in an analysis of the CAS decision. He saw the findings as 'flawed and contradictory on points of procedure', arguing City's failure to provide a key document was a violation of UEFA's rules that 'should have resulted in a ban'. Hessert found the decision all the more 'unfortunate' since it serves to 'punish the compliant clubs'.[117] It was a triumph of technicality, as well as the second time that UEFA had been defeated in such a way. The confederation had again been prevented from applying its own rules by the legal power of state-linked clubs.

At City, assistant Manel Estiarte posted a social media picture of Guardiola and key staff members beaming with delight in front of TV headlines. A club statement said their stance had been 'validated', while an internal Soriano email spoke of vindication and an 'unwelcome distraction'.[118]

It certainly occupied the minds of virtually everyone else in the game. Major club executives demanded a UEFA appeal. Klopp said it was a 'bad day for football', with Mourinho describing it as a 'disaster' and that it may as well be time to 'open the door of the circus . . . there is no control'.[119] 'If City are not guilty of it, to be punished by some million is a disgrace,' the Portuguese added.

Guardiola pointedly talked of a 'good day for football' and said if 'whispering' rivals wanted a Champions League place to 'go and do it on the pitch'.[120] Tebas was sarcastically dismissed as an 'incredible legal expert' as the Catalan also demanded City 'be apologised to'. As long as Guardiola's tirade was, he was less reluctant to discuss the fine for obstruction. The question nevertheless persisted alongside many others about the case, particularly when *Der Spiegel* released new emails two weeks after the CAS judgment. These leaks appeared to directly contradict Pearce's testimony. He had been asked at CAS if he had 'ever arranged any payments to be made to Etihad in relation to sponsorship obligations of Manchester City Football Club.' Pearce responded: 'Absolutely categorically not.' CAS had made a point of stating he 'did not strike the panel as being an unreliable witness' and 'did not find his testimony to be false' in their crucial interpretation that his testimony was more credible than the emails. However, *Der Spiegel* published an email from December 2013 that showed Pearce writing from his Executive Affairs Authority email to Etihad COO Peter Baumgartner stating that he was 'forwarding' the airline £91 million of £99 million owed to the club for sponsorship, with Etihad providing only £8 million.[121]

City described this as a 'cynical attempt to publicly re-litigate and undermine a case that has been fully adjudicated'. That only further fired the frenzied lobbying for UEFA to appeal. That they didn't is one of a number of questions that have only increased since then. Interviews that Čeferin gave in early 2024 added to the confusion, as he said UEFA 'knew we were right'.[122] When asked if there was any route for further proceedings, Čeferin stated: 'No, I don't think so.[123] Our Club Financial Control Body decided. City succeeded with CAS, then, for me, the story was over.'

These statements are strongly disputed by figures within the

CFCB, since the body didn't conduct the CAS appeal. Former United States Soccer Federation chief Sunil Gulati was eventually put in charge of the CFCB Investigatory Chamber as UEFA decided not to reopen the case. The justification was that 'legal opinion' indicated there would be 'limited chances' of success, but it was felt to be 'absurd' not to even try.[124]

There was another crucial question from the start of the case that was relevant to the decision on time-barring. Why didn't UEFA object to City nominating Portuguese lawyer Rui Botica Santos as chairman of the three-man arbitration, in addition to Andrew McDougall QC? Both sides are permitted to select one panellist each, with UEFA putting forward German law professor Ulrich Haas, but the confederation did not ask for the third to be chosen independently. McDougall was from the law firm White and Case, who have worked for Etisalat and Etihad Airways.[125] Botica had done CAS arbitration in the past, but the YouTube documentary noted how he is a practising lawyer in a firm specialising in oil and gas.

UEFA responded to such questions by stating their 'full trust in all arbitrators' appointed by CAS, and 'no doubts about their independence or impartiality'.[126] Two further questions related to the process. Why did UEFA cease pursuing City's emails just before the CAS hearing began? Why did UEFA allow CAS to call new witnesses and evidence when both are against UEFA's rules? A UEFA statement said they were 'satisfied with the way the procedure was conducted' while pointing to how the necessary speed 'aligned with the wishes of the nine Premier League clubs who applied to intervene in the proceedings' and were keen for a decision before the 2020–21 season.[127]

Concerns over the transparency of proceedings have also been raised, especially as to why UEFA never published their own full judgment from the Adjudicatory Chamber's decision in February 2020. The confederation explained the CAS decision rendered this 'moot', a stance 'in line with UEFA's consistent publication policy for decisions overturned by CAS'. This rationale is widely viewed as 'unsatisfactory', especially since revised rules oblige UEFA to publish such decisions. Rummenigge spoke of how he'd heard UEFA's defence was not well 'organised in advance',[128] as Maduro criticised a 'systemic conflict of interest at the heart' of the ruling body.[129]

In April 2022, *Der Spiegel* produced another set of leaks that were perceived by CFCB investigators as the run of emails they had been asking for all along. As well as showing how the finance director of the Executive Affairs Authority was described as 'very important and helpful in facilitating our financial administration of City', they revealed that part of the sponsorship money from Abu Dhabi was in 2012 booked as 'owner investment'.[130] In 2013, then, Pearce requested Chumillas put together a summary of ADUG payment obligations and asked they be organised according to 'club direct payments' and 'partner supplements'. For the 2013–14 season, Abu Dhabi supplements added up to £92.5 million. 'We mustn't show the partner supplement if it is going outside the club,' wrote Widdowson, head of finance at the time. In 2014, he and Chumillas discussed money still to be paid by Etisalat and Aabar. The emails show a differentiation between the amount being paid by ADUG and the sums to be covered by the companies.

'But actually, formally, we want all of these amounts to be paid by Aabar and Etisalat right?' Chumillas wrote.

The response was: 'Yes if they can.'

The 2022 leaks were published within the deadline for appeal, either to CAS or Swiss courts. UEFA could have done that or, according to one legal source, 'opened a new case on the basis of new evidence'. City repeated the statement about cynical attempts to publicly re-litigate. It was also in these leaks that *Der Spiegel* revealed details of the Premier League investigation into City, which was the first time there had been information in four years. The length of time was in part because the Premier League were having as much difficulty getting information out of City as UEFA had. In October 2019, the Premier League sought a court order for the club to 'deliver up documents and information which were being withheld'.[131]

City challenged this, questioning the Premier League's very jurisdiction to investigate it and stating 'that the tribunal did not have the appearance of impartiality'. That failed, and the club and Premier League also both failed – after going to the Court of Appeal – to prevent the decision being made public. Lord Justice Males rebuked the entire situation, stating it is 'a matter of legitimate public concern' that 'so little progress has been made after two and a half years – during which, it may be noted, the club has twice been crowned as Premier League champions'.[132] That became five times.

The eventual charges included allegations that the club obstructed investigation. In the Court of Appeal, the Premier League had accused City of 'making as many procedural applications and complaints as it possibly can to slow the day when it will actually have to provide the information'.[133] Other clubs had long been pressing for updates, to the point that executives would occasionally make impromptu calls or mention it out of nowhere at shareholders' meetings.[134] A common view was that it was ridiculous that something so serious to the history and the future of the Premier League could be so drawn out, which many believed to be City's specific strategy.

CFCB investigators had warned the Premier League what it was like to be on the 'receiving end of a UAE onslaught', where they were left open to allegations of bias or incompetence. It was also why the Premier League were repeatedly counselled they should establish a wholly independent unit to investigate and prosecute big cases. All of this was amped up when the Premier League finally published the 100-plus alleged breaches on 6 February 2023. It couldn't even be called an 'announcement', since the statement was quietly put up on the competition's website, in quite a contrast to the furore it was about to create. City only found out when a courier delivered legal papers.

The investigation went back to 2009–10, since the Premier League didn't have the same time limits as UEFA. The originally reported charges included: 50 alleged breaches of providing accurate financial information 'in the utmost good faith'; 24 breaches regarding the provision of details of manager and player remuneration; five breaches of rules requiring clubs to comply with UEFA FFP regulations; six breaches of the Premier League's profitability and sustainability rules; and 30 breaches of rules requiring member clubs to co-operate with Premier League investigations. Confusion over some of the rules listed in relation to specific seasons later saw the Premier League issue a correction, so the charges amounted to 130, rather than the now notorious number of 115. The release actually served to tighten the tension, especially when it became apparent that the process by an independent commission could take at least two years before any appeals. Although the case had no option to go to CAS, there was the possibility of going to the High Court and possibly even the Supreme Court.

City stated they were 'surprised' by the charges 'particularly given the extensive engagement and vast amount of detailed materials' provided, but again welcomed the possibility for 'the comprehensive body of irrefutable evidence that exists in support of its position' to put the matter 'to rest once and for all'.[135]

A lot of the football world was extremely agitated, especially when the YouTube documentary came out in June 2023 publicly revealing details of the Adjudicatory Chamber's judgment for the first time. Yves Leterme, the former Belgian prime minister who had chaired UEFA's seven-strong investigatory team, had already said in February he was 'convinced that fraud has been committed by Manchester City' and noted the Premier League's lack of time-barring.[136] As one UEFA figure put it, the investigation was given to the English competition 'on a plate', and should never have taken five years.

City, of course, assembled the strongest possible legal team, led by Lord Pannick QC. He had previously attempted to defend the former British prime minister Boris Johnson in the 'Partygate' scandal over gatherings in government during the Covid-19 pandemic, and subsequently became the first barrister to have a banner unveiled in their honour at a football stadium. The otherwise anodyne Premier League anthem was booed. Guardiola meanwhile came out with an even more robust backing of the club's hierarchy than in 2020, while rounding on those he saw as driving action against the club. He even referenced the Tottenham chairman by name. 'I'm sorry but I rely on the words of my people,'[137] Guardiola said. 'You have to ask the CEOs, Daniel Levy, these kinds of people . . .' One City official later sought to explain to other clubs that this was just Guardiola's 'passion', but tension was worsening. City resisted the appointment of Murray Rosen KC as chair of the disciplinary commission due to the fact he is a self-declared Arsenal fan, among a number of legal challenges.[138]

It later emerged through a Freedom of Information request by

The Athletic that the UK Foreign Office and the British embassy in Abu Dhabi had discussed the charges, but refused to disclose correspondence because it 'could potentially damage' the UK's relationship with the UAE.[139] Only a month before the charges, the then secretary of state for business, energy and industrial strategy Grant Shapps said the UK expected to raise tens of billions of investment from the UAE.[140]

On the day that the initial Champions League ban had been overturned, Klopp had already mentioned how a failure to curb spending could 'lead to a World Super League with 10 clubs'.[141] He was closer than he might have imagined.

10.

THE LAND OF THE FEE

If some at UEFA had their way, the 2024 Champions League final would have been in New York, with an even more ostentatious 'kick-off show'. It would also have been the first of several major fixtures across America, as written into detailed plans and pitches for sponsorship. This is one of many reasons why Elon Musk wanted Manchester United. It's why La Liga and the Premier League have still talked about fixtures there.

The United States is already hosting a series of international tournaments over the next half-decade, all centred around the 2026 World Cup, that has duly bloated to 48 teams. Such an expansion is partly a consequence of a widespread American takeover of European clubs, in a way that would have been unimaginable even through the build-up to the country's last World Cup, in 1994. That tournament nevertheless made investors realise just how popular football is. In the time since, virtually every possible American business model has bought a European club. Most of these ownerships have different approaches and ambitions, but they're all in it for the same core reason: profit. That isn't money for the game, either. It is simply the accumulation of wealth for its own sake, turning the 1 per cent into the 0.1 per cent. Football has already had its own Gordon Gekko knock-off moment with AC Milan owner Gerry Cardinale declaring at one summit, 'Capitalism is great.' Community institutions have been reduced to 'investment opportunities'.

That is why capitalist ownership is seen as almost as much of a concern as state ownership. They involve some top-down state influence, too, even though these are private companies in liberal democracies. It is the inevitable by-product of US economic policy and the financial world that has been wrought where politics and business are so intertwined. Just as autocracies had looked around the world and realised football's political capital, financial interests realised the same in terms of actual capital.

Perhaps the most pertinent point isn't whether it's better or worse than state ownership, but how it is another major force combining with geopolitics to change football. The most extreme version of this ownership even represents an intersection point. Most sovereign wealth funds have stakes in private equity groups, as illustrated when Clearlake Capital had to reassure the Premier League that Saudi Arabia's Public Investment Fund – who are also the majority owners of Newcastle United – had 'no part' of Chelsea despite providing capital to the overall group.[1] Supporters of some clubs aren't even able to definitively say who the ultimate owners are.

One major reason this type of ownership has increasingly focused on football is that America's own sports are comparatively closed off. Private equity is only allowed to purchase small stakes. Anyone seeking to buy into the National Football League can leverage no more than $1.2 billion of the purchase price, which works out at under 25 per cent of the $5 billion-plus average value of teams. That's quite a contrast to the 66 per cent the Glazer family bought Manchester United with. It is also where football's sporting strengths have fostered weak points. While US competitions don't have promotion or relegation, ensuring they have become closed cartels with huge collective bargaining agreements, the European game's pyramid structure lowers the value of clubs. Relegation brings risk, but also huge opportunities since lower-league clubs can be bought cheaply with the achievable ambition of rising to the Champions League.

A common view within the US is that football clubs and competitions are badly run, and that efficiency could yet triple the financial size of clubs. The aggregate value of the 32 most prominent European clubs already increased by 96 per cent between 2016 and 2023, which is performance that exceeds the FTSE 100 index.[2] Major clubs are now viewed as high-level media companies, in an evolution of the classic 'content provider' stance. It has even come full circle, with Disney paying for a documentary covering Wrexham A.F.C., a club owned by Hollywood stars Ryan Reynolds and Rob McElhenney.

This is all before the onset of new technology, micro-payments and . . . and if all this sounds like the pitch for a start-up company and far removed from the grass, that is the point. There is no real concern from the majority of these interests about the wider health of football. It is all about maximising commercial opportunity now. One executive who has worked with capitalist ownership almost spits about how they think they are geniuses who can 'identify inefficiencies' only to realise the reality of football and leave behind a mess. Such groups may be already creating a critical mass that manifestly changes the face of the game for entirely non-football motivations. That's if we're not already there.

The Glazers have inspired many different descriptions over two decades in football, but one stood out in investment circles by the end of 2023. They were seen as responsible for the most successful sports deal in history by selling a minority stake of Manchester United to British billionaire Sir Jim Ratcliffe's INEOS group. 'People will write books about it,' one rival chief executive said, in an entirely complimentary tone. It is striking that, as American ownership has spread to almost 60 European clubs, the first take-over was still the biggest. There was no steady build-up. The Glazer family just went for the biggest club in the most cynically capitalist manner. Over half a billion pounds' worth of borrowings were loaded onto a great English institution that had been debt-free since 1931, its sustainable model needlessly put at risk by the lax-ness of football regulation. It says much that the Premier League has since voted to cap such leveraged buyouts, although too late for its most successful club.[3]

For all that United's decline has understandably brought glee among rival supporters, it should still serve as a parable for the game. This American financial success is also a great tragedy of English football. An inspirational club identity, nurtured through youth, adventure, defiance and glory has literally been traded off. Even the huge expenditure on transfer fees and wages reflected the vulgarity of the era, as if just money could solve everything. The Glazer ownership led the way in maximising commercial income from football but fell behind in terms of running a team. When one meeting saw a senior decision-maker questioned about why they don't instil a defined ideology like Liverpool, the explanation was they want 'flexibility within broader parameters'.

The style has been so broad that several teams have just strolled through Manchester United's midfield and subjected them to a series of humiliations. Even Old Trafford became a monument to decline. That famous stadium wasn't invested in, leaving it looking dated as the roof leaks. All of this fittingly stemmed from greed, if not without the poignancy that it centrally involved the club's patriarch. In 2003, Sir Alex Ferguson issued legal proceedings against businessman John Magnier over the racehorse, Rock Of Gibraltar. The manager's love of racing had seen a close friendship develop with the Irish billionaire and his Coolmore Stud partner, JP McManus. Ferguson even counselled the duo on building up investment in Manchester United, which led to the longtime belief the group would seek to buy the club. Magnier invited the Scot to become involved in 'the Rock' which was registered as co-owned by the businessman's wife, Sue, and Ferguson.[4] The horse began to win as much as United, and was bedecked in the same colours. Even more tantalising was the estimation that the Rock's breeding rights could earn £200 million on retirement, which Ferguson thought his stake extended to. Magnier felt the manager's rights ended with the horse's last race.

Ferguson was enraged, but this was a vintage case of a football figure out of his depth in the more complicated world outside it. The Coolmore Stud duo literally showed Ferguson who was boss, as they built up their holdings in United to 28.7 per cent and started to subject the manager to increased scrutiny.[5] An agreement was eventually reached with Ferguson settling for a one-off payment reported as £2.5 million, but the relevant part was the money spent elsewhere around the club. The Glazers had been quietly accumulating shares in an institution they saw as the world's biggest sports brand, and the dispute presented opportunity for a full £805 million takeover. Magnier and McManus had no interest in keeping their shares with the case settled. A deal was struck with the Glazers' Red Football, announced on 12 May 2005. The Glazers, at that point led by father Malcolm, told United staff it was an incredible deal. His children – Joel, Avram, Bryan, Kevin, Darcie and Edward – also joined the board.

So began one of the most acrimonious fan relationships in sport. When word got out that Joel and Bryan Avram were visiting Old Trafford in late June 2005, a ring of steel had to be put up. The new owners were given a tour, as 400 fans outside sang about decapitating their father.[6] The supporters feeling most disenfran-chised formed FC United of Manchester, vowing not to return until the owners were gone. Malcom Glazer himself never went to Old Trafford, fostering a sense of absenteeism that frustrated fans but probably helped the owners maintain their resolutely unflinching attitude. All that mattered was how profitable United were, and the Glazers were about to supercharge that.

Their immense confidence even baffled senior staff, who were used to the 'de-risking' model of a Public Limited Company. Since football was seen as a volatile industry, the advisable moves for a quoted company were to future-proof blue-chip sponsorship deals through long-term agreements. Bryan Glazer thought this was lu-dicrous and felt the shirt sponsorship was especially undervalued. The siblings couldn't believe United had lower commercial revenue than the owners' other franchise, the Tampa Bay Buccaneers, given that NFL regulations limited sponsorship to a 75-mile radius.[7]

It was why the Glazers were thrilled when told Vodafone's shirt sponsorship had ended. They could go global.[8] United had lux-urious boxes made up that featured the club shirt with the target company printed on it. Beyond that, the strategy was to divide the club and the planet into more and more sectors, to secure more and more sponsorships. Commercial staff were convinced when a localised contract with Saudi Telecom was secured for the kind of multi-million figures the previous strategy had budgeted for the biggest deals. The sales team was predictably described as a 'cut-throat' environment, although the power of the club helped secure commissions. A different kind of conviction helped. The Glazers had bought the club when United were trailing well behind Roman Abramovich's new Chelsea, and the sheer finances made it look like this was the new order. The Russian's mega-offers ensured Arjen Robben, Michael Ballack and Michael Essien all decided on

Stamford Bridge over Old Trafford. Ferguson and chief executive David Gill nevertheless explained to the Glazers they had a youth-based strategy they were utterly convinced could overhaul Chelsea in the medium-term. The owners, for their part, signed it off and were rewarded. It brought the best era of Ferguson's entire 27 years, winning five Premier Leagues and a Champions League title. That again ensured United were successful at just the right moment, as great clubs were becoming global super clubs. A new commercial office was set up in London that did attract scrutiny from Manchester's Inward Investment Agency, but then the club also had a luxury lounge at the World Economic Forum.[9]

They were soon seen within the game as a money machine like no other. This alleviated financial pressure from interest payments, although there was one moment when there looked like an opening for a takeover. By November 2010, the debt on high-risk payment-in-kind loans stood at £220 million at an interest rate of 16.25 per cent. Fan groups and Qatar circled. Joel Glazer moved to issue a 'voluntary free-payment notice' to lenders, confirming the amount would be paid in full without using money drawn from the club.[10]

The ownership was then stabilised with a public offering on the New York Stock Exchange that saw United valued at $2.3 billion.[11] That rose to $5.4 billion by the time INEOS bought 27.7 per cent of the club in 2023–24. The Glazers had consequently received £1.3 billion on top of an estimated £200 million in dividends, while the club paid out £1 billion in interest. This was why it was seen as such an incredible deal. There were even plans for Old Trafford to be redeveloped without the Glazers investing, which is what had seen them explore offers in the first place.

Although that process was often described as 'like *Succession*', given how the differing views of the siblings resembled the squabbles of the TV show, Joel and Avram never wanted to sell outright. It was why the strangely low bid of Qatar's Sheikh Jassim bin Hamad Al Thani didn't have a chance. The brothers felt the income of United could yet explode. Joel and Avram genuinely enjoyed being the owners of the club, too. They can cut excited figures at big games, although such encounters have led a number of individuals to describe the Glazers as 'the weirdest people' they'd ever met, a reflection of a different level of wealth. So many stories actually got back to the writers of *Succession* that they considered a similar show based on football. Much less was known about Malcolm, although *The Athletic* reported a typical story where he once mocked Bryan for wearing $200 trousers when he preferred $20 department-store purchases.[12]

United became notorious for a similar frugality. Literally every expense had to go through Florida, right down to dumbbells in the gym. Major sports technology companies stopped working with United because they became so frustrating to deal with. It was a reason they were for a long time seen as ponderous in the market. Managers like Jürgen Klopp were put off joining the club by the commercial obsessions.

The argument long made by executive vice-chairman Ed Woodward was that 'playing performance doesn't really have a meaningful impact' on the commercial side.[13] United's great rivals illustrated the opposite. Liverpool were one of many clubs to so outperform United that, on selling the stake to Ratcliffe, the Glazers realised the need to also hand over the running of the football side. Successive managerial appointments summed up the problem. It was always the wrong man or the wrong time.

By that point, in late 2023, American ownership in football generally had more sophisticated strategies than in the wave that immediately followed the Glazers. That was, so to speak, a

Wild West. Ellis Short got Sunderland relegated to the third tier while reducing support to the club's widely lauded charitable arm.[14] Perhaps the most chaotic were the first American owners at Liverpool, since Tom Hicks and George Gillett Jr fell out within six months of buying the club.

The manner in which the Premier League was descending into a land grab was most evident at the club seen as 'the establishment', replete with marble pillars. Arsenal found themselves pulled East and West. On one side, Uzbek oligarch Alisher Usmanov owned 30.4 per cent of the club and wanted to spend like Abramovich. On the other, Missouri billionaire Stan Kroenke owned 67 per cent and wanted the self-sustaining model that had been successful with his other franchises like the St Louis Rams. The conflict ran for over a decade, until Usmanov abruptly sold his stake in 2018. Kroenke Sports and Entertainment had full control and finally felt empowered to go all in on a new strategy. Arsène Wenger was moved on as manager. Significant influence was taken from another American ownership, again at Liverpool, but definitely not Hicks and Gillett.

By 2010, dissent in the Anfield crowd had manifested into a supporter called Joe Januszewski sending a desperate email to his boss with the subject 'save my club!' That boss just happened to be the owner of the Boston Red Sox, John Henry, whose embrace of analytics ended the baseball team's 86-year wait for a World Series title. 'Liverpool FC are a top-five sports brand worldwide and are just begging to be properly marketed and leveraged globally,' Januszewski wrote. The club's troubles under Hicks and Gillett also made it 'the deal of the century', since loans from the Royal Bank of Scotland were put into the bank's toxic assets division.[15] That allowed Henry's Fenway Sports Group (FSG) to buy the club for £300 million, less than two months after the email. Hicks and Gillett were at least united in describing the deal as an 'epic swindle'.[16] Liverpool had been in danger of falling out of football's elite, but FSG immediately realised the club's heritage, fan base and booming global interest could be combined with a winning team to go off like a rocket. It was just the last part that had proven difficult for virtually everyone since Liverpool's last league title in 1989–90. Henry sought to banish such historic hang-ups with the same modern analytics that succeeded at the Red Sox. An early issue was football's fluidity, so opening up a massed defence was much harder to code than getting on base. Early attempts were a little crude. Stewart Downing was one of the best crossers in the Premier League and Andy Carroll one of the best strikers with his head, so they were put together. That wasn't how football worked, though. Burgeoning analytics guru Michael Edwards was brought in from Tottenham Hotspur and began to hone the approach.

It was still a football immutable, in a transformational manager like Jürgen Klopp, that made it all work. The German's almost evangelical ability to inspire people ensured all the science made sense. The signings began to fit, and excel. This has become the model to compete against the wealthiest clubs. Borussia Dortmund, who Klopp managed from 2008–15, had actually been an example for Arsenal in how they honed young talent. There was now further inspiration from Anfield. By 2023–24, Arsenal and Liverpool are the only clubs to properly challenge Guardiola's City in a title race.

Neither is it a coincidence that all three of England's most historically successful clubs came under American ownership. That mythos mattered. The three did display different approaches, mind. Liverpool's wanted to build up, eventually to sell. Arsenal's wanted to sustain. United's wanted to drain. As of the end of 2023, the four most watched Premier League matches in US TV history were meetings between these three.[17] The figures nevertheless inspired other investors to look for more elsewhere.

It was the world stopping that really accelerated US money into football. The Covid-19 pandemic wrought havoc on the European game, causing €7 billion in losses, but it still couldn't do structural damage.[18] Football's social importance ensured a will to keep it going. As one executive put it, 'you couldn't go to a family funeral but there was Fulham against West Brom'. It showed how the industry was 'bulletproof', armoured by the long-term cash flows of broadcast contracts that few sectors could match. That made it a safe place to put money, amid low interest rates. There was also opportunity to go with security. Since the pandemic had disrupted regular income, club values were depressed.[19] The period saw a proliferation of US purchases, with clubs as diverse as Plymouth Argyle and FC Helsingør taken over. As businessman Brett Johnson explained of his acquisition of Ipswich Town, how often do you find a team that has historically won a series of major trophies and is available at £40 million?[20] That price was at least five times cheaper than setting up a new MLS club, and that was potentially within a season of being promoted to the Premier League.[21] It really paid off once they got there in 2024, and that against the odds. Perhaps a more pertinent question should be how we're at a point where pension-fund money is being put into football, as is the case with Johnson's wealth.

Manchester United remained the great example to follow, with the Glazers having been repeatedly cited in summits for investors despite how bad football performance was. This saw interest escalate to numbers more eyebrow-raising than even United's 7-0 humiliation at Liverpool. In 2018, private equity and similar US institutional investment in Europe's five major leagues – England, Spain, Italy, Germany, France – was at €66.7 million.[22] By 2022, it was €4.9 billion. UEFA's own research found that, in 2024, 37 of the 96 clubs in those same leagues have ties to US private capital, with 27 of those involving private equity. That was especially prominent in France, where half of Ligue 1 clubs had private equity among the ownership in 2022–23.[23] Interest is expected to explode in Serie A due to the glamorous history, the tourism and – crucially – a lack of entry barriers. When one senior football executive was approached by two figures from Goldman Sachs at a conference, they happily told him 'it's a great time to bring capital into the game'. The bemused response was 'what for?'

That's a bigger question than it seems. The core concern with private equity is that the motivations are as far removed from football's community ethos as you can get, even if there are admittedly periods when they run parallel. Put simply, such funds take money from investors and puts it into companies perceived as undervalued.[24] Many private equity groups have become notorious for brutal managerial practice in increasing that value, stripping companies to the bone. They would then seek to sell on, although the timescale can be dependent on strategy. Some are open-ended. Ipswich owner Johnson insisted to investment data company Pitchbook that sports are 'not a quick flip'.[25] Those who work in the field would also point to how there has been benefit in longer-term funds improving practice at clubs like Portsmouth. The success story has meanwhile been Elliott Management at AC Milan, who in 2021–22 reclaimed the Serie A title for the first time in 11 years. That was by taking Liverpool's analytics approach to an extreme, and was arguably ahead of schedule given how the squad was perceived as over-performing. It also showcased the previously small world of US soccer given that former Arsenal chief executive Ivan Gazidis took up the same position at Milan, in part from knowing one of the Elliott figures from playing soccer in New York. 'I know you,' came the line when they saw each other at one summit.

There's also the argument that Ligue 1 badly needed the investment after the Covid-19 pandemic. Even this supposed positive, however, was necessary only because of how football's wider capitalist structure had started to leave French football behind. It was still private equity filling gaps that shouldn't have existed. It's also why the broad principles are viewed as 'potentially disastrous' for the game.

The perceptions of the most prominent deal are telling. Clearlake Capital have almost used Chelsea as an experiment, testing football's 'inefficiencies' with a recruitment model that has left supporters feeling disconnected and baffled. Tellingly, finance figures in the US wonder whether the club can bring a 30 per cent return on investment. Co-owner Todd Boehly's early prominence in negotiating transfers has been matched by other private capital groups putting up real celebrities as the recognisable face. Tom Brady has attended Birmingham City and Michael B. Jordan Bournemouth. Much of this follows the example of Wrexham A.F.C, who have become a vehicle for actors Ryan Reynolds and Rob McElhenney. Some rival clubs have been delighted with the increased attention, but that's been tempered by the acceleration of the wage race in England's lower leagues. There have been grumbles about Wrexham getting promoted from the fifth tier through a third-tier budget. Half of Hollywood now wants to buy an English club, preferably with a quirky lower-league identity, so it's just as well so much private equity is willing to involve stars in such football investments.

Private capital has even managed to pick its way into Barcelona and Real Madrid, even though both are supposed to be ring-fenced by supporter ownership, a virtue offset by the desperation to compete. Sixth Street Partners did a €207.5 million deal with Barcelona for 10 per cent of TV rights, and a €380 million deal with Real Madrid for 30 per cent of stadium operations.[26] These decisions led to bafflement within football, but also concern that such 'indirect participation' may be more widespread.

Even Germany's 50+1 rule has been evaded. Controversial US sports fund 777 Partners were able to gradually build up a stake in Hertha Berlin by leaving the club with more than 50 per cent of the voting shares. There was still concern the structure could allow influence.[27] Ares Management have meanwhile taken a 34 per cent stake in Atlético de Madrid,[28] Arctos a 12.5 per cent stake of Paris Saint-Germain,[29] as Oaktree Capital eventually 'assumed ownership' of Internazionale after owners Suning had failed to repay a loan worth €395 million.[30] That was another opportune position from such stakes.

'Even where you don't see it, private equity is there,' analyst Nicolas Moura told *Private Equity News*.[31] What it essentially amounts to is, just like autocracies, buying off institutional chunks of football. This was interpreted by the *Guardian* as a telling example of what economic geographer Brett Christophers describes as 'rentier capitalism', where an investor receives payment 'purely by virtue of controlling something valuable'.[32]

It may go beyond something so passive, though. This new age has coincided with a new idea of a club. Multi-club projects were initiated by Red Bull and perfected by City Football Group, but the model has been most excitedly taken up by US investors. UEFA's 2024 landscape report found over 300 clubs across the planet in such groups.[33] Of those, 777 Partners have probably been the most controversial and cautionary. As well as Hertha, the US group has stakes in Belgium's Standard de Liège, France's Red Star, Italy's Genoa, Spain's Sevilla, Brazil's Vasco da Gama and Australia's Melbourne Victory, having attempted a move for Everton. While the clubs have broadly underperformed, most of the controversy has been about connecting these great names to more serious concerns.

The positive arguments made about multi-club ownerships are they offer small clubs a chance to compete in a financially stratified world. The negative arguments are that this just hardens the very stratification for good. Some clubs will always be smaller partners. It's all the worse since every regulation in European football is based on clubs as individual entities. The rules are not equipped for such blurred lines. This was illustrated in how, despite UEFA's article 5.01 notionally prohibiting clubs who have the same ownership influences from playing in the same league, Leipzig and Salzburg met in the 2018–19 Europa League. Although both are owned by Red Bull, the group managed to persuade the confederation of structural separation.[34] That set a tone for how authorities have struggled with the issue. The rules have since demanded that sister clubs – such as in the cases of Manchester United and Nice or Manchester City and Girona – do not have board members with links to the other if they are in the same European competition. It has significant implications for the transfer industry and sustainability regulations, since both assume market value on all deals. Multi-clubs create the potential for collusion, as Ronan Evain of Football Supporters Europe argues. 'The opening is there for sovereign wealth funds, private equities to test the system. They will always be one step ahead, to the extent the regulation is not fit for purpose any more. It's probably already too late.'

There is some frustration even within FIFA about this, as 'everyone could see multi-clubs coming'. When some staff raised this, there was pushback. Influential stakeholders prefer the vagueness.

It further serves to centralise power, while taking it away from the many. This does all cut to why football is actually popular in the first place. It distorts the identity that supporters attach to. Clubs that are historic community institutions are made subservient to a bigger structure. When A.F.C. Bournemouth owner Bill Foley and his Black Knight Football and Entertainment group purchased a 33 per cent stake in French club FC Lorient, their ultras group rightfully expressed horror at 'a family club' becoming 'a vulgar . . . training centre' for the bigger Premier League club.[35] It shows how the competing forces complement each other in distorting the game. If state ownership uses club identity, private equity subsumes it.

Čeferin admitted that UEFA need to 'rethink' the issue, before stating that rules might even be relaxed.[36] The European body might instead have new realities imposed on them. What is to stop powerful voting blocs evolving? Private equity is already seeking to insert itself into the infrastructure of competitions, let alone clubs. CVC Capital Partners have agreed a €2 billion deal with La Liga for 8 per cent of the competition's revenues for 50 years.[37] The feeling within UEFA was that it 'didn't feel right' a league like Spain's needed such a deal. FIFA have nevertheless sought work with Softbank.[38] Goldman Sachs have considered similar with Serie A.

This is what could really transform the sport. Such interest was already the source of ideas like staging the Champions League final in New York, although Covid-19 and the Super League put an end to that. Those who regularly go to UEFA meetings say that capitalist influence has changed the content of many strategy meetings, so they are increasingly about raising money for the next cycle rather than developing the sport. Echoing Soriano's view on just boosting his own club, many owners have no concept of the

European model of sport, let alone interest. A detail repeatedly brought up is that the NFL gets $13 billion from just 300 million viewers, whereas European football's two-billion-strong audience doesn't produce the same ratios.

The question is still why, though. European football doesn't need this investment. It generates enough money through its own popularity, with club revenues having increased from €15 billion in 2013 to €26 billion in 2023. The possibility is there for a sustainable organic model. 'I look at the big clubs and their endless desire for money and I just think . . . what's the point?' football historian David Goldblatt has lamented. 'What is the point of this death spiral of an ever-smaller number of clubs?'[39]

It perhaps points to two possible paths. Such interests may reach a critical mass where they start to actively control football. That could bring new competitions or changes to regulations. The latter is very difficult to apply when sovereign wealth funds have already been allowed in. If that means capitalist interests can't regulate finance, and private equity funds realise the real money is only concentrated at the very top of the game, there might be a mass exodus that leaves a huge hole. There are already fears this abrupt escalation in investment has created a bubble where an oversupply of funds has driven investors to riskier takeovers. If so, who is left to buy clubs? More states?

This has all been a long-term consequence of the spread of the game to the biggest market with the 1994 World Cup in the USA. It simply took about 20 years for various American interests to calibrate. That initially brought ideas like the International Champions Cup, which came to resemble a pre-season Super League in the US. Figures within FIFA have long predicted an influx of institutional money would see MLS do what the Saudi Pro League has attempted. It is possible Leo Messi's move to Inter

Miami is a first step. What US soccer really wanted, though, was a return of the World Cup itself. That was supposed to happen for 2022, and the initial failure would eventually see the US state itself get involved, to even more drastic effect.

Bill Clinton was so furious that he demanded action. That was the scene in the VIP lounge in Zürich on 2 December 2010 and that, at least, is the popular theory explaining the upheaval in FIFA that followed. Even Sepp Blatter still insists that the US state set out to bring FIFA down because the country didn't get the 2022 World Cup.[40] The truth is that the FBI had been looking at the governing body for months before the vote that awarded Qatar the tournament. The root of the investigation was the questionable way that FIFA went about such decisions, with that day in Zürich only supercharging it.

In his work for England's 2018 bid, retired spy Christopher Steele gathered a lot of information on Russia's activity and felt it should go further.[41] He contacted the FBI, who had already been looking at Russian money-laundering and bribery. They went to legendary football reporter Andrew Jennings, who explained how the entire structure of modern FIFA was geared towards corruption. Together with Adidas's Horst Dassler and advertising guru Patrick Nally, former president João Havelange developed a revolutionary approach where FIFA directly sold World Cup sponsorship to multinationals like Coca-Cola. That in turn allowed Havelange to redistribute money to member associations, creating a system of clientelism that consolidated his power. With Blatter having honed this model through his GOAL programme, the events of 2 December 2010 were its inevitable consequence.

One of the day's prominent figures only accelerated the investigation. Qatar's Mohammed bin Hammam had decided to run for FIFA president, and that race had already been given edge by Blatter's comments about moving the 2022 World Cup. There had been some hope the Swiss might not run again in 2011, perhaps standing aside for Michel Platini. This of course proved fanciful, and provoked aggravation. To Platini's eventual cost, however, it was over this period that the UEFA president began to insist on the unpaid 2 million Swiss Francs from his agreement with Blatter in 1998. A request was put in writing. FIFA's then general secretary Jerome Valcke meanwhile wrote in a leaked email to Concacaf president Jack Warner that Bin Hammam was only standing to 'show how much he hates' Blatter.[42]

It remains remarkable how events of such consequence were started with petty personal differences, but that is football politics. A lot of glad-handing is entailed, since the FIFA presidency is determined by a majority of votes from the 200-plus associations. A meeting of the Caribbean Football Union (CFU) had been arranged for May 2011 in Trinidad and Tobago, so Bin Hammam could meet representatives, who were all under Concacaf. It was from this that word spread that Warner's staff were passing on a literal brown envelope marked 'Bahamas' that contained 400 brand new 100-dollar bills.[43] It appeared to be a classic cash-for-votes scandal, with Bin Hammam seemingly paying the CFU so they could distribute to members. Warner, a devout Catholic who was nevertheless notoriously corrupt, told members 'if you are pious, go to a church'.[44] Bahamas Football Association vice-president Fred Lunn summed up the scene in a message to his boss, Anton Sealey. 'A lot of the boys taking the cash.'[45]

Sealey informed Concacaf General Secretary Chuck Blazer, who had long been Warner's partner, but felt this was too much. It didn't help that their friendship had soured. That stemmed from another moment during the vote for 2022. Blazer looked over Bin

Hammam's shoulder and noticed Warner's name had been ticked off on a list.[46] Blazer now decided to go to Valcke, eventually resulting in Bin Hammam and Warner being called for a FIFA disciplinary hearing.[47]

On 12 May 2011, then Qatari crown prince Sheikh Tamim met with Blatter in concern about all this noise, and even talk of rerunning the 2022 vote.[48] A UK House of Commons inquiry was meanwhile bringing all manner of headlines about the process. Blatter said Bin Hammam's presidential run wasn't easing the situation.[49] The Qatari was eventually summoned to FIFA HQ, where his country's senior royals were present. *The Ugly Game* tells how the message was clear.[50] Bin Hammam bowed out of the presidential race, stating he couldn't allow the game he loved to be dragged 'in the mud because of competition between two individuals'. It got still dirtier. Warner responded in the only way he knew how, leaking incendiary emails by Valcke.[51] Bin Hammam also formally called for Blatter to be investigated due to the claim Warner had told the FIFA president about the CFU payments.

Blatter was the only one of the three to escape a suspension.[52] He was left to stand unopposed but not unsullied, as the entire episode laid bare a culture of corruption. The English FA called for a postponement of the election but lost. All but 17 out of 203 delegates voted for Blatter. Before the election, the returned president held a press conference with a number of remarkable lines, such as 'Crisis? What is a crisis . . . we are only in some difficulties and these will be solved within our family.'[53]

It said much that Blazer was initially hailed as a 'whistleblower' only to be investigated by the FBI and Internal Revenue Service-Criminal Investigation Division (CID). The headlines piqued the interest of football fan Steve Berryman, a methodical IRS investigator, who suggested to US attorneys that the case might fall under the Racketeer Influenced and Corrupt Organizations Act.[54] Widely called RICO, it was thrust into popular culture by *The Sopranos*. Although it seemed this was a case of obscure soccer officials bribing each other abroad, it most likely involved the United States because virtually any international wire transfer usually flows through American financial systems. They just needed someone to make sense of the numbers, which was why the Blazer investigation was invaluable. Based in an office at Trump Tower in Manhattan, Blazer hadn't filed tax for years. His work as Concacaf General Secretary actually meant he had an elaborate network of financial transactions that he assumed left no paper trail. Blazer, in the parlance, was easily 'flipped'. He agreed to explain everything to authorities and wear a wire.[55]

The accusations of corruption related to 2018–22 eventually embarrassed FIFA into commissioning an investigation by former US attorney Michael J. Garcia. The global body initially refused to release it, and the executive summary was dismissed as a whitewash. Russia and Qatar were largely cleared, with England and Australia receiving most criticism. Even Garcia protested at this interpretation when resigning as independent chairman of the Investigatory Chamber of the FIFA Ethics Committee, describing 'a lack of leadership'.[56] Blatter had by then decided to stand again in 2015, although this election took place amid scenes that very much were a crisis.

At 6 a.m. on 27 May 2015, Swiss police approached the Baur au Lac at the behest of an American indictment. They came out with seven officials in custody – symbolically covered in white sheets – as FBI and IRS agents in New York crossed names off a whiteboard with every arrest that came through.[57] The official press conferences of course contained football references that were less subtle than the arrests. 'This is really the World Cup of fraud,' said Richard Weber, Chief of the IRS CID. 'And today we are issu-ing FIFA a red card'.[58] US attorney general Loretta Lynch starkly laid out the allegations, which were $200 million in bribes over 24 years, money laundering and racketeering. 'The indictment alleges corruption that is rampant, systemic and deep-rooted both abroad and here in the United States.'[59]

Incredibly, Blatter was still going to stand for election, albeit with Jordan's Ali bin Al Hussein challenging. This was despite Platini telling him to resign. Even on a basic level, Blatter didn't have term-limit ideas that conformed to good governance. 'What is this notion of time? Time is infinite and we slice it up . . . I would quite simply just like to stay with you.'[60] Blatter won 133 votes, but time was certainly to be sliced.

Just days later, the *New York Times* reported that Valcke had personally approved the transfer of a $10 million bribe to Jack Warner as part of South Africa's bid for the 2010 World Cup. However, Valcke and FIFA have repeated denied any wrong-doing and Valcke was never prosecuted or charged based on the payment to Warner. Even Blatter realised his time was up, con-firming he would go after an 'extraordinary elective Congress' in May 2016. 'FIFA needs a profound overhaul,' he admitted.[61] Blatter didn't get what he most wanted, which was to step down with an honorary lifetime presidency at the moment of his choos-ing. Platini, however, didn't get his own great desire of the FIFA presidency.

In September 2015, Swiss prosecutors found the 2 million franc payment to Platini from 2011. The timing of the payment looked terrible for both. Even in a substantial interview with *Le Monde*, Platini had no explanation. One theory for why he actu-ally requested it was that it was just old-fashioned envy of football administrators, which was remarkable for such a fêted figure.

Both Platini and Blatter were eventually banned from football for eight years for conflict of interest and dereliction of duty over a 'disloyal payment', although cleared of bribery and corruption.[62] Blatter drew some positives. Those who know the Swiss official say that, since he'd been satisfied with his time at the top, he was by that point happier Platini didn't succeed him as FIFA president. Their friendship had dissolved. Platini is meanwhile understood to remain embittered that he suffered the same fate as Blatter, even though he had just one transgression compared to a tenure that facilitated an era of corruption. Platini didn't even get to enjoy his legacy tournament, the expanded Euro 2016 hosted in France. When his image was shown at the final, he was booed. None of it actually led to grounds for removing the World Cups from Russia and Qatar. The US authorities had still caused regime change in football's two highest confederations.

Gianni Infantino meanwhile took his opportunity to stand for FIFA president. Although he was at that point publicly known as the presenter of the Champions League draw, he had developed a reputation within UEFA as a competent – if extremely ambitious – general secretary. Platini is understood to have been livid. Any mirth at Infantino was put into context by the questions surrounding his main competitor. Sheikh Salman bin Ebrahim Al Khalifa was part of the Bahrain royal family, which were accused by human rights groups of 'a campaign of torture and mass incarceration' against the country's pro-democracy movement.[63]

The race still came down to money, which would reflect the absence of true reform. Infantino pledged to increase funds distribution to member associations to $5 million every four years, while promising to expand the World Cup.[64] It was the same patronage system as Havelange and Blatter. 'At the end . . . I am one of you,'[65] Infantino proclaimed at Congress, eventually winning with 115 countries backing him. 'We will restore the image of FIFA and the respect of FIFA and everyone in the world will applaud us. I am convinced a new era is starting.'[66] One of the first major decisions of the Infantino era was to give USA what they wanted all along. They finally got the World Cup again, sharing 2026 with Canada and Mexico. There were more than a few political layers to this, not least with how confirmation came in Moscow on the eve of the 2018 World Cup.

Although the US would usually have been the outstanding favourite due to the commercial potential, especially against an underdeveloped Moroccan bid, there were new complications. One was lingering disgruntlement at the US investigation, and this in a reformed system where the vote was put to all 203 eligible associations. Another was the 'Donald Trump travel ban', which targeted predominantly Muslim nations on the supposed justification of protecting the US from terrorism.[67] This naturally offended a lot of countries, and even more inevitably brought a Trump response on social media: 'Why should we be supporting these countries when they don't support us (including at the United Nations)?'[68] Morocco had momentum, until a crucial swing. As the US bid visited 150 countries, one trip stood out. *Vanity Fair* reported how Trump's son-in-law Jared Kushner went to Saudi Arabia and directly asked Crown Prince Mohammed bin Salman for their vote.[69] The kingdom was more than willing, and it influenced the region. The Trump administration also made clear the travel ban would not apply to qualified teams. Infantino had by then developed a friendly relationship with Trump, having shared dinner at Davos. Trump was in turn keen to facilitate a connection between Bin Salman and Infantino. The US eventually won in Moscow with 134 votes. It wasn't quite the handover between Russia and the USA in Moscow that Blatter had in mind. It was also quite the turnaround, given that the FBI had likened FIFA to the mafia just three years before. Infantino now had grander plans. In 2025, the USA will host the expanded 32-team Club World Cup, which had become a priority of Infantino's presidency. He had seen first-hand how lucrative club football is to UEFA, and felt FIFA could do with its own global Champions League. This was where the money was, which ensured this was where the power was.

The issue was that, in order to attract the super clubs to make the competition viable, any proposal itself needed to be financially attractive. Infantino had agreed the outline of a $25 billion deal with Softbank by 2018.[70] Chaired by Japanese billionaire Masayoshi Son, this massive conglomerate involved money from Saudi Arabia's Public Investment Fund, UAE's Mubadala as well as American and British firms.[71] Infantino's idea from that was to sell streaming rights and replicate the Premier League's success on an international scale. It was like all the ghosts of football's future in one. Present politics prevented it.

Infantino had invited seven of the biggest clubs – Manchester United, Barcelona, Real Madrid, Bayern Munich, Juventus, Paris Saint-Germain and Manchester City – to a meeting in Zürich.[72] Talk of $100 million prize money each saw eyes light up, but raised eyebrows elsewhere. It would be ruinous for competitive balance. Even $50 million for River Plate, say, would have upended the Argentinian league. So much for spreading the wealth of the game.

There was also the philosophical issue of FIFA, the supposed global safeguard, directly selling off competition to private interests. Čeferin, for his part, lambasted unnamed colleagues 'blinded by the pursuit of profit' who were considering selling 'the soul of football tournaments to nebulous private funds'. 'We are not the owners of football. We are not allowed to sell it.'[73] This was just before an explosion of nebulous private funds buying up the clubs under his own organisation's umbrella. Eventually, Manchester United, Bayern Munich, Paris Saint-Germain and Juventus signed a letter from the European Club Association (ECA) supporting Čeferin's position. Infantino backed down but didn't fully buckle.[74] There were discussions with CVC a year later, and FIFA at one point argued to other stakeholders that the idea would ward off a breakaway Super League.[75] It probably did the opposite. The major clubs couldn't stop thinking of the Softbank deal, and how much they could really make.

A 'whole cycle of madness' had actually started.

As Leicester City were closing in on a shock Premier League title amid much fanfare, executives from five rivals left a London hotel a little more furtively. It was March 2016 and US billionaire Stephen Ross had flown in to meet representatives of Arsenal, Chelsea, Liverpool, Manchester City and Manchester United. They just weren't furtive enough, since they were photographed. An Arsenal spokesperson denied it was about a Super League.[76] Karl-Heinz Rummenigge had already brought the idea back into the public consciousness by saying he could see it 'in the future'.[77] It was eventually acknowledged the English clubs were also discussing Champions League changes, but part of the problem was that no one was taking charge. UEFA, in the words of Rummenigge, were 'rudderless'.[78]

Although the FBI had focused on FIFA, the investigations had a much deeper effect on the European game. Platini's fall left a vacuum. The wealthiest clubs surged in. They had long been disgruntled with how the Champions League didn't offer sufficient guarantees of entry or income, so moved to secure both. Mere weeks before Čeferin was elected, at the start of the 2016–17 season, a group led by Bayern Munich and Real Madrid pushed so that the four top-ranked leagues would have four automatic places and that 30 per cent of all prize money would be distributed by performance over the previous decade. Essentially, 'royalties'. Rummenigge praised a 'serious and fair solution'.[79] He later told *Der Spiegel* that the clubs 'had to act' due to 'lucrative proposals for a Super League' through Spain. It was the same old leverage. Football Leaks later revealed that Key Capital Partners had sent a 'binding term sheet' to Florentino Pérez in that same year.[80] Bayern and those five Premier League clubs were to be included.[81] The plan was to start the project in 2021. Executives involved now say the pressure made it essential to placate the biggest clubs, and particularly Pérez. The problem is that that push is now seen as the decision that has had the most drastic impact on the landscape, finally and fully transforming it. It essentially meant that Leicester would get much less European money than Arsenal despite beating them to the Premier League, increasing the gap rather than reducing it.

Much of this had come from Platini's willingness to bring the old 'G-14' deeper into such decision-making. This was the organisation of elite clubs which became the ECA, and the inclusion has been likened to 'inviting a vampire into your house'. The group's control of the World Leagues Forum meant they also had huge influence over FIFA through the stakeholder committee. It's almost ironic now, but that power imbalance was partly how Čeferin became UEFA president. Political blocs within the confederation felt they needed someone who represented smaller clubs and associations. The then down-to-earth Slovenian was seen as ideal, although his presidency is now considered 'an accident of history'.

The challenge Čeferin faced was illustrated in Chelsea's Bruce Buck declaring his opposition to 'dumbing down the large clubs in order to make all clubs the great unwashed'.[82] The Premier League's 'big six' were at the same time making their own intentions clear, convening in a corner during one discussion over a £564 million TV deal with Chinese broadcaster PPTV. Tottenham Hotspur's Daniel Levy later declared 'we only want what's fair', which was a greater share of the income they felt they created. City's Ferran Soriano was a very strong voice. The tension eventually resulted in a first ever change to the Founder Members Agreement, with one-third of all future international rights distributed according to finishing position.[83] It was around this point that Premier League chief executive Richard Scudamore decided to leave. A problem was growing.

By 2019, the Premier League was also resisting attempts from big European clubs to alter the Champions League to four groups of eight, with promotion and relegation from two other competitions.[84] The idea was savaged, with UEFA's own analysts saying it would produce less revenue overall due to the dilution of domestic leagues. Juventus president Andrea Agnelli, who had led the move, rowed back after the wider ECA body voted against the plans. The Italian did make a point of stressing that the NFL represented an 'even better' model, as he abrasively spoke of the need to change for the future.[85] Agnelli was seen as having a constant need to prove himself, by proving Juventus's stature. 'He is part of a long family dynasty who have been stewards of Italy's biggest club,' former UEFA executive Alex Phillips says. 'But he's only there because they wouldn't put him in charge of the real family business, the cars. Agnelli then turns out to be as bad as any American oligarch.' It's true that UEFA began to work on different models for the Champions League.

Another interpretation is that this was the moment when the European Super League project decided to accelerate. The Covid-19 pandemic had exacerbated huge tensions by putting financial stress on the game, while showing the major clubs how fragile their power was. It didn't help that this was the hubristic peak of the wage race. In the summer of 2019, both Real Madrid and Barcelona had signed 28-year-olds for over €100 million each, in Eden Hazard and Antoine Griezmann, respectively. Both now look irrational moves from a previous era, as they almost caused top-heavy squads to topple over. Juventus had meanwhile deviated from an agile transfer policy to mortgaging the future on a 33-year-old Cristiano Ronaldo. All three made losses into hundreds of millions over the 'lockdown season' of 2020–21, as the debts of the two Spanish clubs grew to at least €1 billion each.[86] The Super League's founding statement even cited how the 'global pandemic accelerated the instability' in European football's economic model.[87]

UEFA's power rankled the super clubs, too. The confederation were seen as a huge commercial operator in their own right, making billions off the big clubs, but who weren't even enforcing their rules as a regulator. Resentment was made worse by Manchester City's ban being overturned at the Court of Arbitration for Sport. It was another pivotal moment. The rival clubs were convinced the Abu Dhabi project had cheated them, with that expenditure inflating the economy. Barcelona had been driven to a form of football madness. Pérez brazenly complained it was difficult to 'compete on a level playing field'[88] after Real Madrid's wage bill jumped by 32 per cent in one season just to keep their Champions League-winning squad together.[89] City and PSG reasonably argued these clubs were responsible for their own bad decisions, but the core point was that more money was required to compete. It only fired American owners' utter astonishment that the game was, in truth, financially unregulated. 'How is everyone losing money,' was one screech from an executive. The conclusion was that UEFA weren't fit for purpose. The clubs wanted to control European football themselves, since they were taking the financial risk.

Initial moves weren't so far-reaching but were still revolutionary. In October 2020, Manchester United, Liverpool and the English Football League – who represented the three divisions below the Premier League – agreed on an idea that would afford more power to the big six while increasing redistribution to the wider pyramid. The latter was essential after the effects of the pandemic. It was titled 'Project Big Picture', but those in the middle inevitably resisted. So, the super clubs went all in. They looked to fully Americanise the European game.

Rumours immediately resurfaced about a Super League.[90] Martyn Ziegler even reported the entire plan in January 2021.[91] UEFA insisted they weren't taking it seriously, but that was because of the ruse of final discussions over Champions League reforms for 2024. Agnelli even hailed the idea of 'sporting merit', before later stating the new competition model would kill the breakaway.[92] It was utterly shameless, especially as the Juventus chairman was a central figure in the Super League. Alarm bells should maybe have sounded when a request was made to delay final decisions on prize money and qualification, for Monday 19 April.[93] UEFA were still oblivious.

Since so many of the plans had been agreed at expensive restaurants like New York's Locanda Verde, it was maybe fitting that the world found out about the plan to carve up football through a lunch between Javier Tebas and Joan Laporta. La Liga's president was informed that Barcelona were in a plan to break away from the Champions League, and it was very real, since the announcement was initially supposed to be that Thursday they were eating. By that late stage, Liverpool and Manchester United were the main English drivers, with Arsenal offering counsel. Tottenham were seen as having 'hit the motherlode', but they were hugely popular in the US, while executives admired Levy's acumen. City and Chelsea were hesitant but were ultimately told 'the train was leaving the station'. By Friday, the Premier League learnt the Super League had all six.

It is remarkable to think now the breakaway clubs felt they could just do a deal with UEFA and proceed, even though that would have destroyed the 66-year-old Champions League. Such audacity was partly based on the confidence in FIFA sanctioning the plan. This prospect was actually described in documents seen by the *New York Times* as 'an essential condition' due to the legal protection it brought.[94] Laporta later revealed Infantino was open to the idea.[95] Those involved in the plans even say there was a point when it might have been called 'the FIFA Super League'. In return for such support, the competition would provide eight clubs to Infantino's expanded Club World Cup. While FIFA are described as never giving full support, their public statements were perceived as open to interpretation.

The English clubs did think they had the categorical support of Boris Johnson's government through Chief of Staff Dan Rosenfield. It was a major reason City and Chelsea agreed. JP Morgan were similarly persuaded to offer $4 billion in credit. This was after all the 'free-market fundamentalism' that fitted with traditional Conservative economic policy. Johnson's abrupt U-turn later stunned the Super League clubs, but fitted with his own personal populism. There was even the scene of a Conservative prime minister decrying the influence of bankers on a call to supporters groups. Then again, the entire story of the Super League is one of strange alliances, that reflected how distorted the game had become. Aside from ascetic American owners coming to an accommodation with state-owned clubs, it was also an agreement with the money-burning Spanish giants. This was a compromise between control and excess. Within that was Liverpool's partnership with Manchester United, as John Henry took to phoning the Glazer hierarchy late into the night, as well as Barcelona's alliance with Real Madrid. At the root of everything was Florentino Pérez insisting on Real Madrid staying on top of the world. He just knew he needed Barcelona there, too. Their fixtures, known as *El Clásico*, had been the real television spectacular for over a decade. That aligned with the American owners' desire to increase the profitability and valuation of their purchases.

After 40 years of the same clubs eroding football's unpredictability, they found there still wasn't enough predictability for business. The digital revolution hadn't yet happened. Executives had meanwhile seen how the closed-shop nature of MLS meant their franchises could trade at eight to 10 times their revenue. European football's variables restricted clubs to three to four times their revenues. The Super League was the attempt to change this at the stroke of a pen. One of the arguments they'd even planned for their imagined deal with UEFA was that this would serve the pyramid, since it would stabilise the wage race. The NFL-style structure would mean the elite clubs would no longer be trying to kill each other, and it would only require them to stay on top in perpetuity.

It was merely a happy coincidence this served as a mass refinancing for the Spanish and Italian clubs. Barcelona and Real Madrid were even to receive an extra €30 million each for the first two seasons.[96] They would similarly be afforded the means to control the state-owned clubs and oligarchs, who in turn needed to stay at the top of the game for their own political purposes. This was where there was another intersection, and an overlap in non-football motives. Both the state-owned and US-owned clubs were looking at this on a scale of 30–50-year periods. It was why so much was made about how Generation Z consume sport. The example that kept being cited was that the Chicago Bulls show how easy it is for a brand to just fall away.

Underpinning it all, however, was an 'intense resentment' at some bureaucrats in Nyon telling them how to run their businesses. 'We know how to make this 100 times better,' one executive argued. It's been variously described as 'real masters of the universe stuff' and 'self-made men dismissing regulators who hadn't put in a penny'. The overwhelming counter-argument, of course, was that this was the collective system they'd bought into. The group had even been advised that the Champions League reforms, which they were still ostensibly negotiating, would give them everything they wanted anyway.

It was no longer enough. Pérez, with the backing of Joel Glazer, was insistent on launching the Super League as soon as possible. Although an early issue was the lack of a figurehead, there was little doubt who the driving personality was. Pérez, in so many ways, personified Real Madrid. The abundance of entitlement was only matched by the absence of self-doubt. 'We created FIFA,' he'd say. 'We are the reason the Champions League is what it is.' Some actually saw the entire Super League as an act of desperation, rather than power, out of the fear Real Madrid might be losing their supremacy. Pérez himself was a very specific product of his country's socio-economic history. Spain was one of only two European dictatorships that hadn't been toppled in the Second World War, along with Portugal, and General Franco attempted to rebuild the economy on three main pillars: services, tourism and entertainment. Banks, construction and football were integral to this, with that supercharged by prime minister José María Aznar's reprogramming of Spanish capitalism in the 1990s. Pérez traversed all of this, primarily through his construction company, ACS. The club's international profile also helped secure contracts around the world.[97] It was through ACS he developed a relationship with Key Capital Partners.[98] The nexus is *el palco*, the presidential box at Real Madrid's Santiago Bernabéu stadium, which is described as like Davos in a royal court. It was from there that Pérez, himself viewed as a 'Spanish oligarch', is reported to have told one politician that 'Real Madrid is a Spanish brand standing above the government'. So much for it being the people's club owned by members who vote on presidents. The reality is that Pérez has made the statutes so limiting – time served as a director, a huge deposit – that he is one of few possible candidates. It is within this context, as well as the media-industrial complex around the club, that Pérez is completely unquestioned. One Real Madrid legend, Emiliano Butragueño, describes him as 'a superior being',[99] another in Roberto Carlos says he is a 'grand visionary'.

Driving this vision is the idea of '*ilusión*', which broadly means excitement from spectacle. It is why Pérez became obsessed with stars, often to the detriment of his team. The first Galacticos unravelled when the president insisted on sacrificing the defensive Claude Makelele for David Beckham. Pérez has belatedly empowered Brazilian technical director Juni Calafat to realign the club around precocious talent such as Jude Bellingham, but that decision was a necessity from the new world. Pérez needed to reshape it again. The Super League was the ultimate idea of *ilusión*.

That just wasn't the emotion when the story broke. There was shock and then, as one director put it, 'a tsunami of shit'. There was also betrayal and fury. Čeferin realised the launch of the Super League was happening when, after weeks of denials, Agnelli was asked to draft a statement finally killing the growing rumours on

Sunday 18 April. The Juventus chairman just turned off his phone. It was all the worse since the two men had been so close that Čeferin was godfather to Agnelli's daughter. By Monday morning, the UEFA president was calling him and Woodward 'snakes' and 'liars'.

The bombshell news was finally broken by Ziegler on Sunday afternoon, and the rest of UEFA and the ECA understood how big it was when they saw many empty seats at an emergency meeting. The announcing press release didn't actually drop until close to midnight, because the project needed legal clearance from Spain. That was never in doubt with Pérez. The Super League was to be launched 'as soon as practicable', directly competing with the Champions League in midweek, and involving 12 clubs who at that point had won the old trophy 40 times in 65 years. Atlético de Madrid, AC Milan, Internazionale and Juventus were to join the English big five and Spanish *Clásico* pair. Bayern Munich, Borussia Dortmund and PSG had been offered places but all three demurred. 'The German clubs didn't sign up due to the 50+1 rule,' Phillips says. It was the clearest benefit possible of fan ownership and direct participation. PSG, who are widely seen as having been willing to join, perhaps sensed different opportunities. Nasser Al-Khelaifi, for his part, is seen as having an appreciation for tradition.

Each of the breakaway clubs were to immediately get €400 million each, which was five times what the Champions League winner received. They were also going to evade what was inferred as FIFA's coded disapproval of a 'closed' competition by opening up five places of a planned 20 for other clubs. The competition would be split in two, before a knock-out and grand final. A solidarity payment of €400 million would be doled out to the rest of the game.

Although the Super League had been strenuously advised to make more of a public argument justifying it, media officers didn't have the data. The haphazard launch reflected how, for all the secret talks going back years, there hadn't been enough consideration of the one essential requirement: audience. Even before the Super League was announced, the public narrative had been set. This was a greedy and hostile takeover. The response within the game was just as vociferous. Players at the English clubs demanded answers from their bosses, as the managers all distanced themselves in stirringly direct words. Manchester United's Ander Herrera bemoaned 'the rich stealing what the people created.'[100]

It was staggering that a handful of men had caused such upheaval for clubs that had existed for over a century, reshaping a world game. Except, it was that very universality that worked against them. The game came together. Čeferin admirably invoked that spirit in a strident press conference that Monday morning.

'The disgraceful, self-serving proposals,' he began, referencing how 'this nonsense of a project' was 'a spit in the face of all football lovers'. 'We will not allow them to take it away from us.'[101]

Impressive as Čeferin's speech was, he was also navigating the political nuances. There were clear olive branches around the personalised attacks on Woodward and Agnelli. Čeferin had already changed his speech because he'd heard City and Chelsea were wavering. Their ownerships after all prized public relations as much as anything else.

Prince William joined a swell of establishment opposition across Europe, amplifying the fury of fans. FIFA finally confirmed they were not supporting the project, as Infantino and Čeferin set aside growing differences. The Premier League meanwhile held several meetings without the six, in which it was decided only executives responsible would be punished. There was insistence it was 'an owner thing'. 'It's not what you think,' Levy had desperately pleaded to Brighton's Paul Barber.

Agnelli was meanwhile repeatedly called a 'Judas' in a Serie A meeting, the tone turning febrile. Spain had the most muted response because the football culture was so in thrall to the big two – at least until Pérez finally became the first major figure to publicly defend the project. On late-night football shows, he theatrically demonstrated trickle-down economics with hand gestures. 'This is not a league for the rich, it's a league to save football.' Executives at his partner clubs had their heads in their hands. There was one truth to something Pérez later said, which was that 'one of the English clubs ... affected all the rest'. That was City. Johnson's special envoy to the Gulf, Lord Udny-Lister, warned the UAE that the club joining the Super League could damage the relationship with the UK.[102] That came from Johnson's instinctive decision when the story broke. The UK prime minister literally just turned to advisors. 'Is this good or bad?' When told 'bad', Johnson immediately made a staff member ring a Super League executive to say it was off.

The episode ended up as one of the best polling issues for Johnson that year, and a rare subject that '100 per cent united the UK parliament'. The response was already impossible to resist when the prime minister promised to drop 'a legislative bomb' on the Super League. Abramovich was meanwhile wary of perception in Russia. The Gazprom-sponsored 2022 Champions League final was due to be staged in St Petersburg and here was Russia's most famous oligarch saying it wasn't good enough for his club? Chelsea's decision was announced to protesting fans who had gathered outside Stamford Bridge for a match against Brighton, and celebrated as if it were the Champions League itself. City were actually the first to officially confirm, with all English clubs quickly following. Woodward resigned. A fan-led review of football had already been announced. A spate of apologies followed, with even JP Morgan going as far as saying they 'misjudged how this deal would be viewed'.[103] As the clubs fell over themselves to admit a mistake, some specific errors stood out. It was a tactical misstep to cut out major broadcasters, since that made it open season for criticism. Perhaps the biggest lesson, however, is that it's a mistake to be too brazen even in football. Advisors had warned this was far too soon. A grand display of hubris meant the Super League had detonated their one long-held nuclear weapon in the wrong place at the wrong time. They'd also failed to learn from their own experience over the course of 30 years, where they got more through suggestion rather than brute force.

Except, as they were also counselled, they'd already got what they wanted. The post-2024 Champions League was set up to be the Super League institutionalised, and that had been announced on the day of Čeferin's 'snakes' speech. The disparity was displayed at the end of that same 2020–21 season, when Chelsea beat Leicester to the last Champions League place. Had Leicester won, they would have been guaranteed €1.5 million. Chelsea's qualification guaranteed at least €30 million. Backed by such resources, the London club won the Champions League itself just six days later, beating City in the final. A moment to reset had been lost. The Super League has since been described as 'just a parenthesis'. There was one other immediate outcome that emphasised how patient politicking was more effective. After PSG stayed loyal to UEFA, Nasser Al-Khelaifi was elected chairman of the ECA. By 2024, the Champions League final may not have been held in New York, but the European club body's assembly was held in Doha.

11.

MEET THE NEW BOSS . . .

Gianni Infantino had barely finished speaking about one of his grand new initiatives, but Aleksander Čeferin couldn't wait to dismiss what he said as 'shit'. For the UEFA president's part, it's not like Infantino's seemingly endless spool of ideas are met with enthusiasm. Čeferin's aside to colleagues, however, didn't come from any rigorous critique of this latest presentation to stakeholders. It mostly derived from a petty personal antipathy, that itself developed simply because they were in the two most powerful positions in football. Infantino's initial attempt to expand the Club World Cup ensured the two didn't speak properly for a year, and that added an awkwardness when Čeferin had to call Infantino about the Super League.

It shows how the relationship between two relatively random men has somehow come to condition the contours of football, but that itself is a product of an inexplicably unsuitable governance model. Geopolitics and capitalism may be the two forces that have transformed the game, but only because the sport's authorities have allowed them. Football, in the words of everyone from executives to legal professors, 'has failed to govern itself'. That is because the system has given these two positions extraordinary power. For the UEFA president, it is the power from the gravitas and wealth of the European club game. For the FIFA president, it is the wonder of the World Cup.

What that has produced is a system where, in terms of competing at the top level, so many matches have become less unpredictable than Infantino vs Čeferin. If there's a fair temptation to pin this on the two presidents, as was the case with Sepp Blatter and Michel Platini, this is really about what football does to people. As one federation head rolls his eyes, 'names change but the culture continues'.

The positions bring proximity to real power without sufficient checks, which blinds authorities to the various forces on the game, ensuring it is driven by this endless need to accumulate. The only solution to anything seems to be to just keep expanding competitions, because that brings more money, which allows more political promises. That has most visibly translated into a battle over the fixture list. Former FIFA Council member Moya Dodd describes the calendar as 'a wealth allocation mechanism upon which the game hinges'. The central pieces are the big clubs, since they now bring the wealth. FIFA want more of that, while the big clubs themselves have wanted to supplant UEFA through the Super League. Through that, the governing bodies fittingly resemble the Organization of Petroleum Exporting Countries (OPEC) in its facilitative relationship with the oil companies. Seeking to deal with clubs rather than regulate them, FIFA and UEFA instead derive power out of bestowing World Cups and Champions League finals on hosts, which becomes more alluring than what the bodies are supposed to be about. That is ensuring 'integrity' and 'competitive balance', according to former FIFA Governance Committee chairman Miguel Maduro. 'They are failing miserably on both.'

This has been the case for decades, but has evolved into an existential threat to football when so many sophisticated actors seek to exploit its political and financial capital. Football has never had greater need for strong and well-structured governing bodies. Instead, FIFA and UEFA are relics. Their rudimentary structures, subject to the whims of over-indulged middle-aged men, can't cope.

Since so few leaders are attuned to this, there is little hope of a unifying vision for football. That should be all the more frustrating given that this is a sport that has the distinctive benefit of being a unified global pyramid, unlike boxing. There is an argument that the very global aspect makes the sport ungovernable, because it is so porous. The true issue is how petty squabbles turn those gaps into chasms, and create problems of immense scale.

It was no less a figure than the FIFA president who declared the presidential structure should change. Blatter proclaimed the need for 'a profound overhaul' as he announced his exit.[1] FIFA now fairly say it is absurd to argue they are in any way similar to the old regime, and would point to how the governing body was recognised as a 'victim' by the US Department of Justice in a 2021 announcement about forfeited funds being remitted. It is still undeniable that elements of the political structure have persisted from 2015, despite both new presidents of FIFA and UEFA being hailed as 'reformers'. The reason for that is really the story of how football changes those in charge. Infantino had even been part of a group tasked with addressing governance after 2015, where one recommendation was that many presidential powers be adopted by a general secretary who would be more like a chief executive. That was what the Swiss official himself had been under Platini at UEFA, but it hasn't worked out like that since he got the top job. Infantino has been a de facto executive president, although is described as behaving like 'a supreme leader'. Some of the very first moments of his presidency had considerable foreshadowing. A big show was made of

Infantino travelling by budget airline Easyjet for his first trip, but he was soon investigated by FIFA's Ethics Committee for use of private jets amid a series of early controversies and complaints about breaches of rules. Some of the latter appeared to come out of a civil war following so much upheaval, with Infantino even grumbling that his 'enemies want to make me look greedy'.[2] He looked farcical when it was reported he became infuriated on being asked to pay a laundry bill for underwear. Infantino was eventually cleared, although there were soon ructions about the independence of such bodies.

Maduro was fired as chair of the governance committee, just eight months after his appointment was hailed as a symbol of reform. He had attempted to block Russian deputy prime minister Vitaly Mutko from rerunning for FIFA Council due to rules on political neutrality, while also highlighting other democratic deficits.[3] Four other committee members resigned in protest. This was all as that same FIFA Council was afforded the power to appoint and dismiss members of such notionally independent committees.[4] The body had been the replacement for the 24-person ExCo, although only after new Ethics Committee chair Domenico Scala advised the latter be completely supplanted by just 12 officials with no links to the past. The disgruntled response was to just make it a 36-person council. Scala eventually resigned.[5]

Infantino had meanwhile declared, 'FIFA is back on track.' He had certainly intuited the main route to power. It is the same as that followed by Blatter and João Havelange, and that is increasingly visible in UEFA. That is to appeal to the smaller nations, with promises of more money creating mega-blocs of vote. This is the primary reason the World Cup has bloated to an unwieldy 48 teams, and there has been a crisis over where to fit the Club World Cup into the calendar. It is to generate more money for patronage. Such an approach ensures it doesn't matter if Europe doesn't back him, since Germany have the same voting weight as Comoros. The tiny country is one of 54 votes in Africa, where Infantino's influence is so pronounced that FIFA is basically seen as running the Confederation of African Football. He has similarly played to the Asian Football Confederation, which brings another 47 votes, together with Africa making up almost half of the 211 members.

The same pattern was inverted in UEFA. Čeferin was pushed as someone who was 'perfect' to represent interests outside the elite, given he is a Slovenian who wasn't considered a company man. Platini had similarly been elected after telling David Conn his job was to 'help the children of Georgia, Armenia, Lithuania ... not the games between Arsenal and Manchester but between the smaller clubs'.[6] And yet virtually every single president ended up facilitating the biggest influences, taking votes from the poor to give power to the rich. There's even a parallel with US neoliberalism in how constituents are persuaded to vote against their own interests. Except, that's where the intrigue lies. There can be a lot of interest for individuals.

One of the persistent criticisms of Blatter's FIFA was how it was run on first-class travel and clientelism. As the federations benefited from the GOAL programme, their heads enjoyed great luxury around FIFA events. The ExCo members had a VVIP lifestyle beyond even that, with a $10,000 per month honorarium and $500 per day expenses. Blatter meanwhile set up a lot of committees that meant administrators got to wear the FIFA suits for two-hour meetings around three-day junkets. There are similar boards at UEFA, that officials push to get on. It's a charmed life. Infantino initially intended to evolve away from this, but it didn't go much further than symbolically moving the official Zürich hotel away from Baur au Lac. The new president wanted to immediately move away from five-star hotels and business-class flights for his first Congress, too, only to then note how members 'liked it so much'. Why irritate those who vote for him?

The 2023 FIFA Congress in Kigali actually included police escorts and a team of chefs flown out.[7] The only real difference is FIFA Council members receiving $250,000 a year rather than the $300,000 from the ExCo. One of Infantino's first controversies was actually when he rejected a first salary offer of $2 million as insulting,[8] as he elsewhere sarcastically grumbled about perceptions of 'a Rolls-Royce with a chauffeur'.[9] He maybe shouldn't have, since it has been noted how some senior FIFA officials have insisted on first-class over business while 'never opening their own car door'. Norwegian federation president Lise Klaveness feels it is 'a very big problem' that the system 'serves everyone so well with money and travels'. UEFA isn't so lavish but isn't exactly austere, and it began to be noted how their HatTrick programme worked in a similar way to GOAL. Distribution figures significantly went up twice in Čeferin's time, by almost 30 per cent and then another 22 per cent.

The smallest federations, according to one such association chief, 'sell their votes cheaply'. The money makes a huge difference. Staging an event like a Super Cup can make a historic difference. This is where the self-perpetuating circle of interest goes beyond individuals. The confederation president funds projects that make him and national associations look good. The national associations return their votes. The word used to describe this by Maduro and Klaveness is 'cartel'. It is made worse by the lack of diversity, which means there are few alternative viewpoints. The general profile is still 'a man, over 55' and 'preferably to have played football'.

'There's still a lot of admiration for alpha-males,' Klaveness explains, 'you still hear a lot about what people got paid when they played ... I'm often challenged, being the first woman, so I feel lucky because I don't have yes people around me.' Klaveness has even been taken aside and told it's smarter to play a longer game. She argues that game is so long there's never any outcome. Far from nuanced politicking, in fact, there is never real discussion. It's not like the game's direction is robustly debated. Some representatives have become infamous for never saying anything. Many look like they're 'just happy to be there', with no actual principles. The president generally speaks for an hour with little response. Klaveness outlines 'a very clear culture of keeping your head down'. One football politician complains that it's almost like people turn up and ask 'what do you want me to vote for?'

That means any presidential vision, if there actually is one, isn't honed. Outside influence has a far greater effect than internal challenge. It ensures decisions are generally taken by fiat, without consultation. It's not real 'democracy', either, because there's no 'opposition'. Groups don't coalesce. Every major decision becomes zero-sum. If the field thinks you are going to win, they often rush behind to produce unanimous results. 'It is real *Game of Thrones* stuff,' one executive confides. 'You win or lose, and you've got to kill any rivals with one strike.'

That is translated into how there is usually only one candidate. Since the initial FIFA upheavals over 2015–16, 12 of 13 presidential elections across seven confederations have been uncontested. No one else tries to win because there's too much to lose. Those who attempt reform are cast out. That was seen with how those who moved against Mohammed bin Hammam in the AFC were even ousted by the next regime. Debate that is just healthy political process in normal systems is generally seen in football federations as insubordination and a breakdown of trust.

A vintage example of how it all works was the UEFA Congress in Paris in February 2024. Čeferin's administration attempted to push through statute changes that could feasibly allow him to stay in office for 15 years. This had caused huge unease among the majority of member associations but they felt they couldn't vote against it because of the potential repercussions, especially for the smaller federations. A European final could suddenly be taken away. It was only the English FA who voted against. All of this conditions an inherent protection of the system. Every function, in the words of law professor Petros Mavroidis, 'is confused in the name of the president'. Other than dissenting insiders like Klaveness or Croatian playing legend Zvonimir Boban, one of the few times they are questioned is by journalists. That is partly why Čeferin is said to have become obsessed with the English media, but then there are so few press conferences. A series of major decisions are made without any public explanation. Descriptions like 'Stalinist' and 'authoritarian reflexes' are instead used inside.

It is in turn what makes football more susceptible to autocrats. Many have sought personal relationships. That was less subtle with Infantino, since his 'new FIFA' needed money from the 2015 overhaul. Autocracies were more than willing to offer it. By the 2022 World Cup, 40 per cent of sponsors were from China or the Gulf.[10] A year later, Rwanda's Paul Kagame praised Infantino for his 'exceptional leadership' after uncontested re-election at that FIFA Congress in Kigali.[11] UEFA meanwhile granted a Champions League final to Turkey's Recep Tayyip Erdoğan, having already been accused of acquiescing to Hungarian Prime Minister Viktor Orbán's autocratic tendencies at Euro 2020. When a request was made to illuminate Bayern Munich's stadium with rainbow colours in protest at a Hungarian law that was criticised for targeting the LGBT community, UEFA refused. So much for the official messaging of the tournament being 'for everyone'.[12]

It is from all of this that UEFA and FIFA presidents come to see themselves as more than football administrators. They fly all over the world, bestowing glamorous events on eager countries, and are fêted by the highest offices. Infantino is said to have realised the 'enormous power' of his position as he walked around the World Economic Forum. Little wonder Blatter used to tell people he was 'essentially a head of state'.

'FIFA sees itself as a parallel world government,' Amnesty's Steve Cockburn says.

Insiders would go further. The role of president is described as more like that of a monarch or, yes, an autocrat.[13]

It inevitably becomes intoxicating. The presidents begin to feel they are individually responsible for what the role brings, and irreplaceable. Most become obsessed with legacy. Some close to presidents talk of 'power corruption' rather than financial corruption. 'Football makes people mad,' Blatter once said. That's especially true at the top.

Having initially spoken with such pride, Gianni Infantino went into a strop. The FIFA president was telling staff about his invite to the White House, when one executive interjected, 'It's not the person, it's the position.' Infantino insisted it was also him. This blurring of the personality with the role is one important way the presidency becomes warped. It's also why Infantino and Čeferin offer such instructive case studies. An irony is that Infantino's specific experience as UEFA General Secretary has informed a vision with some merit. He wants at least 50 club sides around the world of equal quality, and even figures within UEFA have admired – some begrudgingly – how he has started to level up the game in Africa and Asia. An improved Club World Cup is probably overdue. The problem, in the words of one senior executive, is that many of Infantino's ideas are 'terrible'. The inclination is always to expand, and that doesn't necessarily bring equality. The Club World Cup's prize money could even increase disparity, and all of this is generally perceived as a way to bring in more money just to consolidate Infantino's power.

There was always an ego in the former lawyer, too, that was witnessed in those Champions League draws. At one UEFA Congress, he bounded into a meeting 15 minutes late and insisted on shaking everyone's hand. 'It was the Gianni show again.' He even requested a more prominent speaking slot at a technology summit that wanted him and Arsène Wenger, FIFA's head of global football development, to speak. This led to one unfavourable comparison with Blatter, who was at least seen as having a certain romance for the game. With Infantino, 'it's all about him'. FIFA employees still roll their eyes about the president arranging football matches with 'legends' like Luís Figo then appearing as the playmaker. Platini once derided Infantino as 'a good lawyer' and a 'good number-two but to be president, it's a joke'.[14] There was then the kicker: 'But I'm not bitter.' A perceived buffoonery has been all the more incongruous given Infantino's willingness to orbit some of the most criticised figures on the planet. There is so much symbolism to that image from the opening game of the 2018 World Cup, where the FIFA president was delightedly sitting between Vladimir Putin and Mohammed bin Salman. He maintained contact with both. An attempt to step into a more complicated world has seen Infantino put his foot in it. He has offended women's football by going to a match in Iran that only men could attend, amid resentment that he didn't move forward on pushing reform.[15] There was then the claim that changes to football's calendar can 'give hope to Africans so they don't need to cross the Mediterranean in order to find, maybe, a better life but more probably death in the sea'.[16]

Those who work with Infantino say part of the issue is that he's 'a showman' and 'you have to realise he just gets up and goes with it', often without notes. The widespread view is that he now shares one of Blatter's ambitions, at least, which is to win a Nobel Peace Prize. That could be divined in initial suggestions the 2030 World Cup be shared with Israel and its neighbours, potentially including Palestine.[17] There remains a belief this could be revived in the long build-up to Saudi Arabia 2034.

The more severe Čeferin doesn't have such ambitions but then he doesn't have much vision at all. There is even a suspicion he is more of a fan of martial arts and basketball. Čeferin has admittedly faced more challenges than virtually any other president, with a global pandemic, the Super League and the mass encroachment of nation states and private equity. A fair question is whether his leadership made the fallout worse. Čeferin is described as lacking Infantino's instinct for detail. He did initially try to cater to smaller nations, keeping more actual domestic champions in the Champions League while sharing the Super Cup around smaller capitals. The Nations League has been a success, but that was Platini's idea. The Conference League is valuable for smaller clubs, but that was the ECA's idea. They were also seen as low-cost superficial measures. Čeferin, like Infantino, began to move in higher circles. As someone who has driven across the Sahara, Čeferin was suddenly mixing with motoring royalty like Andrea Agnelli. The UEFA president developed what he felt was a close friendship with the former Juventus president, although there was a perception this just made him easier to influence. Agreeing to become the godfather to Agnelli's daughter was a misguided but typical blurring of the professional with the personal, where he didn't see the potential issues. Čeferin had been warned, but he felt he had the measure of Agnelli. Many believe the same is happening now with Nasser Al-Khelaifi.

Čeferin was 'in denial' about the Super League until it was staring him in the face in the form of 'call failed' notifications from trying to phone Agnelli. The Slovenian did navigate the crisis well, but this is said to have gone to his head. Čeferin began to see himself as 'the man who saved European football', with the pretensions to go with it. It was noted that, in the aftermath, he appeared much keener to thank politicians like Boris Johnson and Emmanuel Macron than football figures. This was despite a wider perception he 'got out of jail' due to the English response, having been an enabler of the big clubs for years. Čeferin rarely mixes with staff or federation heads, and is constantly surrounded by security. That is regarded as absurd for someone virtually unknown outside football – although it was seen as quite Infantino-like in how Čeferin was front and centre of the draw for the newly expanded Champions League in 2024–25, even making edgy jokes in a video with Zlatan Ibrahimović. Such a sense of insulation otherwise plays into a perceived 'rudeness' to the point of obnoxiousness. Čeferin was infuriated when a prime minister couldn't meet him on a trip to a smaller European country. UEFA figures admired this abrasiveness when he lambasted Super League organisers in a meeting at Nyon in 2023. They were less impressed when he reacted furiously to UEFA Treasurer David Gill questioning the 2024 statute changes. It was something else he seemed to make personal, even though this was an ExCo meeting where the duty was to football.

A common statement now is that he's become 'lost in power'. His antipathy towards Infantino is one of many tensions at the top of the game.

*

It was both peak drama and, evidently, the height of UEFA's self-satisfaction. In the second leg of the 2018–19 Champions League semi-final, Jürgen Klopp's Liverpool raucously won 4-0 against Leo Messi's Barcelona, having lost the first leg 3-0. There had rarely been a game like it, until the very next night. Tottenham Hotspur scored a 96th-minute winner to complete a three-goal comeback against Ajax to win their semi-final on the away goals rule. The sudden silence in the Amsterdam Arena had a cinematic quality the most accomplished directors would struggle to recreate. Little wonder broadcasters were clamouring for this, given it capped a half decade of full chaos in the Champions League.

This led to a surprisingly bombastic statement from Čeferin at the UEFA Congress in March 2022, as he crowed about how their confederation was now the biggest sports organisation in the world by revenues and audience. The Slovenian made a point of stating how the €15 billion made between 2016 and 2020 was at least twice that of FIFA and the IOC. 'The UEFA Champions League final is the most watched annual football club event in the world ... should we be ashamed of this commercial success?'[18]

There are fair questions over why this should matter so much to Čeferin, beyond whether such money goes back into the game. It's difficult not to link it to the dubious dynamic that comes from being both a regulator and competition organiser, as is also the case with FIFA. This creates commercial competition between the federations as well as the very clubs they preside over, with huge potential for conflict of interest. It is one of the defining issues of the last decade as global income has exploded. The Super League clubs have certainly fixated on this, as well as the moments when it looks like UEFA and FIFA act as sports entertainment companies rather than governing bodies. Human and financial resources mostly go into organising events that make money. The tension is even more historically ironic given how the structure developed. The old European Cup was actually devised in 1955 by French newspaper *L'Équipe*, and willingly taken on by big clubs. The most enthusiastic figure was Florentino Pérez's predecessor as Real Madrid president, Santiago Bernabéu, after whom their stadium is named. The original plan was for a league. It all sounds familiar. UEFA, formed just the year before as a union of national associations, were initially lukewarm. That only changed when FIFA said they would sanction the competition if the national federations approved. They did, so UEFA were simply handed the competition that would become the Champions League and their golden goose. It was out of such happenstance that the body began to swallow up more and more power.

Manchester City's Ferran Soriano wrote how 'they exercise their powers in very favourable conditions'.[19] They organise the calendar, the rules and use the clubs' employees – the players – for international competition without paying them. 'The same guys are executive, administrative, legislative and judiciary,' Mavroidis says, 'all without observing the minimal constitutional restraints.' This perpetuates the cycle that big clubs already enjoy because the competitions become financially dependent on them. It is partly why there was no great reset after the Super League. The justification was that UEFA could 'still lose everything' so had to encourage buy-in from the big clubs. One of the conditions of the surprisingly rushed deal was commitment to Champions League changes, which was what those big clubs wanted anyway.

For Čeferin's part, this was a situation he largely inherited. He was barely a year into the role when Wenger told Arsenal's 2017 AGM that concentration of resources had 'killed the unpredictability of football'. By 2018, of the €17.3 billion prize money that UEFA had distributed in the 25 years of the Champions League, €6 billion went to just 12 clubs. Those 12 were of course the Super League clubs. This was a result of what Crystal Palace's Steve Parrish described as 'gerrymandering' of the system.[20] It created an uncatchable lead at the front of the wage race. Such discussions involve dry terms like 'solidarity money' but they have a crucial effect on the excitement of football. This is the cash given to clubs who don't qualify for European competition, theoretically to prevent financial gaps developing. One conservative calculation is that solidarity money needs to be at least 20 per cent of all cash UEFA give out in order to preserve some stability. It instead hovered around 4–5 per cent between 2015 and 2024.

The result of this has been one of the great tragedies of modern football, and where UEFA have dismally failed in their mission. The federation responsible for the health of European football has instead overseen a situation where most of the continent is a club football wasteland. It's virtually impossible to compete at the top level if you are east of Munich and, increasingly, in large swathes to the west. There are now profound concerns within UEFA over whether the hierarchy are actually worried about the future of European football. By 2022–23, over half of the continent's entire football economy was appropriated by just seven urban areas: England's northwest, London, Madrid, northern Italy, Munich, Barcelona and Paris. Even northern Italy, at just under €1 billion, is less than half the economic size of London clubs or England's northwest. It was as far back as 2015 that Silvio Berlusconi, of all people, said it was impossible for him to sustain Milan at that level. 'It is clear that a family cannot compete with a state,' he lamented, before admitting he'd 'had to reluctantly take note of the situation' and sell up.

Even great names are in this strange sporting purgatory. The Champions League has become almost pointless for previous winners such as PSV Eindhoven and Celtic, other than giving them money that distorts their domestic league. It should always be stressed that this is an entirely new and unnecessary situation. UEFA were repeatedly warned of this by more concerned analysts but didn't heed the messages. It is why some of the criticisms of the Bundesliga for the 50+1 rule are misplaced. The argument has been that it has fostered a one-team competition, but that is an issue in many leagues around Europe. It's correlation not causation. The problem is that Bayern operate in that globalised system, which has been consumed by Champions League prize money but is now starting to eat away at the competition itself.

We've gone way beyond Red Star Belgrade or Benfica not being able to win it, or Leeds United taking on Valencia in a semi-final between hugely exciting teams, as in 2000–01. Even the Super League clubs of Juventus and Internazionale are considered underdogs. Ajax, four-time winners, are viewed as a sensation for reaching the semi-finals. They remain the only club from outside the 'big five' leagues to get that far since PSV in 2005. The lament here isn't that former powers can't win. It is how difficult it is for anyone else to win if they can't.

There is a profound sadness to this. For all the reservations about the modern Champions League, it has a thrilling mystique. That very theme conjures memories of exhilaratingly tense occasions. It was one reason the Super League felt so hollow, because it wasn't part of that lineage. The great ambition to succeed Alfredo Di Stefano or Johan Cruyff ensured the sudden silence from an away goal felt all the more grave. That world now feels so small. There aren't enough competitive clubs. Pérez actually was proven right that 'no one has interest in the Champions League until the quarter-finals'. This is the other side of that peak of 2018–19. Concentration of wealth had reached a point where these super-squads spectacularly collided, but the problem with concentration is that it only goes one way.

All of this makes it even more remarkable that UEFA have never done a proper economic analysis of the European game. There have never been any targets set, such as whether it is desirable that a certain number of clubs win the Champions League every decade. Even though the five that won it between 2019 and 2023 looks diverse, they were all among those invited to join the Super League. Rather than directly confront the causes of this, however, UEFA sought to just sidestep them. The group stage was rendered uncompetitive so they simply got rid of it. So many fixtures were mismatches so they just staggered the competition. This is what the compromise of the Swiss system for 2024–25 represents, but it's one nobody is really happy with. It involves a 36-team opening stage in one table – a super league, if you like. Such convolutions were driven by Agnelli, who once wondered whether it was 'right' that Atalanta got 'direct access to the highest European club competition' through 'great sporting performance' alone.[21] This was who Čeferin listened to for a long time. The Swiss system certainly means big clubs can gain access to the latter stages without such performance. It's why this is all being described as an institutionalised Super League, but with UEFA's stamp of approval. The compromise almost reflects the mess UEFA itself is in, as Čeferin has deviated from his own election promise on competitive balance. Ronan Evain, of Football Supporters Europe, worries an opportunity has been lost. 'There was a moment when we were hoping there might be a different system and what we see is actually getting worse.'

That doesn't necessarily mean it's going to stop there.

*

As it was becoming clear the Super League was falling apart, Nasser Al-Khelaifi hugged Aleksander Čeferin. It was to be a lasting embrace. The European Club Association (ECA) needed a new leadership since most of the senior figures had left in trying to push the Super League. Al-Khelaifi stepped up, but it might have been different. Paris Saint-Germain had initially been invited to the project, with Al-Khelaifi even telling clubs it was 'a brilliant entertainment product'. He did insist it should be under UEFA, which was also the plan for an earlier idea called 'Bohr' which the Qatari had with Agnelli, reported by *L'Équipe*.[22] The Italian told the *Financial Times* that Al-Khelaifi agreed that 'a new competition' was needed 'because if we didn't react, we were dead'.[23] It was still based on clubs with the highest revenues, which reflects a rather different view to Al-Khelaifi's hackneyed description of a 'not-so Super League' a few months after the failed breakaway.[24] In February 2022, when Agnelli was talking up another such project, Al-Khelaifi used the clown emoji in messages about him. The Qatari had instead made the shrewd move to stick with UEFA, strengthening his relationship with a grateful Čeferin.

There were already enough connections due to Al-Khelaifi's different roles as broadcast executive and club president, which should really have inhibited his rise to ECA chair due to conflicts of interest. It was quite a turnaround from a situation where PSG had twice been investigated over Financial Fair Play breaches and Al-Khelaifi had publicly complained about the rules. He now has what is seen as 'the most important seat at the table of European football'. That came after years of the Super League clubs buttressing the ECA, only to leave it vacant for one of the clubs they were most concerned about. The chair similarly afforded Al-Khelaifi an office in Nyon as well as a seat on the Executive Committee.

Symbolic little tales are even told of how UEFA were asked to change the furniture.

There's another more important perspective on this, too. It represents precisely the capture of European football by autocratic states that had long been feared.[25] This was deeper integration. It also happened as Qatar was accused of seeking to corrupt and influence the European Parliament, in one of the EU's biggest ever scandals. The predictably titled 'Qatargate' even involved Brussels politicians conspicuously defending the country's human rights record in the build-up to the 2022 World Cup.[26] Now, as one official complains of the ECA, 'the doors have been opened for Qatari investments'.

Mavroidis is another aghast at the potential issues. 'This is the same guy presenting the broadcaster from Qatar, who now negotiates with Čeferin on the working schedule and how many teams qualify from France.' It shouldn't be forgotten, either, that Al-Khelaifi's single main priority is answering to the emir of Qatar.

Far from sounding like he has considered these conflicts, Čeferin has only engaged in mutual flattery. Al-Khelaifi praised 'the resolve and strength' of the UEFA president in standing 'up to the midnight coup'.[27] Čeferin meanwhile described 'a man I can trust'.[28] This was how Čeferin used to speak of Agnelli. The internal concern isn't that Al-Khelaifi is the same type of personality, but more how the UEFA president leaves himself open. It is already a joke within UEFA that the Qatari is so powerful. There is a widespread belief within UEFA that the relationship has conditioned Čeferin's non-existent stance on state-owned clubs. The view is that it's impossible for him to speak out on it, since Al-Khelaifi is ECA chairman, but he's also been persuaded that it isn't a real problem. 'I'm not worried about state-owned clubs as long as they respect the rules,'[29] Čeferin told the *Guardian* in

January 2024. This was despite the UEFA president having direct experience of two of the state-owned clubs being involved in cases about alleged breaches of FFP rules, having used expensive legal might to prevent the confederation applying those rules. Čeferin had even said in that same week that UEFA knew they were 'right' in initially punishing City in 2020.

Almost more astonishingly, when asked about Newcastle United's questioned relationship with the Saudi Arabian state, the head of European football admitted 'to be honest I didn't know that' about the issue. He immediately followed by stating his belief that state ownership can be acceptably 'transparent'. So much is actually muddied. After the Super League fiasco, Čeferin described Al-Khelaifi as 'someone who has shown he is capable of looking after the interests of more clubs than his own'. This is despite Ligue 1 being rendered a joke and PSG drastically inflating the transfer market.

The bulk of European clubs meanwhile do not feel they have any voice at UEFA level. In 2023, UEFA extended a memorandum of understanding with the ECA, meaning both recognised each other as the sole institution governing European football and the sole representative of the clubs, respectively. Although the ECA broadcasts that 500 clubs are part of its family, only 137 have full voting rights. This has led to the absurdity of some clubs actually putting up their hands at ECA meetings even though they didn't have a vote. The promotion of figures from clubs such as Legia Warsaw has meanwhile been interpreted as a superficial response to the foundation of the Union of European Clubs. Hundreds have flocked to this group to make themselves heard. Čeferin, however, won't even answer the phone to them. One of their founders, Lokomotiva Zagreb's Dennis Gudasic, says this entails the confederation overlooking one of its main responsibilities. 'UEFA's role is not only to communicate with clubs in their competitions, but to safeguard the interests of clubs of all sizes and wealth.'

The stratification of European football has instead worsened, and hardened. It is not just that the Champions League quarter-finals have become the preserve of a handful of clubs. The suspicion is the Conference League is intended to silo 78 per cent of Europa League clubs into a third tier, despite acknowledgement of the competition's positives. An added concern is that there's long been a stratification in terms of punishment, too. The 'settlements' that Manchester City and PSG agreed in 2014 were not extended to clubs like Macedonia's FK Vardar. 'It's never the biggest clubs,' former executive Alex Phillips says. 'Why couldn't smaller clubs come up and say we'd rather pay a settlement? A settlement to clubs with unlimited money is great because the only thing they fear is exclusion. The simple fact that UEFA is also the organiser of the Champions League means they have an interest in preserving teams like PSG and City.' They make the rules but also make money off the competitions.

The FIFA president of course contributed to this situation. It was Infantino who was revealed by Football Leaks to have accommodated City and PSG when general secretary of UEFA. He defended this when the leak came out, stating: 'we were doing our job and saved the system, and we saved European football.'[30] 'Let's be positive,' as Infantino said in a leaked email to City.

It is notable how many resignations there have been from supposedly independent bodies between 2014 and 2019, with many of them among the most respected names in football finance and law. Insiders talk of a repeated pattern where an esteemed individual is initially flattered to be invited to a football body only to realise their reputation has been used after a few years. Blatter's mentoring of Platini is arguably such an example. While these figures are wheeled out to give a confederation view, others have noted an internal lack of independence. 'There has to be a silo between the executive and adjudicative functions,' Mavroidis argues.

One senior football executive laughs uproariously at the idea, saying, 'Every single "independent" committee in football is 100 per cent politically driven.' It makes it all the more absurd that this structure seeks to regulate state ownerships, as can be seen in how so many decisions at the Court of Arbitration for Sport have been overturned. UEFA's weak defence of their own investigations has been the subject of derision, with the 2018 PSG case seen as a watershed moment.

Klopp later said it looked like FFP was 'more of a suggestion than a rule'.[31] The debate blew up at one UEFA meeting, when regulations were amended so if an owner has more than 50 per cent stake in a club's sponsor they were defined as a related party. Manchester United's Ed Woodward argued so vociferously that the rules didn't work properly he was asked to leave the room.

All of this has seen FFP evolve. 'It was a positive regulation,' Phillips argues, 'but the original purpose got lost over time.' UEFA even felt they had to remove 'fair' from the name, retitling it Financial Sustainability, because the regulations didn't address competitive balance. By then, in 2022, the old rules had been rendered a farce by PSG's flurry of spending in summer 2021. The expenditure was all the more brazen since UEFA had first agreed to change the regulations due to the pandemic. It was seen as unrealistic and unfair to require clubs to break even.

PSG then just inflated the market again, with huge wages paid out to players like Leo Messi and Sergio Ramos. FFP was at least changed again, so clubs will only be allowed to spend 70 per cent of revenue on wages, transfers and agents from 2025–26. To give UEFA their due, the new regulations were seen as having 'bite' as early as 2024, including by senior figures at PSG.[32] Other clubs feel it's better late than never, although it could do with such competence being spread to other issues.

If you were to draw up an ideal vision for football, it would surely feature lofty ambitions like a model for competitive balance, and more fundamental aims regarding participation numbers. There is little of this in UEFA's strategy document.[33] It's mostly box-ticking exercises or vague mission statements like 'promote and develop football infrastructure across Europe'. That is another issue that is about the culture as much as the leadership. There is little long-term thinking, despite the relative security of the president, because fire-fighting until the next election consumes so much energy. This is where the constant pursuit of capital has an effect on more than accounts. UEFA now spends a decreasing proportion of its work on development. Few figures in meetings talk about accessibility to play or watch football. There isn't enough emphasis on data, which is one contrast with the modern FIFA. UEFA have also lost a lot of legal and operational staff to FIFA. 'I told them numerous times to invest in a strong European law office,' Mavroidis says. 'UEFA still doesn't have anything like that.'

Infantino is seen as much more forward-thinking than Čeferin, which has made UEFA a more conservative organisation. Disgruntlement has grown about the nature of appointments within the European body, as the president mostly listens to a small circle. Staff complain about a lack of formal recruitment processes and non-meritocratic promotions. There are accounts of appointments recommended by national associations, to the detriment of professionals who would otherwise be recruited from the market. 'The president is checking on every individual promotion,' one insider says. Decisions are described as 'being made in smoking rooms'. Čeferin has defended the idea of a close circle by again pointing to the Super League, saying that bringing in 'someone I don't know' could just lead to A22 securing 'all my secrets. I don't think that's good governance.'[34]

The 700-strong general staff feel further away from the president's office, with a divide between the operational side of UEFA and the political. Dodd believes the latter increasingly dictates governance in these bodies. 'The ratio of politics to actual business is ridiculous. FIFA does politics instead of strategy, and that's true of a lot of governing bodies.' Čeferin himself spends less time in his Nyon office, and there was shock at his absence from a working group organised to assess the potentially huge implications of the European Court of Justice decision on the Super League in December 2023. The UEFA president doesn't do as much glad-handing as Infantino, who makes a point of going to annual meetings of individual associations. There is still a belief the FIFA president should spend more time in developing football countries, rather than so long in Saudi Arabia.

Both presidents share the same approach to big issues, though, which is to just not confront them. The benign perspective on that is it allows consultation, and a more nuanced relationship with powerful stakeholders. The more critical view is that it means nothing is ever addressed and problems become endemic. Decision-making is almost glacial, and that at a point when football is changing at a drastic pace. FIFA actually struck an agreement with the European Commission in 2001 that principles like solidarity and competitive balance had to underlie the system, but that was based on a model that no longer exists. Private money and states have since transformed the economy, but football hasn't changed with it. It's all the more consequential when these interests have super-qualified professionals looking at every conceivable angle of the game's regulations. This is what has happened with the immense challenge of multi-club projects. It is one of a few issues that brings many of these strands together, since it is only ever going to be immensely wealthy groups with ambitions beyond football that want to create them. UEFA and FIFA were so slow to wake up to it that it's now far too late.

Similar has happened with the transfer market, which even players unions like FIFPro think has become a 'monster'.[35] FIFA attempted admirable if belated attempts at reform in 2023, but the tactic of initially tackling it through the role of agents – and especially their commissions – was largely defeated in the national courts of the 'big five' European countries.

It still remains such a tragic waste that so little of this immense money has translated into development. While UEFA have many good projects, that is almost just an inevitable spillover from the millions generated rather than efficient use of resources. A complacency about the future of the landscape and technology has been mirrored in a complacency about who might actually play the sport. Even though football has gone through a historic boom in terms of global popularity, there is little difference in the number of European clubs that exist today compared to 15 years ago. The UEFA data on pitch:population ratios hasn't changed. Although women's numbers have increased, to go with improvements in coaching and conditions, men's football has stagnated. Some internal data estimates the number of registered European footballers dropped from 24 million in 2010 to 16 million in 2015, although there were some changes in definitions. There is most concern in wealthy Western countries. UEFA, in the words of one association head, stopped making proper reports on this. Čeferin claimed during the Super League crisis that around 90 per cent of the money generated goes back into the game, but numerous figures who work in development say it simply hasn't got near this. It is instead estimated that only 1–2 per cent of Champions League money makes it down to the grassroots, with that level mostly funded by revenue from the European Championships. Many small clubs have similarly complained that FIFA's Clearing House for transfers has led to a significant slowdown in the distribution of money for training compensation. By May 2024, €140 million was still owed to clubs who desperately needed it for day-to-day running.[36]

FIFA's more proactive approach can still be witnessed in women's football. Čeferin didn't even attend the 2023 World Cup final even though it involved two UEFA teams in Spain and England. That tournament in Australia and New Zealand was a sensation, but praise still only goes so far. The women's calendar needs to be drastically improved, especially given the erratic gaps between games. There is frustration that women's football committees were dismantled after the 2015 overhauls, and real expertise in Tatjana Haenni and Mayi Cruz Blanco was not replaced. As with men's football, too, potential is being wasted in terms of participation in major nations. 'Numbers aren't that high,' Dodd says. 'You only have to note discrepancies in rankings between men's and women's teams.'

Similar inconsistencies are illustrated in how the bidding process for 2023 was changed halfway through to expand the competition to 32 teams, and the 2027 World Cup hosts were only confirmed as Brazil less than four years in advance. Saudi Arabia 2034, by contrast, was announced in 2023. There was then the manner that the World Cup in Australia and New Zealand ended, with the glory of Spain's victory overshadowed by the ugliness around their then federation president. Luis Rubiales was eventually banned by FIFA for three years after forcibly kissing striker Jenni Hermoso. His obstinacy in the aftermath, and what the governing body described as 'victim-blaming tactics', were seen as reflecting an accountability crisis in football leadership.[37] Rubiales' power was a product of the system. UEFA were questioned for a hesitancy in criticising a former Čeferin ally.

It was the body's biggest events, however, that perhaps most displayed the symptoms of poor governance. UEFA were seemingly so lacking in expertise that they stopped doing what had become a staple, successfully staging major finals. Four recent showpieces could easily have resulted in fatalities: the Euro 2020 final at Wembley, the 2022 Europa League final in Seville, and then the Champions League finals of 2022 and 2023, in Paris and Istanbul, respectively. They all had different problems but from the same lack of oversight. While the Wembley match witnessed ticketless fans dangerously forcing their way in, and the Seville and Istanbul fixtures involved logistical breakdowns – especially with supplies of water in searing heat – an independent commission found the Paris final 'almost led to disaster'.[38] Failures in planning caused dangerous backlogs for tens of thousands of Liverpool and Real Madrid fans outside the Stade de France, with police responding by using tear gas. UEFA's showpiece event couldn't even start on time. Adding insult to literal injury, fans were wrongly blamed for the 37-minute delay, as French authorities belligerently insisted large numbers of fans had forged tickets. This was later refuted. The report found UEFA had 'primary responsibility' and said it was 'remarkable that no one lost their life'. It was all the more distressing for Liverpool fans attending due to the memory of the Hillsborough disaster in 1989. UEFA Events SA, the body who organise major games, were savaged. 'There were clearly operational mistakes made,' Evain says. 'Maybe the priorities were in the wrong place.'

David Conn reported how UEFA were internally accused of presenting 'completely untrue' evidence to its own independent inquiry, which protected its safety and security unit from criticism. That group was headed by Čeferin's best friend, Zeljko Pavlica.[39] Then operations director Sharon Burkhalter-Lau said the claim that UEFA Events senior management marginalised the UEFA security unit 'is based on statements that were untrue and concerted'. She similarly alleged that Pavlica and his team did not attend vital meetings. It raised further criticisms of cronyism within Čeferin's UEFA. Pavlica still works at UEFA, which is itself considered illustrative of so many issues. Logistical problems continued into Euro 2024, with the English Football Supporters Association complaining of 'dangerous levels of overcrowding' after one game. Visit Qatar were major sponsors of the tournament, but senior UEFA officials privately pointed to how even more money was needed to fund the HatTrick programme, perhaps instead of organisation. Čeferin had promised member associations over 50 per cent more than in Euro 2016, but without the same rise in revenue.

Despite such difficulties in putting on big games, Čeferin's major battle has been over staging more of them. The calendar has felt the weight of so many tensions between UEFA and FIFA. It is how football's single natural resource of players is allocated, which is how money is spread. Control of the calendar means control of the game. One of those tensions comes from how FIFA is notionally the ultimate authority but UEFA has the players in huge matches. Infantino has made his intentions clear, having lamented how 'not many' people are interested in 'supporting the Italian national team' compared to Barcelona and Real Madrid.[40] FIFA even relayed plans to create 'the world's greatest club football experience', in tender offers to investors seen by the *New York Times* in December 2019.[41]

The fact this is driven by individual presidents rather than collective strategies, with that evolving into petty battles, isn't a satisfactory framework for business. It becomes personal. Tebas has been blunt about this, stating 'we all knew that Infantino wanted to kill Čeferin, politically speaking'.[42] Čeferin then didn't even show up for the 2022 World Cup draw in Doha, even though it took place a day after FIFA Congress. It is another area where Infantino is seen as cannier, as witnessed in how he 'rode two horses' during the Super League. He initially sought to include UEFA in discussions around the Softbank plan for the Club World Cup, but Čeferin was resistant. This is also where the tension between their functions as regulator and competition organiser become most apparent. FIFA unilaterally set the calendar, but UEFA are seen as better at planning in that regard. The domestic leagues are then left to work around the remains. 'You've got people who've got no say in decisions bearing the most severe consequences,' Dodd argues.

The calendar, in what has become a familar refrain, could do with an independent regulator. The big clubs have inevitably noted this, and played UEFA and FIFA off against each other. That is partly how the Super League happened. Most clubs use the balance of power for leverage, but some have picked sides. Paris Saint-Germain are UEFA. Real Madrid are FIFA, inasmuch as the Spanish club are anyone other than themselves. It was 'very cold' between Florentino Pérez and Čeferin at Wembley when Real Madrid won their 15th Champions League in 2024.

It's where another questionable financial cycle spins the game off track. Infantino got elected because he promised that huge increase to national associations, but that at a point when sponsors were running away due to the 2015 corruption scandal. So, the president then needed money to fulfil promises. That comes from events, and especially big clubs. Except, to attract big clubs, financial incentives are required. It opens just another entry point for autocratic states and private money. They're willing to turn the taps on. You can map the influence on the game from the headlines. In 2018, amid Xi Jinping's state-influenced football expansion, the plan was for the new Club World Cup to be in China. When asked about the state's human rights record, Infantino merely responded, 'the mission of FIFA is to organise football and to develop football all over the world'.[43]

That convenient explanation is admittedly why there is merit to the Club World Cup. 'What are the rest of us supposed to do,' Concacaf president Victor Montalgliani asked, 'just twiddle our thumbs and send players and capital over to Europe?'[44] Boban, who was then FIFA Deputy Secretary General and had purer football motives, was influential in corralling the big European clubs. He scrapped the Confederations Cup because he felt it was a 'ridiculous' competition, and sold the idea of the Club World Cup on the idea of glory and benefit to the wider game. The Croatian also made sure extra-time would be removed from the competition.

The pandemic ended the plan for China, but Infantino was insistent on expansion. A new pushiness was felt in the campaign for a biennial World Cup. Happily for Infantino, it was his new allies in Saudi Arabia who initially made the official proposal.[45] The FIFA president described that as 'eloquent and detailed', while adding 'you don't need to be Einstein' to know it would 'double the revenues'. A huge number of federations were supportive, as Wenger was put forward as a figurehead. Čeferin responded that this would 'be killing football'.[46]

This came amid fair arguments that the entire calendar needed to be reassessed for 2024, but the problem was that no parties could be trusted to act in the interests of the wider game. No one was ever interested in giving up even a single fixture. The fear within UEFA was that the biennial World Cup was a bait-and-switch to gain leverage in the club game. If so, it was ironically this encroachment that scuppered Infantino's plans. Conmebol chief Alejandro Domínguez, who had been a FIFA ally, became aggravated when Infantino met South American clubs without him. The Paraguayan responded by extending a Memorandum of Understanding between UEFA and Conmebol. A new 'Finalissima' was agreed between the champions of the two continents, and it was signalled they would boycott a biennial World Cup with talk of a new 32-team 'Atlantic Nations League'.[47]

It didn't help that Conmebol was pitching heavily for the 2030 World Cup, to romantically celebrate the competition's centenary given the first had been in Uruguay, but Infantino seemed to prefer China. FIFA, outmanoeuvred, backed down on the biennial plan but a few other ideas were put forward. A political solution to 2030 came with Argentina-Paraguay-Uruguay being given the opening three games of a tournament primarily held in Morocco-Portugal-Spain. UEFA eventually acquiesced to the 32-team Club World Cup, with the first planned to take place in 2025, but not without many lingering resentments and obstacles that include legal action from players representatives FIFPro. Čeferin said it will be 'tiring' for teams, and added that it won't be very interesting as 'the Europeans will win everything'. While the idea is still that this will raise the level of non-European clubs, the philosophical dilemma comes in how that could just see them dominate their domestic leagues. Many have pointed to how problematic the Infantino-influenced African Football League – previously called the Africa Super League – is in this regard. The main fear is that, once the Club World Cup is inevitably a commercial success in the US, there will be a push to make it biennial. Tebas already warned that this will lead to a 'confrontation', but one he welcomes.

And yet the importance of a unified pyramid was seen in the pandemic. It meant competitions could be easily rearranged. Would that have happened if there had been a breakaway? The game had a direct example of how essential it was to stay in one piece. It wasn't the only major lesson to come from that period.

In May 2019, as Gianni Infantino returned to Moscow to accept a state medal after the success of the 2018 World Cup, he exceeded himself in obsequiousness. 'The world has created bonds of friend-ship with Russia that will last forever.'[48] Actual timescale of those bonds: less than four years. By February 2022, as Russia's military went over Ukraine's borders, Infantino spoke of his 'shock'. That reaction is the only real surprise, given there had been months of warning about the invasion, not to mention virtually everything that Putin had done in a long and cynical exploitation of the game. FIFA and UEFA eventually banned Russian teams, although only after the global body's suggestion the national side compete in the 2022 World Cup play-offs without symbols. Poland's federation chief Cezary Kulesza derided this with a phrase that perfectly articulates modern football. 'In a situation of war with Ukraine, we are not interested in engaging in a game of pretences.'[49] If the first casualty of war is truth, it shows how much bullshit there is in football that it took a conflict to bring clarity. It was, of course, only temporary.

Just as the pandemic offered a direct example of why a unified pyramid is essential, the invasion that followed illustrated the actual dangers when you leave sport open to autocrats. The lessons were all there, from tournaments to ownership. The sport suddenly had a lot to untangle. It certainly had to wrestle with the knowledge it had been made complicit, with Putin's nation-building use of the 2018 World Cup serving as a modern version of Adolf Hitler's 1936 Olympics. Football couldn't say it hadn't been warned. Infantino's own aides cautioned against being filmed playing football with Putin as Russia was condemned for civilian deaths in Syria.[50] Even before that, due to the initial annexation of Crimea and the shooting down of Malaysia Airlines Flight 17 in 2014, senior European politicians argued Russia should be stripped of the World Cup.[51] The game still allowed Putin to put on a show.

A lot of European football had become dependent on Gazprom's money, with the hydrocarbon company sponsoring the Champions League for years before agreeing a wider deal including the European Championships. That branding had to be ripped away as St Petersburg was also stripped of the 2022 Champions League final. Putin himself had spoken about how Gazprom was 'trying to help Schalke 04 settle its financial questions' in 2006, on the recommendation of Germany's then chancellor Gerhard Schroder.[52] The politician was later appointed chairman of the Nord Stream board. There was constant chatter of 'rivers of corrupt Russian money' running through the sport.

There were also the last European champions before the invasion, to go with the last World Cup. A mere two weeks before the invasion of Ukraine, Roman Abramovich made an increasingly rare appearance with Chelsea, celebrating the Club World Cup victory in Abu Dhabi. That came after the Champions League had been reclaimed in 2021 from an old-fashioned Abramovich spending spree, which seemed to herald a new era. It was instead the beginning of the end, as the UK government sanctioned the billionaire for 'a close relationship with Putin for decades'.[53]

It showed how even the most powerful owners could be subject to sudden turns of greater forces. A football club was being forcibly sold because an autocrat had invaded a neighbouring country, while threatening the world with nuclear weapons. It is probably underestimated how close Chelsea came to going bust. Everything changed in an instant.

Abramovich's entire era should have been reassessed, especially after the new Clearlake Capital ownership self-reported incomplete financial information between 2012 and 2019 to the Premier League, Football Association and UEFA. Leaked files to the *Guardian* subsequently raised further questions over secret payments related to transfers and managerial appointments, possibly breaching Financial Fair Play rules.[54]

Abramovich wasn't the only figure sanctioned – Everton financier Alisher Usmanov, more publicly aligned with Putin, suffered a full asset freeze and travel ban.[55] In the first Premier League match after the invasion, Everton faced Manchester City, with Ukrainian flags everywhere. Also visible at Goodison Park was the branding of MegaFon, a company owned by Usmanov.

As for the owners of the opposition, it was as soon as the following year that Sheikh Mansour and City chairman Khaldoon Al Mubarak were part of the welcoming party for a state visit from Putin to Abu Dhabi.[56] Mohammed bin Zayed proudly spoke of 'the ties between our two nations', as Putin praised the UAE's international role, especially in the UN Security Council. There, the Gulf state had 'raised eyebrows' among those in the West when it abstained on a vote deploring the invasion.[57]

If football has learnt any lessons from all this, they aren't clear. Čeferin later enraged many UEFA member associations when he attempted to reinstate Russian youth teams in 2023, only to be shocked by the resistance. The plan had to be abandoned.[58] Čeferin had received early Russian support when he was first broached as a potential president. The issue had been a rare occasion when there was open dissent within UEFA. This was something higher powers were watching.

It was shortly before Christmas 2023 and the UEFA hierarchy were furious. That was because of the press release from the European Court of Justice on the so-called 'Super League case', brought by A22. The judgment was actually about whether UEFA can continue to monopolise the organisation of pan-European competitions. The official press release stated that FIFA and UEFA are 'abusing a dominant position', which was presented as a victory for the Super League. It wasn't, but the authorities were typically concerned about the wrong thing. Far more relevant to UEFA and FIFA was how the judgment called for a review of the European body's procedures, raising points about sporting merit, distribution, good governance and – above all – collective selling with a real commitment to solidarity.[59] It left that huge lingering question over whether football can be trusted to regulate itself. That consequently meant this form of UEFA and FIFA hadn't won either. The European Union was suddenly attuned to its jurisdiction's most popular cultural pursuit, as well as issues like foreign investment and state ownership in community assets. Al-Khelaifi's centrality to UEFA decision-making at the time of Qatargate was not looked upon with sympathy in EU circles. There was then the farce that was UEFA's first Congress after the judgment, in Paris. Despite all of the issues facing the game, the main subject was one specifically concerning the term and age limits of UEFA presidents, and reforms that feasibly allow Čeferin to stay for 15 years. It is why many in the game see the European Court of Justice judgment as 'quite exciting', as far as these things can be, especially

298

combined with an independent regulator in the UK. FIFA should of course form that role for the wider game, but have been too compromised by other motivations. It is instead instructive that most football policy – be it Bosman or rules on homegrown players – is forced on the sport by court decisions. That runs parallel to how the most profound changes in sport – Lance Armstrong, Calciopoli and FIFA – only come when state bodies with proper legal powers get involved. Sporting bodies, for their parts, generally aren't equipped to deal with such complexities. Some compare elite football to digital platforms, and how the EU's General Data Protection Regulation served as a de facto regulator. The game can only be reformed from the outside. The problem is that other external factors continue to exert even greater force.

12.

KINGDOM COME

For all the chaos the Saudi Pro League caused in the summer of 2023, there could have been more. One intention was to change the football map, which could have influenced the geopolitics. Around the time that Saudi Arabia's Public Investment Fund bought Newcastle United in October 2021, discussions were held over a combined Gulf region super league. They just couldn't strike agreement on share of clubs. Saudi Arabia insisted the league should be based on population, but Qatar felt that would see their clubs outnumbered. Unable to agree a deal, the Saudis pressed on with their own plans.

They almost went in a different direction with Newcastle, too. When Chelsea became available due to the sanctioning of Roman Abramovich in March 2022, a Saudi takeover was explored. The prospect of selling Newcastle was even broached. Most alluring was the idea that Stamford Bridge could become a global hub of influence given its West London location. The Saudis couldn't make it happen, though, and there was a satisfaction with how Newcastle was going. That still didn't prevent interest when Manchester United were up for sale later that year. The country's sports minister, Prince Abdulaziz bin Turki Al Faisal, even said, 'If there is a private investor that wants to come in, why not?'[1]

The belief was that Saudi Arabia should have the biggest club, and the wider point was the state was thinking of everything. Nothing was off limits. This was arguably the concept of sportswashing taken to a final form. Saudi crown prince Mohammed bin Salman even took the unprecedented step of acknowledging the term, simply saying 'I don't care'. 'If sportswashing is going to increase my GDP by way of 1 per cent, then I will continue doing sportswashing,'[2] he told Fox News. 'Call it whatever you want, we're going to get that one and a half per cent.' What they want now is much more than ownership of clubs. It is, in the words of one football president, 'to buy football itself'. Saudi Arabia want to own competitions and intertwine the state with the infrastructure of the sport, as they have already done with LIV Golf. The deal-maker in the latter, Roger Devlin, has already relayed how they are confident of getting whatever they want 'because of almost limitless financial resources'.[3] There's already been a shift in football circles from calling it 'the decade of Saudi' to the 'era of Saudi'. The state is similarly thinking on a bigger scale. The centrepiece will be the 2034 World Cup, so easily facilitated by a burgeoning relationship with Gianni Infantino. Saudi Arabia has what the FIFA president needs most, which is a willingness to spend on football. That money might help Infantino's expanded Club World Cup compete with the UEFA Champions League, and represents an evolution of the Qatari approach. A World Cup may be a start rather than an end point for what is planned to be a global 'destination' for sport. The vision is for a game where all roads lead to Riyadh.

Many in the Gulf had been waiting for Saudi Arabia to expand into football for a long time, especially since this is the region's dominant country, where the state had noted the success of Qatar and UAE. It was a new level, but driven by a new type of leader.

The ripples around football in 2023, right up to audacious offers for Kylian Mbappé, all trace back to one man: Mohammed bin

Salman. 'There was no ability to do it before because power was so diffuse through the Al Saud family,' Nick McGeehan explains. 'Nobody had enough control.' Saudi Arabia had little will to assert itself, either, despite representing the biggest country in the Gulf in terms of size, population, economy and military. Gross domestic product per capita barely grew between 1980 and 2010.[4] This was due to an inherent conservatism, conditioned by the influence of the ultra-repressive movement within Sunni Islam, where clerics viewed music and film as 'evils'. Such values were punitively enforced by the Committee for the Promotion of Virtue and Prevention of Vice (CPVPV) and their enforcers, *mutaween*. Their hold on the population meant the huge ruling Al Saud family submitted to the clerics in order to preserve power, but at the cost of any progress. It ensured monarchs came to power at advanced ages, such as Mohammed bin Salman's own father, the 79-year-old Sheikh Salman, in 2005.

That contrasted with the notoriously decadent international lifestyles of young Saudi princes, although Mohammed bin Salman was distinctive there. He stayed at home and consumed fast food and video games, particularly *Age of Empires*.[5] Bin Salman also became obsessed with billionaires like Steve Jobs and Bill Gates, specifically seeking out the latter on coming to prominence. 'It's almost like he sees billionaires as a club he wants to be part of,' says human rights activist Iyad el-Baghdadi. He stated his role model was Niccolò Machiavelli.[6] As ironic as it was that a gilded prince prized the will of self-made men, Bin Salman's rise was sparked by the realisation his indulged lifestyle might be finite. The sensational book *Blood and Oil* details how worried he became on learning a related royal didn't have a proper personal fortune.[7] Bin Salman became obsessed with investments and applying the thinking of these billionaires he idolised. That impetus made other pretenders nervous. When his father came to power in January 2015, Bin Salman was more eager than most crown princes to use his authority, and this was just when he was deputy crown prince before the 2017 promotion. He'd been given control of the state oil company, Saudi Aramco, which offered a crucial insight into the unimaginable scale of wealth the state really had. The open spigots of money kept thousands of extended Al Saud family relatives living in luxury. By 2022, aided by the invasion of Ukraine, Aramco had profits averaging almost $13.5 billion a month.[8] Bin Salman's long-term plan has been to transfer this to the Public Investment Fund, so as to make it the largest sovereign wealth fund on the planet.[9]

Bin Salman served notice of such expansive ambitions in his first major decision when placed in charge of the military. After just eight weeks, he shocked the region by leading an invasion of Yemen, in an attempt to stem Houthi rebels. This was interpreted as a proxy move against Gulf rivals Iran, but such a proactive attitude was still unprecedented from Saudi Arabia. 'Send in the F15s,'[10] Bin Salman declared, with the backing of UAE. Mohammed bin Zayed started to see a protégé in a young man who was 24 years younger than him, but also sensed opportunity to influence Saudi Arabia. The Abu Dhabi ruler began to promote Bin Salman to Western governments, ensuring the perception quickly went from that of an abrasive kid to the de facto ruler of the country. Khaldoon Al Mubarak, the Manchester City chairman, worked with the Saudis on a similar project of economic diversification.[11] Bin Salman's plan was duly titled 'Vision 2030', just as Abu Dhabi's was, but he wanted to go further than any neighbours. He wanted to make Saudi Arabia a Silicon Valley-style hub, culminating in the 'gigaproject' of the futuristic city of NEOM. The idea was that tourists would leave with a sense of wonder.

Expensive Western consultants started to talk about how the period between 2016 and 2030 would go down in history as the greatest national transformation since the urbanisation of China. The grander political plan was to place Saudi Arabia as the power between the West and the Russia–China axis. A line commonly heard is that, if even 60 per cent of plans are fulfilled, they will be breathtaking. Simply listening to such ambition was mind-boggling to US officials, since they'd been so used to Saudi leaders petrified that even minor change would bring down the whole state.

It was just that, like Qatar and UAE, Bin Salman realised that change was essential to ward off the risks from both a post-oil future and the type of Arab Spring unrest that caused violence in Yemen in the first place. Tension with Iran, and suspicion over the state's influence, weighed over much of this. Such fears were even more pronounced for Saudi Arabia than their neighbours, due to a 30 million population where more than 60 per cent of subjects were under the age of 30.[12] They were better educated than the other 40 per cent of the population but with fewer job prospects due to an economy still based on fossil fuel extraction. Restrictions on social interactions also ensured the younger generation lived their lives on the internet, as illustrated by the fact that Saudi Arabia had the highest number of YouTube views in the world.[13] This in turn made them more susceptible to tech-savvy political Islamic influences. A realisation of the need to tackle this with new thinking was one reason why Bin Salman was promoted in the first place. He understood the weight of it all, and began huge everyday reforms. The CPVPV faded. Cafés, cinemas and even music festivals began to light up. This new entertainment sector was made more vibrant by women walking around with more freedom. 'He wanted to Dubai-ise Saudi Arabia,' El-Baghdadi says. Sport was an inevitable part of this, especially with how football was a national obsession. The game could offer many solutions at once, not least a social outlet. The wider project led Bin Salman to initially be seen as the great reformer. People did genuinely enthuse about the immense difference greater openness made on their everyday lives.

There was some cynicism behind this beyond internal politics, though. Bin Salman had sanctioned international polling to pinpoint the main criticisms of Saudi Arabia, and it appeared as though the state was gradually addressing these with measures that made headlines. Allowances on women driving was a prime example. Entertainment meanwhile worked against the image of conservatism. Civil and political freedoms, however, were never to be part of this. If Bin Salman went further than any previous ruler in opening the country up, he went deeper in securing power, too. The two were almost hand in hand, iron fist in velvet glove. On a basic level, Bin Salman felt he couldn't afford any dissent to distract from the scale of his plans. Even criticism of policies could be a crime. 'The shift has really been to allow social freedom while decreasing political freedom,' former diplomat Arthur Snell says.

This was made clear with the moment that secured his power. In 2017, the billionaires and captains of industry that essentially constituted the Saudi political and financial elite were corralled into Riyadh's Ritz Carlton in what was essentially a mass arrest. Amid a series of interrogations and allegations of abuse and torture, the most influential figures in the state were ordered to hand over assets and fortunes or lose everything.[14] Dubbed the 'sheikhdown', it was like a blunter equivalent of Vladimir Putin co-opting the oligarchs.

The old consensus-based structure was smashed. In its place was what diplomatic circles saw as the second most centralised state in the world after North Korea. No one in Saudi Arabia had ever had as much power as Bin Salman, and he wasn't yet king. State security began to crack down on any criticism of government. Dozens of intellectuals were arrested for not offering total support to the blockade. Women's rights activist Loujain al-Hathloul was deported to Saudi Arabia from UAE, and eventually charged for 'attempting to destabilise the kingdom'. That felt even harsher when Bin Salman approved reforms she'd been calling for.

The climate had unnerved Saudi commentator Jamal Khashoggi, who went from an advocate of Bin Salman to a critic. He'd even moved to the US because he was 'beginning to fear' for himself.[15] A first column for the *Washington Post* was headlined 'Saudi Arabia wasn't always this repressive. Now it's unbearable'.[16] Reflecting the use of new technological approaches, Khashoggi became the target of disinformation campaigns. The state in the meantime attempted to limit his criticism or co-opt him, until Khashoggi went further than expected. He started to speak to an investigator working for American families suing Saudi Arabia over the September 11 attacks, on the basis so many hijackers were from the kingdom. Khashoggi believed his country should 'take responsibility' for 'tolerating and even supporting radicalism'. The state, and especially Bin Salman's deputy, Saud Al-Qahtani, were furious. Khashoggi had meanwhile fallen in love, adding a greater poignancy to his story. It was why he travelled to the Saudi consulate in Istanbul on 2 October 2018, for documents in order to marry Turkish graduate student Hatice Cengiz.

The details about what happened that day remain shocking, as a 15-man killing squad had already assembled. Shortly after his arrival, Khashoggi was sedated, suffocated until he died and then dismembered. The bone-saw used was later revealed to have been brought into Turkey on a private jet belonging to PIF. One of the killers then put on Khashoggi's clothes and went past the CCTV cameras.

Turkish president Recep Erdoğan was appalled by what his state security told him, especially since he had previously met the journalist. Tension was further stoked by the public statements. 'He's a Saudi citizen and we are very keen to know what happened to him,' MbS said that very night. Erdoğan, an ally of the then-blockaded Qatar, began to order the drip-feed of information to increase pressure. It reached such a level that Bin Salman wailed about being perceived as a 'journalist killer'. He tried to peddle the story of 'rogue killers', particularly to a receptive Donald Trump, but it wasn't working. US interests dropped out of events like the Future Investment Initiative at the Ritz Carlton. Jeff Bezos, whose phone Saudi Arabia later had to deny hacking through a message by Bin Salman, pulled out of Davos in the Desert.[17]

Bin Salman eventually took responsibility for the murder, but only on the basis he 'may have caused some of our people to love our kingdom too much'. UN investigator Agnes Callamard reported that the crown prince either condoned or ordered a 'deliberate premeditated execution', concluding it was probably the latter. This all happened as Qatar was resolutely navigating the blockade, and the war in Yemen was descending into a humanitarian disaster. The brief moment of modernising glamour had gone. 'This high risk was not an environment investors wanted to put money into,' FairSquare's James Lynch explains. 'These are things you can't put a price on.'

Bin Salman also greatly valued his reforming image. 'He still wants that back,' El-Baghdadi says. 'He wants to be loved. We kind of discount that.' There was now an additional incentive to commit to the plan for sport, that had taken off at speed with the launch of Vision 2030. Saudi Arabian influence had already spread to golf, tennis, boxing, Formula One, mixed martial arts, snooker, chess and e-sport. Football was only seeing the start of it.

UEFA have not been concerned by the Saudi Pro League's expansion, because of one specific precedent. 'It's not a threat,' president Aleksander Čeferin claimed. 'We saw a similar approach in China.'[18] It was at least superficially similar. The summer of 2023 brought echoes of winter 2016. An autocratic state started to spend astounding figures on players, while representing a new frontier for football as it looked to host Club World Cups and even the World Cup itself.

Chinese leader Xi Jinping ordered a 'football reform and development programme' in 2015, complete with a 50-point plan to rebuild the game from the ground up. There was to be mass construction of pitches and the inclusion of football in the school curriculum. At the top end, billionaires did what they felt Xi expected and pumped hundreds of millions into the Chinese Super League, mostly on foreign stars. Carlos Tevez was made the best paid in the world, at reported wages of £634,000 a week for Shanghai Shenhua.[19] Since the money seemed endless, debate rose – even in dressing rooms – over whether this would gradually hollow out European football. Many players resisted since the Champions League still mattered too much. The influence was nevertheless so strong that talks were held over the Chinese football federation having an office in UEFA. By 2019, Infantino was talking China up as potential hosts of the 2030 World Cup.[20] A year later, he was announcing China as the first hosts of the newly expanded Club World Cup for 2021.

The Covid-19 pandemic ended such plans, while hastening the sudden collapse of Chinese football's moment. The country's stringent regulations brought existing problems to a tipping point.

There were constant allegations of corruption, as the authorities grew frustrated with the money spent on largely uninterested stars living in seven-star hotel complexes.[21] The abrupt loss of crowds and sponsors hastened financial struggles, which were turned existential with the collapse of the Chinese property market. By February 2021, reigning champions Jiangsu went bust.[22] There were numerous complaints to FIFA about unpaid wages. Football figures who once enthused about the league were soon deriding how lacking in expertise it was.

A few years later, many of the same people were extolling how the Saudi Pro League is nothing like China. There is admittedly one huge difference. Football was popular in China but it wasn't a national obsession like in Saudi Arabia. That adoration was witnessed in a superior World Cup pedigree, crowned by Saeed Al Owairan's famous goal against Belgium that brought a last-16 finish at the 1994 World Cup. Two years before, the kingdom had organised a competition between all continental champions called the King Fahd Cup. It was named after the Saudi ruler, but soon became known by its more familiar name after FIFA appropriated it: the Confederations Cup. Two decades later, Saudi Arabia were seeking to appropriate FIFA's events, as the Confederations Cup was abolished to make way for the new Club World Cup. It didn't matter to the kingdom whether UEFA cared about them. They were going directly to the top.

One of the world's biggest clubs already had a relationship with the country, since state-owned Saudi Telecom Company were Manchester United's partner from 2008.[23] This evolved into discussions about Saudi Arabia buying the club, but the Glazers were never willing to sell more than 30 per cent. Many figures close to the talks say that the crisis over Khashoggi prevented what would have been a much more concerted attempt to buy United.

'It was going to be a prince, so it looks more detached from the state,' one prominent source claims. One of Bin Salman's distant relatives actually beat the state to ownership within the Premier League, as Prince Abdullah bin Mosaad bin Abdulaziz Al Saud completed a takeover of Sheffield United in 2019–20.[24] That came after an ugly legal battle with lifelong fan and previous co-owner Kevin McCabe.

There were then the more colourful moves of Turki Al Sheikh, who was considered a political enforcer. He bought Egyptian club Al Assiouty Sport and moved them to Cairo to be renamed Pyramid FC, before selling up amid abuse from ultras. Al Sheikh instead bought UD Almeria in Spain, although Javier Tebas was typically forthright about insisting on cost controls to 'avoid what PSG and Manchester City are doing'.[25] It was Al Sheikh's role as chairman of the new Saudi Entertainment Authority where he was more central to the grander plan of bringing global football to Riyadh, organising Argentina–Brazil friendlies in 2018 and 2019. The Super Cups of Spain and Italy soon followed. It meant that, for the price of over £100 million to the organisers, half of the European Super League clubs would be regularly going to Riyadh. The rules were even tweaked one year when Real Madrid hadn't qualified, to allow for 'historical' criteria.[26] Qatar's beIN SPORTS were especially affronted, since they had a contract with Serie A and this was the height of when the channel was being pirated by beoutQ.

The Spanish federation, rather than La Liga, organised their Super Cup and it led to one historically ironic line by then president Luis Rubiales. He claimed Saudi Arabia could be changed 'if we flood them with equality' and that this would 'be the Supercopa of equality!'[27] Tebas, who loathed Rubiales, discussed how distasteful it was after the murder of Khashoggi. 'We should not forget what happened,' the league chief said. Tebas seemed to do precisely that three years later, as La Liga signed a sponsorship deal with Visit Saudi. 'We are here because of the money,' then Barcelona manager Ernesto Valverde said in 2020. That didn't just apply to the Super Cup.

It also explains Infantino's increasing presence in the kingdom, after a first visit in December 2017. Both the FIFA president and Bin Salman had come to power at the same time, and there was a mutual benefit. There was also a mutual friend, as Donald Trump encouraged a relationship. The link initially came through Saudi Arabia's help in USA winning the bid for the 2026 World Cup. Bin Salman and Infantino kept messaging. Potential complications were illustrated when, after Khashoggi was killed, FIFA tried to play down Saudi Arabia's part in the SoftBank offer for the Club World Cup. Except, Infantino more than played his part in normalising Saudi Arabia. There he was in Riyadh the day after Bin Salman ended the Gulf blockade, 'waving a sword', in the words of one involved figure. Here he is beside the crown prince for the heavyweight bout between Oleksandr Usyk and Anthony Joshua in Jeddah. Al Sheikh described Infantino as 'a dear friend for whom the Kingdom and I hold a great respect'.[28] It had been noted how FIFA were not as proactive as other federations in trying to shut down beoutQ, even though it was also pirating the World Cup. In defence of the relationship, FIFA point to how Saudi Arabia now has departments for the women's game. Many pieces were being put in place for a huge expansion.

For all the romance that people like Amanda Staveley tried to evoke with the Saudi takeover of Newcastle United, the reality was much simpler, and more cynical. The club was available. The country was in a hurry to catch up with Abu Dhabi and Qatar.

Government officials admitted as much. 'These are things we have seen with Paris Saint-Germain and Manchester City,' the Saudi ambassador to Norway said. 'This is not a trend we started.'[29] The actual process was nothing close to simple, as the Newcastle take-over became one of the most fractious sagas in the modern game, while also serving to tell the story of the Gulf blockade.

It is striking, then, that former club owner Mike Ashley rejected a Korean investment fund's offer because the deal would have taken at least six weeks. 'Fuck that,' the retail billionaire supposedly said. 'That's too long.' This was a man who had become notorious for challenging subordinates to drinking competitions, one of which culminated with Ashley vomiting into a fireplace.[30] Newcastle supporters certainly didn't think Ashley was running their club as a serious team. He just represented another form of the capitalism appropriating the game. Newcastle only ever spent the minimum amount required to keep them in the Premier League. Staff mean-while complained of facilities that were falling behind rivals'. That brought understandable animosity from fans, but there was never any indication Ashley was affected. He was open to selling up, but potential buyers were aware he could change on a whim. An earlier attempt from Staveley to buy Newcastle with Chinese investors led Ashley to dismiss her as a time waster.[31]

This fitted with the general perception of Staveley in the game, where she is widely seen as an attention-seeker and opportunist whose main talent is 'walking into a room confidently'. Staveley has a charm, although many have become wise to how she will say whatever is needed to ingratiate herself. 'I can't stand her,' one major club figure says. Others are more benign, insisting Staveley allows herself to be underestimated. That doesn't quite explain her 'legendary' performance at Premier League meetings, where she often baffled other company executives with her comments. Even those who dislike Staveley, however, would admit a begrudging respect at how she facilitated the Saudi takeover. It involved perseverance, if a lot of controversy. The episode points to how ad hoc these decisions can be, even amid state sophistication. Staveley, usually described as a former girlfriend of Prince Andrew, went to Newcastle in October 2017 to watch a 1-1 draw with Liverpool. The story Staveley has told since is that she was immediately bewitched by the passion of the supporters. The club had a lot of positives. They were the only team in the city, just like PSG, but with a more distinguished history. Supporters also packed the stadium despite a lack of recent success. That offered another potential advantage, since any success would bring gratitude.

Other Premier League executives are still dubious as to the business logic of it all, describing the purchase as 'a total mystery'. One joke was that, while Chelsea games attract the biggest business figures, Saudi officials at Newcastle 'would be introduced to Ant and Dec'. Ashley was open to a sale for just £300 million, though. A widespread view is that Staveley saw the club as a way to reinvigorate her career and profile. She had been trying to buy a club for years, including Tottenham Hotspur. Staveley had actually been loaned £10 million by Ashley to facilitate the purchase of her stake in Newcastle.[32] She paid it back in October 2023, after the former owner had taken legal action. That case revealed that at least £2 million was paid from the takeover to reality TV figure Carla DiBello, who had gone from 'one of Kim Kardashian's best friends' to an investment consultant in Dubai. DiBello knew PIF governor Yasir Al Rumayyan well enough to do something that was still rare for a woman in Saudi Arabia. She directly pitched ideas, which was how a takeover of Newcastle was first broached in February 2019. DiBello's contact, Staveley, was able to fill in the details. Al Rumayyan was sold, agreeing a deal where the PIF would buy 80 per cent, Staveley's PCP Capital 10 per cent and Reuben Brothers – the investment body of one of Britain's wealthiest families – the remaining 10 per cent.

Staveley finally had the backing she long desired. Saudi Arabia, more suddenly, had a club to buy. Ashley agreed a £305 million deal in April 2020 and there were expectations it could be done in weeks. It took a year and a half. There was extreme pushback. The most emotive came from human rights groups and families who have suffered from Bin Salman's rule. Amnesty International's UK director, Kate Allen, wrote that the Premier League was 'at risk of becoming a patsy' for 'dire' human rights abuses and values at odds with 'the global football community'.[33] The families of campaigners held in Saudi jails such as Al-Hathloul, Abdulrahman al-Sadhan, Aida al-Ghamidi and Dr Salman Alodah signed a letter 'begging' the Premier League to 'do the right thing' and use its 'unique opportunity to demand change'.[34] The widow of Khashoggi, Cengiz, even went more direct by pleading with Newcastle fans to oppose the takeover on social media. She was met with swathes of abuse. El-Baghdadi felt much of this was instigated by 'bots'.

There was strident opposition within the Premier League, too, albeit for less altruistic reasons. They still had merit, as 18 of the clubs were concerned about what another state ownership could do for competition and cost controls. Others had lamented how the City takeover had just been waved through in 2008, which created a precedent. Still, nobody wanted to publicly relay complaints that were being made with real vociferousness in private. It summed up a lot of modern football, however, that the real obstruction wasn't regulation or backlash. It was media rights and the bottom line.

Through beoutQ's illegal broadcasting of games, the Saudi state was accused of undermining the business of the Premier League. And since PIF was the sovereign wealth fund, with Bin Salman as its chairman, that meant lawyers had to be consulted to determine whether the sale could be sanctioned. BeIN SPORTS, who had become the Premier League's biggest international partners after extending a £400 million-plus deal – with Saudi Arabia their biggest market – urged the blocking of the takeover and warned it could affect future contracts.[35] 'It is no exaggeration to say that the future economic model of football is at stake,' a letter to the clubs said. Rivals were by then even more animated about how this might affect income.[36]

There was finally a concrete development when the World Trade Organization (WTO) ruled in May 2020 that Saudi Arabia facilitated the piracy of Premier League matches by failing to prosecute beoutQ and blocking attempts to shut it down.[37] This had considerable significance. It would have meant the competition being asked to approve the sale of one of its clubs to a country where their games couldn't even be watched legally. Frustrating everyone further, Premier League chief executive Richard Masters refused to offer any comment, leading to criticisms over a lack of transparency.

The nub, however, was that PIF didn't sign a key document. 'Form Four' of the infamous Owners and Directors' Test was never actually filled in, which meant nothing could proceed. This vacuum had come as the Premier League concluded the state of Saudi Arabia would become the ultimate owner, after legal firm Bird & Bird counselled there was no separation between PIF and the state. It raised the unprecedented prospect of a state having to be cleared by the Owners and Directors' Test.[38] This was rejected by the consortium and the crucial form was left blank. One quip was that Bin Salman might be the first person to fail the test. It certainly could have opened a world of complications. The Premier League's rules had been tightened in 2018 so buyers could be disqualified if they had engaged in conduct that would be seen as dishonest in the UK, let alone if they had a conviction. Even before issues like Khashoggi, piracy constituted a crime in the UK. Worse, as one irate executive put it, 'it was a crime against the Premier League itself'.

There is still amazement the takeover was approved, but football was becoming subject to greater forces. The Saudi government argued to the WTO that their stance in blocking beIN was actually a national security issue, on the basis that Qatar messaging was being beamed into their borders at the height of the blockade, and that the country was sponsoring political Islam.[39] As one figure involved in discussions quipped, Barnsley–Millwall was presented as a threat to national security.

The story was going to even higher levels. On 27 June 2020, as reported by the *Daily Mail*, Bin Salman personally messaged prime minister Boris Johnson about the takeover. 'We expect the English Premier League to reconsider and correct its wrong conclusion.'[40] The two were reported to have developed a 'bromance'[41] but it didn't stop the Saudi crown prince warning of 'a negative impact' on 'both our countries' economic and commercial relations'.[42] This probably referred to a 'long-term partnership' reported by *The Athletic*, where the UK would support Vision 2030 and PIF would invest $30 billion into the UK economy over a decade.[43] The deal was all the more important given Britain's vote to leave the European Union.

Ahead of an earlier call with Bin Salman, Johnson had been advised to outline the Premier League's independence if the takeover was raised, but to make clear he 'welcomes continued Saudi investment'.[44] Freedom of Information (FOI) requests later revealed the significant pressure the government were actually putting on the Premier League. With the impasse described by state officials as an 'immediate risk' to engagement with Saudi Arabia, a 'senior interlocutor' was to be nominated to 'impress HMG interests with the Premier League'.[45] That appears to have been Lord Gerry Grimstone, with *Open Democracy* reporting how the then minister for the Department of International Trade personally intervened to liaise between the Premier League and the Saudi government in pursuit of a 'solution'.[46] Messages from Grimstone to Premier League chairman Gary Hoffman reveal a priority was to 'bring this matter to a conclusion as quickly as possible', amid talk of how 'any new "failure" would be highly embarrassing'. Grimstone later rejected the idea this represented pressure, and stated he was only speaking in the context of his ministerial responsibility to keep 'abreast of large investments potentially coming into the UK'.

This was all amid a frenetic spell of frequent meetings on the issue, some involving the British ambassador to Saudi Arabia and Foreign Office minister James Cleverley.[47] Johnson was still stating in parliament as late as April 2021 that the 'government was not involved at any point in the takeover talks on the sale of Newcastle'.[48] Masters had similarly told a parliamentary enquiry there had been no government pressure.[49]

Whatever the interpretation of the constant dialogue, it wasn't enough to make the takeover happen at that point. The Premier League offered arbitration but that was declined. Form Four was left unsigned. Staveley let the tears out, angrily blaming rival clubs and the Premier League's insistence on making 'the state of Saudi a director'.[50] The financier insisted all the necessary questions had been answered while claiming 'piracy was not an issue'.[51] The Premier League argued otherwise on the former while Qatar were adamant on the latter. There was actually immense pride in the smaller Gulf state's resolve, as one official beamed 'this was Saudi Arabia's first moment to integrate into football after Khashoggi and it got blocked by the state they think the least of'.

By then, Bin Salman wanted to end the blockade, as it was increasingly backfiring. The International Court of Justice had given another major ruling in Qatar's favour, this time on airspace restrictions.[52] Meanwhile, beIN SPORTS pressed ahead with a new Premier League deal in December 2020, which again covered Saudi Arabia. Newcastle, who had by then brought legal action against the competition over the takeover, were the only club to vote against it.[53] The Premier League even released a statement refuting the club's claims the takeover had been formally rejected. Such tension was calmed by the actual geopolitics, as the emir of Qatar was invited to the Gulf Co-operation Council summit in January 2021. By late July, PIF were talking to beIN and the Premier League again. A provisional agreement was struck in early September. 'Way above Staveley's head,' one official makes a point of saying. Saudi Arabia also announced new anti-piracy measures, which the British Foreign Office notably commended them for.[54] BeIN was back on Saudi screens. The deal was back on.

The Premier League came to an agreement with PIF. Form Four was signed, and a three-man panel unanimously passed the deal. The news leaked on 6 October 2021, sparking scenes of delirium in Newcastle. The takeover was completed on 7 October, as the decision was explained with a phrase that would become notorious – and potentially consequential. The Premier League spent an entire day briefing everyone that it had received 'legally binding assurances' that PIF is a separate entity to the Saudi Arabian state, with the consortium agreeing to consequences if this was proven otherwise. It was never clarified how this could be monitored. 'We would know,' was one line. The Premier League declared itself 'comfortable' with the way the structures were presented.

At the same time, the Foreign Office prepared responses to likely questions, among them how 'the government allowed a country responsible for the murder of Jamal Khashoggi to take control of one of the north-east's most important cultural assets'.[55] The push was to show Saudi progress. This was the game of pretences in full glare. As recently as six months beforehand, the Premier League was given expert counsel that it would be virtually impossible to get independent legal advice within the kingdom that PIF is any way separate to the state. Former diplomat Arthur Snell just laughs about the 'assurances'. 'The Premier League must have literally had to lie to themselves because there is no way that any sentient person could draw that conclusion. It's an active decision to ignore the evidence.'

Other clubs were now even more irate, especially at the lack of information on the takeover for so long. Some executives believed the 'absurdity' about assurances was concocted after the fact. It has been suggested that the Premier League's insistence on separation led to Al Rumayyan becoming a mere non-executive chairman of Newcastle.[56] Since he was also the chairman of Aramco, no previous football director ever held such power. Publicly, the power at the club was with Staveley. Those with knowledge of the discussions say a plan had initially been to just keep her for a year, or even cut her out altogether, but she did a good job and stayed for almost three. Crucially, Staveley was also a woman heading an internationally famous Saudi asset. One rival club executive derides 'the most acquiescent puppet possible'. Staveley beamed as she spoke with media in the lucrative Jesmond Dene House hotel. More appeals from human rights groups had been waved away by the Premier League. Some fans who gathered at St James' Park waved Saudi colours. A giant flag had been planted in the Premier League.

When Staveley and her husband Mehrdad Ghodoussi finally got to sit with Newcastle United's club staff, they already knew what to say. The ambition was to win the Premier League and Champions League, but within just a few years. Employees left the room 'buzzing'. The response within the Premier League wasn't quite so enthusiastic. That immediate hostility to Newcastle was one major difference between PIF's takeover and Sheikh Mansour's of City in 2008. The years in between had been an education. The Newcastle takeover served as an abrupt wake-up call.

Although the previous thinking among other clubs had been to resist restrictions on state ownership in case owners wanted to sell, there was a sudden realisation of the threat to the competition. It was why time represented the main tension in the Newcastle hierarchy's first few seasons. They wanted to go as fast as possible, the rest of the Premier League were intent on slowing them down. Newcastle began to dominate all discussions among clubs, at least when they weren't about the investigation into City for alleged breaches of FFP rules. The so-called 'other 18' had already de-manded answers from the Premier League about how the sale had been sanctioned, but the explanations didn't placate them. Gary Hoffman's ousting as chairman of the Premier League followed, despite an acceptance that he was under immense pressure throughout the process. The clubs simply felt they hadn't been properly informed. They now feared the takeover could again inflate the market, and that Newcastle might just sign sponsor-ships with Saudi companies to get round financial regulations and then just go spending. One immediate proposal was to temporar-ily freeze deals with 'related parties' – termed Associated Party Transactions – until clubs could vote on new rules to widen the definition of the term. This was especially an issue with state own-ership due to the blurred lines in autocracies. As an example, Etihad hadn't been registered in this way with City, although rivals felt they should be due to the state connection. They now didn't want a situation where Aramco could just emulate the Qatar Tourism Authority with PSG and do a Newcastle sponsorship deal at an inflated figure.

Staveley was furious. She couldn't understand how they'd waited so long to spend all this money on the club, and then weren't allowed to invest. The obvious answer, of course, is that they should have known the system they were buying into. Other executives felt this was typical of how autocratic states had little respect for regulations, especially when outgoing managing director Lee Charnley was sent to a Premier League meeting to threaten legal action if such a vote was passed. That just enraged the 18 clubs into immediately voting for temporarily suspending such deals. City, notably, abstained.[57] The eventual decision ruled that any sponsorship worth more than £1 million had to be assessed over whether it was fair value, with that expanded to include payments from associated parties to staff. This would have greater repercussions.

The actual running of Newcastle had been similarly stop-start, if for different reasons. The hierarchy insisted in the early days they wanted to just watch and listen, and the necessity for this was illustrated when one senior figure asked what the difference is between a head coach and sporting director. There was then a delay in dismissing the existing manager, Steve Bruce, who fans saw as Ashley's man. That had some poignancy since the former Manchester United captain was a boyhood Newcastle fan. Other criticisms of perceived outdated coaching were fairer. It was one reason there was such accelerated improvement when Eddie Howe was appointed. The squad immediately benefited from progressive modern coaching and quickly got out of the relegation zone.

Howe was the right appointment in the circumstances – and maybe for the circumstances. The English coach had spent his time since being sacked by Bournemouth working to update his methods, with Diego Simeone's Atlético de Madrid a particular influence. They were a notoriously abrasive side, and Newcastle started to display similar cynicism through time-wasting and aggression. This fed into animosity from opposition clubs, as rival fans greeted Newcastle with chants and banners about Saudi Arabia's human rights record. Howe himself was pressed on the issue when debate rose about ownership after the sanctioning of Abramovich. Newcastle happened to visit Chelsea in the very next game, which was also the day after Saudi authorities had executed 81 men. People couldn't fail to spot the Saudi flag in the away end.[58] After initially pleading he would 'stick to football', Howe gave a stilted response. 'I'm well aware of what's going on around the world but my focus is on trying to produce a team to win football matches . . .'

Having clearly ruminated on the criticism he received for that, Howe said a few days later he was 'definitely' reading up on the subject and that it was difficult 'for everyone concerned'.[59] He insisted he just made decisions based on the people he met. It was one of the few times anyone had really been questioned on working for a state project, but that partly came from the far greater controversy about Newcastle. Howe had ultimately agreed to become their public face, as manager. Newcastle then had the audacity to select a new away kit that looked strikingly like that of the Saudi Arabian national team. That was after a warm-weather training camp that was of course in the kingdom.[60]

The notorious legally binding assurances then didn't look so watertight when, in quite an about-turn, there were other legally binding assurances in the USA that seemed to say the exact opposite.[61] In March 2023, as part of the legal battle over LIV Golf that underlay Saudi Arabia's other most controversial sporting project, a federal magistrate judge ordered PIF to turn over documents and ruled that its governor – Al Rumayyan – must sit for depositions. The fund's lawyers argued against that on the basis that both Rumayyan and PIF were 'a sovereign instrumentality of the Kingdom of Saudi Arabia'.[62] 'The parties agree that PIF is a "foreign state" within the meaning of the Foreign Sovereign Immunities Act.' It was humiliating for the Premier League, given what Masters had said the month after the takeover. He had insisted there was a 'corporate difference' between PIF and the Saudi state. 'If we find evidence to the contrary, we can remove the consortium as owners of the club. That is understood.'[63]

This sparked another flare-up for the 18 clubs, who demanded the Premier League look at whether assurances had been breached, with Amnesty backing the calls. There was never any update on that, though. The ownership had largely been normalised. That's what regular games – and especially wins – do, with even talk of 'a fairytale'.[64] Newcastle did over-perform in going from survival in 2021–22 to reaching a League Cup final and then qualifying for the Champions League the next season. Rival clubs didn't share the admiration. The dressing-room photos after wins, with Staveley and Ghodoussi prominent, provoked deep irritation.

There was similar aggravation at the praise Howe received for supposedly managing this without spending money. The Champions League qualification had been fired by £350 million-worth of signings. They included five of the six most expensive in the club's history, including Alexander Isak and Bruno Guimarães. Newcastle would say that came through greater FFP allowances from Ashley's frugality. Recruitment was similarly sharpened by the appointment as sporting director of Brighton's Dan Ashworth. That reflected another tension with state ownership. Newcastle's owners can afford to wait, even if they would prefer not to. This was what Bin Salman articulated when asked about sportswashing.

Like City's owners, he wants financial growth in the long term. 'They have the empirical data,' in the words of one insider. It is said to be about pure 'return on investment'. Newcastle may not be able to go as quickly as City or PSG did but they can go more quickly than almost any other ownership. Limitless funds allow patience and greater expenditure on infrastructure. They are monitoring what happens with multi-club regulations, with plans to mirror City's project, including interest in Valencia and Olympique Marseille. Even early on in the ownership, Newcastle tried to market themselves as a world brand. The short sponsor search was contracted to global agency CAA, who had arranged Aramco's deal with Formula One.[65] The process still ended with the deal won by Sela, a Saudi events management company also ultimately owned by PIF. Despite the numbers representing 'fair market value', other clubs were irate.[66]

Newcastle were enduring a battle at every point, including in their first Champions League campaign for two decades. As cost-control rules restricted spending on a small squad, Howe lamented rivals' refusal to agree loans: 'I'm not sure we have many friends in the market.' Newcastle went out in the group stage, which was made even worse for the owners as they finished behind Qatar's Paris Saint-Germain. It was all the more ironic since Qatar had actually considered selling the French club as part of a new strategy, but abandoned that once Newcastle were taken over. They couldn't just leave club football to their regional rivals.

Newcastle were meanwhile caught in that increasingly familiar tension around time. In February 2024, Ashworth said he wanted to go to Manchester United. There were accounts of different views on approach. While Ashworth favoured steady project-building, the Saudis wanted to go faster. All decisions ultimately had to go through Riyadh. It was already a new pole for the sport. Howe was becoming frustrated about not signing a higher quality of player, but there were no such concerns for the owners in an even bigger football project.

It was one of those moments when those around the table couldn't help glancing at each other in disbelief. In late May 2023, Karim Benzema and his entourage met Saudi Pro League representatives, and kept listening as the wage offers kept going up. It was essentially about getting to a number the player said yes to. The actual club could be confirmed later. Benzema ended up joining Al Ittihad, although an initial idea was to pair him with Leo Messi at Al Hilal. The ambition was for the Saudi Pro League to stage the last act of the Messi–Ronaldo rivalry. The whole summer was supposed to be built around it.

The problem was that Messi was by then on a level of his own. He'd already settled the rivalry by winning the World Cup, so went to Major League Soccer partly because their plans were based solely on him. There was fury within the Saudi Pro League about the failure to bring Messi, including sackings, but it didn't disrupt momentum. Al Nassr's January signing of Ronaldo had already accelerated long-term plans, since the state had realised the opportunity. Other stars felt if it was good enough for Cristiano, it was good enough for them. They were told this was the moment to join, since they would be pioneers, and this was when the offers would be best because everyone was eventually going to want to come. All of Neymar, Sadio Mané, N'Golo Kanté and Benzema followed Ronaldo, adding up to £728 million of expenditure by the time the window closed. It was still less than the Premier League spent, but a crucial difference was the source of the money. This wasn't broadcasting revenue, but Mohammed bin Salman sanctioning the outflowing of billions of dollars to reshape football around Saudi Arabia.

The inflated fees and wages had already massively disrupted the market. It was all the more jarring because this represented a new power in football. The view in boardrooms was, if Saudi Arabia couldn't just buy parts of the sport in the way they did with golf and boxing, the state could simply invest so much money it put the country at the centre of football. FIFA analysts estimated it was the biggest ever domestic investment in the game.

In the months before Benzema's meeting, virtually every prominent football executive or agent was invited to high-end meetings in either Riyadh or London. Saudi Arabia wanted to fast-track plans by consulting all insiders on what works, what doesn't, and to avoid the mistakes China made by developing an 'authenticity'. Executives were also keen to smooth concerns over previous cases of unpaid salaries that went to the Court of Arbitration for Sport. Above all, the message was 'we're coming, so get used to us'. One early suggestion the Saudi Pro League really ran with was the idea you need at least four big clubs competing, to make a compelling league. That was ready-made in the giants of Al Hilal, Al Ittihad, Al Ahli and Ronaldo's Al Nassr but they were going to institutionalise it. On 6 June, it was announced that PIF had taken over the country's 'big four' to formally confirm the state's plans to 'be among the top 10 leagues in the world'.[67] They were really aiming higher, and to sit just behind the Premier League, at the least. It was also announced the competition would expand to 18 teams, as four other clubs received investment from other state-owned companies. There have been some internal frustrations at how Neom Sports Club have been backed, due to the political focus on the city. The long-term aim is actually for them all to become fully private, and 'Westernise' the league away from the Gulf model.

That is to gradually condition long-term returns over a generation, by building brands that rival the European clubs.

This announcement was the first part of a broader step-by-step plan, with virtually all figures consulted declaring themselves 'blown away' by the scale of ambition. Most, of course, stood to earn well out of it. This was an extra benefit of all these meetings, as they served to co-opt some of the game's most influential voices. Many were soon talking about the progress the country was making, while responding to criticisms by pointing out problems in the West.

There was a clear logic to the football side, though. As well as a massive fanbase, Saudi Arabia has good-sized stadiums and the third most successful record in the Asian Champions League after Japan and Korea. Yannick Carrasco attracted a huge crowd in a restaurant. Al Hilal got up to 60,000 fans at games, as visitors noticed street football everywhere. This, like many established football countries, was for a long time the Saudi grassroots. For all that the purchase of declining stars seemed to be the same old story, the aim was to gradually make the league younger by working down through age profiles. Phase one was players in their thirties who were satisfied at elite level, such as Benzema and Kanté. Next were those in the 25–30 age bracket, like Ruben Neves, who accepted they were never going to be in that elite category. That was to make the league more palatable for most promising young stars, who were the next phase, with Celta Vigo's highly rated Gabri Veiga a surprising early signing.

Structures and facilities were to be improved, for the standards of Saudi players to be gradually raised. Every contract was intended to be three years, so that all players would be in the league for the build-up to the 2026 World Cup.[68] The plan for the seventh year is for every single game to be 'holistic entertainment events', with fireworks and DJs, extending Saudi Arabia's burgeoning entertainment industry. A parallel target is that the number of registered male footballers rises ten-fold to 200,000.[69]

This all syncs with the official explanations for the expansion, which is to improve public health. It should also be stressed that an entirely legitimate element of the project was building up its own league, since it comes from the people. That is something the big European clubs absolutely couldn't complain about. The issue is that, in such a centralised society, it's impossible to disentangle from state intentions. Lynch says it's actually a 'redrawing of the social contract'. 'The domestic politics shouldn't be overlooked. The deal has long been that you get a share of the oil revenue for not having political participation. Meanwhile, revenue is going to Newcastle and gigaprojects. Football gives something back to the nationals. That's something missed with sportswashing, where there is another audience.'

There was also another international audience. Talk of football in Saudi Arabia helps displace talk of repression in Saudi Arabia. As the transfer window closed and the fees were excitedly counted up, Amnesty International stated that the regime had already executed 100 people that year.[70] During the same period, retired Saudi teacher Mohammad bin Nasser al-Ghamdi was sentenced to death for social media posts. Former Liverpool captain Jordan Henderson was savaged for essentially endorsing a country where homosexuality was criminalised by moving to Al Ettifaq, due to previous advocacy for LGBTQ+ rights. It was seen as even worse when Henderson defended himself by talking of creating 'positive change'.[71] Meanwhile, there was Ronaldo in a video declaring Riyadh as 'one of the best places I have ever been, with the most quality restaurants'. More critical questions led to Saudi Pro League sporting director Michael Emenalo drastically changing tone after an interview with STV. 'Always about sportswashing,' he said, thinking the mike was off. 'Sports-fucking-washing.'[72]

Emenalo would doubtless have preferred to focus on the football, but there were complicated questions there. The market was reshaped. Top European clubs suddenly had to wait for Saudi bids to see what they could spend. Even the European champions, in Manchester City, couldn't make transfer decisions until they knew if Riyad Mahrez was the only player going. The backlog ensured mid-level clubs who rely on selling high were worried about breaking even. Some were left waiting. Others had cost-control problems immediately solved, through multiple high sales. Chelsea were among those who benefited, with £33 million-worth of sales, which briefly led to questions about PIF influence on owners Clearlake due to investment in the private equity firm.

The entire league structure was confusing even to its consultants. Clubs had loose internal set-ups, working under the umbrella of the competition. Deals for top stars would be negotiated centrally, with clubs who want a player then expressing interest. Although there was an encouragement to think collectively, internal politics meant individual presidents and princes would often just offer huge wages to players they desired. Many agents meanwhile claimed to be representing the league when they weren't, while players would naturally use interest to generate better deals. They were advised to firmly reject the first and sometimes second offer, because it could double or even treble.

That unique chaos apart, the centralised structure is relatively common across Asian football. FIFA had no issues for decades, but it presented new problems when it interacted with Europe. Newcastle attracted even more focus when winger Allan Saint-Maximin was sold for £30 million to Al Ahli, who are also owned by PIF. Some English rivals meanwhile feared bids were coming in to destabilise them. Others were keenly watching for collusion, and wanted greater transparency on how fair market value was established in moves between clubs under the same ownership. An openly voiced fear was that PIF's four Saudi clubs could just sign an expensive star and loan them to Newcastle – although the truth was it was actually the Saudi Pro League clubs who were considered top of the structure. That was where the state's real focus was, as they sought to make Saudi Arabia this sports destination. Attempts were still made to push through a vote banning such temporary deals in the Premier League, but it was narrowly defeated due to the number of clubs in these multi projects.

The Newcastle situation was still unprecedented. It wasn't clubs from various different countries but one club from a major league linked to four clubs from a single league, that was itself a state project seeking to change the sport. FIFA statutes do include a general obligation for member associations to ensure the same group or person don't have control over several clubs, or to act whenever the integrity of competition could be jeopardised, but the current regulatory framework places the onus on the individual federation.

It is where the entire issue falls through fault-lines in the game, like the gap between FIFA and UEFA. Some officials openly argue FIFA were 'rubbing their hands' at the disruption caused to European clubs. On the other side, there's a belief UEFA is more stridently against the kingdom due to the Qatari influence through Nasser Al-Khelaifi. Čeferin was frustrated at incorrect reports UEFA were considering allowing Saudi clubs into the Champions League. The Saudi Pro League still dominated discussion at the European Club Association's general assembly in September 2023, although Čeferin eventually echoed Al-Khelaifi in saying they were 'not worried'.[73]

While there is a risk of complacency there, it's still true when figures like the UEFA president and Masters talk of European football's history mattering more. It was why the Champions League inviting Saudi clubs was a non-starter, since it would have afforded them the advantage of this prestige. When Veiga became the first young talent to go, Real Madrid's Toni Kroos labelled it 'shameful' on the new Al Ahli player's own social media post.[74] Kylian Mbappé meanwhile had no interest in talking to Al Hilal after a £259 million bid to PSG in 2023, and Mohamed Salah was another who rejected a move that same summer. Numerous sources say Liverpool were open to a deal. Vinicius Junior's camp simply said 'now is not the time' for an astonishing £1 billion deal. PSG did sell Neymar to Al Hilal, which Qatari officials felt displayed a political maturity. It also did them a favour. The 31-year-old travelled on Prince Alwaleed bin Talal Al Saud's private jet, which was dubbed a 'flying palace'.[75] Trappings like a spa and grand piano on board were seen as a symbol of a player who'd lost his way. Neymar represented a cautionary tale, especially in how he was supposed to be the successor to Messi at Barcelona.

If other signings didn't quite get that level of luxury, the general insulation was one similarity with China. Stars have sequestered lives in gated compounds. Although some of their families lived in the more liberal Bahrain, it wasn't enough. Many players regretted going. Henderson played one game with just 696 fans, quite a drop from Ronaldo doubling Al Nassr's average attendance.[76] An underdeveloped infrastructure frustrated elite players, as one team had to warm down in a media room. Some clubs were just the president and the coach, with few staff in between. England players were still quizzing Henderson about the wages, but they weren't enough to make him stay. He left to go to a traditional club in AFC Ajax, forgoing huge money.

That money still only takes you so far – but there are plans for the rest.

It was a rare occasion when Saudi Arabian officials were left frustrated. Visit Saudi had agreed a deal to sponsor the 2023 Women's World Cup in Australia, which seemed typically targeted. While the kingdom has been specifically criticised over women's rights and criminalisation of same-sex relationships, the women's game has become a bastion of feminist and LGBTQ+ empowerment. That drove profound resistance to the deal, with Dutch striker Vivianne Miedema articulating a mood when saying FIFA should be 'deeply ashamed'.[77] FIFA were desperate to keep one of Infantino's main allies happy, and even suggested an alternative Saudi sponsor, but eventually had to admit defeat.

It marked such a contrast to the men's game. As well as ownership, Saudi entities have sponsored the World Cup, Asian Cup, Asian Champions League, African Super League, Roma, La Liga and Messi himself.[78] December 2023 also brought the kingdom's first international tournament, as host of the smaller-scale Club World Cup. That ended with Infantino dancing across the pitch in white trainers and handing the trophy to Manchester City. The VIP section of the King Abdullah Sports City stadium was filled with high-profile business figures for the final. That is after Saudi Arabia got what it wanted most, in the 2034 World Cup. Infantino simply announced it on his Instagram account, of all places, in October 2023.[79] That was maybe fitting for how farcical the 'process' was, especially compared to the complications of 2010. So much for FIFA's claims of 'an open and transparent selection' from 2016. This had seemingly all been agreed behind closed doors. Having been outmanoeuvred for 2030, Saudi Arabia didn't have to do much at all for 2034. Australia and New Zealand had been expected to challenge but they weren't given any advance notice on the launch of the mere three-week window to register interest and then found they didn't have enough venues to fulfil the new rules on stadiums. That would have required a quick agreement with a third partner in the Asian Football Confederation, but the confederation had already announced full support for the Saudi bid.[80] The kingdom didn't even need to revisit earlier plans to involve Italy in order to layer the announcement with some romance. There was surprise within UEFA that Čeferin didn't request that the FIFA Council extend the deadline. Other officials questioned what happened to human rights requirements that were supposed to come in after the 2018 and 2022 bids. FIFA instead had 11 years of guaranteed sponsorship from Saudi entities, as the kingdom had all that time to prepare. Senior figures within the governing body have been made uncomfortable with the 'cosy' relationship. This culminated in FIFA announcing Aramco as a 'global partner' in 2024, which is seen as a decision potentially as significant as anything that happened in 2010.[81] It essentially made Saudi Arabia the financial engine of global football. FIFA's view is that collaborative work with such states aids progress. It is not a universal view outside of FIFA. If it becomes a primary funder of the Club World Cup, and that competition does properly grow with that money, then that means Saudi influence on the game will only grow with it. It is precisely this integration into infrastructure which is at the core of sportswashing. The bid for 2034 meanwhile ensures all of these efforts are only going to be turbo-charged.

'The World Cup will be MbS's advert to the world about everything his government have been able to achieve,' Davidson says. It is hoped to be Vision 2030 fully realised in 2034. The wonder is how many lessons will be learnt from 2022.

13.

FOOTBALL WITHOUT
FANS IS NOTHING

It's an image that now sounds utopian, but used to simply be normality. A supporter of almost any club could go into a season genuinely hoping that, if things just came together, their team might challenge for the league. That optimism added to the summer sun, as they returned to meet fellow fans. It was a giddy combination of unpredictability on the pitch and familiarity off it. The big clubs often got their way, sure, but even Manchester United, Real Madrid and Bayern Munich finished mid-table. There were no greater complications to consider, other than maybe disgruntlement with certain directors. Fans in countries like Spain weren't just going to a club they supported, either, but one they owned. This was what football was all about.

It was a vision so appealing that, at the turn of the millennium, some UEFA staff talked about trying to create it everywhere. Plans were discussed so all European clubs could eventually be supporter-owned in some form. While it was understood the model wasn't perfect, it immediately removed a lot of issues at source. UEFA even managed to gather €50,000 to establish Supporters Direct Europe, which evolved into Football Supporters Europe (FSE). Such numbers sadly had no effect against the huge sums already creating other incentives in the game. By the early 2020s, the idea of achieving that laudable aim was laughable.

After Roman Abramovich was sanctioned, the United Kingdom's Conservative government had no interest in even acknowledging proposals that could have put Chelsea in control of fans. It could have been a great example for the game's future. Instead, there were many examples of how warped football culture had become.

In the 2022–23 Champions League, Manchester City hosted Bayern Munich in a quarter-final between two perpetual domestic champions. For all the German club typified a modern problem, though, their fans have retained a traditionalist view due to their country's 50+1 rule. They were already pushing against Bayern's association with Qatar Airways, which would finally end in June 2023.[1] Banners were now held up that read: 'Glazers, Sheikh Mansour, all autocrats out! Football belongs to the people.' At the very sight of that, there was a distinctive sound. Manchester City fans began to sing Mansour's name. It seemed a distillation of modern football and its conflicts. As one group called for clubs to be given to supporters, the other hailed the influence of a senior royal from an autocratic state. The latter seemed like sportswashing in live action, but there was naturally more to it.

Part of it was an instinctive defence of a benefactor. Part of it was basic tribalism, and defence of your community from perceived attack. Some fans just wanted to enjoy a bit of football banter. Others just wanted to watch the game. Individuals have more nuanced feelings. It is still all of these emotions that various interests are seeking to capitalise on. Gareth Farrelly, now a football lawyer but once a midfielder who scored to keep Everton from being relegated in the 1997–98 Premier League, has an apt phrase. 'The game is now the commodification of feelings.'

It's why it's all the more important to appreciate what actually drives that emotion.

For some people, it was the sight of the green grass and pristine white lines. For others, it was the sound of older fans roaring abuse. There was then the mass of humanity as a goal went in, and the aroma of beer and burgers. Such senses from childhood all create the Proustian rush that fosters emotion and that connection to the game. If a common lament among fans is 'I don't know why I keep coming', everyone has an instinctive idea. That sense of connection drives professional football, which makes it even more surprising FIFA have never actually defined what a club is.

When staff question that, they talk of stipulating basic technical and legal elements. Even if FIFA did that, though, it couldn't get to the essential nature of a club. That is something more philosophical. From putting that core question of what a club is to scores of people, one word stood out: 'Community'. 'That's what every football club has in common,' FSE's Ronan Evain says. It is a gathering of people with a common bond, forged by unifying identity. That identity is passed down generations, through different squads, kits, badges and even stadiums. This is what football is actually for, which should never be forgotten. It is the playing of a sport in the spirit of representing an area and its people. That has afforded clubs a crucial role as social institutions. Authorities in small towns especially lean on them, as an increasingly rare place where people gather. This is the fabric of society. Going even deeper into those threads, Tranmere Rovers executive chairman Mark Palios says 'the fans are the club'.

'We've grown old with them,' as Manchester City fanzine writer Simon Curtis puts it. That's also why owners can never be the club, since they're only ever transitory. Similarly, the legal structure can be altered indefinitely but the core community can't. It shouldn't need saying but all of that extends beyond just 'a business'. It's beyond trophies, too.

Norman Riley is a Newcastle United fan who relays the joy that comes from the simple match-day routine. 'It'll be a couple of pints before the match, the buzz, the flags and – for six or seven hours – nothing comes into it other than the football, your mates and the enjoyment.' This is why people talk of football as an 'escape'.

There is still what everyone is coming together for, which is the game itself. The simple kicking of a ball is release and expression, which is why football has spread around the planet like nothing else in history. Its simplicity fostered a universality, where anyone can kick something resembling a sphere against a wall. It has the power to move anyone watching. Real life, to paraphrase Nick Hornby, doesn't offer last-minute winners.[2] It doesn't even need to rise to such drama. There are the different responses that come from applauding a cross-field pass to agonising over a close miss. As Palios says, 'You get a tremendous sense of responsibility when you see people standing up with veins bulging.' An appeal to such aggression reflects the darkly humorous view that the real emotional core of football is 'suffering'.[3] Supporters often endure rather than enjoy, but the latter is still the life of it. 'The game itself is beautiful,' Riley enthuses. 'You can go to any match and see a moment you enjoy.' That in turn fosters experiences to share with those around you and build relationships and communities.

One moment stood out for Dom Rosso of the Chelsea Supporters' Trust before a game against Brentford. 'Ten of us were around a table, all different backgrounds, ages and nationalities. There's no other situation in the world we'd be doing this.' Martha Newson is a psychologist who has studied group bonding through football, and points to how such experiences show something that goes beyond the game. 'It's not just identity or even family. It's what we refer to as identity fusion, where your personal identity is

completely immersed in the group identity. It's got this evolution-
ary angle, of propagating groups.' That connection can go beyond
your own club. Every fan has had the experience of not speaking
the same language as someone but communicating by just naming
footballers. These days, that can involve showing a phone video of
a great atmosphere.

These experiences are exactly the feelings that cynical interests
seek to commodify. Such influences start to warp the core impetus
of wanting to win. That is the essence of football, too, after all.
Competition brings a focus to that identity fusion. Fans want to
feel their team is growing, to challenge, because that's what brings
excitement. This was a major issue with Mike Ashley's Newcastle
United, since it felt like the club was merely existing. Such a sense
of drift has become a wider problem, due to the increased financial
stratification that locks clubs into position. Most fans know they
can't even think of challenging for a league.

That commodification becomes more problematic at this point,
since clubs can be bought and sold and have their shape changed.
An extreme was AFC Wimbledon, who were the English game's
first true victims of football's economic transformation. The
former Premier League club were taken over and taken 90 kilometres away, moved from south-west London to Milton Keynes,
while being renamed MK Dons. That led to supporters like Niall
Couper establishing a fan-owned phoenix club. 'Owners started
to see football as the potential rich commodity, and the inconven-
ience of it all was the fans,' Couper says. 'It was this conflict between community asset and the business part. What happened
at Wimbledon was that one part went rampant and completely
ignored what the club was actually about.' Even Michel Platini
recognised this. 'My philosophy is that football is popular because
of the identity of the clubs,'[4] the former UEFA president told David

Conn. 'Now, because football is popular, people are coming to take control of this popularity, to make money. That is not correct.'

Pure profit-making can align with supporter aspiration since winning has become so commercially valuable, too, but the problem is fundamentally different aims. That divergence was best witnessed in the Super League. Where it gets even more complicated, however, is where the most questionable owners give fans exactly what they want.

It was long ago as 1955 that Len Shackleton's autobiography featured a chapter titled 'The average director's knowledge of football', consisting of one blank page. Executives were for a long time figures that seemed to personify a class tension within the game; them against us. That is one element the game's embrace of neoliberalism has exacerbated, at least in some quarters. One of the biggest clubs became the worst example of supporters feeling disenfranchised. At Manchester United, the Glazers appeared to be making decisions far away from fans.

Chelsea fans were going through similar over the course of 2023–24 with the Clearlake hierarchy, who are the highest-profile private equity ownership. While Rosso acknowledges they afford the supporters' trust an audience, there are worries over whether concerns are actually heard. It is compounded by uncertainty over who actually funds Chelsea, due to the nature of private equity.

'That's quite challenging for fans, and many clubs might have this,' Rosso says. 'There's been no publicly explained overview. Fans don't know what they're trying to achieve, which has led to a lot of anxiety.' The latter just shouldn't be an emotion fans feel about their club, but it is increasingly widespread. One exception is the ownership profile considered the most problematic. The supporters of state-owned clubs tend to be those least critical. That shouldn't be too surprising. Such owners put in as much money as they can to win, because they want the wider benefits. That gives fans what they think they want most, which is success. There is often more than that, too, since such ownerships are keen for further good-will through community work. That is still sportswashing, if in a rudimentary form. Many people who talk about the concept often mean fans celebrating owners in the way that has been seen with City and Newcastle. An irony is this probably wasn't really considered by Abu Dhabi when buying City in 2008. It was instead a surprising auxiliary benefit, that ensured PIF did factor it in by the time they were looking at Newcastle in 2020. Some of the evidence even predated the era. Psychologist Dani Pollicino points to studies that show how people used to vote for Silvio Berlusconi 'just because AC Milan were successful'. City fans had banners thanking Mansour even before they won trophies. This evolved into supporters defending UAE's much-criticised conviction of British academic Matthew Hedges on the accusation of espionage.[5] 'A guy like Simon Pearce would have noticed something remarkable, that a British guy could be thrown in jail, without consular access, and we've got guys in the UK defending us,' says human rights activist Nick McGeehan.

By the first Newcastle game under the PIF ownership, against Tottenham Hotspur in October 2021, there was a scene more reminiscent of North Korea. When it was announced new chairman Yasir Al Rumayyan was present, virtually the whole crowd turned to dutifully applaud an autocracy's senior figure. That only followed the huge support for the takeover. Despite the inclination to defend fans as conflicted, huge numbers aren't. Tens of thousands will actively call these autocratic states 'great owners' and attack critics. One otherwise amicable discussion about modern football with Newcastle fans before the 2023 League Cup final brought the following interruption. 'Fuck off. Fuck off. Just fuck off. We don't fucking care about human rights.'

Alex Hurst, the host of *True Faith* podcast, explained wider sentiments with creditable honesty to the *Independent*. 'The easy thing would be to sit here and say I'm conflicted but the feeling of everyone I know who supports Newcastle is one of massive excitement . . . Maybe there is a line but Newcastle fans aren't the ones to draw it. Many won't care.'[6]

Curtis has similar feelings regarding City's owners. 'I don't really think about them too much at all . . . it's not a feeling of gratitude, elation, it's wonderment that my shit little City have managed all this. And I know what it's backed by and partially therefore where it's come from. But, gratitude, no . . . I'm just happy I've lived through City actually being half-decent and if they went back to being absolutely shite again tomorrow, it wouldn't alter how I relate to the club at all.'

Paris Saint-Germain fan Cyril Dubois says fans do care about human rights questions regarding their Qatari ownership but they 'care more about their rights as supporters – which are often violated'.

'Fans have decided not to get involved in geopolitics at a time when understanding the world is more complex.' That isn't difficult to do, psychologist Nils Mallock says, due to the distance. 'The actions of the owners are very far away. They're not something that you as an individual have to interact with, unlike the positive experience of the game.'

That does touch on something fundamental – the sport shouldn't have subjected fans to this. 'It's supposed to be a simple thing, isn't it,' Curtis says. 'You've worked your bollocks off all week and want a few beers with your mates and to go to the football, and then we're confronted with Middle East politics and sportswashing, and whether we really should be there or whether we should be ashamed of ourselves.' There are those who can't help but consider it, like Riley, who has worked for human rights charities. 'Every day to me personally is a bit of a struggle, because of the Saudi factor. The football club is owned by an entity that runs counter to everything I believe in.'

Another is Steve Cockburn, a long-time Newcastle fan who works for Amnesty International. 'It was a genuine emotional turmoil for me. I've been going to games since I was seven with my dad and brother, it's part of your identity, your culture. I'm still unable to give up my ticket . . . but the other part of my identity is about being a human rights activist so these come into conflict. We spoke out against it, but I understand why most people didn't. There was the feeling the club and the city had been neglected.'

A more pointed question is how fans feel when this is discussed. 'Well, it has to be covered,' Curtis says. 'Unfortunately, City will be mentioned in dispatches every time this subject comes up for obvious reasons so that's a bit of a pain in the arse. I understand why . . . the spotlight should be maintained as long as it's done fairly and there's no underlying stuff that means it's being dragged over, in City's case, more thoroughly than anyone else's.'

Curtis does have a theory on coverage. 'There's a kind of gentle bias, just purely because of the numbers of people in the media who kept an eye on United and Liverpool in the 1990s, so that tends to mean, for City, being United's rivals and one of the teams keeping Liverpool out of the successful spots, that there's a bit of resentment there I guess. So I wonder whether there's a little undercurrent in some of the media circles . . . City broke the cartel, so they became a pretty easy target I think; Newcastle will get a bit of this dished at them now.' Curtis does add how 'City used to be a lovable rogue disaster club.' 'It's completely changed . . . which is a bit difficult to take sometimes as we all like to be loved, don't we?'

Riley almost has the opposite response to media discussion. 'I was listening to a podcast discussing how Saudi has just sentenced a man to death for a couple of tweets and that regime owns my football club. This is a horrible thing to listen to. I do feel on a regular basis like a complete hypocrite. I would like to have the strength to say I am actually going to boycott supporting that football club, I consider it on a daily basis . . .'

But. 'I see Alexander Isak take out three players with a pass, I'm out with my mates and I'm lost in that moment.' Such reactions do raise the pertinent question of what the appropriate response to all of this is, if there even is one.

Riley is far from the only person who wonders about not going. Many other fans believe it should be the automatic response, although that is often when it's not their club. If it was, they might understand that it's difficult to just disconnect, given that Newson describes the psychological link as 'irrevocable'. It is thereby asking a lot for any fan to just abruptly give up something that has been their life.

'If I had the guts to do it, I would probably feel better in myself,' Riley says, 'but there are friends and family who I've got literally nothing in common with other than a love for Newcastle United. To cut that off would be to cut off people I love dearly.' There is also just the club they love dearly. Given that autocratic states seek to warp a club's identity, it's arguably even more important for fans to keep going to preserve the true identity. 'There's this cognitive dissonance,' says Cockburn. 'You're never quite sure how you're justifying it to yourself but I was there before them. I feel it's mine, not theirs. A lot of people felt the same about Mike Ashley and then got burnt because people started boycotting and then they give 10,000 tickets away to fill the stadium. That was one of those signs we're cannon fodder, that deflates my ideas about protests.'

Human rights activist and dissident Iyad el-Baghdadi has come to see the fans 'as victims'. Newson describes how these states seek to tap into these connections, with her research detailing how the psychological connections are similar 'sacred values' to religion. Your stadium is your holy land. Your chants are your hymns. Your support is your belief. 'There's an irrationality to it,' Evain says. 'I can't think of another sector in society where a person would suddenly advocate for an authoritarian regime but it's unfortunately possible in football. These sportswashing projects rely on the fact we are a captive audience.'

It's why McGeehan echoes El-Baghdadi's view, especially given the 2008 economic crash that accelerated these dynamics in the first place. 'I think we have to be careful with supporters. When you look at places like Newcastle and the crippling effect of austerity and deindustrialisation, the decimation of jobs, the loss of hope, and the club is the focal point, I think it's unwise to expect fans to take a principled stance on an owner who provides them with the one thing they want to make their life better.' He likens it to how political populism works. 'You strip people of hope and then you give them an easy solution. That's not to absolve people of the responsibility to speak out, I think they should, and many have, but fans have to be protected.'

A poignant part is how that has extended to attacking critics. Anyone who has even glanced online will be familiar with how these discussions go. The responses are the same across multiple clubs. The most instinctive is good old-fashioned 'bias', and the view that criticism is only made because of hatred of the club or support of another. That extends into accusation of a graver form of prejudice, which is usually 'racism' against the state in question.

When specific reasons for criticism are outlined, the response to that is generally whataboutery and pointing out problems in other ownerships and countries. There is then the highlighting of how clubs' home governments have geopolitical relationships with these autocratic states, which usually feeds into some attempt to accuse critics of hypocrisy.

A different avenue is merely that fans 'deserve' success after years of struggle. Newson also describes it all as 'cognitive dissonance', arguing 'doctrinal messaging is a classic clue of identity fusion'. 'The loyalty to identities is precisely the reason you see this defence of autocratic states and systems and structures that people don't really have any understanding of other than it has an overlap with their own identities.'

El-Baghdadi believes there is evidence of a clear evolution in how state actors view all of this, as he has studied how online discussion is instigated. 'The Saudi and Emirati disinformation networks, this starts with them, and fans start repeating what they're saying. It proves disinformation campaigns can work. There are state-sponsored troll armies, and bot factories.' A low was the swarm of abuse that Hatice Cengiz, the widow of Jamal Khashoggi, received when criticising the Newcastle takeover. 'So you see football fans with basically no context, trying to argue this because a state owns your club,' El-Baghdadi says. 'I feel sad. This is not even your fight.' It's an under-considered consequence for the game. As well as making clubs complicit, such ownership poisons the entire discussion around football. Serious issues become part of fan rivalry. It goes from commodification of feelings to the toxification of football. 'This tribalistic thing worries me, that human rights become a culture war,' Cockburn says.

It should be stressed this doesn't extend to the majority of fan discussions, and many see it for the grave problem it is. 'The discussion should be how to fix this,' Cockburn adds. This is where there are other tensions. A fair complaint is that fans have little power, with resignation about that then just feeding more division. The great irony is the game has a huge recent example of fans coming together to assert their power for a common good.

It was a cinematic scene, that modern club owners would usually have been delighted to monetise as content. Except, in this, they were the villains. On the third day of the Super League crisis, as Chelsea hosted Brighton behind Covid's closed doors, thousands of fans gathered outside Stamford Bridge. Their protest had initially been a thrilling venting of righteous anger. Then, shortly before 7 p.m., the area suddenly went quiet. Word came through that Chelsea were preparing to withdraw. In a scene reminiscent of George Bailey joyously running down the street in *It's a Wonderful Life*, one supporter sprinted through the crowds shouting 'We're out!' He was accompanied by rapturous cheers that rippled around Fulham Broadway until it was one mass celebration. A story that seemed to show everything wrong with football ended up displaying its most uplifting virtues. The people had beaten the billionaires.

Frustrated Super League figures spitefully claimed Boris Johnson's intervention was 'the tipping point' but that was only the populist in the UK prime minister responding to unprecedented public outpouring. The reason this emotion had such impact was because it was unified. Fan groups actively came together to try and corral the response into something meaningful; initially, to just *do* something. They all felt betrayed, as Tottenham Hotspur supporter Martin Cloake articulates. 'We'd been asking the club board in meetings we had with them for over 18 months, "Have you got any plans", "there are rumours" – and they lied to us.'

The supporters' trusts of England's six Super League clubs set up a WhatsApp group titled 'ESL', while making sure to keep contact with other fans. 'It was about more than our clubs,' says Cloake. 'It was about the pyramid, the principle that you can go from the bottom to the top and what happens on the pitch is what matters. It wasn't Chelsea or Spurs fans saying "we went to be there". That's the great thing. It was an amazing act of solidarity.' That should have been the moral of the story. Fans from everywhere unified to lobby everyone they could think of. 'We knew we had to make a big noise,' Cloake explains. 'It was a well-established network but we didn't really have to argue the case because people felt it. Those sentiments on the placards, it was a very organic thing. It was easier than we expected.'

Executives at Super League clubs were shocked at the extent of the reaction. Some believed they could brazen out anything, but didn't see this coming. 'It was a very clear authentic rising,' Cockburn says, 'incredibly powerful.' Liverpool supporters demanded banners be removed from the Kop,[7] the Arsenal Supporters' Trust posted about 'the death of a sporting institution'.[8]

'The Super League was defeated because football has much stronger links in communities,' Palios says. The widespread view within UEFA was that it was 'down to English fans'. The German fans might have been influential, too, except they didn't need to be. The 50+1 rule meant it never got that far. There couldn't have been a better illustration of the importance of the supporter stakes. It was a safeguard.

That contrast even said something about better-received capitalist owners like Liverpool. They might generally try to do what fans want but the Super League showed how there will always be a disconnect. FSG have had to apologise for a few decisions. At the least, the game finally seemed to be listening. A fan-led review was

called for. The 'German model' was part of the public consciousness, even mentioned by Boris Johnson.[9] Owners were so shaken
they were committing to better fan dialogue. Except, the energy
inevitably dissipated. It's a lot harder to get animated about obscure
football governance than about a heist of the game, even though
both end up with similar effects. 'The Super League should have
been a turning point,' Rosso says. 'Now, a lot of football clubs are a
very long distance from where we want to be on fan engagement.'

Less than a year after the Stamford Bridge protest, a small group of
fans were at Westminster to harness the same spirit for the future
of their club. Roman Abramovich had been sanctioned for ties
to Vladimir Putin and Chelsea were up for sale, leading to fan
representatives regularly meeting with government. An obvious
solution was suggested. Why not set a pathway that would eventually allow supporters a stake in Chelsea?

It seemed like exactly the moment. That same Conservative government had received a huge polling boost from the Super League,
and overseen a fan-led review. The entire Abramovich crisis had
meanwhile made the issue of ownership incredibly acute. It had
shown a club's future could be threatened overnight. And yet the
government had no interest. Rather than Chelsea becoming the
first major English club to be fan-owned, they became the first
major club to be owned by private equity. It was a wasted opportunity, although not to make money. The new Chelsea hierarchy
told fans in May 2022 that match-going costs wouldn't be affected
until they had exhausted all potential revenue streams but, as
Rosso explains, 'that pledge was quickly broken'. 'Anything from
programme cost has gone up, food and drink . . . Chelsea women
prices have gone up by record amounts. The affordable coach subsidy has been removed entirely – and it doesn't weigh up because

supporters see expenditure on the pitch, and then they're making cuts behind the scenes.' That expenditure was often astonishing, as Chelsea shocked football by spending over £270 million net in January 2023 alone.

It plays into a more philosophical contrast. Clubs were founded for their communities, and the idea was naturally to be positive local influences. Many modern owners instead want to raise profits, which means prioritising commercial decisions. Clubs don't fulfil their community role in the way that should be idealised. This is similarly where the wage race is so corrosive. Chelsea were one of countless clubs who constantly chose to notionally try and improve the squad rather than trying to improve life around the club. With the average wage:revenue ratio in the Premier League at 68 per cent, it is astonishing excess, and for what? Just to keep up with other clubs? It's all the more incomprehensible when the average wage of just one Premier League player – around £3 million a year – could make a huge difference to community work. 'Fans need to be at the very centre of everything a football club does, be that its ethos and identity to the match-day experience,' Rosso argues. 'It's a real shame the way football has gone and the reason is the money at stake, which wasn't there 30 years ago. It's too valuable for these owners to resist.' Couper, who works with fan group Fair Game through his support of AFC Wimbledon, goes even further than that. 'The trouble with the way football operates in England is you're encouraged to overspend. That goes against a sustainable community-based club'

Tony Ernst has monitored all this from Malmö FF, a club his family have been members of for a century, and can't comprehend the lack of say English supporters have. 'I find it remarkable there's no way to put pressure. We have AGMs where we elect the board and we can hold them responsible and raise concerns, often about highly specific sums. That's because it is much more important to keep the club afloat as an active part of the community than winning.' That contrasts with a dynamic in English football culture that is almost a contradiction. Fans are immensely invested, but that generally only extends to attending matches, and not supporter activism. That has occasionally frustrated supporter representatives like Cloake, even if he understands how it happens. 'There's the cliche, shit job in a factory then on Saturday go and watch your team. That was your break. But then you ask people to get involved and it's "really"?' That is far from exclusive to England. It doesn't help that, just as capitalistic owners become apoplectic at 'being told how to run their business' by Swiss sports bodies like UEFA, they don't feel they have to answer to fans. 'The attitude is still "this is my business, why do we need to talk to these people",' Cloake says. Even then, fan engagement can become just another marketing tool. It all serves what Ernst describes as these 'fantasy' transfer fees they pay. That fantasy then creates another absurd cycle. Supporters have always demanded that their clubs 'spend some fucking money' but football's evolved economic model has created a deeper obsession with financial performance. Some fans fixate on where their clubs finish in the Deloitte Football Money League and, just like with serious geopolitical issues, phrases like amortisation over player contracts have become part of the game's language. It is why the financial returns of reaching the Champions League have far outstripped the historic glory of a domestic cup in terms of importance. An adjunct to all of this is how the transfer media industrial complex has almost developed into a separate business. Social media accounts that specialise in speculation generate followings and engagement numbers into tens of millions. A strand of fans seem to care much more about potential signings – in effect, imagined football – rather than actual matches. This has real-world effect, as Palios notes how it has increased pressure. 'Expectation is exacerbated by social media, to the extent the game has become so much more short-term. I used to think a manager would get 18 months but, nowadays, social media enables people to raise a posse.' Another chief executive confides how he was abused by fans because the club hadn't shown enough 'ambition' in the market, even though they'd just had one of their most successful recent seasons. 'Some fans correlate spending with a desire to win and that is more important than actually winning! It's a fascinating but infuriating phenomenon.' The Saudi Pro League almost serves as the perfect product of this era, since it is all big headlines for mega transfers, with little attention to the actual football.

It does show how younger generations consume the game differently, but that has always been the case. Children have rarely sat down to watch full 90-minute games that often. New effects, however, are the further concentration of focus on the wealthiest clubs. Those wealthy clubs are then further unmoored from their communities. More people in France become fans of Paris Saint-Germain rather than their local club because of the glamour. It is just another problem of financial polarisation. Fans might become more interested in their local club if they have a good season and there's a buzz, but the chances of that recede in a stratified game. None of this is to castigate young supporters for being bewitched by the biggest names. That is natural. What is not natural is how the football economy has been engineered this way. The sense of community is at risk. There's a drift, that leaves a gap, and a hollowed-out centre. 'If we're paying more wages, we have to make cuts,' Couper says. 'And the first things to be cut are the community projects like walking football, the dementia clubs. That's all a direct result of Manchester City having spent a lot of money on one player's wages. It has a knock-on effect all the way down. That is a really obvious link but a lot of football isn't seeing that.'

It makes squabbles over minor redistribution of money from the big clubs all the more unseemly. And this, as a charity worker such as Riley points out, at a time of 'grinding social inequality'. The worst part is the excess doesn't satisfy a lot of supporters. Anger is the overriding emotion of online discussion. Even Manchester City, whose owners actively aim to generate goodwill for political reasons, have been criticised by fans for ticket price rises.[10] Such increases infuse a belief that many owners just want to create international vehicles, where tickets can primarily be sold for high prices to tourists. There's then the lack of jeopardy to many of the games. 'It does change the experience of being a fan and watching your team,' Curtis says. 'It's not quite so hair-raising any more.' City Football Group have changed the experience of clubs like Troyes to a much more profound degree. Fans furiously protested their relegation to the third tier of French football in 2023–24, chanting 'merci City'. That came after boycotts and former player Jérôme Rothen saying they were sick of being 'used like a floor cloth'. 'They perhaps think that because it's Troyes, we're not going to be vigilant . . . I just want to tell them, "Get out! French football doesn't need you!" A community institution had lost its independence.'[11]

It is another self-defeating element of modern football. External interests want to capitalise on the spectacle but their approach serves to dilute it. 'The more you kill off the life of the pyramid, and that ability for the underdog to succeed, the more it becomes like cinema,' Couper argues. Ernst echoes that sentiment. 'That's not football. That's Hollywood, Netflix. It has nothing to do with community or your sense of belonging. It could be anything.' Ernst's own Swedish league, however, shows there is an alternative.

About 15 years ago, the general feeling around the Swedish league was to not watch it at all. Fans were drawn to England and Spain, because that's where the stars were. That's where the Champions League usually went. The Allsvenskan seemed so staid in comparison. One study revealed that only 11 per cent of Swedish fans followed it as their favourite competition.[12] 'And then, gradually,' Ernst says, 'the wheels turned.' Swedish football had already steered down a different route. In 1999, the state ruled that all clubs had to be 51 per cent owned by members, which ended up proving opportune by the time of the 2008 financial crash. As the rest of football was looking outward for investment to keep the model going, Sweden looked inward. Forward-thinking officials like Mats Enquist and Lars-Christer Olsson sought to translate fan ownership into events every supporter would want to go to. Evain, who works with fans all around Europe, found the experience exhilarating. 'We're often told football is a business but what Sweden did was look at what they had that was different, which was fan culture, and invest a lot into it. It was really smart. Why try to imitate the Premier League and produce a lesser spectacle when you can build on what makes you different? It's a good lesson for the rest of Europe.' It was also, predictably, good business in itself. Revenues trebled as crowds doubled, because it was a great experience. 'The atmospheres are incredible because the fans are really active,' Ernst smiles. 'We have standing sections at every game, there's pyro. It's organic.'

It's also more organic in terms of competition. Investors can put money in, but they can't take anything out, which is one of many factors that has fostered a more stable football economy. There are minimal financial gaps, leaving the Allsvenskan with a competitive balance that has brought 11 different champions in

20 years. The Premier League has had seven in 30, La Liga just nine in its entire history. 'I work with the FSE and supporters all over Europe look at Sweden as some kind of paradise,' Ernst says. Many fans would simply like any stake in their clubs. It is only really seen in Europe in Sweden, Norway, Germany, Austria and the socio models of Spain and Portugal. The dysfunction of major Iberian clubs such as Barcelona show how this can be abused, although Evain argues this is a problem of structure rather than principle. 'The presidential model leads to populism, but there is no real direct democracy. It's more consultation. Florentino Pérez acts like an owner rather than an elected custodian.' Athletic Club and CA Osasuna represent more progressive structures, but there still isn't as strong a supporter stake as in Germany.

In basic terms, fan ownership means clubs are run by interests whose sole concern is the health of the institution. That's all the more powerful if it is the common model in a league, because they don't have to compete with other motives. There are similarly no debates about owners, or moral concerns about just supporting your club. The incentives to involve questionable sponsors such as cryptocurrency are lessened. Bayern's 11 successive titles show the Bundesliga clearly needs better redistribution of money, but that is the case for all of Europe. Fan ownership isn't perfect but can be far superior to other models when combined with other measures.

It is instructive that German fans have collectively campaigned against changing the 50+1 rule, anyway. Since Bundesliga clubs competed at Champions League level, they had to embrace economic expansion in the way Swedish football couldn't. Clubs were allowed to turn their professional divisions into limited companies. In order to preserve their community role, however, the Deutscher Fussbal-Bund added a statute that required 50 per cent of the shares, plus one extra, to remain in the possession of the parent club.[13] This 'third way' ensured companies or individuals could invest in German clubs but never own or control them. Fans saw football as a public right.

This also ensured, like Sweden, they do more than just turn up. 'The ultras play an active role in creating the atmospheres at games,' long-time fan representative Michael Gabriel says. 'It's much more than sport, especially in times when neoliberalism is getting stronger and people are left isolated. Football is a place you can feel like you are home . . . but there's more in Germany. There's a possibility to be involved in the decision-making.' This could be seen at the biggest club. Despite Bayern competing with Super League clubs, supporters don't prioritise profit at any cost. Quite the opposite. The end of Bayern's association with Qatar Airways followed an AGM where the directors got booed for defending the sponsorship. Their fans were later among mass protests against the Bundesliga selling off marketing rights to private equity. Borussia Dortmund meanwhile used the biggest game in their modern history, the 2024 Champions League final, to protest against the club's sponsorship with arms manufacturer Rheinmetall AG. The contrast with the Premier League couldn't be clearer, but there are seeds.

When the Glazers investigated the sale of Manchester United in 2023, only 17 per cent of club fans in an *Athletic* poll voted for a Qatar-linked bid.[14] Community spirit can be developed. The Allsvenskan's health is the proof of that. Riley would love similar for Newcastle United. 'I'd rather that Newcastle United was owned either entirely by fans or it was based on the German model,' says Riley. That is a sentiment that is spreading. More fans are attracted to the local element. In 2022–23, the English Football League saw its highest attendances for 70 years, with 21.7 million through the gates.[15] It's like people crave the earthier connection. Even Rosso only partly jokes that he tells people to 'go and find a National League team'.

England is one of a few European countries that would need a complete change of regulation. Germany has long been the example, but Sweden goes a level beyond.

'Even though Germany has 50+1, there are ways around it,' Ernst says. 'There are no ways around ours. There's that philosophical question as well, why do we have football? A lot of Swedish fans think it's because the club should represent the city and do good community work. That's more important than having stars or winning the Champions League. And what we've seen around Europe, clubs are going to go bankrupt, maybe even leagues. This is not sustainable. I know my club is going to be here in 50 years because that's the way the system is set up. We'll still be standing.' There was one more turn of the wheel. By the time the Saudi Pro League and multi-club ownership evolved, even those in Sweden backing private investment began to change their mind. They saw what they had and told Ernst as much. 'A lot of powerful people were saying "maybe this is a good idea".' It was for the good of the game.

If the realisation is spreading, the hope is it might eventually become normality.

14.

CATCH 2022

The World Cup trophy is an image so familiar that, when actually seen up close, there's a surreal wonder to it. The gold is so brilliant that it's impossible to take your eyes off, even as the greatest player in history cradles it. Leo Messi certainly found it impossible to take his hands off, as he came through the Lusail media area three hours after the most spectacular final of all. In keeping with the sensory overload of the match, the victorious Argentina squad were heard before they were seen. The new world champions were made to go this way to fulfil media duties, but they only sang at the press – or, really, about them. 'It doesn't matter what those whore journalists say, the whore that gave birth to them.' This happy little tune, sung with glee as Messi lifted the trophy above, had come from previous tension with the media. Some of the FIFA and Qatar officials watching on might have approved of the message, given the tone of that World Cup. There was even one last awkward question for Hassan Al Thawadi, the chief of the Supreme Committee for Delivery and Legacy, as he walked through the same area with the satisfied sense of a job done. The smile vanished when he was asked about Abdullah Ibhais.

Ibhais is a World Cup whistleblower imprisoned after what human rights groups described as 'an unfair trial', and whose family allege had been tortured.[1] The Jordanian advised that the Supreme Committee should acknowledge its role in a failure to pay striking workers at a camp in 2019. His family, including two young children, just wanted contact again. When Al Thawadi registered the question, there was a meek thumbs up before he walked off. The mood was too celebratory, as the jubilant Argentinian procession went by. There was that World Cup trophy itself, the single reason we were all here in a small desert country at all.

Just as the arms on that gold stretch out to 'receive the world at the stirring moment of victory', in the words of designer Silvio Gazzaniga, this was where it all came together. Those few minutes underneath Lusail Stadium distilled the entire tournament, after the tournament itself had distilled the previous 15 years. This football event horizon went beyond the World Cup's status as a mirror for the state of the game. Usually, this grandest of competitions is an enthrallingly self-contained event. To attend a World Cup is to feel like nothing else matters for the month, especially amid the global party of the group stage. That's when everyone is still there in a great festival of colour off the pitch, as nation-defining moments happen on it. An evocative line is that people measure their lives in World Cups. Everyone can remember their first. The World Cup at its best is a celebration of humanity, exactly as founder Jules Rimet intended, invigorated by its nature as a pinnacle of sporting excellence.[2] That fosters a sense of completion that befits a world champion, a status enriched by so many moments that have made the competition's mythology. You only have to glimpse hazy images of Diego Maradona in Mexican heat or Pelé triumphantly lifting his fist to feel that excitement. These are moments looked back on for decades, and watched by billions at the time.

This is what Qatar wanted to buy, at a cost of around $220 billion and the lives of countless migrant workers.[3] It's that moment as the centre of the planet, and a place in history. Nobody should be under any illusions about how clouded that history is, mind. Qatar was only following a complicated lineage. Part of every World Cup's story are the various controversies that shape it, with the image especially darkened when held in non-democracies like Italy 1934, Argentina 1978 and Russia 2018. Qatar's criminalisation of homosexuality sadly had many precedents, too, such as England 1966. What was especially shameful about 2022, however, were the extremes that so many problems were taken to. There was the motivation of it, the winning of it, the running of it and the nature of it. For all that a frustrating moral relativism has been invoked in debates about this, only one fact really matters. This World Cup could not have taken place without considerable human suffering. That was because Qatar had to build an entire infrastructure to host the tournament, but did not reform the labour system at the centre of it. That will always be unconscionable. As FairSquare's Nick McGeehan puts it, 'People *should* be angry about a football tournament that puts hundreds of thousands more migrant workers into this system.' It is even more poignant that, for all the World Cup's historic problems, a genuine emotional purity has been compromised. People spend four years waiting for that sense of wonder, but any conscious thought about this one made it impossible to get excited about. FIFA failed to protect the spirit of their competition, to go with the failure to leverage proper reform in Qatar. If this is the 'greatest show on earth', as FIFA president Gianni Infantino proclaimed, this was the worst possible version. It also undermined what would have been nobler elements of this tournament. It was the first World Cup in the Gulf, the first in an Arab country and the first in the Muslim world. This was overdue. Even Qatar's defiant rise as a small country amid imposing neighbours added another story to it. It just wasn't worth this.

Really, the idea of 'worth' was central to all of this. The

universal revelry that vivifies a World Cup has been recognised by FIFA's tenets of inclusivity, as figures like Infantino boast of 'bringing people together'. That inclusivity just wasn't extended to the LGBTQ+ community since homosexuality is illegal in Qatar. Three Lions Pride were among many fan groups who said they didn't feel comfortable going.[4] They weren't afforded the same worth, which is also true of millions of migrant workers. Their presence on the fringes, everywhere, but often overlooked, made Qatar feel like what the Deep South must have during slavery. It should be considered a moral absurdity that a mere football tournament could be held in these circumstances in 2022. And yet that comes back to a different idea of worth. The football world's willingness to facilitate this was merely its embrace of global capitalism taken to a logical conclusion. Autocracies with financial power can sit very comfortably within that system.

It all meant this wasn't really a distortion of football. It was the direction of travel. That was something that became so apparent in the long wait for the 2022 World Cup, as it weighed over the entire game. By the time the trophy was brought out for the opening game, the image in the brilliant gold was only football's own reflection.

Even as late as the World Cup draw in April 2022, with construction still disrupting Doha, it was almost impossible to imagine how this global mega-event could fit into an area the size of Greater London. It was typical of the doublespeak that surrounded the tournament, though, that this very thought was being recast. Rather than a host ill-suited to a modern World Cup, the setting supposedly recalled the competition's founding. It was to be the first since Montevideo 1930 where everything was in a 'global village'. There just wasn't that much of 'everything'. There was little to do, which meant a lot of tourism to the architecturally dazzling National Museum of Qatar. There, fans saw one of the most important documents in the state's history. That was the envelope that Sepp Blatter opened on 2 December 2010. It said much more than just confirming Qatar would be hosts. It announced the country's arrival on the global stage.

Qatar's strategy might have ensured that victory was inevitable, but it was still far from certain the decision would be fulfilled. There were times when it instead seemed inevitable the country would be stripped of the World Cup. Qatar had to withstand an awful lot during those 12 years, including a regional cold war. That itself could have been recast as a miracle, in different circumstances, about the defiance of a small country. This is certainly the narrative the museum promotes, with exhibits revering the emir for guiding the country through the Gulf blockade. Much of the criticism was of their own making, though. There was still an entire infrastructure to build, as made clear in the original FIFA evaluation report. Qatar needed seven brand new stadiums as well as a new transport system and hospitality industry.[5]

Through all this, the bid team liked to show another image, of two photographs side by side. One was from 1981, and an aerial shot of Doha's pyramid-shaped Sheraton Grand, surrounded by sand. The second is from the twenty-first century, but now with an entire city around it. The will was that Qatar could do the same again. Except, there was no miracle to this, just a grim reality. The $220 billion cost was over five times what China spent on the 2008 Summer Olympics.[6] It might have been tens of billions more had the decision not been taken in 2015 to move the World Cup from summer to winter. This is the kind of unimaginable scale that only dictators can mandate. It is almost biblical, as made clear by the millions in indentured servitude doing the building. Migrant labour came to define the Qatar World Cup, even more so than the corruption accusations. An irony was that an escalation in criticism came from Qatar doing what neighbours like the UAE refused and allowing human rights groups in to scrutinise. Investigators realised the system was so ingrained that Qatar didn't actually understand there was a problem. That was to change, amid a series of damning reports.[7] Specific issues with the kafala system were also made clear by a personal football story, as one of Qatar's early controversies was over French-Algerian striker Zahir Belounis. He endured a pay dispute with SC El Jaish, but then couldn't secure an exit visa without their agreement.[8] Unable to work but unable to leave, Belounis went on hunger strike, eventually suffering suicidal thoughts.[9] He even wrote letters to former World Cup ambassadors Zinedine Zidane and Pep Guardiola, before eventually being allowed to go.

Qatar was initially shocked by the extent of criticism over the wider migrant labour issue. There had admittedly been a realisation of the need for reform, as press officers insisted the country's issues were born of political immaturity rather than malice. This was sensed in another tension around the tournament. Qatar had an anti-World Cup rump largely driven by the same ultra-conservative Wahhabism that underlay Saudi Arabia. A line commonly heard by the tournament team from less progressive elements was, 'I don't recognise my country any more.' Such irredentism was also heard in the argument that the World Cup was a white elephant project for foreigners, that would make Qataris a smaller minority.[10] This was a rump the more liberal generation, led by figures like Al Thawadi, had to work around. They listened to diametrically opposed criticisms from inside and outside Qatar, then had to publicly speak to both, which perhaps explained so many mixed messages. It was difficult diplomacy, amid wider state-building. The emir ultimately corralled everyone to play their part for the greater good, emphasising a pride in what Qatar had achieved. It was still migrant workers from the poorest countries doing the actual work. As much as that criticism aggravated Qatar, insiders say the primary concern was 'overall brand enhancement' against Abu Dhabi and Saudi Arabia. That rivalry posed by far the most tangible obstacle to the World Cup, with the blockade. It could have caused havoc to construction, especially through a pandemic. Qatar kept going. They were also going to stand their ground.

It all goes some way to explaining why fighter jets roared over Lusail ahead of the World Cup final. They were part of a force that had 23 US Apache gunships, 24 British Typhoons and various other military hardware with names that denoted devastating force.[11] Qatar was packing heat and making that explicit. As the blockade faltered, regional rivals had nowhere else to turn but the information war. There were funded campaigns on social media, as well as a report by a pro-Saudi consultancy claiming the World Cup would be moved.[12] Such noise amplified many legitimate criticisms, that for a time created an expectation Qatar really would be stripped of the tournament. It never got to that point, even when FIFA surprisingly admitted there had been bribery, through the publication of a court testimony on the body's own website.[13] One huge disincentive was the threat of massive legal action.[14] The position of the 'new' FIFA through this was that they 'inherited' Qatar and had to navigate it. This was a stance given credence by Infantino's closeness with Mohammed bin Salman and attempts to expand the World Cup around the Gulf. They ran aground against the blockade.

The final obstacle was moral. Once the qualification campaign started, momentum for a boycott developed in northern Europe.

Germany's ProFans alliance asked their national federation not to participate, stating it would be a 'lavish festival on the graves of thousands of migrant workers'.[15] Norway at least discussed the idea, leading their squad to wear T-shirts saying 'human rights – on and off the pitch' before a match against Gibraltar.[16] Such generic words were still revolutionary in elite football. For the players' part, activists like Human Rights Watch's Minky Worden said teams were 'effectively hostages' to the situation. This was in many cases their only chance to fulfil a dream, and it coincided with a decision taken way above their heads. It was seen as a huge societal burden to put on young men. Qatar were nevertheless at one point 'petrified' that 'someone like Marcus Rashford' could start campaigning. That isn't to hold one player to unfair expectations, but it reflects a wider sense of wasted power. Qatar had already realised that, and used it in another way. In September 2021, as debate about a boycott continued, Neymar and Kylian Mbappé were among Paris Saint-Germain stars appearing in a Qatar Airways advertisement for the World Cup.[17]

It was the first of many moments of alignment.

Just a month before a World Cup that Russia had been excluded from, amid global revulsion, the emir of Qatar hailed his relationship with Vladimir Putin. This was from a summit in Kazakhstan where the 2018 hosts were thanked for logistical help with 2022.[18] The two World Cups will forever be intertwined but, by 2022, this went far beyond what happened in Zürich on 2 December 2010. The actions of one World Cup host geopolitically empowered the next. At a time when Qatar might have faced a barrage of political criticism over migrant labour, Russia invaded Ukraine, to bring international ostracism but also a huge Western requirement for different sources of gas. Qatar Energy's annual net profits rose by

£18 billion in 2022.[19] Political commentary decreased. If there are future versions of books like Daniel Yergin's *The Prize*, explaining the profound impact of fossil fuels, the World Cup will surely have a significant place. The tournament has both illustrated how this works and driven it.[20] By 2022, the events of December 2010 – not to mention so much of the club game – made much more sense. Fans watching the World Cup were meanwhile struggling to pay electricity bills. It was blankets and circuses.

Along the same lines, just as Roman Abramovich's purchase of Chelsea foreshadowed ownership to come, Russia's World Cup framed Qatar's. The 2018 tournament involved many of the same themes, if initially in greyer tones. Questions were asked about racism, homophobia, LGBTQ+ treatment and human rights, as well as autocratic use of sport. There were even reports of migrant workers being treated like 'slaves' in preparations. Inspectors for the Building and Wood Workers' International trade union said North Korean labourers on the St Petersburg site were housed in storage containers and forced into 16-hour shifts, with pay sent to their government. Norwegian magazine *Josimar* reported one worker was found dead in a container. FIFA had been made aware of evidence and demanded improvements.[21] Previous calls to boycott the World Cup meanwhile escalated after the poisoning of former spy Sergei Skripal and his daughter in Salisbury, which had been blamed on the Kremlin.[22] The British government didn't send representatives while FA officials refused to applaud Putin's opening address.[23]

No such issues for Infantino, who merrily sat between Mohammed bin Salman and the Russian president, as Putin insisted on 'not mixing sport and politics'. It was in your face as eyes were averted. Russia had essentially erected a Potemkin village that could have served as a blueprint for Qatar. The Federal Security

Service cracked down on groups that might incite violence, while loosening usually strict policing on public congregations.²⁴ That allowed Moscow's Nikolskaya Street to feel like Copacabana in 2014, that global party, spread by welcoming locals all over Russia. This appreciation for the country was made all the more poignant after the invasion of Ukraine, but the 2018 World Cup was an important reminder that the people are always separate to the state. Argentina 1978 is another example worth remembering. The criticism was for the state, not a country now beloved as a tourist destination.

Russia 2018 was also celebrated as a brilliant tournament on the pitch, although this was portrayed as if someway influenced by the hosts, just like Qatar. Since the quality of football is independent of the surroundings, that was really just another attempt to appropriate the sport. The opening game set out much of this. After Bin Salman and Putin watched the hosts thrash Saudi Arabia 5-0, the Russian president rang national team coach Stanislav Cherchesov to congratulate him. At virtually the same time, prime minister Dmitry Medvedev introduced a proposal to controversially raise retirement ages.²⁵ Protestors had meanwhile used the loosened atmosphere of the World Cup to stage rare demonstrations in non-host cities, but the flip side was that the focus remained on the football. Putin's spokesman, Dmitry Peskov, later described the celebrations for Russia's last-16 victory over Spain as 'comparable to images of 9 May 1945'.²⁶

There was then a considerable twist to one of the stories of the tournament. Croatia had been the World Cup's revelation, defying expectations of their mere four million population to reach the final against France. They beat Russia on penalties in the quarter-finals, at which point some of their squad defied state-approved sentiments on the 2014 annexation of Crimea. Defender Domagoj Vida and assistant Ognjen Vukojević were filmed declaring 'glory to Ukraine'.[27] While Vida escaped with a warning, Vukojević was sacked. The Croatian federation later claimed the message was not political but 'unfortunately left room for interpretations'. The entire issue would be put in binary terms four years later, as Russia became the first World Cup host to be banned from a subsequent tournament for non-football reasons. That similarly put a different spin on Infantino's previous scolding of criticisms of Russia.[28] The lesson was that the tail doesn't wag the dog here. Autocratic states change football much more than football changes autocratic states. By November 2022, Qatar was staging the world's premier sporting event, while helping sustain the global economy.

If the romantic line is that people measure their lives in World Cups, the tragedy of Qatar 2022 was that this was a World Cup that could be measured in lives. Except, the state refused to ever properly investigate how many died in the long build-up. The lack of numbers only emphasises that criticisms of all this are no mere words. They are pain and human suffering, families crying at airports at the unexplained loss of loved ones. The deaths were only the gravest consequence of a structure that is both Orwellian and Kafkaesque.[29] A huge underclass of people toil in an autocratic surveillance state, amid a network of abuses. That made it impossible to attend the World Cup and be untouched.

Many will point to comparable issues in the West, but a difference is they are failures of the system. In Qatar, this was the system, as well as an extension of the global capitalist structure. It was exploitation of the poorest people on earth, in the wealthiest nation. As Worden put it, the range of abuses were 'not normal for a World Cup'. It is why Qatar had a dismal claim to be the most problematic tournament in history, surpassing Argentina 1978.

The scale was illustrated when various human rights groups went to qualified teams looking to share concerns, but there were so many they were told to come up with common causes. One of the easiest to relate to was a heartbreaking realisation. In an affecting documentary called *The Workers Cup*, a Ghanaian called Kenneth talks of how a recruitment agent deceived him into thinking he was going to Qatar to be a professional footballer.[30] The 21-year-old instead found himself trapped by the country's labour system. It is almost dystopian, in how desperate people were lured to an autocracy on false pretences, and put in a system the workers themselves say keeps them 'against their will'. The majority did travel of their own volition, since salaries of $220–350 a month in Doha can be transformative in the West African and South Asian countries the labourers are mainly from.

They all still suffered the same 'cycle of abuse', as described by Isobel Archer of the Business and Human Rights Centre. The first step was in their home country, and the payment of illegal recruitment fees that usually extend to thousands of dollars. Archer describes this as 'the worst driver of abuse', primarily from the financial trap that is set by debts that workers can't possibly pay off. 'Stories of how families had to sell a daughter's jewellery stay with you.' Men would go years without seeing their children, watching them grow up on smartphones.[31] On arrival, workers found themselves in an infrastructure so shaped by the notorious kafala system that it was still virtually the same, despite its legal abolition on paper. This was illustrated by the way many had to hand over passports, even though laws prohibited this. Their lives were under complete control of employers, who would often place them in what Amnesty UK described as 'squalid, overcrowded accommodation with no air-conditioning and exposed to overflowing sewage'. There were common complaints about not receiving overtime or outright 'wage theft', which was not getting paid at all. Examples also exist of workers who tried to take sick days being told they would be docked pay, amid fears of deportation.

Such descriptions constitute forced labour under the International Labour Organisation Convention on Forced Labour. Professor Tendayi Achiume, the UN's Special Rapporteur on Contemporary Forms of Racism, wrote of 'indentured or coercive labour conditions' that recalled 'the historical reliance on enslaved and coerced labour in the region'. The Business and Human Rights Resource Centre meanwhile echo many workers in simply calling it 'modern slavery'. This, as human rights groups stress, is only from the testimony of the few migrants who investigators were able to actually build relationships with, and weren't afraid to speak openly. They still had to be under pseudonyms. They formed two million people in this situation before the World Cup, comprising 95 per cent of the workforce.

That sat amid concerns about 'structural racial discrimination' and 'a quasi-caste system', from Professor Achiume's description of how Western and Arab nationalities 'systematically enjoyed greater human rights protections than South Asian and sub-Saharan nationalities'. More than a third of interviewees in one Amnesty report cited pay discrimination on the basis of nationality, race and language. West Africans received the least. South Asians faced the most hazardous jobs. This also prevents worker solidarity. Amnesty cited one of the most vulnerable groups as the women that make up 60 per cent of the 175,000 domestic workers. Out of 105 interviewed, 15 said they were physically abused and five sexually abused. There's then the heartbreaking psychological toll. Nepal estimated just before the World Cup that 10 per cent of the country's 2,000 deaths in the 12-year build-up came from suicide.[32] Such numbers align with the *Guardian*'s report of 6,500 worker deaths, a number which long raised the angriest pushback from Qatar. The disputing of the figures is itself an outrage, since the only reason doubt could be cast was because Qatar never properly investigated how many died. The painful reality was illustrated in images from Dhaka's Hazrat Shahjalal international airport every Friday, when long queues gathered for flights to Doha, at the same time as bodies were returned.[33]

Part of the scandal, McGeehan says, was the 'negligence and the rate of unexplained deaths'. That stood at approximately 70 per cent, according to a 2021 Amnesty report. Deaths were reported with terms like 'natural causes' or 'cardiac arrest', phrases that pathologist Dr David Bailey said 'should not be included on a death certificate'. The wording also meant those deaths were not recorded as World Cup-linked. All of this occurred as people within the game dutifully insisted on how 'we must recognise the reforms made' by Qatar. The reality was they were minimal, mostly amounting to some improvement in accommodation and prevention of the most basic wage theft. Employers just found ways around the rules. That lack of reform was down to a nexus of private interests seeking profits, state politics and the wider culture. You didn't have to be at the World Cup long to see an ex-pat speak to a migrant worker obnoxiously. It wasn't universal but it was noticeable.

The most galling aspect was that Qatar could so easily afford to pay workers properly. A few hundred million could have been spared from the $220 billion, rather than going on indulgences like air-conditioned stadiums that added to the immense environmental cost. Climate expert Mike Berners-Lee claimed the 2022 World Cup was 'going to be the highest carbon event of any kind, apart from a war, that humans have ever staged'.[34]

Although money was clearly no object, the constant argument

against reform was that Qatar couldn't do it 'at the stroke of a pen'. It was internally seen as 'mind-blowing' to expect a company to hire 15 migrant workers, train them up and see them change job. Qatar was apparently too used to decades of treating labour as they wished. That lack of protection was ultimately just an extension of autocracy and the suppression that comes with it. Freedom of expression and assembly are greatly limited. Ibhais has become one of the most sadly prominent examples of what can happen to whistleblowers or dissidents. His family claimed he was imprisoned in a cell a short walk from Al Bayt Stadium, where preparations for the opening game were alleged to coincide with Ibhais being subjected to 'complete darkness in solitary confinement' with near-freezing temperatures so he couldn't sleep for 96 hours.[35] Throughout all of this, people have made appeals to moral relativism, and hailed the most minor concessions. Even if that were all valid, that doesn't mean a state should just be given a World Cup. The bottom line was that the competition perpetuated suffering. That basic reality required a lot of spin.

After Gianni Infantino finished his jaw-dropping media appearance on the eve of Qatar 2022, acquaintances expressed surprise. 'I know, I know,' came the FIFA president's response. Infantino was supposed to hold a 45-minute press conference but that became a 90-minute address, with the shift signposted by the show-stealing opening remarks. 'Today, I feel Qatari. Today, I feel Arab. Today, I feel African. Today, I feel gay. Today, I feel disabled. Today, I feel a migrant worker.'[36] It was a brazen appropriation of the issues FIFA had been accused of betraying with this World Cup. As was how Infantino said he knows 'what it means to be discriminated' against, due to his 'red hair and freckles' as a child.

'What do you do then? You try to engage, make friends. Don't start accusing, fighting, insulting ...' That was almost more brazen, since Infantino seemed to be abrasively accusing Western companies, human rights groups and – above all – the media that sat in front of him. FIFA said he was highlighting 'hypocrisy', but it was difficult not to think that served a greater motivation. Infantino relayed the same sentiments – even about red hair – to human rights groups the year before. He'd evidently been thinking about it. It was why the key sentence wasn't 'I feel ...' but 'I think for what we Europeans have been doing around the world for the last 3,000 years, we should be apologising for the next 3,000 years, before starting to give moral lessons.' Infantino was pitching to his new power base, outside Europe. It illustrated how Qatar 2022 wasn't just a controversial World Cup but a battle in a culture war enveloping the game. That battle was fired by the two parties responsible for the World Cup, whose relationship wasn't frictionless, either.

On one side, FIFA sought to completely depoliticise all discussion of the tournament. This was made clear in a letter two weeks before the World Cup signed by Infantino and secretary general Fatma Samoura, imploring federations to 'focus on the football'.[37] It pleaded not to allow the game to be 'dragged into every ideological or political battle', which somewhat went against Infantino's own previous argument that 'football can change the world'.[38] That created an inherent contradiction to the letter's own logic, given it spoke of 'respecting all opinions and beliefs', in a spirit of 'mutual respect and non-discrimination', yet here was Infantino scolding those criticising discrimination. The FIFA president had remarked grandly on how 'no one people or culture or nation is "better" than any other', even though the idea of superiority is central to Qatar's migrant labour system and monarchical structure. Amnesty International's Agnès Callamard called it what it was, which was a 'crass abdication' of FIFA's responsibility.

Infantino's arguments only fit with the doublespeak that defined the host's own position. Qatar echoed the FIFA president in talking of depoliticising the World Cup, while at the same time politicising absolutely everything. That was emphasised by a line that was never supposed to come to light, in a voicemail from Al Thawadi to Ibhais. The latter had complained about lack of payment to workers, to which Al Thawadi's response was 'to come up with a narrative . . . explain we have taken steps beyond any other institution . . . That needs to be clarified, figure it out, if it's a delay of a month, then put a narrative on it, put a spin on it . . .'[39]

'Put a narrative on it' could have been the 2022 World Cup's slogan, rather than 'now is all'. The soundtrack of the tournament was whataboutery, post-truths and moral relativism.[40] It was how Infantino could claim the World Cup was safe for LGBTQ+ fans, while former Qatari international Khalid Salman described homosexuality as 'damage in the mind'.[41] It was how this World Cup wasn't actually an environmental 'disaster', but somehow 'carbon neutral'.[42] FIFA was later ruled to have misled fans with that latter claim, by a Swiss regulator.[43] It was how Iran manager Carlos Queiroz could respond to questions about the Iranian state's suppression of protests by imploring media to ask England counterpart Gareth Southgate about Afghanistan. It was also how it couldn't just be that a World Cup built on modern slavery was wrong. This was orientalism. The accusation of racism, usually wielded alongside hypocrisy, was one of the most heavily used weapons in that culture war. It is a media tactic that has grown with the influence of autocracy on football, but was expressed with increasing force in the last few months before the World Cup. Qatar's foreign minister Mohammed Al Thani described Western criticisms as 'very arrogant and very racist'.[44] This was where the energy crisis had empowered Qatar. World Cup chief executive Nasser Al Khater had already warned Southgate to 'pick his words carefully' after the England manager voiced concerns about migrant workers and LGBTQ+ fans.[45] Qatar had nevertheless sought to portray itself as a 'champion of the non-Western world', in the words of Amnesty's Steve Cockburn, all while the migrant workers who suffered most were from outside the West. It was a battle that surprisingly unified Gulf leaders, despite some of the criticism emanating from the regional blockade's information war. The entire approach was summed up by sportswashing of the most rudimentary type: public relations. Rather than fully address the key issues, Qatar instead paid figures like David Beckham a reported £150 million to soften their image.

Meanwhile, Infantino echoed his comments about Russia in claiming criticism bore little relation to the reality. This was a man who had stated to the European parliament that there had only been three worker deaths in the construction of World Cup stadiums.[46] Infantino evidently wasn't afraid of getting burnt again, but neither were individual football federations. Despite many remaining furious with FIFA's letter, 200 of 211 still endorsed the president for re-election before the World Cup. A group of European countries privately claimed that was 'conditional'.[47] Human rights groups meanwhile distilled their concerns into the PayUpFifa campaign, which made two requests: investigation into deaths and compensation for workers. It was felt these were easy to immediately grasp and could bring tangible effect from this World Cup. There was still very little pick-up from the game, particularly from FIFA. Only Australia actively backed the campaign, although Belgium, Denmark, Germany and the Netherlands expressed support for the sentiments.[48] Few matched the words of the forthright Dutch coach, Louis van Gaal: 'It's ridiculous that the World Cup is there. FIFA says they want to develop football there. That's bullshit. It's about money.'[49]

Such moral fortitude was all the more admirable since Van Gaal was recovering from prostate cancer. Other federations insisted they were negotiating a collective statement, and privately said they wanted something with more authority than 'just wearing a T-shirt'. They came up with literally less than that, in an armband. Featuring a 'One Love' message on multicoloured backgrounds, it gestured support for LGBTQ+ movements but didn't even name them. This would still provoke another battle. 'Don't criticise the players, don't criticise anyone,'[50] Infantino had also said in that speech, eventually extending his arms. 'Criticise me. Here I am. Crucify me . . . because I'm responsible for everything.' Not even that was true.

FIFA were in a panic. Despite protestations that all was under control, staff were shocked at Qatar's sudden decision to ban the sale of beer at World Cup stadiums just two days before the opening game.[51] The decision had greater complications since it impacted one of FIFA's most loyal partners, Budweiser, who were by then paying them £63 million to continue their presence at all World Cups since 1986. Qatar insiders were surprised at FIFA's naivety, as 'the decision could have been predicted from day one'. Since alcohol can only be sold out of public sight, the emir was never going to risk upsetting religious factions by having Budweiser in the open. There was still political intrigue to the decision, given it went to the wire and was reported to have been ordered by Sheikh Jassim, the emir's brother.[52] This was why the story was about much more than whether fans could drink beer.

There was merit to Infantino's otherwise dismissive statement that fans would 'survive' if 'for three hours a day you cannot drink a beer'.[53] A Muslim country hosting a World Cup was overdue, and it's entirely reasonable that actual cultural sensitivities such as those over alcohol are respected. FIFA probably shouldn't have had it as a requirement, but Qatar did agree to the terms on winning the vote, before reconfirming plans multiple times over 12 years. This, then, was a display of power. It showed who was really running the tournament. That was all the more jarring for FIFA since the World Cup had previously involved the railroading of hosts' constitutions. In 2014, the Brazilian government had been pressured into precisely this decision: to sell beer in stadiums.[54] All of this cut across Infantino's other claim in the press conference that all decisions were made jointly and he 'feels 200 per cent in control of this World Cup'.[55] It is instead cited as the moment 'FIFA lost control'.

There was already a sign of that in how the start date had been brought forward a day, with just 101 days' notice. That was so Qatar–Ecuador could be the opening game, but involved the happy coincidence of overshadowing the Abu Dhabi grand prix. Senior FIFA staff felt that 'backfired' through the sight of scores of local fans leaving early as the hosts were easily beaten 2-0 by Ecuador. That sense of farce continued for at least a week, with even the ticket app crashing. Those involved with planning were frustrated that so many decisions were taken late, with few written guarantees and many then reversed.

The tournament did settle after a few days, and fan groups praised the transport for those who sought to go to multiple games in one day, as the setting allowed. That was until the knockouts, when big crowds started to appear for the first time from Morocco's surprise run. It almost led to a crush outside Education City for the last-16 victory over Spain.[56] Heavy-handed Turkish police were deployed, but flights from Morocco still had to be cancelled. There was considerable tension between FIFA and Qatar right through this. That was spiked when, despite a 12-year build-up, the Death Star-like Fairmont hotel wasn't immediately ready for FIFA officials. The punchline to that was grumbles about the lack of alcohol in the temporary replacement of the Chedi.[57]

The frustration within FIFA was that it felt like anything could change on a whim. Many put this down to the various layers of power in the Qatari state under the emir, extending through royals, then senior staff and wider circles of power brokers. This was compounded by internal rivalries, and constant attempts to exert influence on the country's big show. Two different groups were fighting over the handling of Beckham. In conversations over whether rainbow hats should be allowed, positions were agreed upon in one part of the power structure, only for someone at a higher level to decide the opposite.

Going to the wrong person for the wrong issue could lead to problems, as FairSquare's James Lynch outlines: 'These are completely authoritarian systems but then you have factional in-fighting because it's about how you can get to the top and get the decision through.' And yet, even the controversy over alcohol illustrated other realities about that system. Some fans could actually buy Taittinger Champagne and Chivas Regal 12-year-old whisky – whatever about Budweiser – so long as they paid enough for VIP or VVIP tickets.[58] Another difference with this World Cup was how it displayed a whole other level of power.

Southgate described Qatar as a World Cup characterised by 'external noise', and that was literally true at games. To go with 90s musicians like Chesney Hawkes performing at half-time, a constant sound was helicopters. One was predictably called the 'Giannicopter'. You generally didn't see them land, as there was a level of attendee insulated from the rest of the noise.[59] Al Bayt even had a grand thoroughfare going all the way through to a special entrance. The most lavish suite was Lusail's Pearl Lounge, complete with golden teapots, going at packages of $35,000 for the semi-finals and final. The intersection of FIFA VVIP level and Gulf wealth created a rarefied air even for the international football circuit. One elevated figure who experienced it was US secretary of state Antony Blinken, who the *New York Times* said encouraged diplomats to use the games as an opportunity for politics.[60] That was the real business, which reflected the real point of this World Cup. Blinken gushed at a press conference with Qatar's foreign minister about a 'high point of the five-decade long diplomatic relationship'. It was the high point of Qatar's role as a geopolitical intermediary. This was exactly why the envelope was so revered in the museum. Qatar was not just the centre of the world but also welcoming global figures. That was only accentuated by the timing, since it was a tense period in modern history. Gatherings in marble-floored executive boxes or glamorous restaurants like La Mar allowed senior politicians to discuss issues like Ukraine and the global supply chain.[61]

Those in the middle talked of 'private jet after private jet arriving'. It was described as 'the ultimate Davos', of course, and 'really a political summit'. Connections were made, deals struck, ideas planted. Manchester United owner Avram Glazer was constantly there and 'transfixed', which became all the more intriguing when Sheikh Jassim – the son of Qatar's former prime minister, Sheikh Hamad – tried to buy Manchester United a few months later. Executives had to learn a lot of protocol to greet the various heads of state. Even by the World Cup's standards, the opening game was a geopolitical who's who, particularly from the Gulf. Guests included Egypt's Abdel Fattah El-Sisi, Rwanda's Paul Kagame,

UN Secretary General António Guterres and Igor Levitin, aide to Putin. Also present in a VVIP box at one point was Eva Kaili, the recent European Parliament vice president charged in Qatargate.[62] The final did feature, well, a business end with all of Elon Musk, Jared Kushner and Indian billionaire Lakshmi Mittal mingling.[63] In between, when USA scored against Wales at the Ahmed bin Ali Stadium, Blinken made a point of looking to the president of Liberia. That's because it was George Weah, himself a football legend, whose son Timothy scored. The Liberian premier later had to defend the amount of time he spent in Doha, saying he had secured funding for a highway project. The US-Iran match didn't witness shared moments like that, with diplomats not even speaking to each other.

It was in these situations that Beckham was said to be worth the money, as global figures were 'starstruck' when introduced. There was no such reception for restaurateur Nusret Gökçe, otherwise known as Salt Bae, when he bundled into elite areas. FIFA was forced to explain how the Turkish national got onto the pitch after the final.[64] Even Emmanuel Macron was criticised for going onto it to commiserate with a disinterested Mbappé. Gökçe was seen holding the trophy, which is supposed to be reserved for winners and heads of state. It laid open accusations of cronyism. Infantino had earlier said that, like football, 'Nusret unites the world.' Perhaps in derision. It was later reported that Infantino had un-followed Salt Bae on Instagram.[65] As an illustration of how even diplomatic incidents like that could be overcome, there was also the main political focus. That was the appearance of Mohammed bin Salman at the opening game, in a grand show of unity with Qatar. Not even the football could escape what this World Cup was actually about.

There is no feeling in football like the night before a World Cup. It still conjures that nostalgic magic, a feeling only accentuated in the modern game. That is ironically because the club game has become so dominant, entirely shaped by bigger forces and finances in a way the international level can't be. Managers have to do with what they have, players do it for the glory. There's a new purity to it, which makes it all the more regrettable that tournaments are held in countries that compromise that. So it was with Qatar, where politics ran through every element of the World Cup. This was even the case with the vacuous official slogan of 'now is all', shouted by a pitch-side presenter every match. The audience were implored to only look at the football, and not consider anything behind or around. It was almost impossible to look away, though, because of how consistently the tournament confronted everyone with political dilemmas. The opening ceremony, suitably dazzling and given gravitas by Morgan Freeman's narration, even had a clear message. 'Instead of accepting a new way, we demanded our own way.' There were moments when that first game felt like something other than a football match, particularly when Ecuador easily beat Qatar 2-0 in a non-contest. The result formed the worst ever performance by a World Cup host, as the team lost every game, but it would be wrong to deride them. This was really a squad playing way above their level because of decisions taken way above their heads. Most importantly, some players could never be at the social level of their supposed compatriots.[66] Qatar naturalised 10 of the 26 players through 'mission passports', which gave them the citizenship necessary for international football but not full state benefits.[67] The term is *muqimin*, Arabic for resident. It meant the national team didn't just represent Qatar but also the country's major issues, like migrant labour.

It was inevitable, then, that the World Cup's first moments of tension came outside the pitch. That was from arguments that Iran should never have been allowed to play due to the state's suppression of nationwide protests over the murder of Mahsa Amini. She was beaten in police custody over allegedly breaking religious rules on head coverings. All of this was complicated by Qatar's cordial relations with Iran, as security guards later seized anti-regime banners.[68] That their first match was being held in Khalifa International Stadium, where Englishman Zac Cox had become one of just three officially recognised World Cup deaths after a 40-metre fall, only added to the complexity.

The complexity of national representation was then illustrated in how the Iranian players stood with the people. They refused to sing the national anthem before the opening match against England. It was all the more admirable since Iran had issued death sentences over demonstrations, and Ayatollah Ali Khamenei's state was hoping the World Cup would present an image of normality. The players instead broke protocol.

It was far more than their opponents did. England's players had been part of a group with Belgium, Denmark, Germany, Netherlands, Wales and Switzerland that planned for their captains to wear One Love armbands. A meeting over this in the Fairmont had much more tension than the Qatar–Ecuador game it preceded, as potential sporting sanctions were raised by FIFA for the first time. This was seen as of a piece with the Budweiser decision, because it had been felt for months the armbands would be fine. Except, this was FIFA alone, acting according to the hosts' assumed wishes. Samoura told the group the armbands would be against regulations but also considered a provocation.[69] The *New York Times* reported that she told one Belgian delegate it might prompt African teams to wear armbands protesting colonial abuses, articulating one of the World Cup's bigger schisms.[70] The talk was initially of yellow cards but that escalated to 'unlimited liability', understood to be a one-game suspension.[71] The German federation cited 'extreme blackmail'.[72] It meant an otherwise meek gesture had accrued an even greater significance as a political symbol of defiance – until it was rendered powerless. The European federations felt they couldn't make their players unfairly responsible for such a choice. The captains instead wore FIFA-approved armbands with bland messages like 'No Discrimination'.

Criticism of that wasn't really about the armbands but the fact this was the only actual statement planned – and it didn't happen. Whatever about a boycott, the players hadn't used their considerable leverage once. French captain Hugo Lloris did reflect the sentiments of other players, when he said he wouldn't engage in such gestures because he wanted to respect Qatar's culture and rules.[73] Similarly, there was tension within the Germany squad over the focus on 'politics'. The players had covered their mouths in reference to being 'silenced' during the controversy, before losing 2-1 to Japan. Midfielder İlkay Gündoğan later had a pointed line stating 'now the politics is finished'.[74] Germany's World Cup soon followed in a shock group-stage elimination, which Qatari TV presenters mocked by covering their mouths and waving goodbye.[75] The laughter came amid reports that supporters were having rainbow-coloured items taken off them at games, in another divergence from previous guidance. England fan Anthony Johnson even complained he had been forced to 'strip naked' for wearing a rainbow T-shirt.[76] This led to federations directly complaining to FIFA, and Qatari missives being sent around that the colours be permitted. It was stressed, however, that 'welcomed' should not be used in the messaging.

One political cause was very much welcomed, and it happened to fit with Qatar's foreign policy. That was solidarity with Palestine, whose colours were seen everywhere from armbands on senior figures to flags waved by winning teams. Palestine was often described as the World Cup's '33rd country'.[77] The cause fitted with the spirit of Qatar 2022 in driving an admirable Arab solidarity but it did reflect another split in how some political statements were allowed but others not. A more unexpected form of unity came with the World Cup's biggest shock, and a moment that would have been considered stunning even months beforehand. As Salem Al-Dawsari scored the goal that saw Saudi Arabia beat Argentina 2-1, there was the emir of Qatar celebrating. And not just celebrating but waving the Saudi flag. It returned the gesture of Mohammed bin Salman carrying the Qatari flag at the opening game. That's all it was, though: a gesture. Some of the blockade had actually been revived an hour before that opening game, as beIN's streaming service was abruptly blocked in Saudi Arabia. There was confusion, especially since all of the kingdom's state institutions had been directed to support the World Cup.[78] There were also a few interpretations of that move. One was that Saudi Arabia didn't want such nation-defining moments presented to their population through a Qatari prism, no matter how much tensions had cooled. Another was that it was an attempt to drive down the price of beIN given that Saudi Arabia had been trying to buy a stake. The station's streaming service had become the most popular in the kingdom.

The greatest confusion was over why FIFA didn't act, given this was their broadcasting contracts. On learning of the block at the opening game, beIN officials marched over to FIFA to tell them to 'pick it up with your president now'. They were told they'd find him. It wasn't quite a case of the door comically swinging open to reveal Infantino but, pretty close by, there he was with Bin Salman. A wider regional unity did persist behind Morocco, who became the first Muslim country – and first African country – to reach the semi-finals. Their fans also did something else novel for the tournament. They offered an authentic atmosphere. When Portugal tried desperate last attacks in their quarter-final, they were soundtracked by deafening whistles. That bustle had been missing from the World Cup, as it must have been one of the poorest attended in the modern era. The Souq Wakif was the single place that felt like the global party it should be. It was still only really fans from Argentina, Mexico and Saudi Arabia joining Morocco. That was another area that fitted with the theme of image management. Just as the Souq Wakif had actually been rebuilt to look historic, there were constant debates over 'fake fans' and how many people actually attended.[79]

The Supreme Committee angrily rejected claims that groups greeting major squads had been paid.[80] Although there was unexpectedly raucous fan choreography at Qatar games, it later emerged around 1,500 supporters from Lebanon, Egypt and Algeria had been offered a free trip to support the hosts.[81] It essentially represented appropriated football culture. Another accusation was manufactured attendance figures. Official announcements never seemed to match the numbers of visible empty seats. Other seats were filled by a 'Fan Leader programme', where some supporters were paid to attend and create atmosphere, as well as report critical social media posts by other fans.[82] There was unfortunately no doubting the authenticity of England fans who displayed the cultural insensitivity of dressing up like medieval crusaders. Some locations only added to the sense of simulacrum. Lusail City had imitations of landmarks like the Champs-Élysées, while the Villaggio Mall featured a recreation of Milan's San Siro stadium. There was even birdsong piped into air-conditioned parks like Al Gharrafa. Some players felt they were in a 'theme park', as staff worked to ensure they would not be confronted with any of the hosts' more jarring realities.

This pointed to a core conflict within this World Cup. Either you didn't really think about the migrant workers, and enjoyed the gleaming comfort of Qatar. Or, you did think about the workers, and it was difficult to enjoy anything. Sure, the stadiums were fantastic, but could they really be complimented if you considered how they were built? There was an underlying air of oppression. There were also moments when reality hit, like when taxi drivers pleaded for a tip because they had 'no money to eat'. These were the people essential to making Qatar work but receiving the opposite of gratitude if they were even considered at all. Headlines that should have forced people to confront the reality still appeared throughout the month. For the opening game, more than 200 workers hired for concession stalls were left without food, water and toilet facilities for seven hours.[83] A Filipino migrant worker later died in a tragic accident at a World Cup training base.[84] Samoura felt it would be 'inappropriate' to comment on.

Al Khater's response was that 'death is a natural part of life', amid indignation at being asked given how 'successful' the World Cup had been.[85] He did add it was something they 'feel very sad about'. No emotion was conveyed about BHRRC's report that there had been at least 26 abuses impacting migrant workers by the third week of the World Cup, and this was again only those who had the outlet to complain. Norway's Lise Klaveness refused to attend games, stating 'the build-up was unacceptable and the consequences unacceptable'. It was the stain that couldn't be cleansed, no matter how many times workers were ordered to mop a floor that hadn't had a chance to accumulate dirt. A greater wash was needed. Qatar's World Cup had offered good football and looked great on TV. They could still have done with real legacy, to be part of the game's lore rather than just another World Cup. Brazil's quarter-final elimination was internally viewed as a 'disaster' as it denied the prospect of a semi-final derby with Argentina. There was instead the brief possibility of a Croatia–Morocco final, but this World Cup wasn't about the underdogs. It wasn't about Qatar's first big star, either. Neymar had scored in Brazil's exit to Croatia but was seen by some within the squad as tactically disruptive.

If so, that was arguably a consequence of what modern football had done to his career. Neymar's move to Paris Saint-Germain was a transfer that changed the game, on the back of a World Cup bid that changed geopolitics, but it had also changed him. The Brazilian's face was ubiquitous in Doha but he was now nowhere to be seen when it mattered.[86] It was just as well PSG had two major stars left. It was why the French champions had been so desperate to keep Mbappé in summer 2022, when he seemed certain to leave for Real Madrid. That had involved significant political influence with the player flown to Doha for one last pitch and even Macron involved. The reported pay was €250 million over three years. Unlike Neymar, PSG's sense of drift had actually driven Mbappé at international level, and inadvertently served the tournament. The French star has a keen sense of football history and wanted to emulate Pelé in winning the first two World Cups of his career. He drove France to the final with a series of brilliant goals. The problem for Mbappé was that there was an even deeper sense of history on the other side of the draw. It felt like the world was willing Messi to finally lift the trophy. Messi was also willing himself to win it. He had lost the 2014 final to Germany, and admitted to friends he still woke up thinking about it. This was perhaps the greatest player of all, just lacking the greatest prize of all to poetically crown his career. Such a quest was already being cast alongside the most stirring sporting stories, and there were also echoes of Diego Maradona in 1986 with how Messi was driving a limited team. The Argentina squad were fully aware of their responsibility, as there was almost a sense that helping him win the tournament was more important than even the country winning its third. World Cups come along every four years, after all. A player like Messi may never come along again. 'We know what Messi means for Argentina and for world football,' teammate Julián Álvarez said.

It was a measure of the reverence for Messi that he could straddle the blockade, as an employee of a Qatari-owned club but also a tourism ambassador for Saudi Arabia. The Argentinian had been praised for becoming more outspoken during the World Cup, as he castigated opponents like Netherlands' Wout Weghorst on live television. 'What you looking at, idiot?' That didn't extend to big issues like migrant workers, which was poignant given the weight his words would have had.

Those two autocracies ended up influencing Messi in other ways, too. His first season at PSG, in 2021–22, had actually been one of the worst of his career as he surprisingly struggled with the French league's robustness. This caused Messi to sharpen his physical programme, which helped perpetuate a long unbeaten run for Argentina. That was until they suffered one of the biggest ever World Cup upsets with a 2-1 defeat to Saudi Arabia in their opening match. The humiliation ended up being the best thing for the team. Messi gave the speech that calmed the squad, but also hardened them. He then scored the goal against Mexico that saved their World Cup. Argentina began to claw their way through, with Messi applying the exacting elegance. There was a weight of history on every game, amid the awareness each one could be Messi's last at a World Cup. The sense of release was seen in long dressing-room celebrations after every win, shirts twirled over heads, hands flicking in rhythm with chants. By the time Messi emerged, always the last out, the congregations of journalists were almost events in themselves.

Not everyone was so effusive. Van Gaal, whose Dutch team were beaten on penalties by Argentina in the quarter-final, raised more eyebrows. 'When you see how Argentina scored the goals . . . when you see how some Argentine players crossed the line and weren't penalized, I think it's all premeditated.'[87] He refused to elaborate, but no one could say the final was premeditated. It soared, then spun, then evolved into one of football's most dramatic ever spectacles. It really couldn't have gone better for the hosts, right down to having a star on either side. Whoever lost, Qatar would win. The showpiece was taking place on the country's national day, and this was a culminating moment. That was a final that didn't just surpass all before it, but had echoes of all before it.

Argentina first of all emulated Brazil 1970 by just flowing to a commanding lead. Ángel Di María's goal to make it 2-0 was even reminiscent of Carlos Alberto's. France then followed 1954 and 1986 with a two-goal comeback. After another Messi strike, Mbappé then succeeded England's Geoff Hurst in 1966 by scoring a hat-trick in the final. His volleyed second was one of the fixture's finest ever goals. So to penalties, but this wasn't to be one of those World Cups like 1954 or 1974 where the rightful champions were to be unsatisfactorily denied. As with 1958, 1970, 1986 and 2002, there was a romance to the final victory. Messi finally had the World Cup. As he lifted the trophy, he became the first captain to do so wearing anything other than his country's own shirt. Messi was wearing a bisht, an otherwise honourable garment here politicised as a gift from the emir. The emperor had given new clothes. This World Cup might have cost $220 billion but Qatar had a picture beyond value. Messi didn't care, but the world should have. This was Qatar 2022 encapsulated. The purest of football moments had been compromised. It was the best of football and the worst of the sport. It was the modern game.

Qatar will now always be linked to Messi and sporting grandeur, just like the Azteca with Maradona and Pelé. 'It just becomes part of football history,' McGeehan says. 'All that will be remembered is Messi.' That is why it is worth recognising the wider legacy. Qatar got even more than they wanted, and it is internally seen as a 'huge success'. Even the 'awkward moments', as Human Rights Watch's Michael Page puts it, were 'absolutely worth it' for the state. That was especially true for deeper intentions such as global positioning, as insiders speak of how Qatar enhanced its role as an interlocutor between the US and the Taliban. The World Cup even influenced how the regional tension evolved from Saudi-Qatar to Saudi-UAE.

And yet, as proud as Qataris are of this success, those in the country now speak of a sense of drift. A great purpose is gone. That lingering hollowness has been reflected in the emptiness of Lusail, described since as a 'ghost town'. That makes it apt to consider the absurdity of what this actually was. Incomprehensible money was spent on a World Cup that could have been held anywhere, meaning that $220 billion could have been spent on virtually anything else. It could have helped to try and cure cancer or dementia, while aiding any number of human ills. It instead ensured a football tournament was inexplicably held in the desert, in one of the few areas of the world that had no infrastructure for it, with that very fact actually perpetuating human suffering through so many migrant workers.

A coalition of human rights bodies described FIFA as a 'global embarrassment' for their complicity in this,[88] especially for having 'failed to fulfil its human rights responsibilities' by refusing to commit to a compensation fund for labourers and their families. The *Guardian* went even further, citing 'corporate manslaughter'.[89] So much for Infantino's own description of an 'incredible success', let alone the long-term justification that it would lead to grand reform. This is almost the most infuriating element for human rights groups. Even late on, there was a chance for some positive effects. Everyone from Amnesty International to FairSquare now just cites it as a 'wasted opportunity'. It fundamentally disproves one of the primary arguments made in response to accusations of sportswashing. 'We don't have to work on a theoretical model,' Page says. 'The Qatar World Cup did happen, and improvements did not emerge.' Abuses have instead continued. A mere month after the World Cup, security guards that worked at FIFA's main media centre and two other key sites protested over unpaid wages, redundancies and evictions. Three Pakistani nationals were imprisoned, with other workers deported.[90] A year later, an Amnesty report on the anniversary cited the continuation of 'recruitment fee-charging, unpaid wages, contract substitutions, extremely poor housing, intimidation and physical violence in the workplace as standard'.[91] While Archer notes there have been positives that wouldn't have happened without the World Cup, such as the establishment of the Universal Reimbursement Scheme, none of this is reform.

In reality, Qatar got away with it. They got the rewards without the reforms. The World Cup served to embolden that. It also put the tournament, and the game, at the centre of a growing split between the global south and the West. 'Sport became the public face of a broader realignment,' Cockburn says. Not all of that is bad in a football sense, as more of Europe's resources should be spread. Infantino still took the opportunity to further bloat the game, by announcing a raft of new competitions, including the expanded Club World Cup. That was at a closing press conference that struck a very different tone to his opener.

That sense of action, rather than feeling, didn't quite apply to the World Cup's bigger issues. Months after the anniversary, there were still no details on any kind of remedy fund for migrant workers,[92] nor had FIFA released any review on the impact of human rights in Qatar.[93] Action was instead taken on the hosts of two future World Cups, the latter of which is in Saudi Arabia in 2034. It's hard to see how that will comply with demands for stronger criteria around human rights, which had been cited by some federations as a condition for endorsing Infantino in 2022. It is instead likely to bring all the same issues as Qatar, but on a far greater scale. Meanwhile, Qatar was building on bigger plans, including a bid for an Olympics, and more of a footprint in the Premier League. In the latter, concluding the same season that featured the Qatar World Cup, a state-owned club won the Champions League for the first time in Manchester City. All of the major Gulf states had their day, taking the rivalry and maybe the game to a new stage. The long build-up to the World Cup ensured the tournament itself had a fin de siècle feel. It might just have opened a new era.

15.

AND IT'S LIVE . . . AND KILLING EVERYTHING ELSE

In the Premier League's first few years, there was already so much concern about its growing financial power that the UK Office of Fair Trading suggested it be split in two. The body was rightly told the idea was 'insane' from a football perspective, since there can only be one English champion, but that doesn't mean there weren't fair concerns about concentration of wealth. The Premier League has since become divided and tiered in a number of ways.

It is maybe telling that, when executives travel around the world promoting the competition, they often point to mid-table. Anyone can supposedly beat anyone, which makes everyone want to watch. That's a slightly dubious pitch, since academic studies show most fans just watch the biggest clubs.[1] It is still the mid-table, mind, that shows how modern football works. In summer 2021, Celtic were open to selling Norwegian defender Kristoffer Ajer as part of their economic model, which is basically the only one that can work outside the elite. That is buy low, sell high and be smart about recruitment. AC Milan wanted Ajer but this was not Silvio Berlusconi's AC Milan. The seven-time European champions were outbid by recently promoted Brentford. It was seen in Italy as 'humiliating', with Paolo Maldini complaining how Milan were 'competing against the Premier League's lower teams'.

Andrea Agnelli wasn't quite so downbeat. When the former

Juventus chairman attended Premier League games, he would go wide-eyed at the packed stadiums and colour. 'This is what football is supposed to look like,' Agnelli enthused. The Premier League is certainly one vision of football fully realised. This is Berlusconi's 'television spectacular', the point emphasised with how it has been fired by spectacular television deals. It's the virtuous cycle in full effect, spinning faster than ever imagined. With income from broadcasting contracts having increased by over 2,500 per cent since 1992, the Premier League was collectively spending over £2 billion more on wages than any other league by 2024.[2] Its economy is now three times the size of FIFA's, while its clubs have taken half of all Champions League final places since 2018–19.

There will be occasional lean years, as in 2024, but every trend shows the Premier League has reached a position of historically unprecedented supremacy. It has far surpassed Serie A of the 1990s and La Liga during the Leo Messi–Cristiano Ronaldo era. This was what Manchester City's Ferran Soriano meant when he used to talk in meetings about turning the Premier League into 'the NBA of football'. 'It's that idea you *have* to be in England,' he'd tell other clubs. If you're not there, you're nowhere. La Liga president Javier Tebas used the same point as a warning, stating 'the Premier League will be like the NBA and none of the other championships will be relevant any more'.[3] It already feels like that for managers. The majority now see the Premier League as the ultimate aim, and every other job a stepping-stone. The megastars are starting to follow, with Erling Haaland's rejection of Real Madrid for Manchester City a landmark. Only a handful of European super clubs can compete, and the concentration of international talent is why the Premier League is now being described as the Super League in all but name. It isn't really an 'English' competition in any of its defining characteristics, other than location and how it has taken on its home state's economic politics. Everything has been for sale. Oliver Bullough astutely articulated the UK's nature in *Butler to the World*, and so many descriptions within that book could easily apply to the Premier League. That's especially so with the pattern of 'allowing something, making money from it and attempting to solve the problems it causes after they've occurred'.[4] This has ensured the Premier League is not just an international league but also a prism for every single major international football issue, which probably went hand in hand with its global supremacy.

Problems from competitive balance, regulation, neoliberalism, ownership to what Aleksander Čeferin described as 'globalisation-fuelled revenue polarisation' have reached extremes in England.[5] By summer 2023, amid constant debate about the Saudi Pro League, senior football figures were keen to stress that the Premier League spent more. Of course, the Saudi state also has a club in England, which doesn't feature one state-linked ownership but two. The other has completely dominated the competition while also being investigated for a huge regulatory case that weighs over the Premier League's reputation. This is where that vision becomes clouded. The same neoliberal factors that accelerated the Premier League have also institutionalised long-term problems. Concentration only goes one way. We've already seen how football has hollowed out every other sport, Europe has hollowed out South America, Western Europe has hollowed out the rest of Europe and now England has hollowed out Western Europe. Next, the Premier League might cannibalise itself.

As Khaldoon Al Mubarak and Soriano started to get things right at City, they also realised something distinctive about the Premier League. It was the first competition to really see 'the potential of foreign audiences' and work on it. The bombastic pronouncements that can entail make it fashionable to dismiss the Premier League for shallowness, but there is no illusion there. It puts on a brilliant show. While many other leagues now look to see what they can copy, there were unique historical factors to this. The Taylor Report on the 1989 Hillsborough disaster demanded gleaming new stadiums to house a gleaming new league, quickening a gentrification of football that further accelerated income. Better players arrived, but they were sufficiently spread. A Champions League winner like Fabrizio Ravanelli went to Middlesbrough straight after playing in the final. The dynamic was down to an inspired founding move, fittingly influenced by America, but gradually ensuring an advantage over every other European league. This was the idea to share 50 per cent of all broadcasting revenue equally, with 25 per cent distributed according to league position and the rest by televised games set by a quota.[6] This key decision was scribbled down on a notepad by Rick Parry with the rest of the Founder Members Agreement, but would structurally ensure more competition, which attracted more interest.

Right from the start, Manchester United won their first league title in 26 years, challenged by Norwich City and Aston Villa. Sir Alex Ferguson's new dynasty were beaten by Blackburn Rovers in a race that went to the last seconds of 1994–95, before overhauling the doomed romantics of Kevin Keegan's Newcastle United in 1995–96. The next season saw Arsène Wenger arrive at Arsenal to pioneer the Premier League's internationalisation and give it a compelling personal rivalry with Ferguson. There might have been growing concern about a United–Arsenal duopoly but that made the timing of Roman Abramovich's Chelsea takeover more significant. Many welcomed this dazzling force. Abramovich's Chelsea now look a perfect illustration of Bullough's description of making money from something and solving problems later. By 2018, which was around the same time that structural flaws started to be exposed, executives would crow in sales meetings about how the Premier League hadn't had back-to-back champions for almost a decade.

The point of this potted early history is the capacity for varied storylines that have persisted to this day. An irony is that the Premier League barely had a marketing department. The stories were instead aided by a time zone between the USA and Asia as well as the English language, at a point when both the internet and football were racing around the planet.[7] This was as Richard Scudamore had another inspired insight. On becoming chief executive in 1999, he realised this power for narrative was being sold cheaply. The Premier League in those years sold its international rights as regional packages to global agencies, who would deal with individual countries. Like the Glazers, Scudamore saw the real money was in splitting up those regions and going direct. This brought competition for the rights, which accelerated the cycle. Football economist David Forrest describes it as 'first mover advantage'. The Premier League 'got' satellite broadcasting before anyone. In an echo of how McDonald's saw itself as a 'real estate business', the Premier League was actually a media rights business.[8] The announcement that almost £5.5 billion would be generated from international broadcasting for the 2013-16 cycle, more than trebling that revenue, was seen as 'a real moment'. This naturally went even deeper with the first extensive deal with a US network. NBC's Jon Miller had two main messages in his eventual pitch to the 20 clubs.

'Success for us would be paying the Premier League even more next time.'

'NBC wants to make the Premier League the fourth biggest sport in the USA, surpassing the NHL.'

The club representatives, usually racked by division, were 'giddy'. There was even the attraction of NBC's marketing plan, which was 'pick your team'. Damien Comolli, a current Toulouse executive who worked at Liverpool, says there were always two main topics in meetings. 'One, how do we get competitive advantage? Two, how do we keep entertaining people? It's the only league in the world that talks about it.' Such international success inevitably saw the Premier League trophy brought on trade missions, with heads of states excitedly requesting photos with the trophy. Scudamore even referred to it as 'soft power'.[9]

Finance expert Professor Rob Wilson believes the Premier League has been 'outstanding for the UK government on a macro level', bringing 'a huge amount of tourism and inward investment'. It was certainly a powerful ambassador, as Scudamore enthused about how 'being British is the essence of what we are'.[10] That became only partly true. The Premier League's success couldn't happen without the histories and fanbases of its clubs, but that very identity transformed. The majority of the players (70 per cent), managers (70 per cent) and owners (consistently 75–80 per cent) were international. This openness to money from any-where was arguably the most British aspect of the league, a New Labour sporting ideal. Scudamore was said to 'love' that form of capitalism. 'Everything,' in the words of one executive, 'was about money'. A guiding principle for any decision was whether it added value to TV rights.

Even Michel Platini spoke about the Premier League's 'ultra-liberalisme'.[11] That certainly applied to club ownership. England wasn't just the best place to buy a club but the easiest, thanks to the 1855 Limited Liability Act.[12] Almost two centuries later, the Premier League hierarchy were pointing to laws on PLCs as to why they couldn't stop takeovers. The reality was that most just wanted to be able to sell to the highest bidder. The flow of money bust through any concerns – including the Covid-19 pandemic. The Premier League was the only major competition to come through it unscathed, only reinforcing its position. Broadcasting ensured crowds didn't matter that much. In the summer of 2020 and 2021, the Premier League had a net transfer spend of £905 million and £560 million respectively. The four other major leagues were barely spending at all, with their combined net figure across both windows adding up to a mere £405 million. This investment sharpened a 'flight to quality' from the financial downturn of the pandemic, as NBC did another £2 billion deal in November 2021.[13] Such contracts ensured that income from international rights exceeded domestic for the first time, taking the total value of all broadcasting contracts to more than £10 billion.[14] It was even more staggering since the pandemic had depressed the rights of every other league. Instead, by 2024, the Premier League and Champions League were seen as the two premium products broadcasters had to have.

No one could have accumulated such money, however, without considerable tension arising. The first tremors were from underneath the Premier League. Months before the pandemic, in August 2019, the expulsion of Bury from the English Football League (EFL) for financial collapse had provoked one of the game's periodic moral debates. The outrage was here entirely appropriate, since the decision had ended 125 years of unbroken league membership. While the Bury situation had its own specific problems, and seemed so removed from the Premier League down in League Two, it really displayed the wage race in full effect. Inflation at the top created this financial drag that went all the way down through the pyramid. In May 2019, when Bury's problems were first reported, almost three-quarters of EFL clubs were losing money.[15] Such economics led to unpaid staff at Bolton Wanderers – a Premier League club for 13 seasons – being provided with a food bank.

The Covid-19 pandemic deepened the struggle for survival, with the Super League crisis and resulting fan-led review bringing a quandary over the future of the game. The pressure was on the Premier League to share more of the wealth. Instead, despite immense financial figures, the 20 clubs attempted to claim any independent regulator would discourage investment. The problem was really the opposite. The Premier League was so bloated from so much money it could no longer hold things in place. 'The more revenue that comes in, the more gaps that are created,' Parry explains. 'If you're getting 10 per cent of £100 million that's a hell of a difference to 10 per cent of a billion.' The distribution rules had already been amended so that the increase in overseas deals saw more money go to the highest-finishing clubs. That was a factor in how a revenue gap between the top and bottom Premier League clubs grew from 1.6 to 1 to 5 to 1 in real terms, supercharged by international income. The 'big six' began to stretch, until the Premier League emulated Ligue 1 with City winning six titles in seven years. A race between billionaires, venture capitalists and hedge funds was always going to be won by a state.

And yet clubs were so addicted to the money, and so worried about dropping out of this castle in the sky, that the Premier League reached a *reductio ad absurdum*. It was so lucrative to play in that there were briefly negotiations over whether to play it at all. As the 20 clubs tried to get football back behind closed doors during the pandemic, the six at the bottom argued it would be unfair to be relegated if the season was not completed in the same conditions that the rest had been played. They were Brighton, West Ham United, Watford, Bournemouth, Aston Villa and Norwich

City. Even that group wasn't united, since those above the relegation zone argued for standings to be frozen while those within wanted the season declared void.[16] The situation could have got much uglier than it did, as it is known some clubs took legal advice on curtailing the season. Sanity prevailed, although only because there was too much money at stake. The show went on, but the pressure only increased.

It has become one of the most common complaints in boardrooms across Europe.

'The Premier League is too strong.'

'We need to stop the Premier League.'

Comolli says he 'hears this all the time'. It's a view that's been hardened by a perceived 'arrogance' from the Premier League in not sending decision-makers to European meetings. The other major continental clubs even attempted to use the controversial 2016 reforms to limit the amount of money to England. Sympathy was limited, since this was a rare moment when Bayern Munich and Real Madrid were seeing how the other 99 per cent lived. Comolli says rival leagues 'have been sleeping all these years' and didn't properly plan. Čeferin echoed that, claiming he is 'not worried' about the imbalance and simplistically arguing that the Premier League is 'doing a good job and the other leagues should do a better job'.[17] That is an eyebrow-raising stance from a UEFA president, since the situation totally distorts the landscape they are supposed to preside over.

Before you even get to issues like dominance, there is the threat posed by inflation. Agnelli at one point appealed to Juventus shareholders, complaining that the biggest European clubs have to take more 'economic and sporting' risks to keep pace with the 'unapproachable' Premier League.[18] That puts financial stress on the European ecosystem all the way down to Latvia, in the same manner as the English pyramid. There's also the self-perpetuating effect of the Premier League drawing all playing and coaching talent, which dilutes other leagues.

As long ago as 2014, the 2013 Champions League winners in Bayern Munich earned only half the broadcasting money that relegated Cardiff City did.[19] By the summer of 2021, the Premier League's three promoted teams of Brentford, Norwich City and Watford all spent more than Real Madrid, Barcelona and Atlético Madrid. The next year, newly promoted Nottingham Forest's net spend of €160 million was greater than all of Serie A, La Liga, the Bundesliga and Ligue 1 combined. Broadcasting contracts in Serie A and the Bundesliga have started to decline so much they have contemplated launching their own streaming services.[20] Perhaps the first glimpse of the future was seen in Ligue 1 going for months without agreeing any new broadcaster, after the collapse of a deal with Mediapro.[21] And this is only the major leagues. In many smaller countries, more money goes to Premier League subscriptions than to their domestic competitions.

'It's a grim picture,' fan representative Ronan Evain says. 'Even if the Premier League deserves praise, it's obviously become too big and is a threat to football.' This is why, rather than Čeferin dismissing concerns, UEFA should be proactively thinking about this as much as the clubs. Even if you can't tell the Premier League 'not to take the revenue', as Bayern Munich's Oliver Kahn stated at an ECA meeting, you can limit its effects.

In the meantime, other leagues have been forced into considering responses. Some have been sensible, some drastic, some unreasonable. In Italy, Napoli's irascible president Aurelio De Laurentiis put huge pressure on Serie A to increase income, lambasting 'disastrous' coverage that has been 'an accumulation of total incompetence'.[22] He colourfully rejected potential solutions, asking 'why bring television cameras into the dressing room when the players have half a testicle hanging out'.[23] La Liga tried its own channel abroad, but also sought to take a long-term view. Tebas felt the only way was to replicate the Premier League and introduce more equal revenue sharing. It's still remarkable that La Liga was earning a billion less than the Premier League in an era when Barcelona and Real Madrid had the best teams on the planet. This is why it's referred to as Spain's 'wasted decade', as the big two took too much of the money. Since the effects of that sensible policy will take years to properly see, La Liga has consequently gone for some more questionable approaches. Private equity was invited in through a deal to sell an 8.2 per cent stake of their media rights business to CVC in an unprecedented €1.9 billion contract, while a sponsorship was agreed with Visit Saudi. Although Tebas bristled when asked about the latter, it was private equity that provoked deeper questions due to the potential for future control. Interest in leagues has grown since the pandemic. There were offers to both the EFL and Serie A, and it was only fan resistance that prevented a deal with the Bundesliga. La Liga at least stipulated that 70 per cent of the income had to be spent on infrastructure and innovation, with just 15 per cent for signings.[24] Barcelona and Real Madrid voted against, but in order to pursue their own economic plans.

The Premier League's market dominance meanwhile caused virtually every other club to change model to the buy low, sell high approach. AC Milan reclaimed Serie A through this policy in 2021–22, meaning Ajer missed out. It was over-performance given the value of the squad, and that is actually seen by figures like Liverpool's Michael Edwards as one of the problems of the approach. As with previous Champions League winners like Borussia Dortmund, who eventually abandoned that model, it means clubs stay at a certain level rather than actually catch up. It's impossible to keep selling and sustain the same standard. The model has nevertheless intrigued Premier League owners for another reason. Since such clubs allow young players a lot of competitive game-time, they constitute perfect feeder teams. England after all has more clubs in multi-club ownerships than any other country, and most of them are naturally at the top of such structures. Is this to be the future for the rest of Europe? Instead of challenging the Premier League, will they be subsumed by it? Chelsea have already looked at one of Portugal's biggest clubs in Sporting.[25] That would represent a considerable leap.

As depressing as it all sounds, former UEFA executive Alex Phillips is one of a few football figures not quite so gloomy about the Premier League's power. You only had to look at 2023–24, when there were no English teams in European finals. 'Spanish clubs have won UEFA trophies on half the budget. English clubs are nowhere near twice as good. A lot of players still want to live in Madrid and Barcelona. The market also means that prices go up for English clubs.' In other words, the money isn't used efficiently. English clubs have little need to innovate, because they can solve problems with signings.

It's similar with the competitions. La Liga is seen as the most proactive in trying new ideas, and has long been expected to be the first to introduce the notorious '39th game' idea. This is an extra league fixture in another country, to capitalise on a foreign market. Serie A is enjoying new success in the key market of the US, by appealing to the Italian-American community through the league's cache of 90s cool. The Bundesliga has meanwhile echoed Sweden in leaning further into fan authenticity, with huge crowds generating record revenue of €5.24 billion over 2022–23.[26]

There is also an increasing possibility that UEFA agree to one huge change. That is in sanctioning individual domestic leagues to amalgamate, and form Benelux-style regionalised competitions. It would be so influential because it would suddenly allow scores of clubs to multiply income by being in a bigger market. Phillips first presented the idea to Infantino two decades ago. The then UEFA general secretary was open to it, but it floundered due to debate about European places and the sanctity of domestic leagues. Current realities are forcing change, and renewed exploration of what might work. Such models would immediately solve the 'Celtic problem' of big clubs in small countries, while retaining the basic structure of European football. Meetings about combining leagues do raise another idea that would very much change the structure of European football. There have been numerous discussions over a new Super League that would form a direct challenge to the Premier League. It has specifically targeted that middle class of clubs. Such a strategy would even solve the problem of English clubs being prohibited.

All of this is of course predicated on the idea that it's too late for anyone else to catch up, which is a common view. 'The Premier League is always going to live up to its name,' Tebas argues. 'It has an income nearly double that of La Liga, and they're going to keep that going for ever.' And yet a central part of new Super League plans are discussions about new technology. If the Premier League exploded due to figuring out television before anyone else, the same might happen for streaming. This could be a game-changer, as such innovation is unlikely in England since it is invested in sustaining the current model. La Liga and Serie A, however, are talking about these ideas a lot.

That is still only one side to it. Another reason the Premier League rose was because Serie A fell. The Italian competition was too damaged by controversies, and issues that had been building up for years. The *Calciopoli* scandal, where some clubs and executives were accused of influence-peddling, fatally compromised faith in the league. Juventus were stripped of the 2004–05 title and downgraded from first to last in 2005–06, while other clubs suffered points deductions. Trust was compromised. The wonder is whether something similar will play out again.

Ed Woodward called Joel Glazer and couldn't help but remark on the difference to American sport. Almost two months into the Covid-19 pandemic, English clubs were still locked in 20 hours of talks every week, striving to get football back on. Glazer pointed to how the NFL required just two short meetings, one to sort logistics, another for the broadcasting deals. Job done. Not so in England, where suspicion and in-fighting reigned. Although the pandemic had displayed the financial strength of the Premier League, it also widened fault lines that started to make the foundations unsteady. The old 'big six' alliance was fractured, as other splits spread along disputes that included Project Restart, the Newcastle United take-over, the Super League, the Manchester City case and a series of cost-control punishments. Meetings were described as having two main features. One was of ever-changing rivalries. Another was 'club lawyers making long speeches'.

One American owner, who also has a US franchise, couldn't help but shake his head to a colleague. 'In our board meetings, we basically decide how much money we're going to make for each other. In the Premier League, it's how much we're going to lose!' An obvious difference is that, in England, that partnership is not indefinitely guaranteed. The prospect of relegation, which ensures a vitality that is one of football's great virtues, just brings terror for Premier League clubs. That fear is one of many factors that accelerates the wage race, which grew by an incredible £500 million in the three years after the Covid-19 restart. There were a number of absurdities to this, above all the fact there was no foreign competition, since no one else was spending. The Premier League was already spending over £1.6 billion more on wages than any other league before that. Perhaps a peak – or nadir – was reached when the negotiation for one major star was conducted in an expensive bar, the numbers for their wage going up as alcohol flowed. The player's representatives made sure to take a photo of a napkin with a huge figure written on it for the last – sober – talks. It's hasn't led to any great difference in quality, either. It just means 'more Ferraris for players', in the words of one director. This isn't to complain about young men earning good money but instead ask why? What was it actually for?

Premier League clubs would say it's to keep up in title races or stay up in relegation battles, but the question is deeper than that. Even if you were to take it on those immediate terms, the money has actually ensured the consequences of relegation aren't that great. It has instead created a premier league within the Premier League and a wider Premier League outside it. At the top, the old big six and a Saudi-owned Newcastle United are now fixtures. While a few clubs like Aston Villa, West Ham United and Everton should be capable of always staying in mid-table, the rest form a relatively interchangeable group that extends about six places into the Championship. This has largely been created by 'parachute payments', which were introduced to ensure relegated clubs didn't suddenly struggle to pay an inflated wage bill. What they actually did was reinforce the same group of clubs, as witnessed in how 25 clubs claimed 92 per cent of the 2022–23 English season's distributable revenue. It resulted in the farce of Norwich City and Fulham exchanging places between the top two divisions for four successive seasons between 2018 and 2022. As one went up, the other went down. Fulham eventually accumulated enough money to stay up.

The greatest absurdity is that you could probably take any 14 EFL clubs and put them with the big six and the value of the competition would be the same. It only has to be noted how neither Brighton nor Brentford were seen as Premier League clubs as recently as 2018, but both became 'fixtures'. The average Premier League spell for clubs outside the big six has been a mere five seasons. So, rather than proper five-year plans, the inclination has been to just spend money on more players to stay up. Such short-term thinking dictates everything. That's all the more illogical since the greatest effect is on the rest of the EFL. The inflation caused by the Premier League has led to some lower-division clubs paying more than 100 per cent of turnover on wages.[27] It does become win or bust, as Derby County found. Such outcomes prompted the fan-led review to suggest just doing away with parachute payments and instead change resource distribution so 25 per cent of all broadcasting revenue goes towards the EFL. That would ensure a steadier gradient without huge gaps. The Premier League's position is that this would erode competitive balance and the possibility of 'growth'. The counter-argument is that competitive balance is already an illusion, and this is just an example of clubs never voting against getting more money. Since many of them will inevitably be relegated, it raises the absurdity of clubs voting against their own future interests. Others maintain they would simply see potential rivals in the Championship go out and spend that money on more players.

Executives are mostly keen to maintain a delicate status quo, which has led to a lack of overall strategy. It is how so many splits have occurred within the Premier League. The hardest political division is now between the two state-owned clubs and the other 18. There are 'constant calls' about Saudi Arabia and the City case.[28]

One of the most contentious subjects is financial regulation. The debate is over structure, application and – of course – the perception of consistency. The wage race has shown the need for constraint. In 2022, despite all the money, it was reported that the Premier League hadn't actually broken even at a pre-tax level for five years.[29] A problem for a long time was that the Premier League felt quite unregulated. Clubs barely wanted to be checked on whether they were paying tax every three months. It was only Portsmouth suffering a nine-point deduction for going into administration in 2009–10 that saw that change, although it was still light touch. With virtually everything geared towards revenue creation, the belief spread that the Scudamore-era Premier League didn't want to do anything that would 'damage the brand'. That was what needless complications like points deductions would do. So, every potential issue was 'kicked into the long grass'. The other side was that nobody cared to pry when broadcast deals were getting bigger. Scudamore was even heard to repeat a line from *The Departed* when it came to regulation. It was better to treat the clubs 'like mushrooms: keep 'em in the dark and feed them shit'. The stance was actually that it was better to stay behind the regulatory curve, so they could respond to issues as and when required. At the same time, Scudamore used the threat of independent regulation. The argument was that, if clubs didn't keep order, the 'useless' FA or government would get involved.

Many have since lamented that the FA 'abrogated their responsibility' but the reality was that the Premier League simply became too big for it. Its economic size made it the de facto power in English football, but with almost no interest in exerting that power over the wider game. It was, after all, just a members' group. All this laxness did was create so much leeway that, like in Italy, issues accumulated. As one Premier League owner said when the

City charges were announced in February 2023, 'look, we know everyone bends the rules, but don't take the piss'. It echoes another quote from *Butler to the World*: 'A bit of naughtiness is fine; it's only when it becomes industrialised that it causes problems.'[30] The City of London influence on the Premier League's founding was all too visible. The argument in that sector had long been that self-regulation was essential for growth, only for that to be undermined by scandals.[31] It sounds familiar.

The announcement of City's 115 alleged breaches can now be seen as the start of a new era of litigation in the Premier League, as emphasised by how it was followed months later by Everton becoming the first club to ever get punished for breaking such rules.[32] Everyone was by then obsessed with Profit and Sustainability Rules (PSR), which was what the Premier League's FFP came to be known as. The belief within the game was that this was a belated attempt to show the Premier League could actually self-regulate as it faced pressure from the government. The Premier League itself insisted it was just a matter of time and due process.

This was of little solace to Everton, who were furious about being docked 10 points. The Merseyside club had spent almost £20 million more than permitted over three years, although the hierarchy pointed to numerous mitigating circumstances. The fact this was reduced to six points on appeal over 'legal errors' added to a sense of inconsistency, before another two points were deducted for further breaches. Cynical eyebrows were similarly raised at the very idea that Everton had been the first to breach rules. There was certainly a symbolism to it, as Goodison Park had become a hub for all of the Premier League's major issues. Everton had won the third most English leagues by 1992, with their nine putting them behind just Arsenal and Liverpool. That made them one of the initial 'big five' who pushed for the Premier League's creation, only to become one of its biggest victims. Everton simply didn't have the commercial power. This fostered some questionable football decisions, especially as regards recruitment. It often led to criticism they were the 'worst run club in the Premier League', although there was plenty of competitive balance there.[33] Much of this was just the product of an identity crisis over how to compete at all. As even AC Milan found, it was jarring for old giants to adjust to new realities. Such issues made Everton less attractive to owners, which was a problem in a Premier League largely ordered by the pot luck of who bought your club. There was eventually some good fortune in that, since Alisher Usmanov had attempted to be more closely involved with Everton shortly before the Uzbek oligarch was sanctioned for links to Vladimir Putin.[34] The fact so much of the club's sponsorship income was dependent on Usmanov's companies created enough problems in itself.

By the time Everton were punished, investment firm 777 Partners were in a long takeover process, principally because they saw the club as a 'distressed asset'. It was a lamentable situation for a historic club in the world's wealthiest league.[35] It did ultimately mean jobs on the line and a community institution at risk.

The flood doors were open. The same period saw Chelsea face a Premier League investigation over secret payments made by companies belonging to Abramovich.[36] That was initially launched after the new Clearlake owners self-reported the submission of 'incomplete financial information' they found between 2012 and 2019. Chelsea reached an £8.7 million settlement with UEFA, but the statute of limitations meant it could only look back to 2018–19. Although there had been appreciation at how transparent Chelsea's new ownership were, it didn't escape attention this came amid mega-spending on transfers as the club's hierarchies looked for 'inefficiencies' in the market.

Nottingham Forest's huge spending meant there wasn't much surprise when they were given a four-point deduction for breaches in March 2024.[37] The club had developed a reputation for erratic decisions under their controversial owner Evangelos Marinakis, a Greek shipping magnate who also owned Olympiacos. Just days later, bringing the modern era full circle, Leicester City were charged for allegedly breaching financial rules.[38] This happened when the Thai-owned club were back in the Championship, with many wryly noting how their initial 2013–14 promotion had eventually resulted in a £3.1 million settlement with the EFL over claims of FFP breaches.[39] Two years after that, they won the title. It did foster the sense that it was too good to be true, which was also the case with some of the celebrations in Bangkok. After an open-top bus parade, allegations later emerged that people had been paid to turn up.[40] This was a common tactic for political rallies, and the sensational title victory had certainly afforded the late Vichai Srivaddhanaprabha considerable clout. The sad death of Vichai and four others in a helicopter crash just outside the King Power Stadium in 2018 added a note of tragedy to the Leicester story.

By 2024, the strongest emotion in the Premier League was indignation about the very rules the clubs were accused of breaching. All responded angrily, with Leicester even launching legal action against the Premier League and EFL.[41] This fired a huge debate over whether the regulations were fit for purpose, or simply restricted 'ambition'. It aided the stance of the previously isolated Newcastle United, since they'd spent months complaining about how the rules just kept the established powers at the top.[42]

One of the most remarkable stances was about Kylian Mbappé. All of the major Premier League clubs had a look when he announced he was leaving Paris Saint-Germain and all could probably have afforded him. They didn't move because they knew his wages would put them in breach of rules. It was seen as ludicrous the Premier League couldn't bring in the game's biggest star. This was despite the fact his wages had been artificially inflated by a state project, which was precisely what 18 of the Premier League clubs wanted to avoid, and that another of them signing him would have undeniably brought furore.

The Premier League was full of such circular logic, and the reality was the financial rules were always going to bring conflict. The controls had naturally been introduced in 2013 after UEFA brought in FFP, in order to maintain consistency. Although there was already disgruntlement at it having been pushed by the big clubs, with Manchester United seen as influential, there was a logic. Any ambitious club overspending would almost certainly qualify for Europe, which would require compliance with FFP. The Premier League even had greater allowances than UEFA to facilitate 'ambition', setting the permissible losses at £105 million over three seasons. The rules weren't actually seen as all that robust, since they featured more loopholes than UEFA's. They also had the customary unintended consequence of clubs selling more of their academy graduates, no matter how senior, since they represented 'pure profit' on the books. It was just another way that football's unchecked market forces created dynamics that further worked against the sport's notional community principles. There is usually no greater connection for fans, after all, than a player imbued with a club's identity coming through the ranks. This was all irrelevant, though. The only fact that mattered was that the 20 clubs had voted on them. This was because, for all that Everton or Leicester might complain about restrictions, they didn't want clubs like Newcastle suddenly outspending them. And while

Newcastle's owners complained, this was the model they had bought into. Everton, illustratively, had been one of the strongest advocates of FFP back in 2012.

It was really that model that was the entire problem. The modern history of football has proven beyond doubt that cost controls are essential. Sport requires a sense of competitive tension, which doesn't happen organically, and requires regulation. This is all the more necessary in elite football since the wage race has sent it haywire and fostered an addiction to spending. It required an intervention, especially given football's wider economy. Concentration of wealth means constant expenditure to keep up. It is the circular problem the 'virtuous cycle' inevitably spins into.

Within that, it's always instructive to imagine the alternative. Lax rules would basically mean Abu Dhabi, Saudi Arabia, Qatar and maybe £80 billion private equity funds fighting it out at the top for ever, with everyone else pushing themselves to the limit trying to keep up. This is not a way to run sport. All of this is an argument for more regulation, not less, especially as regards redistribution. Of course, all of that would also necessitate more difficult discussions than simplistic debates over 'ambition', which should really have taken place years ago. Among them are the power of big clubs, redistribution, ownership and multi-clubs. These essential issues were instead simply more problems that got kicked down the road.

Now, to go with concentration of wealth, the Premier League has a concentration of problems. In two seasons, over 2022–23 and 2023–24, the PSR cases fostered uncertainty over the title race, the Champions League chase and the relegation battle. Everton abruptly changed position twice in a few months. The Leicester and Chelsea cases then added to the longer-term questions from City's alleged breaches. There is the potential for asterisks – or at least doubt – over the title winners from 2012, 2014, 2015, 2016, 2017, 2018, 2019, 2021, 2022 and 2023.

That is over a decade of Premier League history open to re-vision. So much for brand protection. The line was that 'it's like Serie A', and Italian football figures would certainly be able to tell the Premier League these perceptions are poison for the sport. Supporters need to be able to trust results. An irony is that, for all Serie A had its image tarnished over such controversies, they resulted in robust regulatory structures. The same was true of the EFL. The Premier League, by contrast, began to put out increasing job advertisements for lawyers. Over 2023–24, almost £30 million was spent on legal counsel in actions against the competition's own clubs.[43] Staff in areas like business development and govern-ment relations multiplied, with more appointments coming in from the civil service and state departments. Such arenas, and especially the courts, were becoming as important as the pitch in determining how English football plays out. The Premier League had actually been repeatedly warned to set up wholly independ-ent units to investigate and prosecute financial cases, but this was not heeded.

It has played into other image problems. The Premier League was by 2024 constantly criticised for a lack of transparency. The standard response to anything was a refusal to comment, right down to the date of the Manchester City hearing.[44] The stands began to be filled with banners proclaiming that the Premier League was 'corrupt', and became so visible that such outlandish sentiments couldn't just be ignored.[45] When Liverpool controver-sially lost to Tottenham Hotspur in October 2023, it was revealed that the officials who ruled on an incorrect offside call had been doing standard extra work in the UAE that same week. While there was no suggestion of anything untoward, it was telling that a simple decision had somehow devolved into a debate about potential conflict of interest and state involvement.

The Premier League similarly makes great play of its Rainbow Laces campaign, and how they proudly promote 'equality and diversity' where 'everyone feels welcome'. That is not something that can be said of the states of Saudi Arabia and UAE, who both had increasing influence on the competition.[46] Then, at the exact same time as Britain was locked in a dismal debate over the much-criticised 'Rwanda plan' – where asylum seekers would be sent to a state deemed incompatible with the UK's human rights obligations – Arsenal wore 'Visit Rwanda' on their shirts. By December 2023, despite much fanfare about a record £6.7 billion broadcasting deal, that broke down to £6.2 million per match, a decline from £8.11 million.[47] The Premier League couldn't even talk of unpredictability in the same way, since City subjected the competition to the most severe spell of dominance it has seen. The unique selling point had gone. Another principle of the league went with it. In 2024, City took the unprecedented step of going against the spirit of the Founder Members Agreement and challenging a vote with legal action. This was because they felt that the proposal, that Associated Party Transactions have to be independently assessed for fair market value, specifically targeted them. A 165-page legal document saw City claim they are victims of 'discrimination against Gulf ownership', while criticising the long-established voting system as a 'tyranny of the majority' and seeking to change it.[48] There was a circular logic to all of this, since it is only really state ownership that poses these sort of problems, and only state ownership that would have the means and will to take such a legal action. The symbolism of a club owned by a senior royal from an autocracy complaining about a democratic process was inescapable. Executives similarly noted how City received increasing support from Aston Villa. Their Egyptian billionaire owner, Nassef Sawiris, had in December 2023 announced plans to move his investment group to Abu Dhabi.[49] These all played into other warnings to the Premier League about geopolitics that went unheeded. There were also echoes of Khaldoon Al Mubarak's notorious leaked emails, where he said he said 'would rather spend £30 million on the 50 best lawyers in the world to sue them for the next ten years' than bow to regulation. This was exactly 10 years on.

It was all interlinked with the most complicated disciplinary case the Premier League has seen, too, right down to how the legal action was viewed as a 'tactic' amid the investigation into the alleged breaches. The predictability of City winning was offset by the uncertainty over whether they would be punished. Such was the scale of the case, that essentially amounted to accusations of fraud and the possibility of expulsion, that it was described as 'an existential event'. It was the story that brought so many strands to a head, so might well bring an entire era to a head. If City are found guilty, it will alter the perception of an entire decade of the Premier League. The entire face of the competition would similarly be transformed if City were to be expelled. If City are found not guilty, however, other clubs may revolt. That might even happen if any punishment from a guilty verdict is deemed weak.

The strength of feeling is that high, the pressures that intense. On one side are a lot of football clubs and stakeholders. On the other are one of the UK's main business partners, which involves the potential for a diplomatic incident. A question that constantly arose was how UAE–UK relations would be affected if one of Abu Dhabi's prize assets was punished like that. Although it was seen as ludicrous that the Premier League's investigation went well past four years, this was the scale of the case.[50] It is into this that an independent regulator will come, compounding the issues for the competition.

This is the mess the Premier League has got itself into, for reasons that go back much further than even the City takeover. It might have real significance for football as a whole, given how central the competition is to the game's global popularity and its economy. It's another storyline the Premier League has thrown up, albeit with a very uncertain ending.

16.

WHAT NEXT?

Over the summer of 2023, there were few discussions as common in football as complaints about the Saudi Pro League. 'The game's ecosystem is fucked,' was the comment from one high-profile figure at the Professional Footballers' Association dinner at Manchester's Lowry Theatre. One discussion more common, however, was willing acceptance of Saudi bids for players. Many executives had gone from throwing their hands up about it all to rubbing them with glee.

Such pretences and contradictions go right to the top in football. In December 2018, FIFA president Gianni Infantino made a grand proclamation while presenting to the G20 summit. 'Football can bring us together and make the world a more prosperous, educated, equal and perhaps even more peaceful place.'[1] Mere months later, Infantino could barely bring the same thoughts together. 'It is not the mission of FIFA to solve the problems of the world.'[2] Even Infantino's empty posturing poses the weighty question of what the mission of football should actually be. There is of course what's good for the game. There is also whether the game is at this moment a net good for the world. Football is after all play, that brings people together in a literal sense. It should bring them together in a more meaningful sense. The people's game – a description never more true, given its global spread – should serve as many as possible.

That philosophical question over what it's for is intertwined with what it should look like. The World Cup certainly feels like it has moved beyond founder Jules Rimet's initial description of an event that can 'unite nations' and 'encourage mankind to be one'.[3] If such words feel quaint now, it's hard not to wonder how history will look back on the current era. One World Cup was central to a state-building project that brought Vladimir Putin's invasion of Ukraine and threats of nuclear war. The hosts of the next World Cup directly profited from Russia's aggressions through gas hikes, as Qatar exploited the poorest people on earth. All the while, a club game greedily grasping for whatever money is coming has been dominated by sportswashing projects and super clubs. This certainly isn't what football is for. And, yet, the game has willingly had its own vanity flattered by fossil fuel economics, amid a worsening climate crisis.[4]

There are parallels that can be drawn in how the game has sped around the world as quickly as a new right-wing populism and culture wars, all propelled by social media. Much of the discussion around the sport actually illustrates how it has become a distillation of the post-truth era. Even if you 'stick to football', as many in the game demand, an obvious question is whether this embrace of hyper-capitalism has actually made the sport better? The best you could say is that extreme concentration of wealth has created a level of quality we have never seen. The Champions League latter stages can be sensational. Such quality isn't necessarily an objective net good, though. It has often come at the cost of competition, drama, development, hope and even attendance, as swathes of society find themselves priced out. In other words, most of the virtues that actually attract fans in the first place. It's why those involved in the Premier League's founding still think of that warning from the NFL. Football is now seeing the problems that come with money, especially a global revenue exceeding £25 billion.[5]

That is more than all three major US sports combined. Unlike those, however, football still hasn't solved this tension between competition on the pitch and co-operation off it. The wage race has driven the modern game to the brink, its impetus inadvertently articulated by Barcelona president Joan Laporta: 'Winning is a universal human emotion.'[6] So are frustration, anger, panic and existential dread, all of which Barcelona have felt in the last few years. Their modern story is quite the morality tale. Barcelona displayed an ideal of football on the pitch, before showing how grim the industry can be off it. As part of the same downfall, they have gone from inspiring the world through their play to potentially undermining trust in the sport. The *Caso Negreira*, where Barcelona have been investigated for payments to a former referee between 2000 and 2018, may change how football's most influential era is perceived. Its potential effects, along with the Manchester City case, could have more drastic effects for its future. Barcelona have insisted this was all 'very normal' and just for 'scouting reports'. City maintain their innocence.

Such uncertainty comes as concentration of wealth causes interest in many leagues and clubs to wane. It doesn't help that the great upheavals of the modern era, the 2015 FIFA scandal and the European Super League, probably ended up making the game worse. That isn't to say the immediate outcomes were wrong. FIFA needed toppling. The Super League wasn't the solution to anything. The problem was that the structures that caused such crises remained in place, and simply evolved in new directions. Far from the different system that had been hoped, as Ronan Evain of Football Supporters Europe says, 'what we see is actually getting worse because there are new streams of money.' That plays into the other persistent question over the game's future. Football's demise has been predicted by editorials and pundits for decades; that the game will eat itself,[7] that the bubble will burst. Such metaphors conjure images of nothingness, but it doesn't necessarily have to go like that for the game to experience profound change. Much of that change has already happened, without people even realising.

More likely is something akin to a *Big Short* moment, where so many of these long-term issues build up a pressure where there is a sudden collapse. There are numerous parallels between football now and the 2007–08 global crash. Concentration has ensured we're now way past talking about Red Star Belgrade or Porto becoming European champions. Five major leagues have become one super league and three others, with France negligible, although all of this only really revolves around 10 elite clubs. That made most of the Champions League so boring it had to be reformed.

All of this can be witnessed in how the opulent top end is better off than ever before but the wider health of the rest has never been worse. Manchester City win the Premier League again. Real Madrid win the Champions League again. Unlike Barcelona, Europe's most successful club astutely navigated the new world so well that they were eventually able to come right back around and pay a huge contract to Kylian Mbappé. Legacy does have a lasting power. That's how it is, as Pérez would say. Government staff who have worked within football, especially regarding community impact, liken it to how globalisation has created vast interchangeable urban centres like London or New York that suck up people and wealth while huge areas around them regress. There's been this vast hollowing out that has run alongside how many influential figures have just disappeared from relevance. Where are Michel Platini, Mohammed bin Hammam or Nicolas Sarkozy, before you even get to AC Milan or Rangers?[8] Meanwhile, Putin is invading countries rather than telling the FIFA Council to keep politics out of football.

La Liga's Javier Tebas actually believes global football may be headed for a moment similar to the Chinese Super League. There, huge investments only really went into player wages, at the cost of football culture and ultimately the competition itself. It is something else that sounds familiar. This is all while the effects of other huge national football projects become more profound, but also come into conflict. On one side, as legal expert Steve Weatherill argues, 'the American model attempts to control costs but the Gulf owners aren't bothered about cost at all. It does suggest a simmering earthquake.' The Super League might have been one of the tremors between these tectonic plates, rather than the earthquake itself.

It would take a lot to shake the foundations of the modern football empire, which often looks impregnable. As with the Premier League that sits at the top, football has an immense advantage over everything else in the world. Stars in other sports complain how they are fighting for coverage underneath. Empires can die, though. In the same way that football's global supremacy didn't just happen, but required a series of concerted decisions, there's a question over whether the game is making the wrong decisions in the other direction. UEFA figures point to a 'complacency' about how football will always be the number-one sport, and are concerned with how younger generations might see through a lack of values, let alone the worries over attention spans. Having been attracted to the very popularity of football, autocratic states and neoliberal forces are only serving to distort what made it popular in the first place. A few wrong turns can mean the sport loses itself, just like what happened with baseball. Certainly, the old qualities and structures that actually made the game popular in the first place contradict the aims of ultra-capitalism. The sport's endless desire for growth has already made huge events feel less 'special' for many players, because they're all just another part in a non-stop rolling football calendar. FIFA should be alert to all of this as the sport's ultimate authority, but have instead got involved in the race, becoming an events company more than a regulator. This is where rulings like that at the European Court of Justice might be so influential. It is described as 'a modern Bosman' but with effects that will take much longer to be seen.

It could cause another shift. The game still has a wonder. There's still nothing like going to your first match. Attendances remain strong. That might bring a move to local football, setting the game as the hyper-local against the hyper-global. Women's football offers such a model. The biggest question that should be driving the game right now is simple, but difficult to answer.

What do you want the future of football to look like?

It was once thought that goals would be made bigger and Crystal Palace would be 'the team of the 80s', which perhaps shows how pointless it is predicting football's future. At the same time, you can clearly see the path that's been laid, between the twin poles of New York and Riyadh. The axis of the game is shifting, even if it continues to spin on European super clubs. FIFA have already moved many key roles to Miami to fit with how the US hosted the expanded 2024 Copa America, and next will host the expanded 2025 Club World Cup, the expanded 2026 World Cup with Canada and Mexico, and then the 2028 Olympics football. This will be as US influence on the club game only increases, with the Premier League getting closer to a point where there's an American ownership voting majority of 14. Those in Major League Soccer are similarly concerned about noises from FIFA that might allow major European leagues to play competitive games in the US. It is why Leo Messi's move to Inter Miami has been so important, creating a classic 'football fever'. The club's sponsorship values jumped five-fold, putting them at Premier League level. Even major American sports are noting football's growing popularity in the build-up to the 2026 World Cup, as it has already leapt ahead of the National Hockey League in prominence. That tournament is likely to only encourage more moves to the US, since the current estimates for income are $11 billion, which is $4 billion more than Qatar. The joint American-Canadian-Mexican hosting may also encourage further collaboration, as there have been plans since the pandemic to eventually incorporate major Mexican clubs into MLS. The belief is this could rival European leagues in the future. That's if Europe's clubs don't get there first.

That runs alongside the widespread expectation that 'Saudi Arabia will eventually take over'. There's just so much money, as well as an immense political will now the kingdom has the 2034 World Cup. That could bring even more profound effect than between 2010 and 2022. Aramco's announcement as FIFA's 'major worldwide partner' means the taps are on. What could effectively be a partnership between Saudi money and FIFA for the Club World Cup might even see that deeper infrastructural integration long anticipated. The Gulf will certainly serve as a wider sports hub to mirror the US, since FIFA have already confirmed Qatar will host five consecutive editions of the expanded 48-team Under-17 World Cup. There are barely any questions about human rights abuses now.

Other small countries are frustrated by this, since hosting youth tournaments aids badly needed developments. Brazil has long been a football culture that required the reorganisation of its immense resources, but there is now anticipation that that could happen after the 'Brazil Football Corporations Act' was passed in 2021, encouraging clubs to act as businesses rather than traditional non-profit associations.[9] There are considerable ironies to that given the debates taking place in Europe. At least, 10 per cent of club structures will still be fan-owned.[10] The ambition is that a club-organised Brazilian league – modelled on the Premier League – can similarly challenge Europe, while becoming a beacon for South American football again. Globally famous clubs will be able to keep more players from what remains the most fertile country for talent in the world. Brazil has already attracted considerable capitalist and state interest, with City Football Group buying Bahia.

That fits into a calculation that football revenues will greatly increase as less developed regions grow. Club research suggests the sport is rapidly gaining traction in India as easily the second most popular sport after cricket. That is in a population that represents almost 18 per cent of the planet.[11] It's why India is seen as the source of the next great ownership wave. The outlook of private equity groups is that this can see major European clubs still expand to three times their current value, to compare with NBA franchises.

A concern with all of this is that it will just increase the interest in the super clubs rather than the local game, which is why City and figures like Andrea Agnelli have preached about looking beyond the European prism. They're intent on catering to different approaches to football. It becomes just another race. That's where evolving technology is so important. Chelsea's owners see the £2.5 billion they paid as good value for precisely this reason.[12] Whoever cracks streaming may crack open the game again. There have already been signs – of course, from the US – in MLS's streaming deal with Apple, and it may lead to a complete reorganisation of sharing agreements. Some executives feel this in itself is being overlooked, as technology structure will 'change sport for ever'. Augmented reality, where fans would pay to see through player wearables, is now cast as a bigger hope than streaming or the Super League.[13] The prediction is that international fans will pay fortunes for this. Infantino and Todd Boehly are hugely immersed in such developments, while the ideas have been central to plans for a revised Super League.

The evolution of the Champions League – in yet another expansion – represents one more potential juncture moment there. If it works, the Super League is finished. If it doesn't, interest in alternatives will be revived. Of course, the widespread description of UEFA's revised format is 'the Super Champions League'. Although so-called solidarity money has been increased to 7 per cent, it comes as the number of matches rises by 50 per cent. That still means more money to the wealthiest clubs. The new system could even see an individual domestic league feature as many as seven teams in the elite competition. It is why European executives say there is 'utter hypocrisy' to UEFA casting themselves as saviours from the Super League, since they are just institutionalising it. The same applies to developments since. The Super League later announced a plan to establish a three-tiered league for Europe's top 64 clubs. Aleksander Čeferin derided this as 'not football', only for UEFA to create a system that at least superficially looks similar.[14] While the Champions League virtually guarantees the same clubs returning, the Conference League is viewed as dragging 78 per cent of the Europa League into a third tier.

Such stratification only further aligns with multi-club groups. It's difficult not to imagine a series of projects with a Champions League club at the top and then teams of other sizes all the way down. The spread of the model will only further consolidate the influence of the main forces on the game, since it is only ever going to be huge capitalist groups or states that can afford this. Worse, the Conference League has the potential to exacerbate the historic problems from the Champions League, in distorting more domestic competitions through prize money. With participants receiving €7 million, that can completely disrupt leagues where revenues are minimal.

This is far from the fluid and varied sport football used to be. It may bring a hard line in this growing tension between healthy crowds and concentration of wealth. How long can the game withstand increased predictability? The perception that sport is in any way predetermined, even subconsciously, is like slow-working poison. And yet this is precisely what is happening with swathes of football. 'You watch a game and you think there is another element that decided the result than what's happening on the pitch,' Evain says. 'It's not match-fixing, but it is a different form of sporting integrity, where the result is the same. And you look at countries that have a massive match-fixing problem, people just stop watching football. There is a threat.' Another destructive consequence is that winning a lot means less. Clubs like Paris Saint-Germain barely value league titles any more. Conversely, it is a tragedy that clubs not being able to win – even massive clubs like Olympique Marseille – has become normalised. 'The emotion of a match is the ABC of our industry and we are destroying it,' Evain adds. It ironically, if inevitably, starts to run against the very business of football, which is putting on competitive matches.

Potential crises of legitimacy, like from the Barcelona and City cases, may consequently become more important. Any erosion of trust, and consequent loss of income, opens the way for private equity or sovereign wealth funds to buy up even more infrastructure. The next step might be entire leagues. The Abu Dhabi sovereign wealth fund, Mubadala, has already proposed a partnership with one model for the new Brazilian league.[15] Meanwhile, FIFA's expanded Club World Cup is viewed as potentially like cricket's Indian Premier League, restructuring the game. In other words, 'a Super League at world level'. It's hard to see how any of this fits with concerns about player workload, which might finally bring the players to say 'stop'. The line could be the legal action taken by FIFPro, who said it was 'challenging the legality of FIFA's decisions to unilaterally set the international match calendar and, in particular, the decision to create and schedule the FIFA Club World Cup 2025'.[16] The competition didn't have an obvious place, and instead looks another potential breakpoint. Other stakeholders wonder whether money will still have the final say. One comment increasingly made is that legal action would have been much less likely to happen without the European Court of Justice ruling.

While FIFA have spoken about how the Club World Cup is essential to global development, 70 per cent of the income is estimated to go straight to players, and most of those will be from major Champions League clubs. That's why the wage race shows no signs of abating. Technology might even mean it accelerates further, especially if wearable technology just sees more go to individual players. That would be on top of a situation where UEFA's 2024 landscaping report showed wages taking 89 per cent of revenue at French clubs, 88 per cent in Belgium. It's instructive that leagues with more fan-owned clubs – such as Austria, Germany and Sweden – keep that at lower than 60 per cent. That may hasten a potential split between the hyper-local and the hyper-global. In the latter, it's impossible not to wonder whether it's going to perpetually be Saudi Arabia v Abu Dhabi; sovereign wealth fund v private equity; state v capitalist.

Whether football becomes a lasting stage for such states partly depends on geopolitical relationships in more vaunted areas. The tensions that led to the Gulf blockade have persisted, but now mostly swirl between Saudi Arabia and Abu Dhabi. The *Wall Street Journal* reported in July 2023 how 'a rift' has opened between Mohamed bin Salman and Mohammed bin Zayed, and they had gone months without speaking.[17] The mentor has grown frustrated with the protégé, who has outgrown him. There had been splits over foreign policy, right up to who exerts the greatest influence on the Gulf, but a core reason was the effects of diversification plans. Virtually every move Qatar and Abu Dhabi made – from tourism to business – has been replicated by Saudi Arabia, but at a greater scale. This affects everyone's bottom line and global visibility. 'Everything Mohammed bin Salman wanted to do was ultimately going to lead to competition with the UAE,' Gulf expert Chris Davidson says. That put football right in the centre, with the *Wall Street Journal* specifically mentioning how Saudi Arabia had encroached into Abu Dhabi's 'realm of soft power' through Newcastle United. The purchase already caused Qatar to abandon any idea of selling Paris Saint-Germain and begin thinking about the Premier League. Such tensions have driven the last 15 years of football, so it's hard not to see how that doesn't escalate before a World Cup in Saudi Arabia.

It is not only between the Gulf states that there is tension, though. There is also friction between the region and the West, as articulated by the culture war within the 2022 World Cup. Diplomats have frequently been 'stunned' by the 'aggression' in the relationship between Abu Dhabi and the UK, as one example. Government sources describe a wariness, even if it has worked for both countries. 'These states are actively trying to export a particular governance model, which is "authoritarian stability",'

McGeehan says. 'Yes, you can go to discos, but you cannot criticise the way things are done.' Just like some of the main influences in football, too, such states are actively targeting the developing world – especially Africa. It offers a growing population and a huge market for energy. This is where positive association from football is all the more important, since Africa is a heartland for the game. 'These are the countries that states like Abu Dhabi want to build its profile in,' former diplomat Arthur Snell says. 'Abu Dhabi isn't trying to curry favour in the north-west of England. It cares about the global south.' African football has already become 'dangerously dependent' on money from fossil fuel economies, in the words of football historian David Goldblatt, most visibly through TotalEnergies sponsorships.[18] The culture war within the 2022 World Cup might consequently shape future discussion.

'There has been this capacity to influence narratives and, right now, they have an accommodating relationship with the West,' activist Iyad el-Baghdadi says. 'But, in 5, 10 years, the West is going to be stepping on their toes, so might be an adversary.' The Janus-like nature of these relationships could be seen in how the major Gulf states all hailed their relationship with Putin in the two years after the Ukraine invasion. The Russian example remains instructive. If you stand back now, it looks like this: Putin's state filled the West with disinformation to further political splits, while then using the World Cup to put on a presentable face, before embarking on a war that directly benefited from those splits. Although this isn't to say the same will happen again, the point is how geopolitical developments can play havoc with football. The very fact that Premier League owners have a direct relationship with Russia opens up huge potential complications. It also brought sportswashing of another form. Rheinmetall's 2024 deal with as romantic a club as Borussia Dortmund was a naked attempt to normalise an arms manufacturer, because of the realistic prospect of war with Russia. Club chief executive Hans-Joachim Watzke even spoke of 'this new normality' as he defended the sponsorship out of concern for how 'freedom' itself must be protected in Europe.[19] Before that, the invasion was a first moment that made many in the Premier League question what might happen if geopolitics shift. It showed the precariousness of the position football has put itself into.

Such problems don't necessarily have to come from shows of power, either. These states can weaken. Climate change will gradually move the world away from fossil fuels, which might become a more pressing problem for Gulf economies than depletion. The impending era of clean energy will redraw the world's map of power. 'It's a bit like with computers,' Snell says. 'As more people flock to different technologies, more innovation comes and the transition accelerates. By the time Bin Salman is in his fifties, the global market for Saudi oil might be a quarter of what it is now.' Along the same lines, Qatar is a country heating faster than anywhere else in the world. Scientific research predicts the Gulf will experience heatwaves beyond human tolerance.[20] As Snell argues, 'What's the point of a tourism industry if it isn't possible to spend much time there?'

There's also the wonder about how workable diversification actually is. Dubai had to be bailed out by Abu Dhabi in the financial crisis. As late as 2023, after billions-worth of investment, a Reuters report said the Saudi economy was only 'edging closer to reducing dependence on oil'.[21] *Blood and Oil* details how White House officials felt economic calculations were overly optimistic.[22] 'It shows there's a limit, because it's difficult to diversify into manufacturing when the industry is built on migrant workers,' Snell posits. 'The economies of scale don't work. Entire societies are structured around a model where a single industry, with not that many people working in it, pays for everything else.'

A barometer might be in how ready the futuristic city of NEOM is for the 2034 World Cup. Ambitions already had to be scaled back by 2024, with Bloomberg reporting the plan was downsized for just 300,000 people to live there by 2030 rather than 1.5 million.[23] The point to all of this is how quickly circumstances change, and the inherent risk of leaving football dependent on geopolitics. 'Black swan events can force a rethink on club ownership in England as well,' Davidson says. 'It's very possible that Gulf states that have increasingly close relations with China and Russia could end up more on their side in broader military or economic conflicts. Where does that leave our sports industry?' One Premier League executive points to how this makes a Gulf-backed Club World Cup, as well as numerous FIFA deals, all the more important.

'If you pull that money out, it's collapse, on a global scale.'

As so many of its great players have shown, football can still be the master of its own destiny. It doesn't need to be so subject to other forces. The sport is popular enough to be entirely self-sustainable. That mostly requires political will, but that is building. With state ownership, governments can pass laws to ban the model. Some clubs already asked the UK government to put in precisely such rules in consultations for the independent regulator. Even if governments refuse to go that far, there are multiple ways from within the game to mitigate the effects of state ownership so as to disincentivise it. Many are linked to the connected problem of concentration of wealth, but that can be incrementally worked back the other way.

Government staff liken the current fan-based movement to how Joe Biden's US administration became so economically interventionist after Donald Trump. There was a snap back after neoliberalism was taken to an extreme. Football has already seen an increasing pivot to the local, as fascination with leagues like Sweden's grows. Ireland, one of the first countries to be affected by English football's popularity, is seeing an attendance boom. Even the Premier League witnessed its first fan-controlled club in Luton Town. That shift still requires a reset of football's system, so it doesn't just perpetuate gaps, and more money goes to development. One simple solution is a levy on Champions League money, or the profits of the super clubs. UEFA could even go further and just allot more of the immense revenue to the rest of the game. Out of the €3 billion that goes to 36 Champions League clubs, a mere €100 million could be put aside for pitches around Europe. That's €1 billion in infrastructure after a decade. Some FIFA figures have similarly suggested a stipulation that any competition selling broadcast rights in a different country have to pay a certain percentage back into local grassroots. There was 'zero interest' at higher levels, due to the potential legalities, despite so much talk about 'development'. More money can still go from the Club World Cup to domestic leagues, while those domestic leagues can look at more equitable redistribution rules. That is easier to action than more drastic ideas like full centralisation of commercial deals, but they wouldn't be so necessary in a world where gaps are reduced. The cycle is spun back in the opposite direction.

It has long become apparent, however, that financial redistribution is not enough on its own. Even in US sport, it's only one mechanism among many. Redistribution of talent is arguably more important. A growing view is that something resembling the pre-Bosman foreign player rule – where teams were only allowed to field three non-nationals and two 'assimilated' players – would be revolutionary. It would eliminate so many issues at a stroke, and is much easier to grasp than any financial regulation. If a major club can only field five foreign players, it immediately means there is less logic in hoarding stars. That ensures more top-level players are available to someone else, with this effect multiplied if it applies to every club in Europe. Every country would consequently keep more talent that bit longer, which would then make their teams stronger, while improving continental performance and generating more commercial opportunities. That redistribution of talent in turn makes money less influential, because it's not a completely open market. Clubs have to be more careful about signings, since super squads can't be developed. FIFA did investigate this idea, but UEFA knew it was incompatible with EU laws on freedom of movement.

That doesn't mean the same effect can't be achieved from the opposite direction. Instead of foreign players being restricted, a certain quota of academy graduates in teams could be mandated. This would be favourable to the EU since it is educational development, but also has multiple other benefits. Fans would enjoy more of a link to homegrown players, and investment in grassroots would be incentivised. It is instantly more organic. A less stringent version might even be squad limits, or restricting transfers.

One major reason that measures like this are never implemented is because of the power structure at the top of the game, but that is now actively being scrutinised by European politicians. There is a new vigilance over whether the executive presidential model works for football. The EU certainly needs to demand fixed-term limits, more diverse representation and greater transparency. If much of this sounds fanciful, people only need to look at how there has already been a legal ruling in the form of the European Court of Justice judgment on the Super League case from December 2023.[24] The effects may be profound.

Most of the focus was on pre-authorisation rules, which may allow for other competitions including transnational leagues. Such events can't supplant the Champions League, though, since that is now ring-fenced as the only competition that crowns the European champions. It prevents a split like boxing. That concept of solidarity is also where the ruling is most consequential. The judgment stated that UEFA and FIFA are monopolies so must display fair, transparent and non-discriminatory rules, which also require the sale of media rights to produce financial solidarity.

The situation could gradually lead to legislation on the shape of sports governance, especially as national sports ministers push the European Commission to articulate a European model of sport that safeguards sporting merit.[25]

European politicians are also looking at limiting direct foreign state investment, on the advice of various stakeholders, since it would form a distortion of markets in any economic sector. There is even increasing talk over whether European football itself needs an independent regulator. Much of the world is looking at how the English example goes. The dismissive talk in the Premier League is that the independent regulator will just find a series of contradictory issues, but that is sort of the point. There's a conflict at the core of football, between competition and partnership. Some of the more progressive voices are now talking about a concept called 'co-opetition', where competitors have a need to co-operate. It is what football is supposed to be about.

There is still a central tension running through the modern game. Is football at this point a net good for humanity? It still has so much beauty, allowing countless children the chance to just play, while affording physical benefits and the mental wellbeing of just belonging to something. For so many people, football brings the happiest moments of their lives. Many might scoff that this just distracts from what is actually important in the world but that is in turn why football is important. It is what we fill the rest of our lives with. Even the pain of defeat brings bonding.

This is also why football is misused. There can sadly be no illusions about its role in the twenty-first century. It has been a force for autocracy, populism, vested interests, commercialism, hyper-capitalism, ultra-liberalism, the fragmentation of the working classes, the overclass, culture wars, tribalism, soft power and hard power.[26] Far from bringing people together, it has stoked direct division. This is only because of what football has been allowed to become, though. It doesn't need to be like this. Women's football, increasingly, isn't like this. Amnesty's Steve Cockburn says it offers 'such a clear example of how it can be a driver of positive change'. It is a more inclusive game, with more activism. Football doesn't have to be misused. The image can be changed. Instead of sportswashing, the game can be cleansed. Football, as is by now abundantly clear, has a power all of its own.

ACKNOWLEDGEMENTS

Given that this was a project that took over a year, but really stretches back many more, there are a lot of people I am grateful to – most of all, for listening to me. Thanks must first go to my editor, Tierney Witty, who offered an immensely important understanding of the subject as well as a considered and patient appreciation of the challenges in writing it. That sentiment extends to the entire team at Orion, including Sian Baldwin, Karin Burnik, Hannah Cox, Beth Eynon, Jess Hart, Tara Hiatt, Louis Patel, Paul Stark, Tom Noble, Esther Waters, as well as Francine Brody for a superb copy-editing job, and Siobhan Tierney and Elaine Egan at Hachette Ireland.

Special thanks also goes to my agent, David Luxton, who was especially crucial in ensuring this book went from years of being talked about, to actually getting written. Like Tierney, he was also very patient with grumbling messages at all hours.

This book directly evolved from my work on various subjects for the *Independent*, so I profusely thank everyone at such a great title, that really supports journalists. Most immediately, there are a series of brilliant sports editors, who persistently backed the articles that formed the core of this book. There was the initial reporting and discussions under Ed Malyon. There was the drive for the subject and backing of Ben Burrows. There was the insightful guidance and constant care of Jack Rathborn. If it wasn't for how each of them valued coverage of these issues, this would never have been written. That same thanks extends to the invaluable support of Chloe Hubbard, Geordie Greig, David Marley, Richard Best, Chris Stevenson and Christian Broughton.

I am also grateful to the sports team past and present for always having my back, who include Lawrence Ostlere, Karl Matchett, Luke Baker, Jamie Braidwood, Alex Pattle, Sonia Twigg, Kieran Jackson, Mike Jones, Richard Jolly, Luke Brown, Jack Austin, Sam Lovett, Vithushan Ehantharajah and Jack De Menezes.

There were a number of people who offered essential journalistic support and advice, but many of these were simply good friends doing what good friends do: Nick Ames, John Brewin, Mark Critchley, Ken Early, Dion Fanning, James Horncastle, Jonathan Liew, Paul Ovenden, Jack Pitt-Brooke, Melissa Reddy, Joshua Robinson, Barney Ronay, Jack Rosser, Catherine Sanz, Lars Sivertsen, Alan Smith, Rory Smith, Jacob Steinberg, Laurie Whitwell and Jonathan Wilson.

I so often felt fortunate about being able to lean heavily on the work of many great journalists who have done supreme reporting on the subjects covered in this book, as well as their advice. They are: Philippe Auclair, Mario Bechler, Andy Brassell, Paul Brown, Martin Calladine, David Conn, James Corbett, Adam Crafton, Joey D'Urso, Simon Evans, Tony Evans, Owen Gibson, David Goldblatt, Nick Harris, Rob Harris, Ian Herbert, Raphael Honigstein, Matt Hughes, Sam Kunti, Bill Law, Sid Lowe, James Montague, Tariq Panja, Dan Roan, Matt Slater, Owen Slot, Kristoff Terreur, Karim Zidan, Martyn Ziegler.

I also apologise for suddenly bothering some of them out of nowhere with obscure questions from work they did years ago. 'When you wrote this . . .' Some I just want to thank because their work was so good.

ACKNOWLEDGEMENTS

General thanks, too, to Gideon Adler, Enrique Aguilar Viñuela, Sam Agini, Duncan Alexander, Noa Bachner, Roger Bennett, Calvin Betton, Benny Berger, Magnus Borgen, Roscoe Bowman, Veronica Brunati, Hendrik Buchheister, Mike Calvin, Jamie Carragher, Mike Collett, Rosanna Cooney, Jason Corcoran, Rob Draper, Fernando Evangilo, Joris Evers, Gareth Farrelly, Megan Feringa, Rachel Frazer, Borja García, Rosie Garthwaite, Jonas Adnan Giævara, Ger Gilroy, Michelle Gulino, Ramzy Haddad, Elle Hardy, Oliver Holt, Vincent Hogan, Paul Howard, Diego Huerta, Simon Hughes, Yasmine Kassem, Paul Kimmage, Nizaar Kinsella, Ben Jacobs, Greg Ian Johnson, Oli Kay, Dan Kilpatrick, Joanna Manning-Cooper, Paul McCarthy, Daniel McDonnell, Priyanka Mogul Petrucci, Mariya Parodi, Keegan Pierce, Jonathan Northcroft, Kieron O'Conner, Mark O'Neill, Paul Quinn, Alvaro Reynolds, Archie Rhind-Tutt, Alan Redmond, Jean-Claude Ribes, Patrick Rochford, Emanuel Roșu, Katie Shanahan, Gary Sinclair, Jon Spurling, Diego Torres, Martin Volkmar, Ian Wright. All offered at least one little piece of help or advice, which can make a huge difference, but it was often much more.

I am also grateful to all of those who agreed to be interviewed for the book or engage with it in any way, either on or off the record. They include: Isobel Archer, Jonathan Barnett, Roberto Carlos, Martin Cloake, Steve Cockburn, Damian Comolli, Frank Conde Tangberg, Adam Coogle, Niall Couper, Simon Curtis, Chris Davidson, Moya Dodd, Iyad El-Baghdadi, Tony Ernst, Ronan Evain, David Forrest, Alex Fynn, Michael Gabriel, Tom Greatrex, Dennis Gudacic, John Hahn, Lise Klaveness, Maksim Krivunecs, Douglas London, James Lynch, Miguel Maduro, Nils Mallock, Petros Mavroidis, Nick McGeehan, Sir Bob Murray, Martha Newsom, Nedum Onuoha, Michael Page, Mark Palios, Rick Parry, Alex Phillips, Daniele Pollicano, Mustafa Qadri, Norman Riley,

Dominic Rosso, Mark Schwarzer, Arthur Snell, Charlie Stillitano, Javier Tebas, Stephen Weatherill, Arsène Wenger, Dr Rob Wilson.

There are numerous others who spoke on background, off the record or simply can't be named out of discretion, and to them I express my thanks here, too.

The Hardly Athletic lads in Battersea were crucial for the release of five-a-side every week, as well as a great laugh, especially long-term team legends like Davy, Jeremy, John, Sean, Paddy, Jim and Joe. As important as help with work on the book were those who helped with everything around it, from listening to me go on about it to just taking my mind off it, and even offering a more detached view: Abigail, Aishling, the two Barrys, the two Brians, Celine, Ciaran, Darragh, Eliza, Ewan, Garret, Iain, Jesika, Joe, Karl, Katia, Lawrence, Lisa, Malachy, Martin, Mike, Olivia, the two Pats, Richard, Ronan.

Then there were those who encouraged me more than anyone: my family. Special thanks to Kevin, Joan, Sinead, Kevin, Claire, Anne, Jack, Senan, Chloe, Aaron, Dave, Patricia, Rosa, Antonio, Miguel and – above all – Aisling, Niall, dad, mum and Éabha.

SOURCES

Introduction

1   Kuper, Simon & Szymanski, Stefan. *Soccernomics: Why France and Germany Win, Why England Is Starting to and Why the Rest of the World Loses.* HarperCollins Publishers, 2022.
2   Tom Holland on 'The World Cup: British Imperialism, South American rivalries, and Mussolini', *The Rest is History*, November 2022.

Chapter 1 – How Football Was Ripe for Takeover

1   Basini, Francesca, et al., 'Assessing competitive balance in the English Premier League for over forty seasons using a stochastic block model', *Journal of the Royal Statistical Society Series A: Statistics in Society*, Volume 183: 3, July 2023, pp.530-556.
2   Deloitte, *Deloitte Football Money League 2024*, 16 March 2022.
3   Conn, David. *Richer Than God: Manchester City, Modern Football and Growing Up.* Quercus, 2012.
4   Hardy, Martin. 'The mad world of Silvio Berlusconi and AC Milan', *The Times*, 13 June 2023.
5   Delaney, Miguel. 'The story of Silvio Berlusconi and the birth of the Champions League', *Independent*, 12 June 2023.
6   Turner, Richard. 'Five Hillsborough myths dispelled by inquests jury', *BBC News*, 28 April 2016.
7   Clegg, Jonathan & Robinson, Joshua. *The Club: How the Premier League Became the Richest, Most Disruptive Business in Sport.* John Murray Press, 2018.
8   Domeneghetti, Roger. *From the Back Page to the Front Room: Football's Journey Through The English Media.* Ockley Books, 2014.
9   Clegg, Jonathan & Robinson, Joshua. *The Club: How the Premier League*

Became the Richest, Most Disruptive Business in Sport. John Murray Press, 2018.

10 Conn, David. *Richer Than God: Manchester City, Modern Football and Growing Up.* Quercus, 2012

11 Dixon, James. *The Fix: How the First Champions League Was Won and Why We All Lost.* Pitch Publishing, 2021.

12 Fletcher, Rob. *1992: The Birth of Modern Football.* Pitch Publishing, 2023.

13 Clegg, Jonathan & Robinson, Joshua. *The Club: How the Premier League Became the Richest, Most Disruptive Business in Sport.* John Murray Press, 2018.

14 Szymanski, Stefan. *Money and Football: A Soccernomics Guide.* PublicAffairs, 2015.

15 Lewis, Michael. 'How USA was chosen to host World Cup 94: the inside story of a historic day', *The Guardian*, 4 July 2015.

16 Dixon, James. *The Fix: How the First Champions League Was Won and Why We All Lost.* Pitch Publishing, 2021.

17 Europa Commission, *Professional Footballers: The Dossier Progresses*, IP/91/316.

18 The Herald, 'Three foreigner rule scrapped', *The Herald*, 20 February 1996.

19 Soriano, Ferran. *Goal: The Ball Doesn't Go In By Chance.* Palgrave Macmillan UK, 2011.

20 Bower, Tom. *Broken Dreams: Vanity, Greed and the Souring of British Football.* Simon & Schuster UK, 2003.

21 Delaney, Miguel. '"He's in his own world": Florentino Perez gripped by delusion amid Super League fiasco', *Independent*, 27 April 2021.

22 Wallace, Sam. 'Exclusive: Real Madrid disclose probably £20m liability in EU illegal state aid case', *The Telegraph*, 8 October 2022.

23 Carlin, John. *White Angels.* Bloomsbury Publishing, 2004.

24 Clegg, Jonathan & Robinson, Joshua. *Messi vs. Ronaldo.* HarperCollins, 2022.

25 Torres, Diego. *The Special One: The Dark Side of Jose Mourinho.* HarperCollins Publishers, 2014.

26 Carlin, John. *White Angels.* Bloomsbury Publishing, 2004.

27 Soriano, Ferran. *Goal: The Ball Doesn't Go In By Chance.* Palgrave Macmillan UK, 2011.

28 Szymanski, Stefan. *Money and Football: A Soccernomics Guide.* PublicAffairs, 2015.

29 Clegg, Jonathan & Robinson, Joshua. *Messi vs. Ronaldo.* HarperCollins, 2022.

30 Szymanski, Stefan. *Money and Football: A Soccernomics Guide*, PublicAffairs, 2015.

31 Moore, Glenn. 'Football: A game in search of its soul', *Independent*, 14 April 1999.

32 Soriano, Ferran. *Goal: The Ball Doesn't Go In By Chance*. Palgrave Macmillan UK, 2011.

33 Parry, Sam. *The Ugly Economics of the Beautiful Game* [Paper Presentation]. International Football History Conference: Cardiff, Wales, June 6-7 2024.

34 Montague, James. *The Billionaires Club: The Unstoppable Rise of Football's Super-rich Owners*. Bloomsbury Publishing, 2018.

35 Ibid.

36 Piketty, Thomas. *Capital in the Twenty-First Century*. Harvard University Press, 2013.

37 Szymanski, Stefan. *Money and Football: A Soccernomics Guide*, PublicAffairs, 2015.

Chapter 2 – What is Sportswashing?

1 Observer sport and agencies, 'Amnesty turns the heart up on "sportswashing" Manchester City owners', *The Guardian*, 10 November 2018.

2 United States Holocaust Memorial Museum. 'The Façade of Hospitality', The Nazi Olympics Berlin 1936: www.ushmm.org/exhibition/olympics/?content=facade_hospitality_more&lang=en.

3 Montague, James. *The Billionaires Club: The Unstoppable Rise of Football's Super-rich Owners*. Bloomsbury Publishing, 2018.

4 Ibid.

5 Ibid.

6 The Moscow Times, 'Russia Imposes Limit to Number of Foreign Players in Football Premier League', *The Moscow Times*, 14 July 2015.

7 Blaschke, Ronny. *Power Players: Football in Propaganda, War and Revolution*. Pitch Publishing, 2022.

8 Miller, Rory. *Desert Kingdoms to Global Powers: The Rise of the Arab Gulf*. Yale University Press, 2016.

9 The United Arab Emirates' Government Portal. 'Abu Dhabi Economic Vision 2030'. 5 September 2023.

10 Crafton, Adam. 'Newcastle's Saudi takeover: The UK government's emails revealed'. *The Athletic*, 6 April 2023.

11 Miller, Rory. *Desert Kingdoms to Global Powers: The Rise of the Arab Gulf*. Yale University Press, 2016.

12 Ibid.

13 Ibid.
14 Montague, James. *When Friday Comes*. Ebury Publishing, 2008.
15 Miller, Rory. *Desert Kingdoms to Global Powers: The Rise of the Arab Gulf*. Yale University Press, 2016.
16 Clegg, Jonathan & Robinson, Joshua. *The Club: How the Premier League Became the Richest, Most Disruptive Business in Sport*. John Murray Press, 2018.
17 Buschmann, Rafael; Naber, Nicola & Winterbach, Christoph. 'Sponsorship Money – Paid for by the State'. *Der Spiegel*, 7 April 2022.
18 McGeehan, Nicholas & Lynch, James. 'Ensuring UEFA Competition Integrity', *FairSquare*, 14 February 2023: fairsq.org/wp-content/uploads/2023/02/Letter-to-Aleksander-Ceferin-14-Feb-2023.pdf
19 Abbot, Sebastian. *The Away Game*, Arena Sport, 2018.
20 ADHRB ADMIN. 'Prisoner Profile: Dr. Ahmed al-Zaabi'. *Americans for Democracy & Human Rights in Bahrain*, 15 December 2015.
21 Delaney, Miguel. 'Should football boycott the Qatar World Cup?', *Independent*, 24 March 2021.
22 Ronay, Barney. 'Qatar calling its critics racist opens a debate that may be worth having', *The Guardian*, 3 November 2022.
23 Conn, David. *Richer Than God: Manchester City, Modern Football and Growing Up*. Quercus, 2012.
24 Miller, Rory. *Desert Kingdoms to Global Powers: The Rise of the Arab Gulf*. Yale University Press, 2016.
25 Conn, David. *The Fall of the House of Fifa*. Random House, 2017.
26 Reuters. 'Saudi population at 32.2 million, 63% of Saudis under 30 years old, census shows'. *Reuters*, 31 May 2023.
27 Wallace, Sam. 'It might leave a stain, but the grim truth is that sportswashing works'. *The Telegraph*, 10 October 2021.
28 Nobie, Josh. 'Can European football clubs ever be profitable?'. *Financial Times*, 17 September 2023.
29 Wallace, Ava & Giambalvo, Emily. 'A timeline of Russia's state-sponsored Olympic doping scandal'. *The Washington Post*, 11 February 2022.
30 Liew, Jonathan. 'Manchester City backers are not the sort to take UEFA's punishment lying down'. *The Guardian*, 17 February 2020.
31 Hope, Craig. 'Saudi Arabia's Crown Prince Mohammed bin Salman urged Prime Minister Boris Johnson to intervene in £300m Newcastle United takeover after it was blocked by the Premier League'. *The Daily Mail*, 14 April 2021.
32 Ramesh, Randeep. 'UAE told UK: crack down on Muslim Brotherhood or lose arms deals'. *The Guardian*, 6 November 2015.

Chapter 3 – All Paths Lead From Roman

1   Montague, James. *The Billionaires Club: The Unstoppable Rise of Football's Super-rich Owners.* Bloomsbury Publishing, 2018.
2   Belton, Catherine. *Putin's People.* HarperCollins Publishers, 2020.
3   Bullough, Oliver. *Butler to the World.* Profile, 2022.
4   Clegg, Jonathan & Robinson, Joshua. *The Club: How the Premier League Became the Richest, Most Disruptive Business in Sport.* John Murray Press, 2018.
5   Duff, Alex & Panja, Tariq. *Football's Secret Trade.* Bloomberg. Wiley, 2017.
6   Law, Matt. 'Abramovich wanted Chelsea training ground in Regent's Park – until he learned the Queen owned it'. *The Telegraph*, 21 March 2023.
7   Midgley, Dominic & Hutchins, Chris. *Abramovich: The Billionaire from Nowhere.* Chiselbury, 2004.
8   Montague, James. *The Billionaires Club: The Unstoppable Rise of Football's Super-rich Owners.* Bloomsbury Publishing, 2018.
9   Midgley, Dominic & Hutchins, Chris. *Abramovich: The Billionaire from Nowhere.* Chiselbury, 2004.
10   Ibid.
11   Kuper, Simon & Szymanski, Stefan. *Soccernomics: Why France and Germany Win, Why England Is Starting to and Why The Rest of the World Loses.* HarperCollins Publishers, 2022.
12   Speare-Cole, Rebecca. 'British journalist sued by Abramovich over Putin claims made MBE'. *Independent*, 31 December 2022.
13   Belton, Catherine. *Putin's People.* HarperCollins Publishers, 2020.
14   Ibid.
15   Ibid.
16   Hansard, 'Lawfare and UK Court System, Volume 707: Thursday 20 January 2022', *UK Parliament*: hansard.parliament.uk/commons/2022-01-20/debates/4F7649B7-2085-4B51-9E8C-32992CFF7726/LawfareAndUKCourtSystem
17   Macaskill, Andrew & Belton, Catherine. 'Insight: Londongrad tries to kick its 30-year Russian money habit'. *Reuters*, 28 February 2022.
18   'Fears raised at Chelsea takeover'. *The Guardian*, 2 July 2003.
19   Midgley, Dominic & Hutchins, Chris. *Abramovich: The Billionaire from Nowhere.* Chiselbury, 2004.
20   Ibid.
21   'Tap-up row: Cole and Chelsea guilty'. *The Guardian*, 1 June 2005.
22   Fifield, Dominic, et al. 'Abramovich and the aftershocks that altered football forever'. *The Athletic*, 28 November 2020.

23 Conn, David. 'Liverpool's American dream looks like a dead end'. *The Guardian*, 6 June 2009.

24 Bower, Tom. *Broken Dreams*. Simon & Schuster UK, 2023.

25 Clegg, Jonathan & Robinson, Joshua. *The Club: How the Premier League Became the Richest, Most Disruptive Business in Sport*. John Murray Press, 2018.

Chapter 4 – City State

1 Kompany, Vincent. *Treble Triumph*. Simon & Schuster UK, 2019.

2 Montague, James. *The Billionaires Club: The Unstoppable Rise of Football's Super-rich Owners*. Bloomsbury Publishing, 2018.

3 Ducker, James. 'Human rights group voices angry opposition to Thaksin takeover'. *The Times*, 1 August 2007.

4 Austin, Simon. 'A fit and proper premiership?'. BBC News, 31 July 2007.

5 Conn, David. *Richer Than God: Manchester City, Modern Football and Growing Up*. Quercus, 2012.

6 Ducker, James. 'Human rights group voices angry opposition to Thaksin takeover'. *The Times*, 1 August 2007.

7 Ibid.

8 Adams, Brad. 'HRW concerned about Thaksin's ownership in Premier League Team, Manchester City'. Human Rights Watch, 30 July 2007.

9 Ducker, James. 'Human rights group voices angry opposition to Thaksin takeover'. *The Times*, 1 August 2007.

10 Conn, David. *Richer Than God: Manchester City, Modern Football and Growing Up*. Quercus, 2012.

11 Ibid.

12 Ibid.

13 Ibid.

14 Ibid.

15 Montague, James. *The Billionaires Club: The Unstoppable Rise of Football's Super-rich Owners*. Bloomsbury Publishing, 2018.

16 Taylor, Daniel. 'City laid bare: from Thaksin's troubles to old-school Hughes'. *The Guardian*, 23 August 2008.

17 Clegg, Jonathan & Robinson, Joshua. *The Club: How the Premier League Became the Richest, Most Disruptive Business in Sport*. John Murray Press, 2018.

18 Dein, David. *Calling the Shots: How to Win in Football and Life*. Little, Brown Book Group, 2022.

19 Clegg, Jonathan & Robinson, Joshua. *The Club: How the Premier League*

Became the Richest, Most Disruptive Business in Sport. John Murray Press, 2018.

20 Al Baik, Eman. 'Lawyer denies cheating Thaksin in club deal'. *Emirates 24/7*, 18 March 2011.

21 Sheikh Mansour Bin Zayed Al Nahyan. 'A Letter to the City Fans From Sheikh Mansour'. ManCity.com, 18 September 2008.

22 Montague, James. *The Billionaires Club: The Unstoppable Rise of Football's Super-rich Owners.* Bloomsbury Publishing, 2018.

23 Ronay, Barney. 'Manchester City fans' defence of UAE shows sportswashing in action'. *The Guardian*, 24 November 2018.

24 Conn, David. *Richer Than God: Manchester City, Modern Football and Growing Up.* Quercus, 2012.

25 Davidson, Christopher M. *Abu Dhabi: Oil and Beyond.* Hurst and Company, 2009.

26 Harris, Paul. 'Outrage at acquittal of Abu Dhabi sheikh in "torture" tape'. *The Guardian*, 17 Janaury 2010.

27 Montague, James. *The Billionaires Club: The Unstoppable Rise of Football's Super-rich Owners.* Bloomsbury Publishing, 2018.

28 Conn, David. *Richer Than God: Manchester City, Modern Football and Growing Up.* Quercus, 2012.

29 Ramesh, Randeep. 'UAE told UK: crack down on Muslim Brotherhood or lose arms deals'. *The Guardian*, 6 November 2015.

30 Clegg, Jonathan & Robinson, Joshua. *The Club: How the Premier League Became the Richest, Most Disruptive Business in Sport.* John Murray Press, 2018.

31 Halliday, Josh. 'Burson-Marsteller: PR firm at centre of Facebook row'. *The Guardian*, 12 May 2011.

Chapter 5 – Drinking It In

1 Conn, David. *Richer Than God: Manchester City, Modern Football and Growing Up.* Quercus, 2012.

2 Ibid.

3 Ibid.

4 Clegg, Jonathan & Robinson, Joshua. *The Club: How the Premier League Became the Richest, Most Disruptive Business in Sport.* John Murray Press, 2018.

5 Carragher, Jamie. *The Greatest Games.* Transworld, 2020.

6 Der Spiegel. 'Chapter 2: The Secret "Project Longbow"'. *Spiegel International*, 6 November 2018.

7   Clegg, Jonathan & Robinson, Joshua. *The Club: How the Premier League Became the Richest, Most Disruptive Business in Sport.* John Murray Press, 2018.

8   Soriano, Ferran. *Goal: The Ball Doesn't Go In By Chance.* Palgrave Macmillan UK, 2011.

9   Der Spiegel. 'Carlos Tevez in Manchester: A Dubious Transfer Gone Sour'. *Spiegel International*, 13 November 2018.

10 Taylor, Daniel, et al. 'Welcome to Manchester – the real Carlos Tevez story'. *The Athletic*, 6 January 2020.

11 Rich, Tim. 'Sir Alex Ferguson refuses to accept "small club" Manchester City as a threat'. *The Guardian*, 26 July 2009.

12 Onuoha, Nedum. *Kicking Back.* Biteback Publishing, 2022.

13 Buschmann, Rafael; Naber, Nicola & Winterbach, Christoph. 'Manchester City's Cozy Ties to Abu Dhabi: Sponsorship Money – Paid for by the State'. *Spiegel International*, 7 April 2022.

14 Der Spiegel. 'Chapter 4: A Global Empire'. *Spiegel International*, 8 November 2018.

15 Ibid.

16 Hytner, David. 'Mario Balotelli: I don't like Manchester and I'm homesick'. *The Guardian*, 1 August 2011.

17 BBC Sport. 'Carlos Tevez says Roberto Mancini treated him "like a dog"'. *BBC Sport*, 13 February 2012.

18 Lowe, Sid. 'Carlos Tevez launches explosive attack on "boot-licking moron" Gary Neville'. *The Guardian*, 21 January 2010.

19 Clegg, Jonathan & Robinson, Joshua. *The Club: How the Premier League Became the Richest, Most Disruptive Business in Sport.* John Murray Press, 2018.

20 Carragher, Jamie. *The Greatest Games.* Transworld, 2020.

21 Carrick, Michael. *Michael Carrick: Between the Lines.* Blink Publishing, 2018.

22 Carragher, Jamie. *The Greatest Games.* Transworld, 2020.

23 Conn, David. *Richer Than God: Manchester City, Modern Football and Growing Up.* Quercus, 2012.

24 Williams, Jennifer. 'Manchester City to put new sports village on map with giant signs visible from above'. *Manchester Evening News*, 8 January 2015.

25 Wearing, David. *AngloArabia: Why Gulf Wealth Matters to Britain.* Polity Press, 2018.

26 Conn, David. *Richer Than God: Manchester City, Modern Football and Growing Up.* Quercus, 2012.

27 Tremlett, Giles. 'Manchester City's plan for global domination'. *The Guardian*, 15 December 2017.

28 https://www.theguardian.com/news/2017/dec/15/manchester-city-football-group-ferran-soriano

29 Soriano, Ferran. *Goal: The Ball Doesn't Go In By Chance*. Palgrave Macmillan UK, 2011.

30 Tremlett, Giles. 'Manchester City's plan for global domination'. *The Guardian*, 15 December 2017.

31 Gov.UK Find and Update Company Information. 'City Football Group Limited 08355862': find-and-update.company-information.service.gov.uk/company/08355862

32 Tremlett, Giles. 'Manchester City's plan for global domination'. *The Guardian*, 15 December 2017.

33 Schetzer, Alana. 'Melbourne suburban club defies UK juggernaut on name'. *The Sydney Morning Herald*, 24 February 2014.

34 Der Spiegel. 'Chapter 4: A Global Empire'. *Spiegel International*, 8 November 2018.

35 Tremlett, Giles. 'Manchester City's plan for global domination'. *The Guardian*, 15 December 2017.

Chapter 6 – How the World Cup Was Bought

1 Ziegler, Martyn. 'Sepp Blatter: Giving World Cup 2022 to Qatar was a mistake'. *The Times*, 8 November 2022.

2 Panja, Tariq & Smith, Rory. 'The World Cup that Changed Everything'. *The New York Times*, 19 November 2022.

3 Ziegler, Martyn. 'What does Michel Platini's detention mean for the Qatar World Cup?'. *The Times*, 18 June 2019.

4 Blake, Heidi & Calvert, Jonathan. *The Ugly Game*. Simon & Schuster UK, 2015.

5 Ziegler, Martyn. 'Michel Platini held over Qatar World Cup bid'. *The Times*, 19 June 2019.

6 Pitt-Brooke, Jack, et al. 'No final glory but PSG are now part of Europe's elite – and they're here to stay'. *The Athletic*, 24 August 2020.

7 Ziegler, Martyn. 'Qataris get dream World Cup final – for $200bn'. *The Times*, 17 December 2022.

8 Abbot, Sebastian. *The Away Game*. Arena Sport, 2018.

9 Wearing, David. *AngloArabia: Why Gulf Wealth Matters to Britain*. Polity Press, 2018.

10 Ramesh, Randeep. 'The long-running family rivalries behind the Qatar

crisis'. *The Guardian*, 21 July 2017.

11 Hope, Bradley & Scheck, Justin. *Blood and Oil: Mohammed bin Salman's Ruthless Quest for Global Power*. John Murray Press, 2020.

12 Abbot, Sebastian. *The Away Game*. Arena Sport, 2018.

13 Ibid.

14 Mason, Rowena. 'Wikileaks: Qatar asked Shell and ExxonMobil for donations'. *The Telegraph*, 22 March 2011.

15 Miller, Rory. *Desert Kingdoms to Global Powers: The Rise of the Arab Gulf*. Yale University Press, 2016.

16 Blaschke, Ronny. *Power Players: Football in Propaganda, War and Revolution*. Pitch Publishing, 2022.

17 Goldblatt, David. *The Age of Football: The Global Game in the Twenty-first Century*. Pan Macmillan, 2019.

18 BBC Sport. 'Fifa rules on eligibility'. *BBC Sport Football*, 18 March 2004.

19 Abbot, Sebastian. *The Away Game*. Arena Sport, 2018.

20 Ibid.

21 Goldblatt, David. *The Age of Football: The Global Game in the Twenty-first Century*. Pan Macmillan, 2019.

22 Ibid.

23 Abbot, Sebastian. *The Away Game*. Arena Sport, 2018.

24 Gillis, Richard; Oliver, Brian & Briggs, Nialls. 'Spoil Sports'. *The Observer*, 11 November 2007.

25 Blake, Heidi & Calvert, Jonathan. *The Ugly Game*. Simon & Schuster UK, 2015.

26 Abbot, Sebastian. *The Away Game*. Arena Sport, 2018.

27 Ibid.

28 Ronay, Barney. 'Was Aspire project a vehicle to deliver votes to Qatar's World Cup bid?'. *The Guardian*, 3 December 2022.

29 Blake, Heidi & Calvert, Jonathan. *The Ugly Game*. Simon & Schuster UK, 2015.

30 Ibid.

31 Ibid.

32 Kay, Oliver, et al. 'The story of England's 2018 World Cup bid – told by those who lived it'. *The Athletic*, 2 December 2020.

33 Ibid.

34 BBC Sport. 'Fifa abandons World Cup rotation'. *BBC Sport Football*, 29 October 2007.

35 Blake, Heidi & Calvert, Jonathan. *The Ugly Game*. Simon & Schuster UK, 2015.

36 Dorsey, James. 'FIFA World Cup: Why Did France's Zinedine Zidane

Support Qatar for 2022?' *Bleacher Report*, 9 February 2011.

37 Kuper, Simon. *Barça: The rise and fall of the club that built modern football*. Short Books, 2022.

38 Blake, Heidi & Calvert, Jonathan. *The Ugly Game*. Simon & Schuster UK, 2015.

39 Press Association. 'Qatar World Cup bid ties up exclusive Africa deal'. *The Guardian*, 7 January 2010.

40 Ronay, Barney. 'Was Aspire project a vehicle to deliver votes to Qatar's World Cup bid?'. *The Guardian*, 3 December 2022.

41 Ibid.

42 Ibid.

43 Press Releases. 'Qatar Airways Announced June 24 Launch Date For New South American Flights'. *Qatar Airways*, 29 March 2010.

44 Blake, Heidi & Calvert, Jonathan. *The Ugly Game*. Simon & Schuster UK, 2015.

45 Ibid.

46 Futterman, Matthew & Clegg, Jonathan. 'Qatar Bests U.S. Bid to Host World Cup, Kicking Up Storm'. *The Wall Street Journal*, 2 December 2010.

47 Blake, Heidi & Calvert, Jonathan. *The Ugly Game*. Simon & Schuster UK, 2015.

48 Ibid.

49 Ibid.

50 Ibid.

51 Ibid.

52 Ibid.

53 Bensinger, Ken. *Red Card*. Profile, 2018.

54 'Written evidence submitted by The Sunday Times Insight Investigations Team': time.com/wp-content/uploads/2014/12/15880.pdf

55 Uersfeld, Stephan. 'FIFA releases full Garcia report into corruption in 2018, '22 World Cup bids'. *ESPN*, 27 June 2017.

56 Corbett, James. 'Inside Russia's plot to buy the World Cup – big consequences for England'. *Off The Pitch*, 6 November 2019.

57 Ibid.

58 Blake, Heidi & Calvert, Jonathan. *The Ugly Game*. Simon & Schuster UK, 2015.

59 Guardian Sport. 'Fifa's Michel d'Hooghe says he is being treated "like a murderer"'. *The Guardian*, 2 December 2014.

60 Panja, Tariq & Draper, Kevin. 'U.S. Says FIFA Officials Were Bribed to Award World Cups to Russia and Qatar'. *The New York Times*, 6 April 2020.

61   Ibid.

62   Bensinger, Ken. *Red Card*. Profile, 2018.

63   Sputnik Mediabank #794606: sputnikmediabank.com/media/794606.
     html?context=list&list_sid=list_65673

64   Walker, Ali. 'Qatar's emir praises Vladimir Putin for World Cup support'.
     Politico, 13 October 2022.

65   Blake, Heidi & Calvert, Jonathan. *The Ugly Game*. Simon & Schuster UK,
     2015.

66   Ibid.

67   Bensinger, Ken. *Red Card*. Profile, 2018.

68   Blake, Heidi & Calvert, Jonathan. *The Ugly Game*. Simon & Schuster UK,
     2015.

69   Ibid.

70   'Written evidence submitted by The Sunday Times Insight Investigations
     Team': time.com/wp-content/uploads/2014/12/15880.pdf

71   Scott, Matt. 'Handbag gifts come back to haunt England 2018 World Cup
     bid'. *The Guardian*, 4 November 2009.

72   Ronay, Barney. 'Fifa's World Cup debacle isn't just about money – there's
     horror and death too'. *The Guardian*, 17 November 2017.

73   Miller, Rory. *Desert Kingdoms to Global Powers: The Rise of the Arab Gulf*.
     Yale University Press, 2016.

74   Ibid.

75   Ibid.

76   Clegg, Jonathan & Robinson, Joshua. *Messi vs. Ronaldo*. HarperCollins,
     2022.

77   Panja, Tariq & Smith, Rory. 'The World Cup that Changed Everything'.
     The New York Times, 19 November 2022.

78   Conn, David. *The Fall of the House of Fifa*. Random House, 2017.

79   Ibid.

80   Montague, James. *When Friday Comes*. Ebury Publishing, 2008.

81   Conn, David. 'A Sarkozy lunch, PSG and beIN sports: questions for Platini
     over Qatar 2022'. *The Guardian*, 18 June 2019.

82   Conn, David. *The Fall of the House of Fifa*. Random House, 2017.

83   Ibid.

84   Panja, Tariq & Draper, Kevin. 'U.S. Says FIFA Officials Were Bribed to
     Award World Cups to Russia and Qatar'. *The New York Times*, 6 April
     2020.

85   Montague, James. *When Friday Comes*. Ebury Publishing, 2008.

86   Conn, David. *The Fall of the House of Fifa*. Random House, 2017.

87   Ziegler, Martyn. 'World Cup: Qatar denies 2022 bid chief offered cash for

votes'. *The Times*, 9 November 2022.

88 Ibid.

89 Conn, David. *The Fall of the House of Fifa*. Random House.

90 Blake, Heidi & Calvert, Jonathan. *The Ugly Game*. Simon & Schuster UK, 2015.

91 Ibid.

92 Conway, Richard. 'Qatar 2022 World Cup a "high security risk", report claimed'. *BBC Sport*, 14 June 2014.

93 Panja, Tariq & Smith, Rory. 'The World Cup that Changed Everything'. *The New York Times*, 19 November 2022.

94 Ibid.

95 Conn, David. 'Panorama: Allegations from the BBC but silence from Fifa's accused'. The Guardian, 29 November 2010.

96 Ibid.

97 Associated Press. 'England to FIFA: Don't punish our bid'. *ESPN*, 14 November 2010.

98 Bensinger, Ken. *Red Card*. Profile, 2018.

99 Blake, Heidi & Calvert, Jonathan. *The Ugly Game*. Simon & Schuster UK, 2015.

100 Bensinger, Ken. *Red Card*. Profile, 2018.

101 'Soccer capital'. *DW*, 16 May 2010.

102 Kay, Oliver, et al. 'The story of England's 2018 World Cup bid – told by those who lived it'. *The Athletic*, 2 December 2020.

103 Gill, Kate. 'David Beckham signs £150m deal to be face of 2022 Fifa Qatar World Cup'. *Independent*, 24 October 2021.

104 Montague, James. *The Billionaires Club: The Unstoppable Rise of Football's Super-rich Owners*. Bloomsbury Publishing, 2017.

105 Dunbar, Graham. 'FIFA ends bribery case against Germany great Beckenbauer'. *AP News*, 25 February 2021.

106 Bensinger, Ken. *Red Card*. Profile, 2018.

107 Whitaker, Brian. 'How a man setting fire to himself sparked an uprising in Tunisia'. *The Guardian*, 28 December 2010.

108 Collett, Mike. '2022 World Cup will probably be in January: Sepp Blatter'. *Reuters*, 7 January 2011.

109 Jackson, Jamie. 'Asian Football Confederation chief: Qatar will host summer World Cup'. *The Guardian*, 14 January 2011.

110 Reuters. 'Soccer-Blatter to set up anti-corruption committee', *Reuters*, 2 January 2011.

111 Kelso, Paul. 'Fifa President Sepp Blatter admits Spanish and Qatar World Cup bid teams did trade votes'. *The Telegraph*, 7 February 2011.

Chapter 7 – Paris Syndrome

1   Pitt-Brooke, Jack, et al. 'No final glory but PSG are now part of Europe's elite – and they're here to stay'. *The Athletic*, 24 August 2020.
2   Elberse, Anita & Moreno Vicente, David. *Paris Saint-Germain: Building One of the World's Top Sports Brands*, Harvard Business School, July 2020.
3   Kuper, Simon. 'Can Paris Saint-Germain become the world's richest sports club?' *Financial Times*, 28 March 2014.
4   Blaschke, Ronny. *Power Players: Football in Propaganda, War and Revolution*. Pitch Publishing, 2022.
5   Conn, David. *The Fall of the House of Fifa*. Random House, 2017.
6   Gibson, Owen. 'Why PSG and the World Cup will not be enough for football-hungry Qatar'. *The Guardian*, 3 April 2014.
7   Blaschke, Ronny. *Power Players: Football in Propaganda, War and Revolution*. Pitch Publishing, 2022.
8   Goldblatt, David. *The Age of Football: The Global Game in the Twenty-first Century*. Pan Macmillan, 2019.
9   Duarte, Fernando. 'Thiago Silva gets used to great expectations with PSG and Brazil'. *The Guardian*. 6 September 2013.
10 Conn, David. 'Qatar cash is stripping French football revolution at Paris St-Germain'. *The Guardian*, 22 November 2011.
11 Guardian staff. 'David Beckham will donate all PSG wages to children's charity in Paris'. *The Guardian*, 31 January 2013.
12 Ancelotti, Carlo. *Quiet Leadership*. Penguin Books Ltd, 2016.
13 Press Association. 'Zlatan Ibrahimovic attacks 'bullshit' criticism: 'I like it in France'' *The Guardian*, 25 March 2015.
14 Fifield, Dominic. 'Chelsea's Jose Mourinho wary of threat posed by the nouveaux riches of PSG'. *The Guardian*, 1 April 2014.
15 Kuper, Simon. 'Can Paris Saint-Germain become the world's richest sports club?'. *Financial Times*, 28 March 2014.
16 Gibson, Owen. 'Manchester City and PSG cannot 'cheat' financial fair play, Uefa warns'. *The Guardian*, 4 February 2013.
17 Duff, Alex & Panja, Tariq. *Football's Secret Trade*. Wiley, 2017.
18 Wallace, Sam. 'Exclusive Peter Kenyon interview: Signing Ronaldo, transforming Chelsea and opposing FFP regulations'. *The Telegraph*, 19 July 2020.
19 Szymanski, Stefan. *Money and Football: A Soccernomics Guide*. PublicAffairs, 2015.
20 'Uefa outlines plans to clamp down on big-spending clubs'. *The Guardian*, 27 August 2009.

21 Gibson, Owen. 'Uefa set to discuss club debt rules as part of financial fair play review'. *The Guardian*, 9 October 2014.

22 Hytner, David. 'Arsene Wenger says FFP rule-breakers should be kicked out of Europe'. *The Guardian*, 8 May 2014.

23 Steinberg, Jacob. 'Arsene Wenger: FFP rules may help Arsenal but can Uefa police system?'. *The Guardian*, 7 August 2014.

24 UEFA.com. 'Financial Fair Play Regulations are approved'. *UEFA. com*, 27 May 2010: www.uefa.com/insideuefa/about-uefa/news/01e5-0ea1848137bd-b1291315b87e-1000--financial-fair-play-regulations-are-approved/#

25 Gibson, Owen. 'Manchester City accept £49m fine and transfer cap from Uefa over FFP'. *The Guardian*, 16 May 2014.

26 Der Spiegel Staff. 'How Oil Money Distorts Global Football'. *Spiegel International*, 2 November 2018.

27 Ibid.

28 Martin, Richard. 'Barcelona extend Qatar Airways sponsorship deal to 2017'. *Reuters*, 19 July 2016.

29 Press Association. 'Manchester City and Paris Saint-Germain face financial fair play fate'. *The Guardian*, 14 April 2014.

30 Der Spiegel Staff. 'How Oil Money Distorts Global Football'. *Spiegel International*, 2 November 2018.

31 Ibid.

32 Ibid.

33 Ibid.

34 'Decision of the Chief Investigator of the CFCB Investigatory Chamver: Settlement Agreement with Paris Saint-Germain Football Club', 16 May 2014: editorial.uefa.com/resources/0258-0e2dedb6bf65-df535c83724f-1000/paris_saint-germain_-_settlement_agreement_-_may_2014.pdf

35 Gibson, Owen. 'Manchester City accept £49m fine and transfer cap from Uefa over FFP'. *The Guardian*, 16 May 2014.

36 Taylor, Daniel. 'Manchester City bank record £400m sponsorship deal with Etihad Airways'. *The Guardian*, 8 July 2011.

37 Der Spiegel. 'Chapter 2: The Secret 'Project Longbow''. *Spiegel International*, 6 November 2018.

38 Ibid.

39 Gibson, Owen. 'Manchester City accept £49m fine and transfer cap from Uefa over FFP'. *The Guardian*, 16 May 2014.

40 Herbert, Ian. 'How are big-spending Manchester city set to pass Uefa's Financial Fair Play rules?'. *Independent*, 31 January 2014.

41 Der Spiegel Staff. 'How Oil Money Distorts Global Football'. *Spiegel*

International, 2 November 2018.

42 Ibid.

43 Ibid.

44 Ibid.

45 Ibid.

46 Ibid.

47 Ibid.

48 Ibid.

49 Ziegler, Martyn. 'Manchester City 'did FFP deal with Gianni Infantino''. *The Times*, 3 November 2018.

50 'Decision of the Chief Investigator of the CFCB Investigatory Chamber: Settlement Agreement with Manchester City Football Club Limited', 16 May 2014: editorial.uefa.com/resources/0258-0e2dedb2acec-2bcb 7225d41a-1000/manchester_city_fc_-_settlement_agreement_-_may_ 2014.pdf

51 Gibson, Owen. 'Manchester City accept £49m fine and transfer cap from Uefa over FFP'. *The Guardian*, 16 May 2014.

Chapter 8 – Cirque du Qatar

1 Delaney, Miguel. 'Remembering la remontada: Barcelona 6-1 Paris Saint-Germain'. *Independent*, 16 February 2021.

2 Burt, Jason. 'Exclusive: Nasser Al-Khelaifi reveals how Neymar and Mbappe can help PSG take on the world'. *The Telegraph*, 11 September 2017.

3 Saeed, Saim. 'Macron looks forward to Neymar's arrival at PSG'. *Politico*, 3 August 2017.

4 Buschmann, Rafael & Wulzinger, Michael. *Football Leaks: Uncovering the Dirty Deals Behind the Beautiful Game*. Guardian Faber Publishing, 2018.

5 Ibid.

6 Kuper, Simon. *Barça: The rise and fall of the club that built modern football*. Short Books, 2022.

7 Buschmann, Rafael & Wulzinger, Michael. *Football Leaks: Uncovering the Dirty Deals Behind the Beautiful Game*. Guardian Faber Publishing, 2018.

8 Ibid.

9 Elberse, Anita & Moreno Vicente, David. *Paris Saint-Germain: Building One of the World's Top Sports Brands*, Harvard Business School, July 2020.

10 Conn, David. 'Uefa opens formal FFP investigation into PSG's transfer activity'. *The Guardian*, 1 September 2017.

11 Brewin, John. 'PSG, Neymar 'peeing' in the 'swimming pool' – La Liga

president Javier Tebas'. *ESPN*, 6 September 2017,

12 Montague, James. *When Friday Comes*. Ebury Publishing, 2008.

13 Hope, Bradley & Scheck, Justin. *Blood and Oil: Mohammed bin Salman's Ruthless Quest for Global Power*. John Murray Press, 2020.

14 Ramesh, Randeep. 'The long-running family rivalries behind the Qatar crisis'. *The Guardian*, 21 July 2017.

15 Mortimer, Caroline. 'UAE Crown Prince asked the US to bomb Al Jazeera during war on terror'. *Independent*, 29 June 2017.

16 Montague, James. *When Friday Comes*. Ebury Publishing, 2008.

17 Hope, Bradley & Scheck, Justin. *Blood and Oil: Mohammed bin Salman's Ruthless Quest for Global Power*. John Murray Press, 2020.

18 Miller, Rory. *Desert Kingdoms to Global Powers: The Rise of the Arab Gulf*. Yale University Press, 2016.

19 Ramesh, Randeep. 'UAE told UK: crack down on Muslim Brotherhood or lose arms deals'. *The Guardian*, 6 November 2015.

20 Miller, Rory. *Desert Kingdoms to Global Powers: The Rise of the Arab Gulf*. Yale University Press, 2016.

21 https://www.theguardian.com/commentisfree/2013/feb/03/qatar-tiny-gulf-state-global-force

22 Montague, James. *When Friday Comes*. Ebury Publishing, 2008.

23 Hope, Bradley & Scheck, Justin. *Blood and Oil: Mohammed bin Salman's Ruthless Quest for Global Power*. John Murray Press, 2020.

24 Wintour, Patrick. 'Donald Trump tweets support for blockade imposed on Qatar'. *The Guardian*, 6 June 2017.

25 'Qatar says state news agency hacked after report cites emir criticizing US'. *BBC News*, 24 May 2017.

26 Hope, Bradley & Scheck, Justin. *Blood and Oil: Mohammed bin Salman's Ruthless Quest for Global Power*. John Murray Press, 2020.

27 Holden, Michael. 'NSO ended Pegasus contract with UAE over Dubai leader's hacking'. *Reuters*, 6 October 2021.

28 Hope, Bradley & Scheck, Justin. *Blood and Oil: Mohammed bin Salman's Ruthless Quest for Global Power*. John Murray Press, 2020.

29 Wearing, David. *AngloArabia*. Polity Press, 2018.

30 Hope, Bradley & Scheck, Justin. *Blood and Oil: Mohammed bin Salman's Ruthless Quest for Global Power*. John Murray Press, 2020.

31 Ziegler, Martyn. 'Just five years to solve issues plaguing the Qatar World Cup. *The Times*, 20 November 2017.

32 Blaschke, Ronny. *Power Players: Football in Propaganda, War and Revolution*. Pitch Publishing, 2022.

33 Wearing, David. *AngloArabia*. Polity Press, 2018.

34 Hope, Bradley & Scheck, *Justin. Blood and Oil: Mohammed bin Salman's Ruthless Quest for Global Power.* John Murray Press, 2022.

35 Miller, Rory. *Desert Kingdoms to Global Powers: The Rise of the Arab Gulf.* Yale University Press, 2016.

36 Ziegler, Martyn. 'Fifa president Gianni Infantino wants 48-team World Cup in Qatar 2022, not 2026'. *The Times*, 31 October 2018.

37 Panja, Tariq. 'FIFA considering Oman and Kuwait to Host Some 2022 World Cup Games'. The Ney York Times, 6 March 2019.

38 Montague, James. *When Friday Comes.* Ebury Publishing, 2008.

39 Grim, Rayn & Walsh, Ben. 'Leaked Documents Expose Stunning Plan To Wage Financial War On Qatar – And Steal The World Cup'. *The Intercept*, 9 November 2017.

40 Ziegler, Martyn. 'Football has become the battleground for conflict between Qatar and Arab neighbours'. *The Times*, 22 March 2019.

41 Panja, Tariq. 'For Qatari Network beIN sports, Political Feud Spills Into Stadiums'. *The New York Times*, 11 September 2017.

42 Ziegler, Martyn. 'World Cup: Saudi Arabia to take legal action over beIN Sports 'biased coverage' of defeat by Russia'. *The Times*, 15 June 2018.

43 Zieglar, Martyn. 'Qatar TV matches pirated'. *The Times*, 10 May 2018.

44 Ziegler, Martyn. 'Saudi Arabia mocked Qatar with piracy of £500m rights'. *The Times*, 22 April 2020.

45 Ziegler, Martyn. 'Uefa and Saudi Arabia row over pirate station showing World Cup matches'. *The Times*, 22 June 2018.

46 UEFA. 'Joint statement by FIFA, the AFC, UEFA, the Bundesliga, LaLiga, the Premier League and Lega Serie A regarding activities of beoutQ in Saudia Arabia'. *UEFA.com*, 21 July 2019.

47 Seward, Jordan. "At Manchester City, Pep Guardiola is in charge. At PSG, Neymar has to be': Unai Emery says he had to change because Brazilian star was the 'leader'". *DailyMail*, 26 May 2018.

48 Crafton, Adam. 'Good luck, Tuchel. Can you ever really manage a team of superstars?' *The Athletic*, 19 September 2019.

49 Burt, Jason. 'PSG want Neymar to stay as long as performances improve beyond current level of '60 per cent''. *The Telegraph*, 25 June 2019.

50 Burt, Jason. 'Neymar is treated like a king at Paris Saint-Germain – so Real Madrid's pursuit already looks a lost cause'. *The Telegraph*, 12 February 2018.

51 Burt, Jason. 'The show poiny who became captain: How Neymar grew up at PSG'. *The Telegraph*, 27 April 2021.

52 Burt, Jason. 'PSG want Neymar to stay as long as performances improve beyond current level of '60 per cent''. *The Telegraph*, 25 June 2019.

53 Crafton, Adam. 'How can Lyon still compete in the age of the superclub?'. *The Athletic*, 14 August 2020.

54 Burt, Jason. '"We have big ambitions': PSG primed to take final step into Europe's elite – and their lofty goals do not stop there'. *The Telegraph*, 22 August 2020.

55 Kuper, Simon. *Barça: The rise and fall of the club that built modern football*. Short Books, 2020.

56 Marsden, Sam. 'Neymar court date over Barcelona's non-payment of loyalty bonus delayed'. *ESPN*, 29 January 2019.

57 Burt, Jason. 'Neymar linked with return to Barcelona after PSG president says he 'no longer wants superstar behaviour' at club'. *The Telegraph*, 18 June 2019.

58 Pitt-Brooke, Jack, et al. 'No final glory but PSG are now part of Europe's elite – and they're here to stay'. *The Athletic*, 24 August 2020

59 Crafton, Adam. 'How Paris Saint-Germain signed Lionel Messi'. *The Athletic*, 10 August 2021.

60 Ronay, Barney. 'PSG and Messi struggling to adjust to one another as City rematch looms'. *The Guardian*, 27 September 2021.

61 Guardian Sport. 'Neymar claims he and Lionel Messi 'lived through hell' at PSG'. *The Guardian*, 4 September 2023.

62 Elberse, Anita & Moreno Vicente, David. *Paris Saint-Germain: Building One of the World's Top Sports Brands*, Harvard Business School, 2020.

63 Burt, Jason. 'Revealed: PSG's plan to infiltrate English football – and take over the world'. *The Telegraph*, 9 March 2022.

64 Burt, Jason. 'Neymar linked with return to Barcelona after PSG president says he 'no longer wants superstar behaviour' at club'. *The Telegraph*, 18 June 2019.

65 Crafton, Adam & Hay, Anthony. 'PSG president: We don't want flashy, bling-bling anymore'. *The Athletic*, 21 June 2022.

66 Panja, Tariq. 'At Top of European Soccer, Fears That Rules Don't Apply to All.' *The New York Times*, 24 August 2022.

67 Ibid.

68 Garcia, Adriana. 'PSG president Nasser Al-Khelaifi has 'too many conflicts of interest' – LaLiga chief'. *ESPN*, 25 May 2022.

69 Crafton, Adam & Hay, Anthony. 'PSG president: We don't want flashy, bling-bling anymore'. *The Athletic*, 21 June 2022.

70 Burt, Jason. 'Revealed: PSG's plan to infiltrate English football – and take over the world'. *The Telegraph*, 9 March 2022.

71 Elberse, Anita & Moreno Vicente, David. *Paris Saint-Germain: Building One of the World's Top Sports Brands*, Harvard Business School, 2020.

72 Clegg, Jonathan & Robinson, Joshua. *Messi vs. Ronaldo: One Rivalry, Two GOATs, and the Era That Remade the World's Game.* HarperCollins, 2022.
73 Smith, Matthew. 'Paris St Germain heroes including Neymarand Kylian Mbappe join forces with the Justic League in promotional video for new DC Comics film'. *DailyMail*, 10 November 2017.
74 Elberse, Anita & Moreno Vicente, David. *Paris Saint-Germain: Building One of the World's Top Sports Brands*, Harvard Business School, 2020.
75 Panja, Tariq. 'In P.S.G. Case, Documents show UEFA Surrendered Without a Fight'. *The New York Times*, 24 July 2019.
76 Ibid.
77 Sky Sports. 'PSG avoid UEFA punishment over FFP rules'. *Sky Sports*, 13 June 2018.
78 Zieglar, Martyn. 'Uefa financial fair play official Petros Mavroidis quits over treatment of Paris Saint Germain'. *The Times*, 16 September 2019.
79 Panja, Tariq. 'As Its Stars Shone at the World Cup, P.S.G. Scrambled to Avoid Financial Punishment'. *The New York Times*, 1 July 2018.
80 Crafton, Adam. "'The Super Bowl should not feel bigger than the Champions League' – PSG's Nasser Al-Khelaifi on how he wants to grow the game'. *The Athletic*, 4 April 2022.

Chapter 9 – Flawed Perfection

1 https://www.dailymail.co.uk/sport/football/article-7042429/Guardiola-Man-City-not-respect-United-Liverpool.html
2 Press Association. 'Manchester City are trying to poach our staff, says the Barcelona president'. *The Guardian*, 15 January 2013.
3 Martin, Lu & Ballus, Pol. *Pep's City: The Making of a Superteam*. BackPage and Polaris, 2019.
4 Ibid.
5 Der Spiegel. 'Chapter 3: Recruiting Pep Guardiola'. *SPIEGEL International*, 7 November 2018.
6 Buschmann, Rafael & Winterbach, Christoph. "'Why Do We Need to Change Anything at All?'. *SPIEGEL International*, 31 May 2019.
7 Perarnau, Martí. *Pep Confidential: The Inside Story of Pep Guardiola's First Season at Bayern Munich.* Birlinn, 2014.
8 Hampson, Andy. 'Pep Guardiola says Manchester City job is 'everything a manager could dream of''. *Independent*, 30 January 2024.
9 Perarnau, Martí. *Pep Confidential: The Inside Story of Pep Guardiola's First Season at Bayern Munich.* Birlinn, 2014.

10 Clegg, Jonathan & Robinson, Joshua. *The Club: How the Premier League Became the Richest, Most Disruptive Business in Sport.* John Murray Press, 2022.

11 Wilson, Jonathan. *The Barcelona Legacy: Guardiola, Mourinho and the Fight For Football's Soul.* Blink Publishing, 2018.

12 Martin, Lu & Ballus, Pol. *Pep's City: The Making of a Superteam.* BackPage and Polaris, 2019.

13 Balague, Guillem. *Pep Guardiola: Another Way of Winning: The Biography.* Orion, 2012.

14 Martin, Lu & Ballus, Pol. *Pep's City: The Making of a Superteam.* BackPage and Polaris, 2019.

15 Ibid.

16 Perarnau, Martí. *Pep Confidential: The Inside Story of Pep Guardiola's First Season at Bayern Munich.* Birlinn, 2014.

17 De Bruyne, Kevin. 'Let Me Talk'. *The Player's Tribune*, 15 April 2019.

18 Clegg, Jonathan & Robinson, Joshua. *The Club: How the Premier League Became the Richest, Most Disruptive Business in Sport.* John Murray Press, 2022.

19 Stafford-Bloor, Sebastian. 'Why £34m agent fees in Haaland deal could soon be a thing of the past'. *The Athletic*, 13 May 2022.

20 Martin, Lu & Ballus, Pol. *Pep's City: The Making of a Superteam.* BackPage and Polaris, 2019.

21 Manchester City, Twitter, 20 May 2023: twitter.com/ManCity/status/1659993727224487936

22 Jack Grealish, Twitter, 13 June 2023: twitter.com/JackGrealish/status/1668609600843595778

23 Ziegler, Martyn. 'Manchester City wage bill rises to English-record £351m'. *The Times*, 9 April 2021.

24 GiveMeSport. 'Pep Guardiola's speech to Man City players after winning 17/18 PL title goes viral again'. *OneFootball*, 13 January 2022.

25 Hunter, Andy. 'Manchester City 'can do what they want' financially despite FFP, Klopp claims'. *The Guardian*, 14 October 2022.

26 Kompany, Vincent. *Treble Triumph.* Simon & Schuster UK, 2019.

27 Harris, Nick. 'New evidence shows Manchester City may have inflated income to get around Premier League financial rules ... so how did Sheikh Mansour's club earn £600m more than their rivals?'. *DailyMail*, 24 July 2021.

28 Manchester City, 'Our Partners': https://www.mancity.com/club/partners

29 Crafton, Adam. 'Special report: Manchester City's sponsors, the links to Abu Dhabi and what it means for Newcastle United'. *The Athletic*, 17

February 2022.

30 Mubadala, Press Releases. 'Nexen Tire and Mubadala Investment Company Sign Memorandum of Understanding'. 20 July 2017: www.mubadala.com/en/news/nexen-tire-and-mubadala-investment-company-sign-memorandum-understanding

31 Crafton, Adam. 'Special report: Manchester City's sponsors, the links to Abu Dhabi and what it means for Newcastle United'. *The Athletic*, 17 February 2022.

32 Martin, Lu & Ballus, Pol. *Pep's City: The Making of a Superteam*. BackPage and Polaris, 2019.

33 Deloitte, *Deloitte Football Money League 2024*, 16 March 2022.

34 Crafton, Adam. 'Special report: Manchester City's sponsors, the links to Abu Dhabi and what it means for Newcastle United'. *The Athletic*, 17 February 2022.

35 Ziegler, Martyn. 'Manchester City under fire for loan deals'. *The Times*, 7 September 2017.

36 Der Spiegel. 'How Clubs Profit By Exploiting Young African Talent'. *SPIEGEL International*, 9 November 2018.

37 Wallace, Sam. 'Expansion of City Football Group knows no limits – question is why they bother'. *The Telegraph*, 28 November 2019.

38 Long, Michael. 'City Football Group posts UK £112m loss despite record revenue'. *SportsProMedia*, 9 April 2024.

39 Ziegler, Martyn. 'Manchester City owners sell £389m stake in football group to US investors'. *The Times*, 27 November 2019.

40 Clegg, Jonathan & Robinson, Joshua. *The Club: How the Premier League Became the Richest, Most Disruptive Business in Sport*. John Murray Press, 2022.

41 https://www.theguardian.com/football/2018/nov/10/manchester-city-amnesty-international-football-leaks

42 Clegg, Jonathan & Robinson, Joshua. *The Club: How the Premier League Became the Richest, Most Disruptive Business in Sport*. John Murray Press, 2022.

43 Observer Sport. 'Amnesty turns the heat up on 'sportswashing' Manchester City owners'. *The Guardian*, 10 November 2018.

44 Pod Save the UK. Twitter, 23 June 2023: twitter.com/podsavetheuk/status/1672200055690780672

45 Collins, David. 'Manchester, the city that sold out to Abu Dhabi.' *The Times*, 24 November 2019.

46 Chakrabortty, Aditya. 'How a great English city sold itself to Abu Dhabi's elite – and not even for a good price'. *The Guardian*, 21 July 2022.

47 Pidd, Helen. 'Housing crisis: 15,000 new Manchester homes and not a single one 'affordable''. *The Guardian*, 5 March 2018.

48 Chakrabortty, Aditya. 'How a great English city sold itself to Abu Dhabi's elite – and not even for a good price'. *The Guardian*, 21 July 2022.

49 'Letters to the Editor: Firms exploiting slaves will be found out'. *The Times*, 29 December 2019.

50 Delaney, Miguel. 'Public land sold to Manchester City's owners on the cheap in 'sweetheart deal,' report claims'. *Independent*, 22 July 2022.

51 'Sir Howard Bernstein appointed Strategic Development Advisor'. City-Football, 7 November 2017.

52 Wintour, Patrick & Batty, David. 'Matthew Hedges: pardoned British academic arrives back in UK'. *The Guardian*, 27 November 2018.

53 Piers Morgan, Twitter, 22 November 2018: twitter.com/piersmorgan/status/1065507115744329729

54 Frank Conde Tangberg, Twitter, 3 June 2023: twitter.com/frankctangberg/status/1664940088717979650

55 'Press Releases. UK: protest plan flown over Man City ground to highlight case of jailed Emirati activist'. Amnesty International UK, 25 November 2023.

56 Delaney, Miguel. 'Box office Erling Haaland's persuasive power stretches far beyond pitch for Man City'. *Independent*, 14 October 2022.

57 Kompany, Vincent. *Treble Triumph*. Simon & Schuster UK, 2019.

58 Crafton, Adam. 'Manchester City, Premier League champions*?' *The Athletic*, 22 May 2023.

59 Ingle, Sean. 'Manchester City and PSG should be thrown out of Europe, says La Liga president'. *The Guardian*, 21 May 2019.

60 Jackson, Jamie. 'Rivals are jealous of Manchester City, says chairman Khaldoon Mubarak'. *The Guardian*, 26 May 2019.

61 McGeehan, Nicholas. ' . . ..football just got a little bit dirtier.' *Medium*. 22 July 2019.

62 Delaney, Miguel. ''A dangerous mess': Uefa under more pressure from fans after Champions League final chaos'. *Independent*, 11 June 2023.

63 Anastas, Katia. 'Turkey's Tilt: Erdogan, Deteriorating Democracy, and the West's Role'. *Harvard Political Review*, 21 August 2023.

64 Saif B Zayed, Twitter, 11 June 2023: twitter.com/SaifBZayed/status/1667768970806546433

65 Ziegler, Martyn. 'Government confirms Abu Dhabi talks over Manchester City charges'. *The Times*, 22 September 2023.

66 Der Spiegel. 'Chapter 1: Bending the Rules to the Tune of Millions'. *SPIEGEL International*, 5 November 2018.

67 Ibid.

68 Ibid.

69 Der Spiegel. 'How Oil Money Distorts Global Football'. *SPIEGEL International*, 2 November 2018.

70 Conn, David. 'From desert skyscrapers to Manchester City's sky blue land of riches'. *The Guardian*, 18 Septemebr 2009.

71 Arbitral Award, CAS 2020/A/6785 Manchester City FC v. UEFA, Court of Arbitration for Sport, 13 July 2020: https://www.tas-cas.org/fileadmin/user_upload/CAS_Award_6785___internet__.pdf

72 Ziegler, Martyn & Joyce, Paul. 'Premier League says it is investigating City after rival clubs demand action'. *The Times*, 8 March 2019.

73 Der Spiegel. 'Chapter 1: Bending the Rules to the Tune of Millions'. *SPIEGEL International*, 5 November 2018.

74 Ibid.

75 Ibid.

76 Ibid.

77 Ibid.

78 Ibid.

79 Britain's Biggest Football Scandal. 'Britain's Biggest Football Scandal?'. YouTube, 29 June 2023: www.youtube.com/watch?v=LlLRWw47HOk

80 Ibid.

81 Ibid.

82 Der Spiegel. 'Chapter 1: Bending the Rules to the Tune of Millions'. *SPIEGEL International*, 5 November 2018.

83 Ibid.

84 Der Spiegel. 'Chapter 2: The Secret 'Project Longbow''. *SPIEGEL International*, 6 November 2018.

85 Ibid.

86 Ziegler, Martyn. 'Uefa: we can reinvestigate City 'breach' of financial fair play regulations'. *The Times*, 13 November 2018.

87 Der Spiegel. 'Chapter 2: The Secret 'Project Longbow''. *SPIEGEL International*, 6 November 2018.

88 Ziegler, Martyn. 'Why Super League collapse if fuelling Liverpool owners' £4bn exit plan'. *The Times*, 7 November 2022.

89 Panja, Tariq. 'President of Spanish Soccer League Lashes Out at Rivals, and Partners'. *The New York Times*, 6 November 2018.

90 Britain's Biggest Football Scandal. 'Britain's Biggest Football Scandal?'. YouTube, 29 June 2023: www.youtube.com/watch?v=LlLRWw47HOk

91 Ziegler, Martyn. 'Uefa chief confirms Manchester City could be banned from European football'. *The Times*, 3 January 2019.

92 Joyce, Paul & Ziegler, Martyn. 'Premier League says it is investigating City after rival clubs demand action'. *The Times*, 8 March 2019.

93 Ziegler, Martyn. 'Manchester City refusing to co-operate with FFP investigation'. *The Times*, 17 January 2019.

94 Ziegler, Martyn. 'Manchester City strategy of saying nothing lands huge win'. *The Times*, 14 July 2020.

95 Panja, Tariq. 'Manchester City and the Bruising Battle to Avoid Losing It All'. *The New York Times*, 15 February 2023.

96 Panja, Tariq. 'Manchester City Cited Media Leaks in Failed Bid to Avoid Ban'. *The New York Times*, 13 February 2023.

97 Ziegler, Martyn. 'Manchester City demanded damages from 'unlawful' Uefa after Champions League ban recommendation, court documents reveal'. *The Times*, 13 February 2020.

98 Wallace, Sam. 'Expansion of City Football Group knows no limits – the question is why they bother'. *The Telegraph*, 28 November 2019.

99 Panja, Tariq. 'Manchester City Defiant Despite Champions League Ban', The New York Times, 19 February 2020.

100 Arbitral Award, CAS 2020/A/6785 Manchester City FC v. UEFA, Court of Arbitration for Sport, 13 July 2020: https://www.tas-cas.org/fileadmin/user_upload/CAS_Award_6785___internet__.pdf

101 Britain's Biggest Football Scandal. 'Britain's Biggest Football Scandal?'. YouTube, 29 June 2023: www.youtube.com/watch?v=LlLRWw47HOk

102 Ziegler, Martyn & Lawton, Matt. 'Man City accused over £30m 'sponsorship' payments'. *The Times*, 29 June 2023.

103 Britain's Biggest Football Scandal. 'Britain's Biggest Football Scandal?'. YouTube, 29 June 2023: www.youtube.com/watch?v=LlLRWw47HOk

104 Ibid.

105 Ziegler, Martyn & Lawton, Matt. 'Manchester City hit with two-year Champions League ban and Premier League punishment could follow'. *The Times*, 15 February 2020.

106 Britain's Biggest Football Scandal. 'Britain's Biggest Football Scandal?'. YouTube, 29 June 2023: www.youtube.com/watch?v=LlLRWw47HOk

107 Wallace, Sam. 'The truth about Manchester City's legal battles over FFP? Uefa blew it'. *The Telegraph*, 10 June 2023.

108 Ziegler, Martyn & Jacob, Gary. 'Pep Guardiola welcomes Uefa investigation on Manchester City'. *The Times*, 5 December 2018.

109 Lee, Sam; Ornstein, David & Crafton, Adam. "We have to show we are talent not money' – how Guardiola, Soriano and City's players reacted to the ban as club study rivals' finances'. *The Athletic*, 16 February 2020.

110 Ziegler, Martyn & Lawton, Matt. 'Manchester City hit with two-year

Champions League ban and Premier League punishment could follow'. *The Times*, 15 February 2020.

111 Lowe, Sid, et al. "Better late than never': European reaction to Manchester City's ban'. *The Guardian*, 15 February 2020.

112 Wallace, Sam. 'The truth about Manchester City's legal battles over FFP? Uefa blew it'. The Telegraph, 10 June 2023.

113 Ibid.

114 Arbitral Award, CAS 2020/A/6785 Manchester City FC v. UEFA, Court of Arbitration for Sport, 13 July 2020: https://www.tas-cas.org/fileadmin/user_upload/CAS_Award_6785___internet__.pdf

115 Ziegler, Martyn. 'Manchester City deserve serious reproach for obstructing FFP investigation, says CAS report'. *The Times*, 29 July 2020.

116 Britain's Biggest Football Scandal. 'Britain's Biggest Football Scandal?'. YouTube, 29 June 2023: www.youtube.com/watch?v=LlLRWw47HOk

117 Hessert, Björn. 'The duty to cooperate – questions arising from the Man City v UEFA decision'. *LawInSport*, 31 July 2020.

118 Crafton, Adam, et al. 'The story of Manchester City's five months in limbo'. *The Athletic*, 14 July 2020.

119 Joyce, Paul; Ziegler, Martyn & Jacob, Gary. "It was a bad day for football': Jürgen Klopp critical of Manchester City decision'. *The Times*, 15 July 2020.

120 Ziegler, Martyn. 'Pep Guardiola lets rip: Whispering rivals should say sorry'. *The Times*, 10 Septemebr 2020.

121 Conn, David.' 'Der Spiegel claims new Manchester City emails cast doubt on Cas verdict'. *The Guardian*, 30 July 2020.

122 Rumsby, Ben. "We know we were right': Uefa chief Aleksander Ceferin sure of Man City's FFP guilt'. *The Telegraph*, 23 January 2024.

123 Ames, Nick. "It was like I became Kim Jony-un': Aleksander Ceferin on Uefa, Super Leagues and Saudi cash'. *The Guardian*, 27 January 2024.

124 Ziegler, Martyn. 'Man City's 115 Premier League charges explained'. *The Times*, 29 June 2023.

125 Ziegler, Martyn. 'Manchester City strategy of saying nothing lands huge win'. *The Times*, 14 July 2020.

126 Delaney, Miguel. 'Man City financial investigation raises old questions and prospect of Champions League ban'. *Independent*, 23 February 2023.

127 Ibid.

128 Wallace, Sam. 'The truth about Manchester City's legal battles over FFP? Uefa blew it'. *The Telegraph*, 10 June 2023.

129 Britain's Biggest Football Scandal. 'Britain's Biggest Football Scandal?'. YouTube, 29 June 2023: www.youtube.com/watch?v=LlLRWw47HOk

130 Buschmann, Rafael; Naber, Nicola & Winterbach, Christoph. 'Sponsorship Money – Paid for by the State'. *SPIEGEL International*, 7 April 2022.

131 Ziegler, Martyn. 'Manchester City launch legal fight against Premier League charges'. *The Times*, 18 May 2023.

132 Ziegler, Martyn. 'Manchester City: the charges explained – and why it has taken so long'. *The Times*, 6 February 2023.

133 Slot, Owen. 'Are Manchester City one of greatest teams or one of greatest cheats?' *The Times*, 19 May 2023.

134 Crafton, Adam. 'Manchester Ctiy, Premier League champions*?' *The Athletic*, 22 May 2023.

135 Man City. 'Club Statement'. Man City Club News, 6 February 2023: www.mancity.com/news/club/club-statement-premier-league-63811282

136 Ziegler, Martyn; Lawton, Matt & Hirst, Paul. 'Manchester City charged by Premier League with breaking financial rules'. *The Times*, 6 February 2023.

137 Jolly, Richard. 'To Pep Guardiola, it's Man City against the world'. *Independent*, 11 February 2023.

138 Ziegler, Martyn. 'Manchester Ctiy launch legal fight against Premier League charges'. The Times, 18 May 2023.

139 Sheldon, Dan. 'Manchester City's Premier League charges discussed by UK government and its embassy in Abu Dhabi'. *The Athletic*, 22 September 2023.

140 Kerr, Simeon. 'UK on course for £10bn of UAE investment after relationship reset'. *Financial Times*, 13 January 2023.

141 Joyce, Paul; Ziegler, Martyn & Jacob, Gary. "It was a bad day for football': Jürgen Klopp critical of Manchester City decision'. *The Times*, 15 July 2020.

Chapter 10 – The Land of the Fee

1   Morgan, Tom. 'Premier League demanded extra assurances Chelsea were not owned by Saudi Arabia'. *The Telegraph*, 22 June 2023.

2   Clifford Chance. 'US Private Equity Investments in European Football'. June 2023:   www.cliffordchance.com/content/dam/cliffordchance/briefings/2023/06/us-private-equity-investments-in-european-football.pdf

3   Wallace, Sam & McGrath, Mike. 'Premier League clubs vote to ban Glazer-style big-debt takeovers'. *The Telegraph*, 14 June 2023.

4   White, Jim. 'How Manchester United's history has been shaped by Rock of Gibraltar'. *The Telegraph*, 24 October 2022.

5   Cambell, Denis & Byrne, Nicola. 'United won't answer the 99 questions'.

The Guardian, 1 February 2004.

6   Fifield, Dominic, et al. 'Glazers under siege after Old Trafford visit'. *The Guardian*, 30 June 2005.

7   Whitwell, Laurie, et al. 'The Glazers'. *The Athletic*, 26 May 2020.

8   Clegg, Jonathan & Robinson, Joshua. *The Club: How the Premier League Became the Richest, Most Disruptive Business in Sport*. John Murray Press., 2018.

9   Reuters. 'Manchester United set up luxury Davos lounge but deny it is to attract buyers'. *The Guardian*, 16 January 2023.

10 Press Association. 'Manchester United owners Glazer family to pay off £220m PIK loan'. *The Guardian*, 16 November 2010.

11 BBC. 'Manchester United shares debut in New York'. *BBC News*, 10 August 2012.

12 Blackhurst, Chris. *The World's Biggest Cash Machine: Manchester United, the Glazers, and the Struggle for Football's Soul*. Pan Macmillan, 2023.

13 Ibid.

14 Wilson, Jonathan. 'US owners understand profit but do they appreciate clubs' tradition and values?' *The Guardian*, 2 October 2023.

15 Scott, Matt. 'RBS moves to force George Gillett and Tom Hicks to sell Liverpool'. *The Guardian*, 9 September 2010.

16 Conn, David. 'Tom Hicks and George Gillett must take 'epic swindle' claim in UK'. *The Guardian*, 17 February 2011.

17 Fansler, Kyle. 'Top 5 most-watched Premier League games in US history'. *WorldSoccerTalk*, 28 December 2023.

18 FT Live. 'The Wealth Gap in European Football'. FT Live (In association with FT Scoreboard), February 2024: brxcdn.com/fts-app-storage/d6e5bd4c-9228-11eb-a414-9a67e462410e/media/original/264f0340-b47f-11ee-907e-da6f08ca277e

19 Schaerlaeckens, Leander. 'A New Wave of American Buyers Has Set Its Sights on European Soccer'. *The Ringer*, 27 January 2022.

20 Ibid.

21 Ames, Nick. 'Ipswich enter new era with £40m takeover by Gamechanger 20'. *The Guardian*, 7 April 2021.

22 Rubio, Jordan, et al. 'Every PE connection to Europe's top football clubs', *Pitchbook*, 13 November 2023.

23 Ibid.

24 Kuper, Simon & Szymanski, Stefan. *Soccernomics*. HarperCollins Publishers, 2009.

25 Hamlin, Jessica. 'More private investors take shots at sports, but do they score?' *Pitchbook*, 5 September 2023.

26 Panja, Tariq. 'Real Madrid Secures $380 Million Investment'. *The New York Times*, 19 May 2022.

27 Veth, Manuel. 'Hertha Berlin: 777 Partners Deal Under DFL Scrutiny?' *Forbes*, 8 May 2023.

28 Club Atlético de Madrid. 'Club Atlético de Madrid General Meeting unanimously agrees 181.8 million euro capital increase'. 25 June 2021.

29 Islam, Arif. 'PSG valued at 'more than €4bn' as Arctos takes minority stake'. *SportsProMedia*, 8 December 2023.

30 Linford, Maisie & Grez, Matias. 'Inter Milan taken over by US investment firm Oaktree after Chinese owners fail to repay loan'. *CNN Sports*, 22 May 2024.

31 McCarthy, Sebastian. 'Football club ownership: 'Even where you don't see it, private equity is there'. *Private Equity News*, 3 August 2023.

32 Timms, Aaron. 'The Glazers' non-exiting exit of Manchester United is the way of the future'. *The Guardian*, 5 January 2024.

33 UEFA. 'The European Club Finance and Investment Landscape'. *UEFA*: editorial.uefa.com/resources/028a-1a2f899177e2-b3619612eaa4-1000/ uefaeuropeanclubfinanceinvestmentlandscape_150224.pdf?utm_ source=substack&utm_medium=email

34 Kay, Oliver. 'Multi-club 'sharks' pose a danger to football – they should be curbed, not encouraged'. *The Athletic*, 19 March 2023.

35 Ibid.

36 Ziegler, Martyn. 'Uefa's rethink of Champions League multi-club owner-ship rules could affect Manchester United sale'. *The Times*, 14 March 2023.

37 CVC. 'LaLiga and CVC Fund VIII sign agreement to set Project Boost LaLiga in motion'. *CVC*, 13 December 2021.

38 Reuters. 'SoftBank among investors for $25 billion FIFA plan: report'. *Reuters*, 12 April 2018.

39 Delaney, Miguel. 'How modern football is broken beyond repair'. *Independent*, 12 February 2020.

40 Conn, David. *The Fall of the House of Fifa*. Random House, 2017.

41 Bensinger, Ken. *Red Card: FIFA and the Fall of the Most Powerful Men in Sports*. Profile, 2018.

42 McCourt, Ian. 'Jack Warner warns of a 'football tsunami' ahead of Fifa elections'. *The Guardian*, 28 May 2011.

43 Bensinger, Ken. *Red Card: FIFA and the Fall of the Most Powerful Men in Sports* . Profile, 2018.

44 Kelso, Paul. 'Former Fifa vice-president Jack Warner is caught on tape offering 'gifts' of £25,000 to Caribbean delegates'. *The Telegraph*, 12 October 2011.

45 Bensinger, Ken. *Red Card: FIFA and the Fall of the Most Powerful Men in Sports*. Profile, 2018.

46 Blake, Heidi & Calvert, Jonathan. *The Ugly Game: The Qatari Plot to Buy the World Cup*. Simon & Schuster UK, 2015.

47 Bensinger, Ken. *Red Card: FIFA and the Fall of the Most Powerful Men in Sports* . Profile, 201.

48 Ziegler, Martyn. 'Re-run of 2022 World Cup vote a possibility says Sepp Blatter'. *Independent*, 19 May 2011.

49 Blake, Heidi & Calvert, Jonathan. *The Ugly Game: The Qatari Plot to Buy the World Cup*. Simon & Schuster UK, 2015.

50 Ibid.

51 McCourt, Ian. 'Jack Warner warns of a 'football tsunami' ahead of Fifa elections'. *The Guardian*, 28 May 2011.

52 Reuters. 'Soccer-Blatter cleared, top FIFA officials suspended'. *Reuters*, 30 May 2011.

53 https://www.independent.co.uk/sport/football/news/crisis-what-crisis-blatter-tries-to-rise-above-corruption-claims-2291083.html

54 Bensinger, Ken. *Red Card: FIFA and the Fall of the Most Powerful Men in Sports*. Profile, 2018.

55 Scott-Elliot, Robin. 'Crisis? What crisis? Blatter tries to rise above corruption claims'. *Independent*, 31 May 2011.

56 Watt, Holly. 'Michael Garcia's resignation statement'. *The Telegraph*, 17 December 2014.

57 Bensinger, Ken. *Red Card: FIFA and the Fall of the Most Powerful Men in Sports*. Profile, 2018.

58 Neate, Rupert. 'Fifa officials pocketed $150m from 'World Cup of fraud' – US prosecuters'. *The Guardian*, 27 May 2015.

59 Gibson, Owen & Gayle, Damien, 'Fifa officials arrested on corruption charges as World Cup inquiry launched'. *The Guardian*, 27 May 2015.

60 Gibson, Owen. 'Sepp Blatter re-elected as Fifa president for fifth term'. *The Guardian*, 29 May 2015.

61 AP News. 'Text of Sepp Blatter Statement'. *AP News*, 2 June 2015.

62 Gibson, Owen. 'Sepp Blatter and Michel Platini banned from football for eight years by Fifa'. *The Guardian*, 21 December 2015.

63 Gibson, Owen. 'Fifa candidate Sheikh Salman al-Khalifa is linked to Bahrain crackdown'. *The Guardian*, 16 October 2015.

64 Bensinger, Ken. *Red Card: FIFA and the Fall of the Most Powerful Men in Sports*. Profile, 2018.

65 Goldblatt, David. *The Age of Football: The Global Game in the Twenty-first Century*. Pan Macmillan, 2019.

66 ESPN Staff. 'FIFA elects Gianni Infantino as new president ahead of Sheikh Salman'. *ESPN*, 26 February 2016.

67 Amnesty International UK. 'A Licence to Discriminate: Trump's Muslin & Refugee Ban'. *Amnesty.Org*, 6 October 2020.

68 Donald J. Trump. Twitter, 27 April 2018: twitter.com/realDonaldTrump/status/989650212380692480?lang=en

69 Fox, Emily Jane. 'How Jared Kushner Helped Bring the 2026 World Cup to North America'. *Vanity Fair*, 15 June 2018.

70 Ziegler, Martyn. 'Fifa Club World Cup may allow only 48 hours' rest'. *The Times*, 25 October 2018.

71 Crafton, Adam. 'Special report: Manchester City's sponsors, the links to Abu Dhabi and what it means for Newcastle United'. *The Athletic*, 17 February 2022.

72 Panja, Tariq. 'FIFA Pitches Multibillion-Dollar 'Project Trophy' to Seven Top Clubs'. *The New York Times*, 9 May 2018.

73 Panja, Tariq. 'In Fine Print of $25 Billion Offer, a Bid for a Stake in FIFA's Business'. *The New York Times*, 25 May 2018.

74 Panja, Tariq. 'FIFA Averts 'Institutional Crisis' by Delaying Mayor Vote'. *The New York Times*, 26 October 2018.

75 Ziegler, Martyn. 'Rugby's big investor CVC Capital Partners sets sights on football'. *The Times*, 6 December 2019.

76 Gibson, Owen. 'Premier League clubs admit to meeting over changes to Champions League'. *The Guardian*, 2 March 2016.

77 Der Spiegel. 'Bayern Munich Explored Exit from Bundesliga and Champions League'. *SPIEGEL International*, 2 November 2018.

78 Buschmann, Rafael & Winterbach, Christoph. "Why Do We Need to Change Anything at All?". *SPIEGEL International*, 31 May 2019.

79 Press Association. 'Europe's top four leagues guaranteed four Champions League places'. *The Guardian*, 26 August 2016.

80 Der Spiegel. 'Bayern Munich Explored Exit from Bundesliga and Champions League'. *SPIEGEL International*, 2 November 2018.

81 Ziegler, Martyn. 'Deal struck with Manchester City saved European football, says Fifa president Gianni Infantino'. *The Times*, 7 November 2018.

82 Ziegler, Martyn. 'Chelsea chariman Bruce Buck tells Uefa: don't turn big clubs into 'great unwashed''. *The Times*, 11 October 2018.

83 Conn, David. 'Premier League's top six win battle for larger share of overseas TV rights'. *The Guardian*, 7 June 2018.

84 Ziegler, Martyn. 'Top-flight clubs gear up to black Champions League expansion'. *The Times*, 6 April 2019.

85 Ziegler, Martyn. 'Closed NFL competition is better model than Premier

League, says Andrea Agnelli'. *The Times*, 7 June 2019.

86 Kuper, Simon. 'Barcelona after Messi'. *Financial Times*, 7 August 2021.

87 Aarons, Ed & Ingle, Sean. 'European Super League: Premier League 'big six' sign up to competition'. *The Guardian*, 18 April 2021.

88 Corrigan, Dermot. 'Florentino Perez: Reduced Real profit down to keeping hold of best players'. *ESPN*, 1 October 2017.

89 Clegg, Jonathan & Robinson, Joshua. *Messi Vs. Ronaldo*. HarperCollins, 2022.

90 Ziegler, Martyn. 'Uefa dismisses threat of Florentino Pérez-backed breakaway league'. *The Times*, 20 October 2020.

91 Ziegler, Martyn. 'Manchester United have been leading the charge for a European Super League – and Uefa fear the worst this time'. *The Times*, 22 January 2021.

92 Ziegler, Martyn. 'Impending Champions League changes 'to end breakaway talk''. *The Times*, 8 March 2021.

93 Morgan, Tom & Wallace, Sam. 'Europe's biggest clubs accused of 'stitch up' over Champions League revamp'. *The Telegraph*, 1 April 2021.

94 Panja, Tariq. 'The Super League Thought It Had a Silent Partner: FIFA'. *The New York Times*, 20 May 2021.

95 Garcia, Adriana. 'FIFA president accused of masterminding European Super League by La Liga chief'. *ESPN*, 11 May 2021.

96 Bartz, Tim, et al. 'Investors Wanted to Make €6.1 Billion with Super League'. *SPIEGEL International*, 27 April 2021.

97 Delaney, Miguel. ''He's in his own world': Florentino Perez gripped by delusion amid Super League fiasco'. *Independent*, 27 April 2021.

98 Clegg, Jonathan & Robinson, Joshua. *Messi Vs. Ronaldo*. HarperCollins, 2022.

99 Lowe, Sid. 'Galactic era that began in triumph ends in disarray'. *The Guardian*, 28 February 2006.

100 Ziegler, Martyn & Lawton, Matt. 'European Super League: Big Six breakaway plot sparks outrage'. *The Times*, 19 April 2021.

101 UEFA. 'President Čeferin: Footballing world and society stand united against closed 'Super League''. *UEFA.com*, 20 April 2021: www.uefa.com/insideuefa/about-uefa/news/0268-1215571df751-a59f73c3216f-1000--president-ceferin-footballing-world-and-society-stand-unit/

102 Zeffman, Henry. 'British envoy warned UAE not to let Manchester City play in European Super League'. *The Times*, 22 April 2021.

103 Panja, Tariq & Das, Andrew. 'JPMorgan Apologizes for Its Role in Super League'. *The New York Times*, 23 April 2021.

Chapter 11 – Meet the New Boss . . .

1   AP News. 'Text of Sepp Blatter Statement'. *AP News*, 2 June 2015.

2   Ziegler, Martyn. 'Fifa president's fury over secret record of laundry bill'. *The Times*, 14 June 2016.

3   Panja, Tariq. 'FIFA President Gianni Infantino Faces New Ethics Complaint'. *The New York Times*, 13 September 2017.

4   Gibson, Owen. 'Fifa's independent audit committee chairman resigns in protest at reforms'. *The Guardian*, 14 May 2016.

5   Ibid.

6   Conn, David. *The Fall of the House of Fifa*. Random House, 2017.

7   Ziegler, Martyn. 'Salt Bae's World Cup gatecrashing angers Fifa sponsors'. *The Times*, 17 March 2023.

8   Panja, Tariq. 'Soccer's Perpetual President: Why Gianni Infantino Can't Lose'. *The New York Times*, 15 March 2023.

9   Ziegler, Martyn. 'Fifa president's fury over secret record of laundry bill'. *The Times*, 14 June 2016.

10 Kissin, Ellesheva. 'The soccernomics of Fifa's changing sponsorship'. *FDI Intelligence*, 3 March 2023.

11 Ziegler, Martyn. 'Gianni Infantino: Rwanda's genocide recovery inspired my first election win'. *The Times*, 16 March 2023.

12 UEFA. Twitter, 3 August 2019: twitter.com/UEFA/status/1157702852413968384

13 Bensinger, Ken. *Red Card: FIFA and the Fall of the Most Powerful Men in Sports* . Profile, 2018.

14 Ziegler, Martyn. 'Tony Pulis shares wisdom with England's rugby coaches'. *The Times*, 29 February 2020.

15 Panja, Tariq. 'The Power Politics of Gianni Infantino'. *The New York Times*, 10 June 2018.

16 Ziegler, Martyn. 'Gianni Infantino: Biennial World Cup could stop African migrants dying in sea'. *The Times*, 26 January 2022.

17 Rumsby, Ben. 'Fifa's Gianni Infantino sparks controversy with 'dream' of Israel and Palestine co-hosting World Cup'. *The Telegraph*, 13 October 2021.

18 Evans, Simon. "Should we be ashamed of our success?' asks UEFA chief'. *Reuters*, 3 March 2020.

19 Soriano, Ferran. *Goal: The Ball Doesn't Go In By Chance*. Palgrave Macmillan UK, 2011.

20 Gardner, Jamie. 'Steve Parish urgers change to Champions League payments due to growing disparity'. *Independent*, 24 April 2023.

21 Wallace, Sam. 'If Europe's elite have their way, the Champions League will become a closed shop for 'big clubs' only'. *The Telegraph*, 8 March 2020.

22 Hermant, Arnaud. 'Quand le PSG et Nasser al-Khelaifi travaillaient à un project de Superligue'. *L'Équipe*, 19 February 2024.

23 Financial Times. 'Andrea Agnelli on Juventus and the Super League'. *Financial Times*, 26 January 2024.

24 Ziegler, Martyn. 'PSG president Nasser Al-Khelaifi attacks 'not-so Super League' rebels'. *The Times*, 6 September 2021.

25 Goldblatt, David & McGeehan, Nicholas. 'Brussels should join the dots between Qatargate and Manchester United'. *Politico*, 17 March 2023.

26 Vinocur, Nicholas, et al. 'When Eva met Francesco: The golden couple at the heart of Europe's Qatargate scandal'. *Politico*, 9 December 2023.

27 Ziegler, Martyn. 'PSG president Nasser Al-Khelaifi attacks 'not-so Super League' rebels'. *The Times*, 6 September 2021.

28 Burt, Jason. 'How PSG and Nasser Al-Khelaifi emerged as the big winners from Super League crisis'. *The Telegraph*, 22 April 2021.

29 Ames, Nick. "It was like I became Kim Jong-un': Aleksander Ceferin on Uefa, Super Leagues and Saudi cash'. *The Guardian*, 27 January 2024.

30 Ziegler, Martyn. 'Deal struck with Manchester City saved European football, says Fifa president Gianni Infantino'. *The Times*, 7 November 2018.

31 Buschmann, Rafael & Wulzinger, Michael. *Football Leaks: Uncovering the Dirty Deals Behind the Beautiful Game*. Guardian Faber Publishing, 2018.

32 Ziegler, Martyn. 'European clubs agree to overhaul of spending rules'. *The Times*, 28 March 2022.

33 UEFA. 'UEFA Strategy: United for Success'. *UEFA.com*: www.uefa.com/insideuefa/about-uefa/strategy/

34 Ames, Nick. "It was like I became Kim Jong-un': Aleksander Ceferin on Uefa, Super Leagues and Saudi cash'. *The Guardian*, 27 January 2024.

35 Duff, Alex & Panja, Tariq. *Football's Secret Trade*. Wiley, 2017.

36 Delaney, Miguel. 'Fifa's statement on UEC meeting reveals hidden meaning behind football's current governors'. *Independent*, 28 May 2024.

37 Garry, Tom. 'Luis Rubiales savaged by Fifa over Jenni Hermoso kiss scandal'. *The Telegraph*, 12 February 2024.

38 Ziegler, Martyn & Joyce, Paul. "Remarkable that no one lost their life' in Uefa's Champions League final shame'. *The Times*, 14 February 2023.

39 Conn, David. 'Uefa accused of presenting 'untrue' evidence to inquiry on Champions League final chaos'. *The Guardian*, 25 September 2023.

40 Delaney, Miguel. 'Football must change now after Saudi Arabia 2034 exposes 'failure' at the very top'. *Independent*, 2 November 2023.

41 Panja, Tariq. 'In Offer to Investors, FIFA Angels for Bigger Role in Club Soccer'. *The New York Times*, 12 December 2019.

42 Ziegler, Martyn. 'Gianni Infantino was open to Super League talks, claims Barcelona president'. *The Times*, 20 January 2023.

43 Bradsher, Keith & Panja, Tariq. 'In China, FIFA's Focus is Soccer, Not Human Rights'. *The New York Times*, 24 October 2019.

44 Panja, Tariq. 'The Biennial World Cup May Be Dead, but FIFA's Fight Isn't Over'. *The New York Times*, 4 April 2022.

45 Ziegler, Martyn. 'Fifa exploring new Saudi Arabia proposal to hold men's and women's World Cups every two years'. *The Times*, 22 May 2021.

46 Ziegler, Martyn. 'Uefa president Aleksander Ceferin: Europe and South America prepared to boycott biennial World Cup'. *The Times*, 9 September 2021.

47 Ziegler, Martyn. 'Uefa and Fifa at war over global competitions'. *The Times*, 15 February 2019.

48 Ronay, Barney. 'Uefa and Fifa are too late: Russia's sportswashing has served its purpose'. *The Guardian*, 25 February 2022.

49 Delaney, Miguel. 'Russia going to war finally removes football's veil of pretence'. *Independent*, 1 March 2022.

50 Panja, Tariq. 'The Power Politics of Gianni Infantino'. *The New York Times*, 10 June 2018.

51 Byrnes, Jesse. 'German lawmakers call for stripping 2018 World Cup from Russia'. *The Hill*, 23 July 2014.

52 Montague, James. *The Billionaires Club: The Unstoppable Rise of Football's Super-rich Owners*. Bloomsbury Publishing, 2018.

53 Bancroft, Holly. 'Chelsea owner Roman Abramovich sanctioned by UK government'. *Independent*, 10 March 2022.

54 Davies, Rob & Lock, Simon. 'Chelsea FC face new questions over how Roman Abramovich funded success'. *The Guardian*, 15 November 2023.

55 Foreign, Commonwealth & Development Office. 'Government announces sanctions against Russian oligarchs Alisher Usmanov and Igor Shuvalov'. *GOV.UK*, 3 March 2022.

56 The National. 'President Sheikh Mohamed welcomes Vladimir Putin to UAE on state visit'. *The National News*, 6 December 2023.

57 Roy-Chaudhury, Rahul & Hokayem, Emile. 'Understanding India and the UAE's abstentions over Ukraine'. *IISS*, 3 March 2022.

58 Delaney, Miguel. 'Uefa torn over plans to reinstate Russian youth teams'. *Independent*, 8 October 2023.

59 'Judgement of the Court'. *InfoCuria Case-Law*, 21 December 2023: curia.europa.eu/juris/document/document.jsf?docid=280765&mode=

req&pageIndex=1&dir=&occ=first&part=1&text=&doclang=EN&cid=
2518235

Chapter 12 – Kingdom Come

1   Ziegler, Martyn. 'Saudis rule out state-backed Manchester United take-over'. *The Times*, 24 November 2022.
2   Richardson, Drew. 'Saudi crown prince says he will keep 'sportswashing' as criticism of the practice grows'. *CNBC*, 21 September 2023.
3   Ziegler, Martyn, et al. 'Can Saudi Pro League change face of world football?'. *The Times*, 25 July 2023.
4   Miller, Rory. *Desert Kingdoms to Global Powers: The Rise of the Arab Gulf.* Yale University Press, 2016.
5   Hope, Bradley & Scheck, Justin. *Blood and Oil: Mohammed bin Salman's Ruthless Quest for Global Power.* John Murray Press, 2020.
6   Ibid.
7   Ibid.
8   Sweeney, Mark. 'Saudi Aramco's $161bn profit is largest recorded by an oil and gas firm'. *The Guardian*, 12 March 2023.
9   Ziegler, Martyn. 'No booze at the World Cup stadiums – unless you spend £19k on a box'. *The Times*, 9 September 2022.
10   Hope, Bradley & Scheck, Justin. *Blood and Oil: Mohammed bin Salman's Ruthless Quest for Global Power.* John Murray Press, 2020.
11   Ibid.
12   Ibid.
13   Miller, Rory. *Desert Kingdoms to Global Powers: The Rise of the Arab Gulf.* Yale University Press, 2016.
14   Hope, Bradley & Scheck, Justin. *Blood and Oil: Mohammed bin Salman's Ruthless Quest for Global Power.* John Murray Press, 2020.
15   Ibid.
16   Khashoggi, Jamal. 'Saudi Arabia wasn't always this repressive. Now it's unbearable'. *The Washington Post*, 18 September 2017.
17   Kirchgaessner, Stephanie. 'Jeff Bezos hack: Amazon boss's phone 'hacked by Saudi crown prince''. *The Guardian*, 22 January 2020.
18   BBC Sport. 'Saudi Pro League 'not a threat' and 'similar to China', says Uefa president Aleksander Ceferin'. *BBC Sport*, 31 August 2023.
19   Duerden, John. 'Carlos Tevez's big-money move to China has proved an expensive mistake'. *The Guardian*, 3 September 2017.
20   Ziegler, Martyn. 'Gianni Infantino opens door to China World Cup bid after re-election as Fifa president'. *The Times*, 5 June 2019.

21   Panja, Tariq. 'China's Soccer Experiment Was a Flop. Now It May Be Over.' *The New York Times*, 29 March 2023.

22   Duerden, John. 'China's football crisis: what happened next after Covid struck?' *The Guardian*, 18 January 2023.

23   Elsborg, Stanis. 'The expansion of Saudi investments in sport: From football to esport'. *PlaytheGame*, 12 January 2023.

24   Ziegler, Martyn. 'High Court forces Sheffield United owner Kevin McCabe to sell 50% share to Saudi royal family'. *The Times*, 16 September 2019.

25   Panja, Tariq. 'La Liga Chief Claims Saudi Arabia Is Using Sports to 'Whitewash' Reputation'. *The New York Times*, 20 January 2020.

26   Wallace, Sam. 'Money talks in Spanish Cup stitch-up'. *The Telegraph*, 12 January 2020.

27   Ibid.

28   Ziegler, Martyn. 'Uefa and Saudi Arabia row over pirate station showing World Cup matches'. *The Times*, 22 June 2018.

29   Giæver, Jonas. 'Er deter fotballens nye makthavere?' *Dagbladet*, 11 December 2022.

30   Neate, Rupert. 'Mike Ashley vomited into fireplace at pub meeting, court told'. *The Guardian*, 3 July 2017.

31   Conn, David. 'Mike Ashley says there is no Newcastle deal with Staveley: 'It's been a waste of time''. *The Guardian*, 16 January 2018.

32   Woolfson, Daniel. 'Amanda Staveley pays back £10m Newcastle United loan from Mike Ashley after row'. *The Telegraph*, 10 October 2023.

33   Taylor, Louise. 'Amnesty say Premier League 'risks being a patsy' on Newcastle takeover'. *The Guardian*, 21 April 2020.

34   Delaney, Miguel. 'Newcastle takeover: Families of campaigners held in Saudi Arabia 'beg' Premier League to block bid'. *Independent*, 12 July 2020.

35   https://www.nytimes.com/2020/04/21/sports/soccer/saudi-arabia-qatar-beIN-premier-league.html

36   Ziegler, Martyn. 'Newcastle takeover: Premier League wanted Saudi Arabia on US piracy blacklist'. *The Times*, 30 April 2020.

37   Ziegler, Martyn. 'New TWO piracy ruling threatens Saudi's Newcastle takeover bid'. *The Times*, 16 June 2020.

38   Amin, Lucas & Conn, David. 'How Tory minister aided Saudi takeover of Newcastle United'. *OpenDemocracy*, 26 September 2022.

39   Ziegler, Martyn. 'New TWO piracy ruling threatens Saudi's Newcastle takeover bid'. The Times, 16 June 2020.

40   Walters, Simon. 'Boris Johnson was lobbied by killer Saudi prince: Prime Minister acted on personal plea from Mohammed Bin Salman over 'axed'

£300m deal to buy Newcastle United football club . . . now it may be back on'. *Daily Mail*, 14 April 2021.

41 Casalicchio, Emilio & Gallardo, Cristina. 'Boris Johnson's Saudi bromance'. *Politico*, 19 March 2022.

42 Walters, Simon. "Brilliant!': Boris Johnson could barely contain his glee when he was told Newcastle deal was back on track'. *Daily Mail*, 15 April 2021.

43 Crafton, Adam. 'Newcastle's Saudi takeover: The UK government's emails revealed'. *The Athletic*, 6 April 2023.

44 Ibid.

45 Ziegler, Martyn. 'Government put pressure on Premier League to allow Newcastle United takeover'. *The Times*, 6 April 2023.

46 Amin, Lucas & Conn, David. 'How Tory minister aided Saudi takeover of Newcastle United'. OpenDemocracy, 26 September 2022.

47 Crafton, Adam. 'Newcastle's Saudi takeover: The UK government's emails revealed'. *The Athletic*, 6 April 2023.

48 Conn, David. 'Revealed: government did encourage Premier League to approve Newcastle takeover'. *The Guardian*, 24 May 2022.

49 Ziegler, Martyn. 'No government pressure to approve Newcastle takeover, insists Premier League chief executive'. *The Times*, 30 June 2020.

50 Hardy, Martin; Lawton, Matt & Ziegler, Martyn. 'The inside story of Newcastle United's Saudi takeover'. *The Times*, 10 October 2021.

51 Ziegler, Martyn & Lawton, Matt. 'Rival clubs accused of undermining Newcastle takeover as Saudis pull plug'. *The Times*, 31 July 2020.

52 McManus, John. *Inside Qatar*. Icon Books, 2022.

53 Ziegler, Martyn. 'Newcastle the only club to vote against new £367m TV deal with beIN sports'. *The Times*, 17 December 2020.

54 Crafton, Adam. 'Newcastle's Saudi takeover: The UK government's emails revealed'. *The Athletic*, 6 April 2023.

55 Ibid.

56 Ibid.

57 Sheldon, Dan, et al. 'Inside the 'incredible' Premier League meeting – and what it means for Newcastle and beyond'. *The Athletic*, 20 October 2021.

58 Human Rights Watch. 'Saudi Arabia: Mass Execution of 81 Men'. *Human Rights Watch*, 15 March 2022.

59 Hope, Craig. 'Eddie Howe admits he IS reading up on the geo-political situation in Saudi Arabia – where 81 people were beheaded last week – after the boss of Saudi-owned Newcastle was accused of dodging the issue at Chelsea'. *Daily Mail*, 16 March 2022.

60 Panja, Tariq. 'Newcastle Players, Saudi Jets and Nagging Questions for the

Premier League'. *The New York Times*, 28 January 2022.

61 Ronay, Barney. 'Newcastle being owned by a nation state: how is this accepted and normalized?'. *The Guardian*, 3 March 2023.

62 Ziegler, Martyn. 'Newcastle Saudi takeover facing scrutiny after LIV Gold court case'. *The Times*, 1 March 2023.

63 BBC Sport. 'Newcastle United: Premier League 'comfortable and satisfied' Saudi state will not interfere'. *BBC Sport*, 26 November 2021.

64 BBC Sport. 'Given hopes for Newcastle 'fairytale''. *BBC Sport*, 6 April 2023.

65 Harris, Graham. 'Aramco deal worth more than $450m to Formula 1'. *MotorSportWeek*, 11 March 2020.

66 Delaney, Miguel. 'Why Man City's FFP case could be another Super League moment for football/ *Independent*, 1 June 2023.

67 Ziegler, Martyn. 'Newcastle owners PIF take over Saudi Arabia's four biggest clubs'. *The Times*, 6 June 2023.

68 Smith, Rory; Panja, Tariq & Al Omran, Ahmed. 'Inside the Saudi Gold Rush'. *The New York Times*, 13 July 2023.

69 Whitehead, Jacob, et al. 'Saudi Arabia, football's big disruptors. The story of the money, the motive and the hidden disputes'. *The Athletic*, 12 June 2023.

70 Amnesty International UK. 'Saudi Arabia: 100 people executed as authorities continue relentless 'killing spree'. *Amnesty.Org*, 8 September 2023.

71 Ornstein, David & Crafton, Adam. 'Jordan Henderson: I strongly believe that me playing in Saudi Arabia is a positive thing'. *The Athletic*, 5 September 2023.

72 SVT Sport. 'Saudi-chefen Michael Emenalo glömmer micken på: "Hörde de min förolämpning?"'. *SVT Sport*, 12 April 2024.

73 Ames, Nick. "It was like I became Kim Jong-un': Aleksander Ceferin on Uefa, Super Leagues and Saudi cash'. *The Guardian*, 27 January 2024.

74 Peiando, Daniel. 'Toni Kroos reacts to the departure of Celta's Gabri Veiga to Saudi Arabia's Al Ahli: "shameful"'. *AS*, 24 August 2023.

75 Fletcher, Harry. 'Neymar slammed for taking a private Boeing 747 flight to Saudi Arabia'. *Indy100*, 23 August 2023.

76 Hankinson, Andrew. 'Jordan Henderson just played in front of 696 people – how small are Saudi Pro League crowds?' *The Athletic*, 28 October 2023.

77 Ziegler, Martyn. 'Saudi fury at row over World Cup sponsorship'. *The Times*, 8 March 2023.

78 Wilson, Jonathan. 'Clownish populist Infantino is complicit in Saudi Arabia's colonization of football'. *The Guardian*, 4 November 2023.

79 Gianni Infantino. Instagram, 31 October 2023: www.instagram.com/

gianni_infantino/p/CzErr6Uo1QJ/

80 Martyn, Ziegler. 'Fifa ready to walk Saudi Arabia down red carpet to 2034 World Cup'. *The Times*, 13 October 2023.

81 FIFA. 'Aramco and FIFA announce global partnership'. *InsideFIFA*, 25 April 2024.

Chapter 13 – Football Without Fans is Nothing

1 Reuters. 'Bayern Munich end deal with Qatar Airways after fan protests'. *ESPN*, 28 June 2023.

2 Hornby, Nick. *Fever Pitch*. Penguin Books, 1997.

3 Davies, William. 'A Dog in the Fight'. *London Review of Books*, Vol 45: 10, 18 May 2023.

4 Conn, David. *The Fall of the House of Fifa*. Random House, 2017.

5 Ronay, Barney. 'Manchester City fans' defence of UAE shows sportswashing in action'. *The Guardian*, 24 November 2018.

6 Delaney, Miguel. "I'm massively conflicted – I still love that football club': Newcastle fans in the face of a tarnished takeover'. *Independent*, 23 April 2020.

7 Spion Kop 1906. Twitter, 19 April 2021: twitter.com/SpionKop1906/status/1384095535854800901

8 Topping, Alexandra. "We did what fans do best – we united': how supporters' groups fought the ESL'. *The Guardian*, 23 April 2021.

9 Walker, Peter & Elgot, Jessica. 'European Super League amounts to a 'cartel', says Boris Johnson'. *The Guardian*, 20 April 2021.

10 Less, Sam. 'Manchester City, ticket price rises and why some of their fans have had enough'. *The Athletic*, 27 March 2024.

11 Hartland, Nick. "GET OUT!' – JEROME ROTHEN CALLS FOR CITY GROUP TO LEAVE FRANCE AS TROYES' SAVIO NEARS MANCHESTER CITY SWITCH'. *Get Football News France*, 6 February 2024.

12 Smith, Rory. 'Swedish Soccer Prioritized Fans Over Finances. Now, Business is Booming.' *The New York Times*, 19 November 2023.

13 Hesse, Uli. *Bayern: Creating a Global Superclub*. Random House, 2016.

14 Whitwell, Laurie. 'Manchester United takeover: Two-thirds of fans went Sir Jim Ratcliffe'. *The Athletic*, 17 February 2023.

15 EFL. 'Highest League attendances for 70 years as nearly 22 million attend EFL competitions'. *EFL*: www.efl.com/news/2023/june/highest-league-attendances-for-70-years-as-nearly-22-million-attend-efl-competitions/

Chapter 14 – Catch 2022

1   Delaney, Miguel. 'The man who was jailed after working on Qatar's World Cup'. *Independent*, 17 December 2022.

2   Spurling, Jon. *Death or Glory: The Dark History of the World Cup*. Vision Sports Publishing, 2010.

3   Whiteside, Philip. 'Cost of the Cup: The toll and cost of Qatar 2022'. *Sky News*: news.sky.com/story/qatar-2022-what-has-been-built-for-the-2022-world-cup-what-it-has-cost-in-lives-and-how-much-was-spent-on-construction-12496471

4   Delaney, Miguel. 'Everything wrong with Qatar World Cup'. *Independent*, 13 December 2022.

5   Panja, Taria & Smith, Rory. 'The World Cup That Changed Everything'. *The New York Times*, 19 November 2022.

6   Goldblatt, David. *The Age of Football: The Global Game in the Twenty-first Century*. Pan Macmillan, 2019.

7   Ziegler, Martyn. 'Qatar World Cup 'built on workers' rights abuse''. *The Times*, 31 March 2016.

8   Montague, James. *When Friday Comes*. Ebury Publishing, 2008.

9   Gibson, Owen. 'French footballer trapped in Qatar asks Guardiola and Zidane for help'. *The Guardian*, 14 November 2013.

10 Abbot, Sebastian. *The Away Game*. Arena Sport, 2018.

11 Ronay, Barney. 'Forget 'sportswashing': Qatar 2022 is about military might and hard sports power'.

12 Ziegler, Martyn. 'Just five years to solve issues plaguing the Qatar World Cup'. *The Times*, 20 November 2017.

13 Ziegler, Martyn. 'Fifa publishes bribe claims but still stands by Qatar'. *The Times*, 6 December 2019.

14 Ziegler, Martyn. 'What does Michel Platini's detention mean for the Qatar World Cup?' *The Times*, 18 June 2019.

15 Delaney, Miguel. 'Should football boycott the Qatar World Cup?' *Independent*, 24 March 2021.

16 Ziegler, Martyn. 'Norway players escape punishment for Qatar T-shirt protest replicated by Germany'. *The Times*, 26 March 2021.

17 Qatar Airways. Twitter, 29 September 2021: twitter.com/qatarairways/status/1443227778690732037

18 Walker, Ali. 'Qatar's emir praises Vladimir Putin for World Cup support'. *Politico*, 13 October 2022.

19 Ronay, Barney. 'No need for conspiracies – World Cup 2030 and 2034 are a plot in plain sight'. *The Guardian*, 6 October 2023.

20 Ronay, Barney. 'Why Qatar is done with saying sorry for human rights and equality issues'. *The Guardian*, 2 April 2022.

21 Ziegler, Martyn. 'Fifa kept quiet about North Korean stadium 'slaves' in Russia'. *The Times*, 25 May 2017.

22 Ziegler, Martyn. "Arsenal fans may be put off going to Russia due to political tension". *The Times*, 16 March 2018.

23 Ziegler, Martyn. 'World Cup: FA chiefs' short shrift for Vladimir Putin'. *The Times*, 14 June 2018.

24 Goldblatt, David. *The Age of Football: The Global Game in the Twenty-first Century*. Pan Macmillan, 2019.

25 Ibid.

26 Reevell, Patrick. 'Moscow erupts into massive street party after Russia's World Cup win'. *ABC News*, 2 July 2018.

27 Ziegler, Martyn. 'World Cup: Pro-Ukraine coach loses Croatia job'. *The Times*, 10 July 2018.

28 Panja, Tariq. 'FIFA Approves New Term for Gianni Infantino as President'. *The New York Times*, 5 June 2019.

29 Delaney, Miguel. 'Everything wrong with the Qatar World Cup'. *Independent*, 13 December 2022.

30 The Workers Cup: www.theworkerscupfilm.com/

31 Panja, Tariq. 'A Migrant's Desperate Day Chasing Work at the World Cup.' *The New York Times*, 25 November 2022.

32 Ronay, Barney. 'As Qatar's World Cup ends it is time for truth: Fifa chose death and suffering'. *The Guardian*, 16 December 2022.

33 Montague, James. *When Friday Comes*. Ebury Publishing, 2008.

34 BBC Sport. 'World Cup 2022: Will Qatar tournament be carbon neutral?'. *BBC Sport*, 23 November 2022.

35 Delaney, Miguel. 'The man who was jailed after working on Qatar's World Cup'. *Independent*, 17 December 2022.

36 Ronay, Barney. 'Gianni Infantino does his Football Jesus act during strange monologue on Qatar'. The Guardian, 19 November 2022.

37 Crafton, Adam. 'Gianni Infantino's letter about the World Cup is lamentable, irrational and dumbfoundingly stupid.' The Athletic, 4 November 2022

38 FIFA. 'FIFA President: Football can change the world'. *InsideFIFA*, 23 May 2022.

39 Delaney, Miguel. 'The man who was jailed after working on Qatar's World Cup'. *Independent*, 17 December 2022.

40 Ronay, Barney. 'The winner is . . . Qatar: curtain comes down on Project Hard Football Power'. *The Guardian*, 19 December 2022.

41 Delaney, Miguel. 'Everything wrong with the Qatar World Cup'. *Independent*, 13 December 2022.

42 BBC Sport. 'World Cup 2022: Will Qatar tournament be carbon neutral?'. *BBC Sport*, 23 November 2022.

43 MacInnes, Paul. 'Fifa misled fans over 'carbon-neutral Qatar World Cup', regulator finds'. *The Guardian*, 7 June 2023.

44 Preussen, Wilhelmine. 'Qatar to Europe: You sound arrogant and racist'. *Politico*, 7 November 2022.

45 Ziegler, Martyn. 'Gareth Southgate told to 'pick his words carefully' after criticizing Qatar'. *The Times*, 31 March 2022.

46 www.youtube.com/watch?v=9coW1A-MvBw&t=1s

47 Ziegler, Martyn. 'Gianni Infantino set to gain from FA's conditional backing for re-election'. *The Times*, 18 November 2022.

48 McNiell, Sophie. 'Australia's FIFA World Cup Team First to Collectively Back Workers, LGBT Rights'. *Human Rights Watch*, 28 October 2023.

49 Ronay, Barney. 'Louis van Gaal's final act will be a gripping piece of World Cup theatre'. *The Guardian*, 17 November 2022.

50 Panja, Tariq. 'On Eve of World Cup, FIFA Chief Says, 'Don't Criticize Qatar; Criticize Me.' *The New York Times*, 19 September 2022.

51 Wallace, Sam. 'Qatar's World Cup has come to a close – what was it all for?'. *The Telegraph*, 18 December 2022.

52 Slot, Owen; Lawton, Matt & Ziegler, Martyn. 'World Cup: Qatar bans beer at all eight stadiums'. *The Times*, 19 November 2022.

53 Panja, Tariq. 'On Eve of World Cup, FIFA Chief Says, 'Don't Criticize Qatar; Criticize Me.' *The New York Times*, 19 September 2022.

54 Panja, Tariq. 'Ban on Beer Is Latest Flash Point in World Cup Culture Clash'. *The New York Times*, 18 November 2022.

55 Panja, Tariq. 'On Eve of World Cup, FIFA Chief Says, 'Don't Criticize Qatar; Criticize Me.' *The New York Times*, 19 September 2022

56 White, Jim. 'Morocco fans escape 'crush' outside stadium ahead of last-16 match with Spain'. *The Telegraph*, 6 December 2022.

57 Ziegler, Martyn. 'Gianni Infantino set to gain from FA's conditional backing for re-election'. *The Times*, 18 November 2022.

58 Lyall, Sarah & Goldbaum, Christina. 'When V.I.P. Isn't Exclusive Enough: Welcome to V.V.I.P.'. *The New York Times*, 30 November 2022.

59 Ibid.

60 Wong, Edward. 'Global Leaders Mix Sports and Diplomacy at the World Cup'. *The New York Times*, 16 December 2022.

61 Glancy, Josh. 'Forget virtue signalling: this World Cup is a magnet for deals in the desert'. *The Times*, 26 November 2022.

62 Wong, Edward. 'Global Leaders Mix Sports and Diplomacy at the World Cup'. *The New York Times*, 16 December 2022.

63 Bennet, Dalton, et al. 'From Jared Kushner to Salt Bae: Here's who Elon Musk was seen with at the World Cup'. *The Washington Post*, 20 December 2022.

64 Ziegler, Martyn. 'Fifa embarrassed as Salt Bae pesters Lionel Messi'. *The Times*, 19 December 2022.

65 Allen, Felix. 'Goodbye, Bae-By'. *The Sun*, 23 December 2022.

66 Burton, Josef. 'Team Qatar Wanted Immigrant Players – Not Citizens'. *Foreign Policy*, 16 December 2022.

67 McManus, John. *Inside Qatar: Hidden Stories from One of the Richest Nations on Earth*. Icon Books, 2022.

68 Rothwell, James. 'Iranians clash over anti-regime flags during World Cup match with Wales'. *The Telegraph*, 25 November 2022.

69 Panja, Tariq. 'How FIFA Silenced a World Cup Armband Campaign'. *The New York Times*, 17 December 2022.

70 Ibid.

71 Delaney, Miguel. 'England feared red card and 'unlimited liability' for wearing OneLove armband at World Cup'. *Independent*, 24 November 2022.

72 Grohmann, Karolos. 'England were threatened with 'extreme blackmail' to ditch OneLove armband, claims German FA'. *Independent*, 22 November 2022.

73 Patrequin, Samuel. 'France goalkeeper Hugo Lloris won't wear rainbow armband at World Cup in Qatar'. *Independent*, 15 November 2022.

74 Delaney, Miguel. 'Ilkay Gundogan proud of first Muslim World Cup 'now the politics is finished''. *Independent*, 28 November 2022.

75 Belam, Martin. 'Qatari TV hosts appear to mock Germany's human rights gesture after World Cup exit'. *The Guardian*, 2 December 2022.

76 Braidwood, Jamie. 'England fans 'strip searched' for wearing rainbow t-shirt at Qatar World Cup match'. *Independent*, 29 November 2022.

77 Panja, Tariq. 'Waving the Flag of the World Cup's Unofficial Team'. *The New York Times*, 7 December 2022.

78 Panja, Tariq. 'Frustrations Simmer as Saudis Are Blocked From Watching the World Cup'. *The New York Times*, 25 November 2022.

79 Abbot, Sebastian. *The Away Game*. Arena Sport, 2018.

80 Ingle, Sean. ''Disappointing and unsurprising': Qatar 2022 organisers reject 'fake fan' claims'. *The Guardian*, 16 November 2022.

81 Montague, James. 'The Fans Screamed for Qatar. Their Passion Hid a Secret'. *The New York Times*, 28 November 2022.

82 Lawton, Matt. 'England fans paid to be 'spies' at World Cup'. *The Times*, 4 November 2022.

83 Panja, Tariq. 'Migrants hired to work at the opening match waited all day without food and water'. *The New York Times*, 20 November 2022.

84 Crafton, Adam. 'Migrant worker died in accident at World Cup base during group stage'. *The Athletic*, 7 December 2022.

85 Ziegler, Martyn. 'World Cup chief dismisses question about migrant worker's death'. *The Times*, 8 December 2022.

86 Ronay, Barney. 'Football turned Neymar's talent toxic: Qatar 2022 feels like an end point'. *The Guardian*, 10 December 2022.

87 Olé. 'La nueva provocación de Van Gaal a Messi'. *Olé*, 5 September 2023.

88 Delaney, Miguel. 'Human rights organisations say Fifa complict in 'serious abuses' over unpaid workers in Qatar'. *Independent*, 12 December 2022.

89 Ronay, Barney. 'As Qatar's World Cup ends it is time for truth: Fifa chose death and suffering'. *The Guardian*, 16 December 2022.

90 Wallace, Sam. 'World Cup migrant workers imprisoned for months in Qatar'. *The Telegraph*, 18 May 2023.

91 Delaney, Miguel. 'A year on from Qatar, this is the real legacy of the 2022 World Cup'. *Independent*, 20 November 2023.

92 Ibid.

93 Amnesty International. 'Global: FIFA must publish its review into compensation for workers harmed delivering the World Cup in Qatar'. Amnesty.Org, 9 May 2024: www.amnesty.org/en/latest/news/2024/05/fifa-must-publish-its-review-into-compensation-for-world-cup-workers-in-qatar/

Chapter 15 – And It's Live . . . and Killing Everything Else

1 Forrest, David; Simmons, Robert & Buraimo, Babatunde. 'Outcome Uncertainty And The Couch Potato Audience'. October 2004: www.lancaster.ac.uk/media/lancaster-university/content-assets/documents/lums/economics/working-papers/CouchPotatoAudience.pdf

2 Clegg, Jonathan & Robinson, Joshua. *The Club: How the Premier League Became the Richest, Most Disruptive Business in Sport*. John Murray Press, 2018.

3 Duff, Alex; Panja, Tariq. *Football's Secret Trade*. Wiley, 2017.

4 Bullough, Oliver. *Butler to the World*. Profile, 2022.

5 UEFA. 'Benchmarking report highlights profits and polarisation'. *UEFA.com*, 16 January 2020.

6 Clegg, Jonathan & Robinson, Joshua. *The Club: How the Premier League*

Became the Richest, Most Disruptive Business in Sport. John Murray Press, 2018.

7   Ibid.

8   Ibid.

9   Ibid.

10 Ebner, Sarah. 'History and time are key to power of football, says Premier League chief'. *The Times*, 2 July 2013.

11 Conn, David. *The Fall of the House of Fifa*. Random House, 2017.

12 Montague, James. *The Billionaires Club: The Unstoppable Rise of Football's Super-rich Owners*. Bloomsbury Publishing, 2017.

13 Ziegler, Martyn. 'Premier League secures £250m South American TV deal'. *The Times*, 18 January 2022.

14 Ziegler, Martyn. 'Premier League's broadcast income to reach £10bn over next three seasons'. *The Times*, 10 February 2022.

15 Ziegler, Martyn. 'Football League clubs lost £388m last season as cash crisis is revealed'. *The Times*, 24 May 2019.

16 Panja, Tariq. 'Premier League's Restart is Held Up by Bottom-Ranked Teams'. *The New York Times*, 6 May 2020.

17 Ziegler, Martyn. 'Uefa's rethink of Champions League multi-club ownership rules could affect Manchester United sale'. *The Times*, 14 March 2023.

18 Ziegler, Martyn. 'TV boom tempting Americans to pay top dollar for Premier League clubs'. *The Times*, 7 October 2022.

19 Hesse, Uli. *Bayern: Creating a Global Superclub*. Random House, 2016.

20 FT Live. 'The Wealth Gap in European Football'. FT Live (In association with FT Scoreboard), February 2024: brxcdn.com/fts-app-storage/d6e5bd4c-9228-11eb-a414-9a67e462410e/media/original/264f0340-b47f-11ee-907e-da6f08ca277e

21 Dixon, Ed. 'What is the domestic TV rights picture in Europe's 'big five' soccer leagues?' *SportsProMedia*, 17 November 2023.

22 Campanale, Susy. 'De Laurentiis slams 'disastrous' Serie A television coverage'. *Football Italia*, 3 February 2024.

23 Ibid.

24 CVC. 'LaLiga and CVC Fund VIII sign agreement to set Project Boost LaLiga in motion'. *CVC*, 13 December 2021.

25 Wallace, Sam. 'Chelsea have spent £1bn and signed 27 players – now they want Sporting CP'. *The Telegraph*, 15 September 2023.

26 Lukasz Baczek. Twitter, 20 March 2024: twitter.com/Lu_Class_/status/1770457068647985462

27 https://www.thetimes.co.uk/article/olympics-on-the-bbc-ofcom-recommends-review-into-rules-on-free-to-air-events-rrgpwpw8w

28 Wallace, Sam. 'Golf's implosion is a reminder of price football nearly paid'. *The Telegraph*, 12 June 2022.

29 Ziegler, Martyn. 'Premier League clubs' income eclipse European rivals – as gap with Championship also widens'. *The Times*, 18 August 2022.

30 Bullough, Oliver. *Butler to the World*. Profile, 2022.

31 Bower, Tom. *Broken Dreams*. Simon & Schuster UK, 2023.

32 Ingle, Sean. 'Everton's deduction is a tremor – City and Chelsea may face the earthquake'. *The Guardian*, 17 November 2023.

33 Delaney, Miguel. 'Everton are a club out of time in every way'. *Independent*, 25 January 2023.

34 https://www.thetimes.co.uk/article/alisher-usmanov-everton-had-a-lucky-escape-from-russian-oligarch-disaster-gdq28pjct

35 Everton FC. 'Everton Release 2022/23 Report & Accounts'. *EvertonFC.com*, 31 March 2024.

36 Davies, Rob & Lock, Simon. 'Chelsea FC face new questions over how Roman Abrmovich funded success'. *The Guardian*, 15 November 2023.

37 Unwin, Will. 'Nottingham Forest appeal against four-point Premier League penalty'. *The Guardian*, 25 March 2024.

38 Fisher, Ben. 'Leicester City charged by Premier League over alleged breach of PSR rules'. *The Guardian*, 21 March 2024.

39 Conn, David. 'Leicester make £3.1m settlement with Football League over FFP claim'. *The Guardian*, 21 February 2018.

40 Montague, James. *The Billionaires Club: The Unstoppable Rise of Football's Super-rich Owners*. Bloomsbury Publishing, 2017.

41 Unwin, Will. 'Nottingham Forest appeal against four-point Premier League penalty'. The Guardian, 25 March 2024.

42 Edwards, Luke. 'Newcastle claim their attempt to join elite is held back by spending rules'. *The Telegraph*, 11 January 2024.

43 Samuel, Martin. 'Premier League spends £30m fighting its own clubs'. *The Times*, 10 June 2024.

44 Ziegler, Martyn. 'Premier League chief Richard Masters refuses to answer Newcastle questions'. *The Times*, 28 March 2023.

45 Wallace, Sam. 'Sorry Everton, but 'corruption' allegations will not be taken seriously'. *The Telegraph*, 26 November 2023.

46 Ronay, Barney. 'Newcastle's Saudi takeover will cause faux morality of football to collapse'. *The Guardian*, 7 October 2021.

47 Llewellyn, Mike. 'Inside the English Premier League's latest media rights deal: What does it tell us about the current state of play of market'. *Sports Legal*, 20 February 2024.

48 Lawton, Matt. 'Man City launch unprecedented legal action against

Premier League'. The Times, 4 June 2024.

49 Ziegler, Martyn. 'Villa in step with City on financial rules after owner's Abu Dhabi switch'. The Times, 7 June 2024.

50 Wallace, Sam. 'Manchester City legal dispute shows why Government's role as football regulator will be so difficult'. The Telegraph, 1 October 2023.

Chapter 16 – What Next?

1   FIFA. 'Infantino highlights football's potential to unite at G20 summit'. InsideFIFA, 1 December 2018.

2   Ronay, Barney. 'Sportswashing and the tangled web of Europe's biggest clubs'. The Guardian, 15 February 2019.

3   Spurling, Jon. Death or Glory: The Dark History of the World Cup. Vision Sports Publishing, 2010.

4   Ronay, Barney. 'Cold comfort get ready to shiver watching a World Cup you helped to pay for'. The Guardian, 17 September 2022.

5   Schaerlaeckens, Leander. 'A New Wave of American Buyers Has Set Its Sights on European Soccer'. The Ringer, 27 January 2022.

6   Panja, Tariq. 'Barcelona Spent Its Way Into Crisis. Can It Now Spend Its Way Out?'. The New York Times, 3 August 2022.

7   Campbell, Denis. 'The game that ate itself.' The Guardian, 24 October 2004.

8   Ronay, Barney. 'Football corruption and the remarkable road to Qatar's World Cup'. The Guardian, 8 October 2022.

9   Paulinelli, Gustavo. 'The Football Corporations in Brazil: evolution and perspectives'. Lexology, 9 April 2024.

10 Wallace, Sam. 'Manchester City leading the way with Brazil ripe for investment'. The Telegraph, 7 May 2023.

11 Kuper, Simon & Szymanski, Stefan. Soccernomics. HarperCollins Publishers, 2022.

12 Ziegler, Martyn. 'Why Super League collapse is fuelling Liverpool owners' £4bn exit plan'. The Times, 7 November 2022.

13 Ogden, Mark. 'What's gone wrong at Manchester United under Glazer ownership?' ESPN, 7 February 2024.

14 Camut, Nicolas & Walker, Ali. 'France shoots to kill the football Super League, once and for all'. Politico, 7 February 2024.

15 'Brazilian football: the next frontier in global sport?' Financial Times, 11 February 2024.

16 Guardian Sport & PA Media. 'Footballers' union starts legal action against

Fifa over Club World Cup'. *The Guardian*, 13 June 2024.

17 Said, Summer, et al. 'The best of Frenemies: Saudi Crown Prince Clashes with U.A.E. President'. *The Wall Street Journal*, 18 July 2023.

18 Goldblatt, David. 'Awash with fossil fuel money, African football is sowing the seeds of its own destruction'. *The Guardian*, 7 January 2024.

19 Early, Ken. 'We no longer try to understand why Real Madrid win the Champions League final – we just accept'. *The Irish Times*, 3 June 2024.

20 McManus, John. *Inside Qatar: Hidden Stories from One of the Richest Nations on Earth*. Icon Books, 2022.

21 Uppal, Rachna. 'Saudi economy edging closer to reducing dependence on oil, IMF official says'. *Reuters*, 3 May 2023.

22 Hope, Bradley & Scheck, Justin. *Blood and Oil: Mohammed bin Salman's Ruthless Quest for Global Power*. John Murray Press, 2020.

23 Fattah, Zainab & Martin, Matthew. 'Saudis Scale Back Ambition for $1.5 Trillion Desert Project Neom'. *Bloomberg UK*, 5 April 2024.

24 'Judgement of the Court'. InfoCuria Case-Law, 21 December 2023: curia.europa.eu/juris/document/document.jsf?docid=280765&mode=req&pageIndex=1&dir=&occ=first&part=1&text=&doclang=EN&cid=2518235

25 Camut, Nicolas & Walker, Ali. 'France shoots to kill the football Super League, once and for all'. *Politico*, 7 February 2024.

26 Ronay, Barney. 'Qatar ready to make history in Asian Cup … but the world is not watching'. *The Guardian*, 28 January 2019.